THE ANALYSIS
OF PSYCHOLOGICAL
THEORY
Metapsychological Perspectives

THE ANALYSIS OF PSYCHOLOGICAL THEORY

Metapsychological Perspectives

Edited by

Henderikus J. Stam
Timothy B. Rogers
University of Calgary

Kenneth J. Gergen
Swarthmore College

○ **HEMISPHERE PUBLISHING CORPORATION, Washington**
A subsidiary of Harper & Row, Publishers, Inc.

Cambridge   New York   Philadelphia   San Francisco
London   Mexico City   São Paulo   Singapore   Sydney

THE ANALYSIS OF PSYCHOLOGICAL THEORY: Metapsychological Perspectives

1 2 3 4 5 6 7 8 9 0   B R B R   8 9 8 7

Library of Congress Cataloging-in-Publication Data

The Analysis of psychological theory.

  Bibliography: p.
  Includes index.
  1. Psychology—Philosophy. I. Stam, Henderikus J., date.
II. Rogers, Timothy B., date.
III. Gergen, Kenneth J.
BF38.A47   1987   150′.1   86-29550
ISBN 0-89116-597-5

Contents

PART 2: STUDIES IN METATHEORY

PART 3: METATHEORETICAL APPLICATIONS

Contributors

ROBERT A. BOUDREAU
The University of Lethbridge
Lethbridge, Alberta

RONALD J. FISHER
University of Saskatchewan
Saskatoon, Saskatchewan

JAMES FOSTER
University of Victoria
Victoria, B.C.

KENNETH J. GERGEN
Swarthmore College
Swarthmore, Pennsylvania

MARY M. GERGEN
Swarthmore College
Swarthmore, Pennsylvania

JILL G. MORAWSKI
Wesleyan University
Middletown, Connecticut

LOUISE PLOUFFE
Carleton University
Ottawa, Ontario

TIMOTHY B. ROGERS
University of Calgary
Calgary, Alberta

EDWARD E. SAMPSON
California State University
Northridge, California

MORRIS L. SHAMES
Concordia University
Montreal, Quebec

HENDERIKUS J. STAM
University of Calgary
Calgary, Alberta

LLOYD STRICKLAND
Carleton University
Ottawa, Ontario

WARREN THORNGATE
Carleton University
Ottawa, Ontario

CHARLES TOLMAN
University of Victoria
Victoria, B.C.

PHILIP WEXLER
University of Rochester
Rochester, New York

ROBERT G. WEYANT
University of Calgary
Calgary, Alberta

Preface

The practice of prefixing *meta* to the name of a discipline is usually meant to designate a "higher," or transcending, discipline. It deals with problems that are both beyond the scope of the original and more fundamental. *Metapsychology,* then concerns itself with the foundational problems of psychology. It self-critically seeks to analyze the basic nature of psychological discourse. While not "higher" than the remainder of the discipline in any sense of fundamental superiority, it does represent an important departure from the day-to-day workings of psychology. Such an enterprise requires an analysis different from that of psychological works. It does not ask questions about specific psychological phenomena: how to assess, how to describe, or explain. Rather, it asks how we came to ask those questions in the way we did, what issues have been overlooked, what problems interfere in the way the question has been asked, and what is likely to result if inquiry continues its present course. To be sure, metapsychological questions have been with us from the inception of the discipline—even if they did not always appear under that name. Wundt, James, Watson, McDougall, and many others have asked questions about the social, historical, and philosophical basis of psychological inquiry.

Therefore, we would hardly claim to be at the threshold of a new discipline. However, we do argue that the present use of the term *metapsychology* usefully separates the work of psychological inquiry itself from the analysis of this inquiry.

It is not the aim of this volume to furnish a full introduction or review of metapsychological analysis. The scope of such an analysis can scarcely be envisioned. Instead, we have attempted to assemble chapters that call attention to critical problems in contemporary psychology, and do so in a way that gives metapsychology a specialized identity and function.

The Introduction lays the groundwork. Here Gergen discusses several major themes with which metapsychological works have been concerned in the past decade as well as future concerns. The remainder of the volume is divided into three parts. The first (The Study of Metatheory) deals with psychology's ubiquitous scientism, its general refusal to examine metatheoretical questions, the various alternatives to current orthodoxy, and a reminder of the ultimate consumers of our prodigious outpourings. The second part (Studies in Metatheory) consists of six chapters treating various aspects of psychology. These include discussions of language, history, folklore, social factors, and philosophy. The very breadth of material covered here is an indication of the scope of metapsychological inquiry. Part 3 (Metatheoretical Applications) outlines several different ways in which metapsychological inquiry can have a direct bearing on the psychology one conducts. Here authors with a wide variety of viewpoints reflect on the outcome of such inquiry within the fields of social psychology, artificial intelligence, and Soviet psychology, etc.

This book was the natural outgrowth of a symposium entitled "Metapsychology: Problems and Prospects" held at the University of Calgary. All of the chapters have been substantially rewritten and edited for this volume. Furthermore, three papers not presented at that symposium (Sampson, Tolman, and Wexler) were written especially for this volume—as was the Introduction. We are grateful to the Social Sciences and Humanities Research Council of Canada (Grant no. 443-84-0011) and University of Calgary Research Services (Conference Grant) for their generous support of the symposium that led to this work.

Henderikus J. Stam
Timothy B. Rogers
Kenneth J. Gergen

THE ANALYSIS
OF PSYCHOLOGICAL
THEORY

Metapsychological Perspectives

Introduction: Toward Metapsychology

Kenneth J. Gergen

If one scans the past century of psychological inquiry one rapidly becomes aware of the steadily increasing dependence of psychological theory on empirical findings. Whereas early theorists permitted themselves the luxury of broadening conjecture, contemporary psychologists proceed with caution. Seldom does a theoretical premise enter the literature unaccompanied by empirical data, and often it seems, theorists limit their theories to a few simple principles out of empirical concerns. As theories are progressively elaborated they run the danger of outdistancing the scientist's capacity to furnish the "necessary" evidence. The reasons for this increasing concern with data are hardly obscure. They are part and parcel of the empiricist program of science to which the discipline increasingly committed itself. From the empiricist perspective the fundamental crucible for assessing the value or worth of a theory is the empirical test. We can even forgive a theory if it is conceptually cumbersome, ambiguous, or imparsimonious so long as it proves useful in generating an array of successful predictions. The great promise of the empiricist account of knowledge was its premise that objective knowledge could ultimately be achieved through the deployment of specified methods. With the assiduous application of such rules of procedure, the scientist could escape the snares of nonsense, opacity and the exotic, and accumulate theoretical propositions of increasing precision and broad applicability.

Yet, within more recent times it has become increasingly clear that the empiricist foundations of the science are deeply flawed. The deployment of empirical data to justify and evaluate theoretical propositions ceases to be broadly creditable. To the extent that this is so, the traditional criterion for assessing the worth of a theory is obviated. Consideration must be opened on alternative theories of knowledge along with alternative criteria for evaluating theoretical contentions. It is just such concerns that form the basis for a discipline of metapsychology. In the present context, the term metapsychology refers to the systematic study of theoretical accounts which make expository use of psychological constructs. Metapsychology is thus primarily concerned with the formal discipline of psychology. However, its justifiable concerns extend to the realm of lay discourse, and to psychological theory as it is employed within neighboring realms such as philosophy, sociology, economics, biology, history, political science and anthropology.

The present chapter will first outline a number of critical arguments against the traditional view that scientific theory is determined, bound or constrained by empirical evidence. These arguments should furnish grounds for the essential liberation of the theoretical enterprise, and for the consideration of alternative criteria of theoretical evaluation. In the latter section of the paper we shall consider the challenges that confront emerging inquiry into metapsychology. What progress has been made, what resources are now available, and what can we anticipate for the future? All shall concern us.

THE LIBERATION OF THEORY FROM OBSERVATION

As philosophers of science have long been aware, it is primarily in the degree to which there is correspondence between theoretical language and real world events, that scientific theory acquires utility in the market of prediction and control. If scientific language bears no determinate relationship to events external to the language itself, not only does its contribution to prediction and control become suspect, but scientific theory becomes invulnerable to improvement through observation. The hope that knowledge may be advanced through continued, systematic observation is rendered problematic. More generally, one would be moved to question the fundamental objectivity of scientific accounts. If such accounts are not grounded in observation, then what furnishes their warrant? On what basis are the sciences to claim special expertise, privilege, or value to the society?

It is in these many respects that philosophers of science have been keen to establish a close relationship between language and observation. At the heart of the logical positivist movement, for example, lay the "verifiability principle of meaning," to whit, the meaning of a proposition rests on its capacity for verification through observation. As it was argued, propositions not open to corroboration or emendation through observation are unworthy of further dispute. The problem was, however, to account for the connection between propositions and observations. Schlick (1934) argued that the meaning of single words within propositions must be established through ostensive ("pointing to") means. In his early work Carnap (1928) proposed that thing-predicates represented "primitive ideas," thus reducing scientific propositions to reports of private experience. For Neurath (1932) propositions were to be verified through "protocol sentences" which were, themselves, to refer to the biological processes of perception. (As all such statements are thus reducible to the language of physics, Neurath argued, there is a fundamental unity among all branches of science.) From yet another vantage point, Russell (1924) proposed that objective knowledge could be reduced to sets of "atomic propositions," the truth of which would rest on descriminable, punctate facts.

Yet, such attempts to establish secure and determinate relationships between words and real world referents eventually came under heavy attack. Were the propositions entering into the verifiability principle themselves subject to verification? And if not, in what sense were they meaningful? Propositions appear to have meaning over and above the referential capacity of the words which make them up. How is such meaning to be understood? Are entire propositions subject to verification, or only single terms? Is verification a state of mind, and if so, in what sense are states of mind themselves verifiable? On what grounds are the basic facts to which descriptors refer to be established? How can rules for linking predicates with particulars be constructed when the terms of the rules themselves remain meaningless until defined by further linking rules? These and other nettlesome questions have remained recalcitrant to broadly compelling solution. Today it is generally agreed (cf. Fuller, 1983; Barnes, 1983) that the manner in which objectivity in meaning is achieved, along with a specification of the rules for when it is not, remains unsatisfactorily explicated.

At the same time, other lines of argumentation have been emerging, the implications of which are of substantial moment. In each of these cases, significant question has been raised concerning the relationship between word and object, or theory and evidence. In each case the arguments grant such substantial autonomy to theoretical discourse that major revisions seem demanded in the traditional account of science. Certain of these arguments are of particular significance to the formulation of metatheory for psychology.

The Contextual Dependency of Meaning

As we have seen, from the logical empiricist perspective critical descriptive terms at the theoretical level should correspond to specifiable or delimited observations. The ideal situation would be one in which discrete particulars at the level of observation stand in a one-to-one relationship with mathematical integers at the theoretical level. The attempt of correspondence theorists is thus to establish foundations of knowledge which are context free. That is, the linkage between theoretical terms and observations (or the objective meaning of propositions) should remain stable across varying contexts—both at the theoretical and observational level. If context invariance is not maintained then the potential for scientific prognostication is severely threatened; one would be unable to specify what facts would be predicted by the theory as theoretical and historical context were altered. The possibility for empirical test is further impugned as one would be unable to specify what observations would count as confirmations or disconfirmations of a theory across varying contexts.

Wittgenstein's *Philosophical Investigations* was one of the first significant works to challenge the possibility for context free correspondence. As he proposed, the meaning of words (or sentences) is achieved through their use in the carrying out of various life forms. Such uses may be viewed as so many language games, each subject to its own particular rules. The precise boundaries of the rules cannot be explicated, as the terms of explication will themselves be context (or "use") dependent.

> There are countless . . . different kinds of use of what we call "symbols," "words," "sentences." And this multiplicity is not something fixed, given once and for all; but new types of language, new language-games, as we may say, come into existence, and these become obsolete and get forgotten. (p. 11e)

Essentially this would mean that any scientific term would derive its meaning from its context of usage, which context could also include ostensive means of securing word-object identities. The term "rabbit" for example, may figure in many different linguistic, social, and environmental, contexts. As a result it would be virtually impossible to determine the truth value of propositions containing the term through observation. There simply is no stimulus event (or class of events), abstracted from context, to which the term is semantically wedded.

When writ large, the contextualist arguments suggest the following with respect to theoretical accounts within the sciences: Descriptive and explanatory schemas remain mute with respect to prediction and empirical evaluation until linked to referents. However, rules as to how such linkages are to be constructed remain generally unexplicated (and indeed there are principled impediments to establishing such rules). Thus, descriptive and explanatory constructions are fundamentally free to vary across contexts of usage. When extended, this is to say that any behavioral theory may, in principle, be applied to (used to describe or explain) virtually any human action. The constraints over such application lie chiefly within the social process through which contextual linkages are forged. In this sense, virtually any theory (Freudian, Skinnerian, social learning, role-rule, cognitive) should be capable of absorbing all empirical outcomes so long as there are communities of scholars capable of negotiating the meaning of theoretical terms across divergent contexts.

The Social Construction of Reality

In the preceding case the semantic link between word and object was weakened by taking into account the contextual dependency of linking practices. A second threat to incorrigibility of meaning has been nurtured in different soil, namely that of rationalist and idealist philosophy. Debate over the origin of abstract ideas has had a long and vigorous history. On the one hand, empiricists such as Locke, Hume and the Mills have argued that such ideas are derived from sensory input, while rationalist/idealist thinkers such as Kant, Spinoza, Schopenhauer and Nietzsche have demonstrated the manifold weaknesses in such a position. As they proposed in various ways, the mind functions as a generative source of ideas. In effect, the mind generates the conceptual basis for interpreting and understanding (and some will argue, perceiving) the world. The implications of this position for a theory of meaning or semantic linkages are far-reaching. To the extent that the mind furnishes the categories of understanding, there are no real-world objects of study other than those inherent within the mental makeup of persons. There are no objects save those for which there are preceding categories. The result is that semantic linkages do not derive from a conjoining of independent realms—object and category—tied through linking definitions. Rather, in the act of comprehension object and concept are one; objects reduce to the mental a priori.

In the present century this tradition has manifested itself in numerous ways. Several are especially pertinent to our proceedings. First, within the philosophy of science the reduction of object to percept occurs, though in muted form, in Kuhn's (1970) influential work. In his most radical moments Kuhn raises serious doubts over the cumulativeness of scientific knowledge. Scientific anomalies are not generally viewed by Kuhn as contradictions to the assumptions of normal science. Rather, they are orthogonal to it. Thus, when a new theory is articulated to render the anomalies coherent, this theory is not so much as improvement over the old as it is essentially a different theory, designed to account for different data, to ask different questions, etc. As Kuhn argues, scientific revolutions are akin to "Gestalt shifts;" one simply sees the world through a different theoretical lens. This form of closet-rationalism gives way to a more complete assault in Hanson's (1958) widely credited *Patterns of Discovery*. As Hanson proposes, what we take to be elementary facts (observables) are determined in significant degree by the conceptual systems we bring to bear. Visual experience is a product of conceptual or theoretical invention.

> The infant and the layman can see—they are not blind. But they cannot see what the physicist sees; they are blind to what he sees. We may not hear that the oboe is out of tune though this will be painfully obvious to the trained musician . . . The elements of the visitor's visual field, though identical with those of the physicist, are not organized for him as for the physicist; the same lines, colors, shapes are apprehended by both, but not in the same way (p. 17).

Although strongly appealing in certain respects, social thinkers (among others) have discerned limitations in the assumption that the forestructure of understanding lies "within the mind of the beholder." To commit oneself to this position is ultimately to end in either the quagmire of innate categories or solipsism (or both). To retain the wisdom of the approach and simultaneously avoid the conceptual pitfalls, many social theorists have shifted their emphasis from the mental construct to the domain of linguistic construction. Thus, the categories of understanding are traced to the social milieu. The forestructure of understanding is generated within the social process of developing intelligibility systems. In this sense, what we take to be the facts owe their existence to the social process whereby meanings are generated and events indexed by these meanings. There are no independently identifiable, real world referents to which the language of social description is cemented.

Deconstructionism and the Figurative Basis of Human Understanding

As we see, the contextualist approach emphasizes the situational dependence of meaning, while the constructionist emphasizes the social origins of meaning within situations. In both cases however, the deployment of a descriptive term is determined less by the features of the object, action or event to be described than it is on extraneous processes. A third line of argument threatens the empirical dependences of theoretical description in an entirely different way. Rather than directly challenging the connection between theory and event, the attempt has been to demonstrate how much that is communicated about events is determined, not by the character of events themselves, but by linguistic figures or forms. To the extent that description and explanation is dependent on such figures or forms, the assumption that science tells us about the "thing in itself" is rendered suspect. Although the threat to the semantic link is thus an indirect one, the implications for correspondence assumptions are nevertheless powerful.

To appreciate more fully the force of this line of argument, one must take into account the structuralist movement—to which deconstructionism is largely a response. Structuralism as an intellectual endeavor has largely been given to a dualistic conception of communicative acts, one that discriminates between surface actions and underlying meaning. Following Saussure's (1979) distinction between the "signifier" (or word) and the "signified" (or the underlying concept which the word represents) it is assumed that the sprawling, ephemeral, and varigated acts of communication may be expressions of more fundamental, structured sets of principles, dimensions, conceptual templates or the like. A penetrating examination of the spoken or written work might thus reveal the more latent, possibly unconscious structure that lies beneath, structure that may serve as the ultimate basis for human understanding itself. On this view, for example, Levi-Strauss (1963) has proposed that wide ranging cultural forms and artifacts can be traced to a fundamental binary logic. Chomsky (1968) has attempted to locate a "deep" grammatical structure from which all well-formed sentences may be derived. Lacan's (1978) persistent concern has been with the structural elements forming the layers of the mind.

In spite of the immense and optimistic challenge furnished by the structuralist movement, mounting criticism combined with the steady accumulation of competing accounts of the "hidden structures" have left the movement crippled. For one, the hermeneuticist writings of Gadamer (1975) and Ricoeur (1974) may be singled out for their debilitating implications. As argued in the former case, the interpretation of texts (i.e., the apprehending of underlying meaning) is largely dependent on historically situated conventions. Thus, what a text "means" can only be determined within the contemporary "horizon of understanding." Whether this understanding coincides with that of the initial author is essentially indeterminate. Although differing from Gadamer in important respects, Ricoeur (1974) echoes this concern in his argument that texts serve as means of "opening up" possible existences. Interpreting a person's words is not a matter of determining with clarity its precise underlying structure. Rather words have a social career that escapes the finite horizon lived by the writer. The critical implications of this line of reasoning for structuralist thought is clear enough: to the extent that interpretation of the "underlying realm" is dependent on historically based conventions, then rendered interpretations give more insight into contemporary practices of interpretation than they do into underlying structure. Or to put it another way, the constraints over what may be said about such underlying structures are not furnished by the structures themselves so much as they are by the acceptable practices of rendering interpretation.

These implications are amplified in the works of deconstructionist writers such as Derrida (1977), Hartman (1975), and DeMan (1979). Here the recurrent concern is with the literary figures (tropes, metaphors, and other rhetorical strategems) that dominate the process of interpretation. If one chooses to interpret or describe, such interpretations must abide by the rules governing interpretation itself. As certain literary forms are selected and others abandoned, the resultant work (whether literary, philosophic or scientific) will not only be delimited by the forms, but the object of interpretation is deconstructed. Thus in adopting a given literary form, the form itself comes to dominate description in such a way that the object of description is obliterated or masked from view. If one attempts to interpret the "underlying intention" of a given author (or actor), the literary form intrinsic to interpretation itself will obscure and replace the object of concern. In Derrida's terms, "Il n'y a pas de hors texte." (There is nothing outside the text.) Or to bring the matter closer to home, behavioral description possesses an autonomy of its own. Once a descriptive form is adopted it carries on an independent existence and the referential implications are obscured. For example, to use the metaphor of the computer to "describe" mental functioning is to restrain the descriptive enterprise in significant ways. Concepts of "creativity," "imagination" and "motivation" cease to be matters of major concern. In effect, once the metaphor has been selected the actual processes at stake are circumscribed. Whatever their properties, they will be replaced by constituents of the metaphor.

From Action to Linguistic Autonomy

Although thinkers in the deconstructionist vein furnish an indirect threat to assumptions of semantic mapping, one final departure must be considered. In this case a principled challenge is launched more directly against the relationship between word and entity. To appreciate the force of this challenge we must turn the clock back to late 19th century Germany, and the intense debate over the character of the specifically human (Geistenwissenschaften) as opposed to the natural sciences (Naturwissenschaften). Dilthey, Weber, Richert, and many others argued that the study of human behavior was centrally concerned not with the objectively given behavior of persons but with the underlying meaning of behavior to persons. The understanding of human conduct thus requires a penetration into the subjective life of persons, into their intentions, motives, and reasons. A similar line of argument was later adopted by Collingwood (1966) in his characterization of historical study. As he maintained, "Unlike the natural scientist, the historian is not concerned with events as such at all. He is concerned with those events which are the outward expression of thoughts and is only concerned with these so far as they express thoughts" (p. 217). Peter Winch's influential *The Idea of a Social Science* elaborates further on this thesis. As Winch maintained, the objects of natural science study have an existence independent of the concepts used to understand them. However, in the case of human action the concepts of understanding essentially establish the ontological foundations. In the former case, for example, the occurrence of something that we term "claps of thunder" is independent of the concept of thunder; however, in the case of human action, without a concept of a "command" or "obedience" such "events" simply do not exist.

Such thinking wends its way into contemporary study in the form of anti-behaviorist thinking. Most important in this instance, Charles Taylor (1964) among others, has distinguished between human behavior (bodily movements *caused* by forces or elements over which the individual has no control), and human action (or movements of the body resulting from intentionality or *reasons*). Human study, on this account, is not principally concerned with the former (such as the velocity of a free falling human body), but is vitally absorbed with the latter. The understanding of human action requires that one take into account the precipitating reasons (motives, intentions). Most of our terms for describing human conduct are essentially wedded to the assumption of underlying reasons or intentions. That is, when an individual is described as aggressive, the assumption follows that he or she must have intended to aggress. If one had no intention to do so, then the descriptor would simply be inappropriate. In the same way the logic of our language does not permit us to say that one "reads a book," "writes a speech," "takes a plane to Calgary," or even "criticizes others" without any intention of doing so. In effect the common language is a language of reasons rather than causes.

The argument that the language for describing human conduct is largely an intentional one has been broadly compelling. A rationale for why such language is required is spelled out elsewhere (Gergen, 1982). However, in the present context we must inquire into the implications of this view for the problem of semantic linkages. Essentially we find ourselves in the following condition: The language of person description is not linked to, defined by, nor does it refer to spatio-temporal particulars as such. Rather, its referents seem largely to be psychological conditions (intentions, meanings, motives, etc.). When we speak of a person being aggressive, helpful, obedient, conforming, and the like, we are speaking not of the overt movements of the body but of his or her psychic dispositions. Yet, if this conclusion is accepted we then confront the problem of grounding the semantic linkage between person description and psychological state. How is one to recognize the occurrence of one form of intention, motive, etc., as opposed to another?

A variety of answers to this question have been posed over the centuries, and there is simply not space enough and time for a review of such proposals and their difficulties. However, that there are difficulties has become most apparent in recent hermeneutic debate. In this context the problem is generally cast in terms of accuracy of interpretation. When confronted with competing accounts of the interpretation of a text, how are judgments to be rendered regarding relative accuracy. How can one interpretation be judged as "missing the author's point" (meaning, intention) and another deemed accurate? Again, attempts have been made to answer this question positively (Habermas, 1983; Hirsch, 1967), but none of these arguments has yet commanded broad agreement (see Gergen, in press). Further the specter of cultural and historical relativism remains robust. We have already touched on the work of Gadamer and Ricoeur in this respect.

In my view there are principled reasons for indeterminacy of interpretation. In particular, it appears that all attempts to clarify or determine with accuracy the intent, meaning or motive underlying a given action are subject to infinite regress. As we have seen, behaviors are indexed by intentional language (e.g., aggression, dominance, helpfulness). In effect the label commits one to assumptions about a psychological state that is not itself made transparent by the movements of the body. If clarification is thus desired concerning the actual motive or intention, we must then rely on other behavioral indicators (e.g. utterances, movements, etc.). Yet, the description of these indicators is subject to the same problem as the initial interpretation: the descriptor commits one to still further assumptions about psychological dispositions. We now approach an infinite regress. For example, interpreting a given action (e.g. delivering shock to another subject) as aggression, is in itself without objective warrant. The experimenter does not truly know what the subject was intending when he pressed his fingers on the button. For clarification the subject might then be asked what he was "trying" to do. Yet, his utterance (e.g., "he had it coming") itself stands in need of interpretation (e.g., are these words expressing anger, moral duty, a need for reciprocation, a need to fulfill the experimenter's expectation or what?). Whatever conclusion is drawn rests on the same quicksand as the initial interpretation: it commits one to yet another objectively unwarranted conclusion—as would all further attempts to clarify or "shed further light" through observation. (For further amplification see my chapter in this volume.)

This analysis leaves us confronting the possibility that the language of person description (and explanation) is generated, elaborated, extended or cast aside in relative independence of the activities it is designed to describe. In principle, its life is essentially autonomous from and orthogonal to the life for which it accounts. This is not to say that we cannot reach agreement (even rapidly) regarding the adequacy of behavioral description. Rather, it is to venture that adequacy in description is not engendered by the character of the acts in question but by the exigencies of social practice. For example, we may readily agree that a person is "dominating a conversation," but with the proper negotiation of terms, the same actions could be viewed as "submissive," "loving," "inquiring," "lazy," and so on. The necessity for shifting from one description to another does not derive from the character of the actions themselves; the actions are identical across descriptions. Rather, they depend on the skills or abilities of the interlocutors to navigate successfully the existing language conventions.

TOWARD A MATURE METAPSYCHOLOGY

As the foregoing analysis has attempted to demonstrate, the traditional crucible for assessing the significance of psychological theory, namely its correspondence with empirical fact, is deeply problematic. The *contextualist* arguments hold that descriptions of the world are in themselves uninformative about the nature of things. Such descriptions may be constrained by observation, but a continuous process of ostensive grounding is necessitated as environmental and linguistic circumstance are altered. The same descriptive term may have multiple referents (or none at all) depending on what language game one is playing at a given time. From the *constructionist* vantage point we find that descriptive languages are not derived from observation; rather, such languages operate as the lenses or filters through which we determine what counts as an object. In the case of the *deconstructionist* orientation it was argued that scientific description is strongly influenced by the linguistic figures (metaphors, tropes, etc.) selected for communication. Once the figure has been selected, certain descriptive practices are virtually required. The language itself functions autonomously—without dependence on the particulars of the world to be described. And finally, in our analysis of the *language of action,* we found that terms of behavioral description cannot in principle be linked in a definitional sense to observed patterns of human activity. By and large, the language of human action simply has no consistent spatio-temporal coordinates.

With the realization of the minimal degree to which psychological formulations are or can be constrained by observation, we stand at the threshold of a new and challenging form of inquiry. In particular, we find ourselves confronting a range of questions that have scarcely been asked over the past century of psychological study, and yet, questions that are of profound consequence to the subsequent development of the discipline. These are essentially questions of metapsychology. How are we to understand the nature and limits of psychological accounts of human conduct, both as these accounts are developed and sustained within the science and within the culture at large? Within this context there are three issues that appear of paramount importance. Each deserves attention, with respect to their underlying rationale, to present and future inquiry within the field, and to the chapters constituting the present volume.

The Origins of Psychological Accounts

As we have seen, there is little reason to suppose that conceptions of the psychological world are in any way derived from observation—either directly or by inference. How are we then to account for the origins and vicissitudes of propositions about the mind? This question is one to which a mature discipline of metapsychology must address itself. Not only is the challenge of significant intellectual proportion in its own right, but its ramifications are many and significant. For one, an understanding of origins is informative regarding the degree of respect that might be awarded psychological accounts. Are they necessitated by any particular circumstance, do they emerge in response to functional needs of the culture, do they inevitably emerge as mystifying devices? Answers to such questions raise or lower the status of psychological accounts accordingly. In addition, explanations of origin inform psychologists of their own potential. Depending on our account of origins, development of new theory is invited or inhibited.

Resources for the exploration of such issues are beginning to emerge, both within psychology and neighboring disciplines. Questions of origins are, for one, of focal interest to those concerned with the evolution of cultural artifacts—both historically and cross-culturally. In their capacity to furnish contrasting accounts to those taken for granted in present day society, such explorations either implicitly or explicitly confront us with the question of origins. In the case of historical analysis, for example, developmentalists have been particularly sensitive to the temporal context in which differing conceptions of the child have emerged. For example, Aries' (1962) well known work traces the social construction of the child through several centuries. Kessen (1979) uses this work as a backdrop against which to venture a theory of the present century's construction of the child. In particular, the modern view of a child's psychological nature is traced to the industrialization of the culture and the associated separation between work and home. Along similar lines, the historian Badinter (1980) has traced the concept of mother love, or the instinctual feelings of attachment that mothers are supposed to feel for their children. As she attempts to demonstrate, the concept of the mother's natural love for her children is of relatively recent origin within French culture and can be traced to a shift in state policies. When human resources became necessary to maintain a powerful state it was essential to convince mothers that child care was a vital function. The contemporary celebration of mother love thus represents the remnants of a state sponsored idealization. Of related concern Verhave and Van Hoorn (1984) have traced the historical emergence of the concept of the self. As they propose, our modern view of the self is vitally dependent for its origins on the development of and broadscale reliance on the mechanical clock. Industrialization, state needs, technology—all are viewed as factors or conditions that foster the development of particular conceptions of the human psyche.

Numerous studies in the anthropological arena elucidate cultural variations in conceptions of the mental world. Certain of these investigations also adumbrate factors or processes giving rise to various concepts of mind. For example, Shweder and Miller (1985) distinguish between rights-based cultures, in which morality is viewed as a matter of personal decision making, and duty-based cultures in which moral actions are those which are consistent with the natural order. As they demonstrate, in rights-based cultures such as that of the contemporary United States, there is a far greater reliance on the elaboration of the psychological realm than in duty-based cultures—such as the Hindu. The elaboration of the mental world is needed, then, for purposes of accounting for one's actions in a rights-based moral system.

Alternative possibilities for understanding psychological accounts can also be located. From the standpoint of critical social theory, conceptions of mental life are frequently seen as derivatives of the economic system (Wexler, 1983; Plon, 1974). Most especially, in the attempt to rationalize a capitalist economic system, it is proposed, the ruling class champions a concept of mental life that engenders activity to sustain the existing structure of power. For those engaged in intellectual history it is possible to locate the origins of various ideas about the mind within the more general evaluation of conceptual systems. Thus, for example, Rorty (1979) traces contemporary views of personal knowledge back to Descartes' treatise on mind as mirror or glassy essence. Graumann and Sommers (1984) find debates in contemporary cognitive psychology to be modern vestiges of nineteenth century mentalist beliefs. It has also been argued that in certain respects the rudiments of our mental language are required by the pragmatic tasks to which language is put within ongoing relationships (Gergen, 1985). For example, the fact that we make distinctions among various aspects of the mental world (e.g., rationality, emotion, motivation) is partly required by the fact that we employ a verbal language for purposes of mental accounting. Verbal language is essentially a differentiating device, and to employ the language will necessarily imply a mental ontology of differentiated entities. Such an ontology would not be required should one employ, for example, dance or symphonic music as a means of representing mental life.

The present volume is in no way an attempt to synthesize or furnish fully developed accounts of origins. Rather, the hope is to bring such issues into focus as important in their own right. Certain chapters, then, attempt to develop ongoing dialogue concerning such matters. Shames (Chapter 1) continues the critical appraisal of objectivity-based formulations, while Foster (Chapter 4) makes an appeal to a form of objectivism. Strickland (Chapter 12) and Morawski (Chapter 7) both explore the extent to which theories are generated by particular social and political conditions (including those within the science themselves). This concern with the social process of science is also elaborated in Roger's (Chapter 9) treatment of folklore in scientific communities. Wexler (Chapter 11) traces a shift in theoretical discourse to a shift from corporate liberal capitalism to a transnational capitalism. Each furnishes a new lens through which to view the origins of psychological discourse.

The Constraints and Potentials
of Psychological Accounts

As one gains sensitivity to the various factors or processes that lend themselves to the development of mental conceptions, one increasingly senses the possibility for the self-conscious molding of mental accounts. If technology, value positions, political and economic climate and the like favor the development of particular theories, then the theorist is invited to reflexive repose. Given one's intellectual interests along with one's passions and commitments, would it not be possible to undertake the self-conscious development of new and specialized mental accounts? Rather than accepting the traditional role of map maker or mirror holder, can the scientist not view him/herself as a creator of perspectives, a visionary, or social change agent who constructs theories for functional ends within society? For many this is indeed an enticing image, and much within the move toward metapsychology would invite the enthusiast to press forward in such endeavors.

Yet, along with such invitations, a mature metapsychology should also furnish indications of the possible limits of psychological accounts. Sensitive to such limits, one can more selectively direct one's creative energies. Again, efforts to explore these constraints have begun to take shape.

It was Wittgenstein's later works that provided the first significant inquiry into the limits of mental language. As Wittgenstein asks, why is it so difficult for us to say "my soul is tired," "he felt deep grief for one second," or he is "considering something mechanically?" Is it because such sentences are untrue? Or is it rather not because our discourse about the mental world is governed by historical convention? Various problems inherent in such conventions have been elaborated by ordinary language and analytic philosophers. In the case of Ryle (1949) and Austin (1962), for example, the attempt was to show how assumptions of mental functioning within philosophy and psychology depended on linguistic conventions—which conventions, when closely examined, revealed deep incoherencies. In the hands of Anscombe (1976) such concerns led to an analysis of the concept of volition as it functions in ordinary language. Her analysis pointed to the profound problems inherent in the attempt to identify the individual's voluntary impulses on any given occasion. Yet, for investigators such as Winch (1958), Peters (1958) and Charles Taylor (1964) the exploration of the language of person description led to the conclusion that the descriptive practices of the natural sciences were virtually irrelevant to the science of understanding persons. Person description in Western culture is inherently based on the assumption of voluntary impulses.

A similar concern with the limits and implications of ordinary language conventions can be found in much ethnomethodological writing. As Garfinkel (1967) realized during his early writing, our talk about people's actions is governed primarily by socially shared methods for generating sense. However, it is in Jeff Coulter's works (1979, 1983) that one finds the implications for metapsychology developed most fully. Coulter explores the kinds of constraints that govern a variety of mental concepts such as thinking and memory and shows how these constraints depend on social convention as opposed to empirical fact. Kessler and McKenna's (1978) inquiry into gender talk is also noteworthy in its relevance. As they are able to demonstrate, the ethnomethods for distinguishing among genders vary considerably from one sub-culture to another. Thus, the reification of the language of gender is shown to be misleading; there are no univocal references for the use of the terms "man" and "woman." And, to the extent that we commit ourselves to one linguistic convention or another we are also molding the character of social life—for good or ill.

While much of the philosophic and ethnomethodological work is useful in clarifying the limits and problems inherent in given concepts of mind, little of it attempts to elaborate a more general framework for understanding the nature of these limits. This latter project has been the concern of a handful of other psychologists. In seminal work on this topic, Jon Smedslund (1980, 1985) is attempting to generate a series of common sense theorems from which all psychological theory must be derived. As Smedslund has demonstrated, with a limited set of such theorems, a theory such as Bandura's social learning formulation can be derived. The theory is not open to empirical test, because propositions that violated the theorems would simply be nonsense within contemporary culture. A similar but more rarefied approach to the problem of essential understandings has been taken by Peter Ossorio (1985) and his colleagues. In this case the attempt has been to locate sets of fundamental distinctions as opposed to proposition or theorems. In order to generate understanding of persons through our discourse, it is argued, it is necessary to draw distinctions between the person, the world, behavior, language and so on. Working with this approach from the abstract to the more particularized, others have gone on to explore the definitional components of other domains, such as love and friendship (Davis & Todd, 1982).

My own work on constraints has had a dual focus. One of them is closely related to the programs of both Smedslund and Ossorio. In this case, the attempt is not to locate basic axioms or fundamental propositions, but to explore the extent to which intelligible propositions about the mind are derivative from the definitional structure of various constituent terms (Gergen, 1984). In effect, it is proposed, mental statements reduce to a set of extended tautologies, a position whose contours will become clearer in my later chapter in this volume. The second approach to limitations derives from a concern with the pragmatic functions to which mental language is put (Gergen, 1985). Language may be viewed as a tool for carrying out human relations, and like most tools has certain structural limitations. These limitations, in turn, will place constraints over the ontology of mind implied by the language.

Ultimately such metapsychological inquiry into the limitations of mental constructions must also take advantage of developments in literary theory, from deconstructionism as outlined above, and to theories of rhetoric. Works in the former domain demonstrate an acute sensitivity to the subtleties of literary contrivance, and the extent to which given theoretical accounts may be dominated by literary tropes. Accounts of rhetoric have begun to outline the kinds of literary techniques necessary to create the realities suggested by our languages. Social scientists have begun to explore the implications of such work. Hayden White's (1978) analysis of the literary limitations over historical writing, and McCloskey (1985) on the rhetoric of economics are noteworthy in this respect. Within psychology David Leary is currently editing a book on the use of metaphor in the construction of psychological theory, and a volume, edited by Theodore Sarbin, on the use of narrative in figuration in psychology, has recently appeared (Sarbin, 1986).

Within the present volume several chapters explore issues of limitation. My own chapter (Chapter 5), attempts to demonstrate the extent to which hypotheses relating psychological constructs to observables rely on extended tautologies. Mary Gergen's offering (Chapter 13) treats the concept of narrative as it informs accounts of social phenomenon. And Weyants' essay (Chapter 14) focuses on the uses of metaphor in applying the language of machines to the understanding of human psychology. In addition, Morawski's (Chapter 7) discussion of the contextual constraints on meaning and Wexler's (Chapter 11) analysis of the semiotic society are relevant and instructive. In each case understanding of the limitations of various theoretical commitments is broadened.

The Construction and Evaluation of Theory

A mature discipline of metapsychology should not only enhance our consciousness of the development and limitations of theoretical constructions. Ideally it should also invite new theoretical ventures. If theories are not derived from nor dependent upon observations, then significant theoretical development should no longer await the establishment of a so called "observation base." Rather, the theorist is fundamentally free to engage in new theoretical departures. To be sure, the aspiring theorist should take into account relevant insights into the process and limits of theory construction. However, in principle, the outcome of a mature metapsychology should be a flourishing of new theoretical implements of greater intellectual and social consequence than hitherto.

Yet, significant inquiry is also needed into the function of such theorizing. If metapsychology is to innervate the theoretical enterprise, to what end? If the function of theories is not mimetic—if good theories are not faithful representations of the world—then what is to favor the development of still further accounts? Why should theoretical flowering be considered a value? And if myriad theories do emerge, how are we to judge their relative merits? If verisimilitude no longer serves as the crucible for theoretical evaluation, then how are we to select among competing accounts? These are indeed critical questions and ones with which a mature discipline of metapsychology should be focally concerned. Inquiry is vitally needed into forms of justification or warrant in psychological theorizing. This need is underscored in Thorngate and Plouffe's contribution to the present volume (Chapter 3), in which they explore the relative insignificance of current psychological investigation in contemporary society. Such insignificance may largely be traced to the delimited view of theory extant within the discipline.

Preliminary exploration is again in evidence. Since the early Frankfurt period critical theorists have made it clear that at least one major concern in the evaluation of theories is the kinds of social institutions which they rationalize or justify. In the initial case, capitalist economic theory was attacked on the grounds that it served as a mystifying device for justifying an oppressive and exploitative structure of society. Since this early period the critical orientation has spawned interesting and enlightening attacks on, for example, exchange theory in social psychology (Plon, 1974), and theories of intimacy and attraction (Wexler, 1982).

Of course this concern with the social implications of theoretical accounts cannot be separated from the more general problem of moral, ethical or ideological standards. Commitments to social forms are inherently valuational; they favor certain ways of life over others on the basis of some criterion of the good. Thus, an important byproduct of critical school analysis has been a more global sensitivity to the valuational implications of psychological theory. Retaining the rhythm but not the melody of the critical school, recent years have seen criticisms leveled against various psychological accounts for their dehumanization of the person (Hampden-Turner, 1970), social class biases (Apfelbaum & Lubeck, 1976), racist implications (Gordon, 1973), sexist biases (Gilligan, 1982), implicit ageism (Gergen & Gergen, in press), their antagonism to democratic principles (Deese, 1985), and so on. Among the most vocal and sophisticated critics of this genre has been Edward Sampson. Of major concern to Sampson has been the extent to which psychological theory champions various forms of self-contained individualism (Sampson, 1977, 1978), and simultaneously suppresses consciousness of social interdependency. In its support of self-contained individualism Sampson sees such theory as inimical to the society's wellbeing and possibly to its longevity.

Several of these themes are picked up and elaborated in the present volume. In Chapter 6, Stam undertakes a critical analysis of the value implications of the psychology of control. Wexler (Chapter 11) continues his analysis of psychological understanding as it justifies and maintains the common order. In Sampson's present contribution (Chapter 2) a search is mounted for a more general rationale for a morally critical science. Finally Boudreau (Chapter 8) presents the scaffolding for a more general model of criticism as it emerges within and changes a discipline.

Although it is vitally important to open broad inquiry into the social and valuational implications of psychological theory, the search for significant criteria of analysis should hardly be exhausted at this point. A mature field of metapsychology should increase the range of critical considerations in theory construction. For one, there are important issues to be raised of a purely conceptual nature. For example, do the various propositions making up a theory possess logical coherence; does a given theory lead to problems of infinite regress, or contain fundamental tautologies? The work of Wittgenstein, Ryle, Austin, and others within the domains of ordinary language and analytic philosophy furnish excellent precedents for such analyses. The chapters by Tolman (Chapter 10) and Weyant (Chapter 14) in the present volume form additional wedges, as they assess the conceptual strengths and weaknesses of dialectical materialism and of artificial intelligence accounts of human action. Strickland's analysis of social psychological concepts in the Soviet Union (Chapter 12) opens the door still further as it outlines theoretical assumptions that could enrich and expand our present undertakings.

The concern with valuational and conceptual criteria together yields still further possibilities for theoretical evaluation. For example, in important degree, we may view theoretical accounts as pragmatic tools for carrying out various forms of social life. Fisher (Chapter 15) argues, for one, that if properly reconsidered, social theory may be directly applied to problems besetting the society. However, there is an important sense in which theoretical conceptions need not await the process of application to change the culture. Such conceptions can enter directly into the common vernacular, and in doing so, become cultural resources for carrying out relationships. To assume, as many psychologists do, that infants are emotionally dependent furnishes a rationale for a particular form of parent-child relationship; to assume that unconscious motives may precipitate criminal actions provides a rationale for defending one's client against the death penalty; to assume that intelligence is innate is sufficient reason to maintain hierarchies in educational systems. In each case the psychological assumption is a constitutive feature of an ongoing social pattern. By this token certain theoretical assumptions serve to maintain already existing institutions, while others open the way to fresh alternatives. In this sense, certain theories furnish tools or devices for the construction of new forms of relationship.

SUMMARY

This chapter has first attempted to demonstrate the need for a fully developed discipline of metapsychology—that is, a form of scholarship devoted to understanding the nature and potential of psychological accounts. The chief impetus for such a discipline is derived from widespread developments concerning the nature of scientific language in general and psychological explanations in particular. As demonstrated in a variety of contexts, the relationship between language and the world is not such that theoretical propositions may be derived from observation. Nor can such propositions be tested against the world except in delimited contexts. The meaning of words is hammered out in specific social situations; the terms are typically imported into these situations—thus prefiguring what is later to be called factual; and the rules or conventions for intelligible word use play a critical role in determining how reality will be portrayed. Further, we find that the vocabulary used to describe human action essentially indexes psychological states; subsequent attempts to delineate such states are reliant on additional inferences to the psychological level. Thus the language of human action, along with psychological states, is not fundamentally falsifiable. The major upshot of these various arguments is that psychological theories are relatively unconstrained by the nature of the world. Thus the chief means of comparing theories in traditional psychology—namely the empirical test—is not adequate to the task of evaluating competing formulations. Alternative means must be sought for evaluating the character of psychological explanations. It is out of such a context that a need for metapsychology emerges. Such a discipline concerns itself with such issues as how psychological theories are generated, the manner in which they may be constrained, and their uses within the culture. Earlier work demonstrates the potential of such endeavors, and the chapters of the present volume attempt in various ways both to bring the endeavor into focal consciousness and to move understanding forward.

REFERENCES

Anscombe, G. E. M. (1976). *Intention.* Oxford: Blackwell.

Aries, P. (1962). *Centuries of childhood: A social history of family life.* New York: Vintage.

Apfelbaum, E., & Lubek, I. (1976). Resolution vs. revolution? The theory of conflicts in question. In L. Strickland, F. Aboud, & K. Gergen (Eds.), *Social psychology in transition.* New York: Plenum Press.

Austin, J. L. (1962). *How to do things with words.* New York: Oxford University Press.

Badinter, E. (1980). *Mother love, myth and reality.* New York: Macmillan.

Barnes, B. (1974). *Scientific knowledge and sociological theory.* London: Routledge and Kegan Paul.

Carnap, R. (1967). *The logical structure of the world* (2nd ed.). London: Routledge & Kegan Paul.

Chomsky, N. (1968). *Language & mind.* New York: Harcourt, Brace & World.

Collingwood, R. (1946). *The idea of history.* Oxford: Clarendon Press.

Coulter, J. (1979). *The social construction of the mind.* New York: Macmillan.

Deese, J. (1985). *American freedom and the social sciences.* New York: Columbia University Press.

DeMan, P. (1979). The epistemology of metaphor. *Critical Inquiry, 5,* 13-30.

Derrida, J. (1977). *Of grammatology* (Gayatri C. Spivak, Trans.). Baltimore: Johns Hopkins University Press.

Fuller, S. (1983). The "reductio ad symbolum" and the possibility of a linguistic object. *Philosophy of the Social Sciences, 13,* 129-156.

Gadamer, H. G. (1975). *Truth and method* (G. Barden & J. Cumming, Trans.). New York: Seabury. [Originally published as *Wahrheit und Methode.* Tubingen: J. C. B. Mohr (Paul Siebeck), 1960.]

Garfinkel, H. (1967). *Studies in ethnomethodology.* Englewood Cliffs, NJ: Prentice-Hall.

Gergen, K. J. (1982). *Toward transformation in social knowledge.* New York: Springer-Verlag.

Gergen, K. J. (1984). Aggression as discourse. In A. Mummendey (Ed.) *Social psychology of aggression.* Heidelberg: Springer-Verlag.

Gergen, K. J. (1985). Social pragmatics and the origin of psychological discourse. In K. J. Gergen & K. E. Davis (Eds.) *The social construction of the person.* New York: Springer-Verlag.

Gergen, K. J. (in press). If persons are texts. In Messer, S. B., Sass, L. A., Woolfolk, R. L. (Eds.), *Hermeneutics and psychological theory.* New Brunswick, NJ: Rutgers University Press.

Gergen, K. J., & Gergen, M. M. (in press). The self in temporal perspective. In R. Abeles (Ed.). *Life-span social psychology.* Hillsdale, NJ: Erlbaum.

Gilligan, C. (1982) *In a different voice.* Cambridge: Harvard University Press.

Gordon, T. (1973). Notes on white and black psychology. *The Journal of Social Issues, 29,* 87–96.

Graumann, C. F., & Sommer, M. (1984). Schema & Inference: Models in cognitive social psychology. *Annals of Theoretical Psychology,* Vol. 1, New York: Plenum.

Habermas, J. (1983). *Hermeneutics and critical theory.* Paper presented at Bryn Mawr College, 19 February.

Hampden-Turner, C. (1970). *Radical man: The process of psycho-social development.* Cambridge, MA: Schenkman.

Hanson, N. R. (1958). *Patterns of discovery.* London: Cambridge University Press.

Hartman, G. (1975). *The fate of reading and other essays.* Chicago: University of Chicago Press.

Hirsch, E. D. (1967). *Validity in interpretation.* New Haven, CT: Yale University Press.

Kessen, W. (1979). The American child and other cultural inventions. *American Psychologist, 34,* 815–820.

Kessler, S., & McKenna, W. (1978). *Gender: An ethnomethodological approach.* New York: Wiley.

Kuhn, T. S. (1970). *The structure of scientific revolution* (2nd rev. ed.). Chicago, IL: University of Chicago Press. (Original work published 1962.)

Lacan, G. (1978). *The four fundamental concepts of psychoanalysis.* J. Jacques-Alain Miller (Ed.). New York: Norton.

Levi-Strauss, C. (1963). *Structural anthropology.* New York: Basic Books.

McCloskey, D. (1985). *The rhetoric of economics.* Madison, WI: University of Wisconsin Press.

Neurath, O. (1959). Protocol sentences. In *Logical positivism.* A. J. Ayer (Ed.). Glencoe, IL: Free Press. (Originally published in 1932.)

Ossorio, P. (1985). An overview of descriptive psychology. In K. J. Gergen & K. E. Davis (Eds.). *The social construction of the person.* New York: Springer-Verlag.

Peters, R. S. (1958). *The concept of motivation.* London: Routledge & Kegan Paul.

Plon, M. (1974). On the meaning of the notion of conflict and its study in social psychology. *European Journal of Social Psychology, 4,* 389–436.

Ricoeur, P. (1974). *The conflict of interpretation: Essays in hermeneutics.* Evanston, IL: Northwestern University Press.

Rorty, R. (1979). *Philosophy and the mirror of nature.* Princeton, NJ: Princeton University Press.

Russell, B. (1924). Logical atomism. In *Contemporary British philosophy.* J. H. Muirhead (Ed.). New York: Macmillan.

Ryle, G. (1949). *The concept of mind.* London: Hutchinson.

Sampson, E. E. (1977). Psychology and the American ideal. *Journal of Personality and Social Psychology, 35,* 767–782.

Sampson, E. E. (1978). Scientific paradigms and social values: Wanted—A scientific revolution. *Journal of Personality and Social Psychology, 36,* 1332–1343.

Sarbin, T. R. (1968). *Narrative psychology.* New York: Praeger.

Schlick, M. (1934). *The foundation of knowledge on logical positivism.* A. J. Ayer (Ed.), Glencoe, IL: Free Press.

Shweder, R. A. & Miller, J. G. (1985). The social construction of the person: How is it possible? In K. J. Gergen & K. E. Davis (Eds.), *The social construction of the person.* New York: Springer-Verlag.

Smedslund, J. (1985). Necessarily true cultural psychologies. In K. J. Gergen & K. E. Davis (Eds.) *The social construction of the person.* New York: Springer-Verlag.

Taylor C. (1964). *The explanation of behavior.* London: Routledge & Kegan Paul.

Verhave, T., & van Hoorn, W. (1984). The temporalization of the self. In K. J. Gergen, & M. M. Gergen (Eds.) *Historical social psychology.* Hillsdale, NJ: Erlbaum.

Wexler, P. (1982). *Critical social psychology.* London: Routledge & Kegan Paul.

White, H. (1978). *Tropics of discourse.* Baltimore: Johns Hopkins University Press.

Winch, P. (1958). *The idea of a social science.* London: Routledge & Kegan Paul. (Originally published in 1946.)

Part One

The Study
of Metatheory

Chapter 1

Lagging behind the Papacy: Whither Psychology's Aggiornamento?

Morris L. Shames

INTRODUCTION

Hume (1748/1965) led the way in proffering his pronouncements on the problem of induction and the problem has not since abated. Notwithstanding the shaky, logical base upon which the pillar of scientific method is founded, it remains a robust and, by most measures, a successful enterprise. To put the problem succinctly, if somewhat generically, there exists a wide chasm between theory and praxis in the matter of scientific epistemology in that one cannot substantiate the scientific enterprise logically in terms of its own criteria; it is an edifice founded upon, in small measure, assumed fundamental postulates and, in large measure, an unarticulated faith. This is not a bloody-minded, obdurate view of science based on a biased reading of the historical, philosophical and sociological record; rather it is the view of scientists themselves—the self-reflective among them—and their commentators (e.g., Foster & Martin, 1966; Kuhn, 1970, 1977; Medawar, 1969; Polyani, 1958; Popper, 1965, 1972, 1973).

It is of no small moment that the great physicist Max Born grounded the

25

"inductive code" on an act of faith thereby reducing induction to a metaphysical principle (Popper, 1965). Thus, it is not by dint of its progress from observation to theory by means of a method which yields probative certainty that science has prospered. Science is at root an institutionalized set of attitudes and beliefs—an ideology (Brown, 1973)—and its prosperity reflects its ideological success rather than its logical prowess. Epistemologically speaking, it is a method no more superior than any other and very similar to most others in ideological form in that "inductivism is a formulary of beliefs, a complex of attitudes and practices having to do with the nature of science and scientific enquiry" (Medawar, 1969, p. 23).

Turn-of-the-century psychology had already turned away from ontic questions to those more readily settled by scientific materialism but the deontologization of psychology—at this point, seriously champing at the bit of scientific respectability—was not rendered complete until Watson (1913) proffered his Behaviorist manifesto. This was a radical, ideological tack and psychology has remained fundamentally ideological, scientifically ideological, ever since. In point of fact, psychology has so embraced the functionalist credo that it has voluntarily and assiduously eschewed theory in the bargain and, in the end, it has become victimized by its own praxical success. As a result, it is not the science which most constructively straddles the bicultural world of C. P. Snow (1959) but rather it is the most ideologically hardened of all the sciences (Doyle, 1965). It has been argued that this obdurate commitment to empirical data—admitting no other virtually—and the experimental paradigm has led psychology to an inverse relationship between the growing precision of its analysis and the shrinking significance, if not the outright factitiousness, of the phenomena it treats. As is the case with most ideologies, psychology has evolved into a triumph of form over matter.

Lest this view be considered mere rhetorical extravagance and unremitting counter-ideology, it should be noted that this view finds support, albeit obliquely in most instances, in the reflections of eminent psychologists. It is to this testimony which the paper now turns.

AN EPISTEMOLOGICAL ASSESSMENT OF SOCIAL PSYCHOLOGY WITH SPECIAL EMPHASIS ON ITS IDEOLOGICAL UNDERPINNING

Twentieth-century psychology has fastidiously clung to method as though it were the sole means whereby apodictic knowledge is revealed. This is evident from the educational regimes which students and psychologists undergo where the primary focus is on research design and statistical analysis and more research design and statistical analysis. This, of course, is to be expected owing to psychology's ideological nature, that is to say, its constellation of group commitments which, taken together, mould it into a "disciplinary matrix" (Kuhn, 1977). To elaborate, Kuhn (1970) has argued for a model of science as a shared community with deeply etched attitudes dictating what research will get done, what will get published and, therefore, what theories will be rife during any particular period. The flavor of this conception is characterized best by the following description:

> When, in the development of a natural science, an individual or group first pro-
> duces a synthesis able to attract most of the next generation's practitioners, the
> older schools gradually disappear. In part their disappearance is caused by their
> members' conversion to the new paradigm. But there are always some men who
> cling to one or another of the older views, and they are simply read out of the
> profession, which thereafter ignores their work. The new paradigm implies a new
> and more rigid definition of the field. Those unwilling or unable to accommodate
> their work to it must proceed in isolation or attach themselves to some other group
> (Kuhn, 1970, pp. 18–19).

Psychology's paradigm, it should be noted, appears to be grounded in formal scientism more than on substantive science and this, notwithstanding the apparent *circulus ad demonstrandum,* is the pillar upon which its ideological superstructure is founded.

There is no cavalier use of the term "ideology" in this analysis. Its application herein to psychology, considered as a disciplinary matrix, rests fully on its connotative richness given the extant social scientific literature on the topic. It is quite straightforwardly a matter of addressing the issue of science—itself a paradigm in the most generic sense of that term—and its much-vaunted disinterest as ideology even in the Marxist tradition where ideology is presumed to be a distortion of reality, a social formula in fact, which masks some specific, delineable interests to the detriment of true consciousness (Marx & Engels, 1927/ 1964). In virtue of Doyle's (1965) empirical test of psychology's commitment to the scientific creed among other even more telling data, such as the unspoken practices of the psychological community, it is clear that science, in general, and especially psychology, in particular, is a "style of thought," a *weltanschauung,* which Mannheim (1936) clearly identifies as a "total ideology." Geertz's (1964) view, unlike Marx, does not impute pejorative meaning to the term ideology; however, psychology in this view,—along with science in general, religion, aesthetics and the like—democratic as it is, is just another cultural system, an ideology.

Attitudes, founded as they are upon beliefs, intentions and behavior, are the foundational material out of which ideologies are fashioned. More precisely, the psychological view holds that "an ideology is a system of beliefs about social issues, with strong effects in structuring thoughts, feelings and behaviour" (Brown, 1973, p. 179). In addition, "ideologies force conclusions that are self-validating, and they control and restrict the behavior of individuals and groups"

(Brown, 1973, p. 180). They are, in short, colored by functional rationality (Mannheim, 1936)—a principal ingredient in this amalgam.

It appears clear, then, that there exists an extraordinary, extra-rational cleavage between what science is and what scientists say it is. Medawar (1969) describes this in the following terms:

> Science, broadly considered, is incomparably the most successful enterprise human beings have ever engaged upon; yet the methodology that has presumably made it so, when propounded by learned laymen, is not attended to by scientists, and when propounded by scientists is a misrepresentation of what they do. Only a minority of scientists have received instruction in scientific methodology and those that have done so seem no better off (p. 12).

This seeming violation of reason is tolerated by the scientific community on extra-rational grounds, that is to say, by dint of functional rationality. It is straightforwardly the case that self-reflection and the criticism that issues therefrom are simply not characteristic of ideology.

That this is an apt characterization of the extant state of affairs in psychology is reflected in the fact that the alarm of self-reflection and criticism has been sounded oftimes—on somewhat different grounds at different times—by the *cognoscenti* in the discipline. The measure of psychology's deep-seated ideological character is related to the extremely meager logical purchase which such well-grounded exhortations have exerted. Ideology, insofar as it is able, remains impervious to change.

Critique of the General Paradigm

There has indeed been something like a revolution of self-reflection in social psychology, in particular, a frontal attack on its perceived fundamental postulates, since the advent of the 1960's (Rosnow, 1981). Among these critics in the discipline there are those who have clamored for self-scrutiny without ever touching a raw, epistemological nerve. The order of criticism has usually been an impugnment of the general paradigm by reason of phenomena such as its synchronic limitations, its general internal or external invalidity, or its lack of detachable values.

In this vein the clarion call came from George Miller (1969) who, notwithstanding his passionate embrace of scientific psychology as "one of the most revolutionary enterprises ever conceived by the mind of man" (p. 1065), called for "giving psychology away" to the nonpsychologist. Instead of this demythologization, in practice, psychology—almost perversely—has continued to mystify those who would otherwise "take it" and avail themselves of it by tenaciously clinging to the linguistic syntax of science as an instrument of legitimation even though "the air of impersonal authority that reigns over such writing is often bogus" (Hudson, 1980, p. 453). It is simply the case that "in choosing one form of language rather than another, one genre rather than another, the psychologist commits himself epistemologically" (Hudson, 1980, p. 456) and in so doing psychology betrays itself as a fastidious, ideologically-grounded epistemology even in the face of exhortations to liberalize itself and, in the bargain, make itself that much more veridical. In short, instead of an *aggiornamento,* the likes of which John XXIII called for and which was authorized in large measure by Vatican Council II, and which would have the net effect of giving the Church back to the laity through, in part, a demystification and reappropriation of liturgy and practice, psychology has stood firm, clinging steadfastly to the language of mystification—"scientese"—as though its ideological existence depended upon it.

Not everyone in the discipline feels saddened over this state of affairs. McGuire's (1965) position, expressed succinctly in the following parable, is widely divergent from this view:

> I always ask an undergraduate inquirer why he feels his vocation lies in social psychology. Sometimes the student replies "I think maybe modern psychology has something to offer (or at least could be made to offer something) on the problem of international tensions, on how to reduce them before we all blow ourselves up, and I'd like to work on it." To such I say gently: "My boy, you have a good heart. I admire you. But unfortunately I myself have little to offer you. Perhaps you should speak to one of my colleagues here. Or have you thought of the law or the ministry?" But sometimes I get that other kind of student who replies: "I'm interested because I've got a hunch that a person might be able to do neat things in social psychology by using a little matrix algebra and difference equations." To this one I say, "My boy . . . welcome home" (p. 139).

Repelled by this total ideological posture and the partial ideologies which flow therefrom, Ring (1967) has been driven to inveigh against this as well as the fashion in social psychology which cultivates "fun-and-gamesmanship" instead of the humanistic, action-oriented discipline on whose behalf Lewin (1939) appealed.

Division Eight of the American Psychological Association, Personality and Social Psychology, has come in for more than its fair share of battering and excoriating self-examination owing to its general "epistemopathy" (Koch, 1981). Nearly a generation ago, Sanford (1965) wrote that:

> Psychology is really in the doldrums right now. It is fragmented, overspecialized, method centered, and dull. I can rarely find in the journals anything that I am tempted to read. And when I do read psychological papers, as I must as an editorial consultant, I become very unhappy; I am annoyed by the fact that they have all been forced into the same mold, in research design and style of reporting, and I am appalled by the degree to which an inflation of jargon and professional baggage has been substituted for psychological insight and sensitivity (p. 192).

Seventeen years later, Sanford (1982) found the ideological *status quo* to have been unrelenting, it seems, based upon his echoing references to the "too-far advanced overspecialization and fragmentation in psychology" (p. 896). This is as expected, in light of Mannheim's (1936) suggestion that ideologies are both insidious and conservative and, thus, resistant to change.

There is no shortage of voices—Cassandra voices it would seem, based on their impact—echoing this anti-ideological refrain. Paull (1980), for instance, has made the case whimsically that laws in science, unlike our cherished belief in scientific epistemology, are not independent phenomena awaiting discovery by some clever realist but are rather human artifacts necessitated only by a particular scientific posture. Such artifactual enterprise, according to Wachtel (1980), has been psychology's bane in that it has placed:

> . . . the emphasis on productivity and its encouragement of quickly doing, at the expense of reflecting on what one does and determining the resources needed to do the job well; . . . and the often exclusive reliance on experiments as the sole means of empirical inquiry—all interact to produce a pattern of research activity that has limited progress in our field. . . . we must reexamine these interlocking social and ideological forces . . . (p. 408).

Moreover, in social psychology this problem is further aggravated by an individuocentric bias that derives not from the nature of its subject matter but mainly from its ideological inclination, that is to say, from "methodological doctrines associated with the concept of psychology as a natural empirical science" (Pepitone, 1981, p. 972).

The general paradigm in psychology and, by dint of ideological success, in social psychology has thus met with a good deal of profoundly reasoned opposition. It is, however, a measure of its success in ideological terms that, praxically speaking, psychology has continued in much the same way as before. It should be noted that the story does not end here. There are significant cuirasses in the methodological armor of psychology which have great chinks yet, in virtue of its practices, psychology again shows itself to be undeterred by such problems.

Critique of Specific Elements of the General Paradigm

The litmus test of psychology's ideological resoluteness lies in its methodological obduracy even in the face of serious, logically-founded refutations of that methodology. For instance, Rozeboom (1960), in a landmark paper, has argued that the omnipresent null-hypothesis decision procedure is "vigorously excoriated for its inappropriateness as a method of *inference*," concluding that "its most basic error lies in mistaking the aim of scientific investigation to be a *decision* rather than a *cognitive* evaluation of propositions" (p. 428); yet psychology, in the true spirit of ideological heedlessness, has continued with this same methodological practice at the same rate as before.

Meehl (1967) expatiated upon this same theme by drawing attention to a paradox which should have proved fatal to psychological methodology. He argued that:

> In the physical sciences, the usual result of an improvement in experimental design, instrumentation, or numerical mass of data, is to increase the difficulty of the "observational hurdle" which the physical theory of interest must successfully surmount; whereas, in psychology and some of the allied behavior sciences, the usual effect of such improvement in experimental precision is to provide an easier hurdle for the theory to surmount. (p. 103)

He reasons, thus, that an improvement in the power of a statistical design yields a scientifically unrespectable result in psychology. As if this was not sufficiently damaging to psychology's methodological cause, he exacerbates the problem further by pointing out that the null-hypothesis testing procedure is founded on the formally invalid case of the *modus ponens*. This fatally damaging argument rests on the most important consideration that:

> inadequate appreciation of the extreme weakness of the test to which a substantive theory T is subjected by merely predicting a directional statistical difference $\bar{d} > 0$ is then compounded by a truly remarkable failure to recognize the logical asymmetry between, on the one hand (formally invalid) "confirmation" of a theory via affirming the consequent in an argument of the form: (T $\supset$ H_1, H_1, infer T), and on the other hand the deductively tight *refutation* of the theory *modus tollens* by a falsified prediction, the logical form being (T $\supset$ H_1, $\sim$ H_1, infer $\sim$ T). (p. 112)

These arguments and their begetter are extremely difficult to ignore and, even more importantly, to dismiss, yet psychology has accomplished both.

This apparent indifference is all the more difficult to comprehend in consequence of the chorus of important voices all harmonizing on the same theme. Bakan (1966), in concert with the above argument, has reasoned forcefully that:

> The test of significance does not provide the information concerning psychological phenomena characteristically attributed to it; and a great deal of mischief has been associated with its use. . . . The null hypothesis is characteristically false under any circumstances. Publication practices foster the reporting of small effects in populations. Psychologists have "adjusted" by misinterpretation, taking the p value as a "measure," assuming that the test of significance provides automaticity of inference, and confusing the aggregate with the general (p. 423).

This point of view is reinforced by Lykken's (1968) postulation that the null hypothesis is never strictly true, "such predictions having about a 50–50 chance

chance of being confirmed by experiment when the theory in question is false, since the statistical significance of the result is a function of sample size" (p. 150). Moreover, he properly claims that statistical significance is almost inconsequential in the grand design of experimental verification, which echoes the arguments of Bakan (1966), Meehl (1967) and, most particularly Bolles (1962) who has suggested that "the effect of any single experimental verification is not to confirm a scientific hypothesis but only to make its *a posteriori* probability a little higher than its *a priori* probability" (p. 645). Buttressing this argument even more, Lachenmeyer (1969) has written that "tests of statistical significance and rules of experimental sophistication must be supplemented with some concept of theoretical significance" (p. 621). Proffering persuasive arguments against piecemeal nomological experimentation, he concludes that this approach is not the most efficient means by which general theories of human behavior are developed. In like vein with Meehl (1967) he makes clear the logical invalidity of this form of experimentation *a fortiori,* by suggesting that despite the avowed bias against committing the fallacy of the *modus ponens* in modern scientific psychology, by dint of practice and as an extra-logical, entirely human theory-building device, "this fallacy is the lifeblood of science." (p. 623)

Such a contradiction between theory and practice in the rational world of science seems, on the surface, inexplicable but, upon closer examination, it reveals itself as rational indeed. As is the case with all ideology, extra-rational behavior frequently is undertaken on behalf of a highly rational institutionalized set of values. Thus, psychology's methodolatrous ideology, as Bakan (1967/ 1974) has characterized it, is sufficiently grounded as to withstand and repel the onslaught of mere logic.

The arguments in respect of particular elements of this methodological ideology have not all turned on this question of internal validity. The laboratory experiment, for instance, has suffered criticism based on the analysis of its limited external validity (Adair, 1982; Berkowitz & Donnerstein, 1982; Harré & Secord, 1972; Mitchell & McKillip, 1982), artifact owing to experimenter effects and subject effects both (Adair, 1973; Barber, 1976; Rosenthal, 1976; Rosnow, 1981; Shames, 1979, 1983; Silverman, 1977), demand characteristics (Orne, 1962, 1973) and evaluation apprehension (Rosenberg, 1969), to name the most prominent criticisms. Yet notwithstanding the weight of this considered opinion, psychology has continued unperturbed in its methodological, scientistic routine. For its strenuous effort in this regard it has earned for itself criticism of the following order:

> Pure research in social psychology is among the most unproductive fields of human endeavor today ranking only with mathematical economics as being a kind of exciting game for people that like exciting games in this particular field, i.e. nobody except those who do it (Scriven, 1964, p. 190).

An Epistemological Critique

As damaging as the above-cited criticisms should have been, it should be noted that the critique runs even deeper. These criticisms bore to the very heart of psychology transcending issues of empiricalism and experimentation, although they impinge on them obliquely. Koch's (1981) thesis is one of the most lucid on the subject, arguing eloquently that:

> a syndrome of "ameaningful thinking" is seen to underlie much of modern scholarship, especially the inquiring practices of the psychological sciences. Ameaningful thought regards knowledge as an almost automatic result of a self-corrective rule structure, a fail-proof heuristic, a methodology—rather than of discovery. In consequence, much of psychological history can be seen as a form of scientistic role playing which, however sophisticated, entails the trivialization, and even evasion, of significant problems (p. 257).

Arguing from the antinomal character of human experience, antinomies in this sense including and exceeding the classic antinomies propounded by Kant, Koch is led to the conclusion that:

> there is a class of questions which have intense meaning to all human beings but which "transcend the competence of human reason." The pervasiveness of such meaningful yet (strictly) undecidable issues in experience leads, in both formal and disciplinary contexts, to forms of cognitive denial that fuel such ameaningful tendencies as the belief in the coextensionality of the undecidable and the meaningless, and the need to exorcize uncertainty by ensconcing inquiry in a spurious "systematicity" (p. 257).

In assessing the scientific status of psychology, Koch—the self-avowed "epistemopathectomist"—holds a variegated methodological view, not the wizened, dogmatic view of the discipline itself. His rhetoric is not merely counter-ideological nor does it pertinaciously call for the exorcism of our experimental epistemopathy. In fact, he recognizes that:

> fields like sensory and biological psychology may certainly be regarded as solidly within the family of the biological and, in some reaches, natural sciences. But psychologists must finally accept the circumstance that extensive and important sectors of psychological study require modes of inquiry rather more like those of the humanities than the sciences. . . . A moral analysis of the past, by inviting a change of heart, is a surer bridge to a tolerable future than any confident methodological manifesto (p. 269).

Koch, apparently, is a more perspicuous epistemologist than ideologist, a fact revealed by the following articulated sentiment:

It is incredible to contemplate that during a century dominated by the tidy imagery of prediction and control of human and social events, the perverse cognitive pathology housed in such imagery has not been rooted out. In fact, such notions have rarely been seen as problematic and still more rarely subjected even to perfunctory modes of analysis (p. 266).

It is not incredible at all in light of our understanding that this is the way of ideology in all intellectual enterprise.

There is a concentration of such opinion adverting to the notion that the existing condition of psychology as a theoretical science is chaotic (e.g. Peele, 1981; Royce, 1982). In the case of social psychology this is grounded in the view of an aleatory subject matter in that:

social psychology is primarily an historical inquiry. Unlike the natural sciences, it deals with facts that are largely non-repeatable and which fluctuate markedly over time. Principles of human interaction cannot readily be developed over time because the facts on which they are based on do not generally remain stable. Knowledge cannot accumulate in the usual scientific sense because such knowledge does not generally transcend its historical boundaries (Gergen, 1973, p. 310).

This view has not been proffered without criticism (Schlenker, 1974) but, based on the evidence of those who pronounce on the subject of metatheory and metamethodology, it does appear to be the prevailing view and it has not since suffered either abatement or recantation. More recently, for instance, it has been affirmed that the investigation of social phenomena, in psychology, is synonymous with the controlled experiment which, to put it baldly, is insufficient for the task owing to the fact that social events are culturally imbedded, sequentially imbedded, openly competitive with other simultaneously occurring stimuli, complexly determined and, in addition, they represent a "final common pathway" for a number of interacting psychological states (Gergen, 1978). Even more recently, in a somewhat more sanguine historiographical treatment of this ungrounded epistemology in social psychology, this same critical approach is brought to bear in an effort to reorient the discipline toward a diachronic, genetic social psychology (Rosnow, 1978, 1981). However, the disciplinary matrix, notwithstanding the weight of this considered opinion criticizing it, has remained unmoved.

THE AGGIORNAMENTO

The *aggiornamento* is fundatorily a call to *phronesis,* to practical wisdom and deliberating soundly, where methodolatry is intentionally sacrificed—exorcised, in fact—in favor of content-grounded theory. Such theory draws attention to the veridicality of the subject matter and prescinds the extant methodological imperative in psychology. This approach is emancipatory, freeing the investigator from his objectivist ideology which unavoidably leads to a rigidified epistemology grounded solely on methodological preoccupation. Further, this call is not unlike the view, in some respects, of that eminent historian, Herbert Butterfield (1931/1963), who advisedly opts for the tendentious historian who makes no attempt whatever to conceal his bias rather than the historian who self-righteously—and mistakenly, in his view—clings to the historiographical myth that he is pristinely objective in his historical account. This call, then, is purely emancipatory and does not, in and of itself, outline a more apposite theory of knowledge than the one modern psychology has embraced.

Gadamer (1975) has undertaken such an epistemological project having recognized that the contemporary view of science "does not see nature as an intelligible whole but as a process that has nothing to do with human beings, a process on which scientific research throws a limited but reliable light, thus making it possible to control it" (p. 211). His hermeneutical theory lays claim to universality, with language as its fundamental substrate, and this frames his bulwark against the positivist hyperbole in methodologically-grounded science. Based upon empirical investigation (Doyle, 1965) this epistemology should speak most poignantly to psychology, yet it has passed wholly unnoticed by the discipline. It rejects dogmatic methodology and invites an *aggiornamento* in virtue of:

> the claim to universality on the part of hermeneutics [which] consists in integrating all the sciences, of perceiving the opportunities for knowledge on the part of every scientific method *wherever they may be applicable to given objects* [italics mine]; and of deploying them in all their possibilities. . . . It has to bring everything knowable by the sciences into the context of mutual agreement in which we ourselves exist. To the extent that hermeneutics brings the contribution of the sciences into this context of mutual agreement that links us with the tradition that has come down to us in a unity that is efficacious in our lives, it is not just a repertory of methods. . . but philosophy. It not only accounts for the procedures applied by science but also gives an account of the questions that are prior to the application of every science. . . . These are the questions that are determinative for all human knowing and doing, the greatest of questions, that are decisive for human beings as human and their choice of the good (Gadamer, 1981, p. 137).

This view, indeed the whole hermeneutic apparatus, irrespective of its origin, should have proved especially germane for a psychology which has recently recognized "an epistemic drive present in man" which "provides the basis for the development of symbolizing activity" (Royce, Coward, Egan, Kessel & Mos, 1978, p. 340). That it has not so proved is a measure of the ideological obduracy of a discipline which apparently prefers the comfort of convention to relevancy.

There is yet another theory that speaks adroitly to the plight of science and psychology, in particular. Jurgen Habermas' (1971) critical theory—

notwithstanding its moorings in the sea of German thought running from Kant to Marx, with its moral-political inspiration and deeply felt intention to transmogrify social systems which prove themselves inimical to the masses of people—is just such a theory. It is first and foremost a general theory of knowledge which "views social theory so broadly as to include virtually the entire range of systematic knowledge about man" (McCarthy, 1978, p. *x*). It is, furthermore, profoundly committed to opposition to the "objectivist illusion" and calls for a clearly self-critical epistemology, one which is rarely, if ever, recognized in dogmatic scientific practice. Such an approach is especially welcome in that it offers the promise of generative theory (Gergen, 1978) in the face of a wizened, sterile social psychology.

Habermas (1971) has taken as his principal task the understanding and explanation of how the dissolution of epistemology has led to the ascendancy of philosophy of science. As a result, critical consciousness has been lost and he takes it as his major undertaking, his radical epistemology, to revivify this— these abandoned stages of reflection. His central thesis is that " 'the specific view points from which we apprehend reality,' the 'general cognitive strategies' that guide systematic inquiry, have their 'basis in the natural history of the human species' " (McCarthy, 1978, p. 55). Moreover, they are inextricably rooted in the "imperatives of the socio-cultural form of life" (p. 55). Thus, he classifies three species of inquiry: (1) the empirical-analytic sciences, (2) the historical-hermeneutic sciences, and (3) the critically-oriented sciences.

The empirical-analytic sciences are guided by the goal of furnishing nomological knowledge and are generally underpinned by "an 'anthropologically deep-seated interest' in predicting and controlling events in the natural environment" (McCarthy, 1978, p. 55). The cognitive strategy to which this enterprise is linked is the technical interest. The historical-hermeneutic sciences, on the other hand, have as their aim the interpretation of meaningful configurations and this process finds itself underpinned by the "anthropologically deep-seated interest in securing and expanding possibilities of mutual and self-understanding in the conduct of life" (p. 56), what Habermas refers to as the practical interest. Finally, the critically-oriented sciences which aim at "emancipation from pseudonatural constraints whose power resides in their non-transparency" (p. 56), are underpinned by emancipatory cognitive interests. This thematization demonstrates how epistemology is guided by general cognitive strategies. More specifically:

> these cognitive interests are of significance neither for the psychology nor the sociology of knowledge, nor for the critique of ideology in any narrower sense; for they are invariant . . . [They are not] influences on cognition that have to be eliminated for the sake of the objectivity of knowledge; rather they themselves determine the aspect under which reality can be objectified and thus made accessible to experience in the first place (Habermas, 1973, pp. 8–9).

In an emendatory shift from consciousness to language, Habermas (1973) has formulated a theory of social evolution and communicative competence, a universal pragmatics, as he calls it, but his aim remains nonetheless emancipatory. He still wishes to free modern, scientized epistemology from its rigid methodocentrism and to radicalize the enterprise by opening up the possibility of critical choice based upon reflection. In this approach, no metatheoretical discourse is free from criticism and potential modification. This theory speaks to science and, especially, psychology, given the methodological monolith it has become; however, our discipline has yet to sit up and take notice of it.

In consequence of the understanding that one congenial exemplar is worth pages of rhetoric, a recent study on *Contemporary Perspectives and Future Directions of Personality and Social Psychology* (Rosenberg & Gara, 1983) recommends itself to the issues under consideration in this paper. Its intent was both historiographical and augural in nature in that it posed the following questions:

> What are the underlying theoretical and methodological dimensions that differentiate prominent figures in personality and social psychology? What are the conceptual and methodological relations between personality and social psychology? What are the relations of personality and social psychology to the rest of psychology? This is followed by the identification of major ideological, substantive, and methodological developments in these two fields. The question that we then take up is what contemporary interest communities have emerged from these developments (p. 58).

However, even though the perceptions and opinions of eminent practitioners in Division Eight of the American Psychological Association were the source of the data generated by this study, the yield—not unexpectedly—was disappointingly meagre indeed, pointing up, for the most part, the ideological character and myopic perceptions of the discipline. It could not possibly be otherwise since the nature of the study itself—notwithstanding its subject matter—was in the mainstream of social psychology, that is to say, it was purely method-centered and this led to predictable, inevitable contentual aridity. It is yet another *conventional* example where content was unable to triumph over form. That, after all, is the way with disciplinary matrices.

REFERENCES

Adair, J. G. (1973). *The human subject: The social psychology of the psychological experiment*. Boston: Little, Brown.

Adair, J. G. (1982). Meaning of the situation to subjects. *American Psychologist, 37*, 12, 1406–1408.

Bakan, D. (1966). The test of significance in psychological research. *Psychological Bulletin, 66*, 423–437.

Bakan, D. (1967/1974). *On method: Toward a reconstruction of psychological investigation.* San Francisco: Jossey-Bass.

Barber, T. X. (1976). *Pitfalls in human research: Ten pivotal points.* New York: Pergamon Press.

Berkowitz, L. & Donnerstein, E. (1982). External validity is more than skin deep. Some answers to criticisms of laboratory experiments. *American Psychologist, 37,* 3, 245–257.

Bolles, R. C. (1962). The difference between statistical hypotheses and scientific hypotheses. *Psychological Reports, 11,* 639–645.

Brown, L. B. (1973). *Ideology.* Harmondsworth, England: Penguin Books.

Butterfield, H. (1931/1963). *The Whig interpretation of history.* London: G. Bell & Sons.

Doyle, C. L. (1965). *Psychology, science, and the western democratic tradition.* Unpublished doctoral dissertation, University of Michigan.

Foster, M. H. & Martin, M. L. (1966). *Probability, confirmation and simplicity: Readings in the philosophy of inductive logic.* New York: The Odyssey Press.

Gadamer, H–G. (1975). *Truth and method.* New York: Continuum.

Gadamer, H–G. (1981). *Reason in the age of science.* Cambridge, MA: MIT Press.

Geertz, C. (1964). Ideology as a cultural system. In David Apter (Ed.). *Ideology and discontent.* New York: Free Press.

Gergen, K. J. (1973). Social psychology as history. *Journal of Personality and Social Psychology, 26,* 309–320.

Gergen, K. J. (1978). Toward generative theory. *Journal of Personality and Social Psychology, 36,* 11, 1344–1360.

Habermas, J. (1971). *Knowledge and human interests.* Boston: Beacon Press.

Habermas, J. (1973). *Theory and practice.* Boston: Beacon Press.

Harré, R., & Secord, P. F. (1972). *The explanation of social behavior.* Totowa, N.J.: Rowman & Littlefield.

Hudson, L. (1980). Language, truth and psychology. In L. Michaels & C. Richs (Eds.), *The state of the language* (pp. 449–457). Berkeley, CA: University of California Press.

Hume, D. (1965). *An enquiry concerning human understanding.* Chicago: Gateway Editions. (Originally published, 1748).

Koch, S. (1981). The nature and limits of psychological knowledge: Lessons of a century qua "Science." *American Psychologist, 36,* 257–269.

Kuhn, T. S. (1970). *The structure of scientific revolutions.* Chicago: University of Chicago Press.

Kuhn, T. S. (1977). *The essential tension: Selected studies in scientific tradition and change.* Chicago: University of Chicago Press.

Lachenmeyer, C. W. (1969). Experimentation: A misunderstood methodology in psychological and social-psychological research. *American Psychologist, 24,* 12, 617–624.

Lewin, K. (1939). Field theory and experiment in social psychology: Concept and methods. *American Journal of Sociology, 44,* 868–896.

Lykken, D. T. (1968). Statistical significance in psychological research. *Psychological Bulletin, 70,* 151–159.

Mannheim, K. (1936). *Ideology and Utopia: An introduction to the sociology of knowledge.* New York: Harcourt, Brace Jovanovich.

Marx, K. & Engels, F. (1927/1964). *The German ideology.* Moscow: Progress Publishers.

McCarthy, T. (1978). *The critical theory of Jurgen Habermas.* Cambridge, MA: MIT Press.

McGuire, W. J. (1965). Discussions of N. Schoenfeld's paper. In O. Klineberg & R. Christie (Eds.), *Perspectives in social psychology.* (pp. 135–140). New York: Holt, Rinehart & Winston.

Medawar, P. B. (1969). *Induction and intuition in scientific thought.* Philadelphia: American Philosophical Society.

Meehl, P. E. (1967). Theory-testing in psychology and physics: A methodological paradox. *Philosophy of Science,* June, 103–115.

Miller, G. A. (1969). Psychology as a means of promoting human welfare. *American Psychologist, 24,* 1063–1075.

Mitchell, T. O. & McKillip, J. (1982). The defense that fails. *American Psychologist, 37,* 12, 1408–1409.

Orne, M. T. (1962). On the social psychology of the psychological experiment: With particular reference to demand characteristics and their implications. *American Psychologist, 17,* 776–783.

Orne, M. T. (1973). Communication by the total experimental situation: Why is it important, how is it evaluated, and its significance for the ecological validity of findings. In P. Pliner, L. Krames & T. Alloway (Eds.), *Communication and affect.* New York: Academic Press.

Paull, J. (1980). Laws of behavior. Fact or artifact? *American Psychologist, 35,* 12, 1081–1083.

Peele, S. (1981). Reductionism in the psychology of the eighties: Can biochemistry eliminate addiction, mental illness, and pain? *American Psychologist, 36,* 8, 807–818.

Pepitone, a. (1981). Lessons from the history of social psychology. *American Psychologist, 36,* 9, 972–985.

Polyani, M. (1958). *Personal knowledge: Towards a post-critical philosophy.* Chicago: The University of Chicago Press.

Popper, K. R. (1965). *Conjectures and refutations: The growth of scientific knowledge.* New York: Harper & Row.

Popper, K. R. (1972). *The logic of scientific discovery.* London: Hutchinson & Company.

Popper, K. R. (1973). *Objective knowledge: An evolutionary approach.* London: Oxford University Press.

Ring, K. (1967). Experimental social psychology: Some sober questions about some frivolous values. *Journal of Experimental Social Psychology, 3,* 113–123.

Rosenberg, M. J. (196). The conditions and consequences of evaluation apprehension. In *Artifact in behavioral research,* R. Rosenthal and R. L. Rosnow, pp. 280–349. New York: Academic Press.

Rosenberg, S. & Gara, M. A. (1983). Contemporary perspectives and future directions of personality and social psychology. *Journal of Personality and Social Psychology, 45,* 57–73.

Rosenthal, R. (1976). *Experimenter effects in behavioral research: Enlarged edition.* New York: Irvington.

Rosnow, R. L. (1978). The prophetic vision of Giambattista Vico: Implications for the state of social psychological theory. *Journal of Personality and Social Psychology, 36,* 11, 1322–1331.

Rosnow, R. L. (1981). *Paradigms in transition: The methodology of social inquiry.* New York: Oxford University Press.

Royce, J. R. (1982). Philosophic issues, Division 24, and the future. *American Psychologist, 37,* 3, 258–266.

Royce, J. R., Coward, H., Egan, E., Kessel, F. & Mos, L. (1978). Psychological epistemology: A critical review of the empirical literature and the theoretical issues. *Genetic Psychology Monographs, 97,* 265–353.

Rozeboom, W. E. (1960). The fallacy of the null-hypothesis significance test. *Psychological Bulletin, 57,* 416–428.

Sanford, N. (1965). Will psychologists study human problems? *American Psychologist, 20,* 192–202.

Sanford, N. (1982). Social psychology: Its place in personology. *American Psychologist, 37,* 896–903.

Schlenker, B. R. (1974). Social psychology and science. *Journal of Personality and Social Psychology, 29,* 1, 1–15.

Scriven, M. (1964). Views of human nature. In T. Wann (Ed.), *Behaviorism and phenomenology* (pp. 163–183). Chicago: University of Chicago Press.

Shames, M. L. (1979). On the metamethodological dimension of the "expectancy paradox." *Philosophy of Science, 46,* 3, 382–388.

Shames, M. L. (1983). Experimenter bias and the biased experimental paradigm. In N. Rescher (Ed.). *The limits of lawfulness: Studies on the scope and nature of scientific knowledge.* (pp. 101–107). Lanham, Maryland: University Press of America.

Silverman, I. (1977). *The human subject in the psychological laboratory.* New York: Pergamon Press.

Snow, C. P. (1959). *Two cultures and the scientific revolution: The Rede lecture.* New York: Cambridge University Press.

Wachtel, P. (1980). Investigation and its discontents: Some constraints on progress in psychological research. *American Psychologist, 35,* 5, 399–408.

Watson, J. B. (1913). Psychology as the behaviorist views it. *Psychological Review, 20,* 158–177.

Chapter 2

A Critical Constructionist View of Psychology and Personhood

Edward E. Sampson

INTRODUCTION

The hegemony of the Western, patricentric worldview, once so much taken for granted that to challenge it was to fly in the face of reason itself, has increasingly come under critical scrutiny. One area in which this challenge has been significantly mounted involves the concepts and ideals of the person (e.g., Geertz, 1973, 1979; Gergen & Davis, 1985; Gilligan, 1982; Lykes, 1985; Sampson, 1983b, 1985; Shweder & Bourne, 1982). Can anything be more obvious or natural than our culture's view of what a person is, where a person's boundaries begin and end, and what the ideal person, that is, the mature adult should be like?

Far from being natural, however, all concepts and ideals of personhood are cultural constructions designed to serve certain purposes and encourage certain kinds of social practices and institutions. In this respect, therefore, the view we hold so dear is but one of several alternatives, neither natural nor inevitable in the larger scheme of human possibilities. This position lies clearly within the

scope of those broad approaches that have come under the rubric of constructionism (e.g., Gergen, 1985; Sampson, 1983a, 1983b). In this view, reality is a
cultural construction with a history and an ongoing social dynamic.

I call my own position a critical constructionism, however, in order to
support that while reality is a sociohistorical construction, and thus many different realities exist within the world, this need not reduce us to mere relativists
who accept any and all social constructions without comment.

All societies construct their concept of what it means to be a person and
their ideals about the mature person. In general, the Western world sees persons
as highly bounded, individuated entities, and, as I noted elsewhere (Sampson,
1977), tends to emphasize a self-contained ideal: that is, the ideal person is not
only highly distinct and well defined apart from others, but in addition is remarkably capable of standing alone, containing within him or herself all the
qualities valued by the culture. This view is by no means universal, either
within the world or for that matter within the West itself. Thus it is not a natural
way of understanding and being a person, but one that has been socially and
historically constructed in order to serve particular institutions and purposes.

If we follow the recent account developed by Heelas and Lock (1981), we
can see an illustration of the two key dimensions of all cultures' indigenous
psychologies of persons and selves. One dimension emphasizes the nature of
the self-other boundary. The second dimension focuses on matters of autonomy,
the degree to which persons are understood to be "in control" or "under
control." The Western view clearly locates itself on the side of a sharply defined
self-other boundary and an emphasis on being in control. Heelas and Lock's
review of several indigenous psychologies suggests a general but by no means
perfect correlation between these two dimensions. Thus in general, cultures
such as our own that emphasize sharp self-other boundaries likewise emphasize
selves in control, whereas cultures, such as the Dinka and the Chewong are
reported to be within the opposite quadrant, emphasizing both less firmly drawn
self-other boundaries and a self under, not in control.

The difficulty in breaking the hold of our own view is well illustrated in
two key papers appearing in the same special issue of the *Journal of Personality*
(June, 1985). The first paper by Franz and White (1985) seeks to extend
Erikson's Western and male-centered theory of human development by bringing
into clearer focus the development of attachment and connectedness. What the
two authors are unable to abandon, however, is their insistence that the course
of development still moves towards individuality. This latter point is very
clearly addressed by Lykes' (1985) paper in that same issue. She reviews what
she terms "female" variations in the "male" model of developmental maturity
and concludes that however much such variations have sought to extend our
understanding, they remain firmly wrapped in the Western notion of an independent and autonomous self, thus retaining "the underlying assumption of
individualism" (p. 361).

These sociohistorical constructions of personhood do not appear in a vacuum as isolated bits and pieces of a culture; they are thoroughly embedded in and permeate almost all aspects of the culture. In particular, personhood occupies a strategic position in that it both arises from the underlying structures and practices of a culture and operates to sustain those very features that give rise to it (see Bhaskar, 1979; Giddens, 1979; Sampson, 1983a). In other words, societies constitute the kinds of person they need in order to reproduce themselves.

TOWARD A CRITICAL CONSTRUCTIONISM

Thus far, my position has been primarily constructionist. A critical constructionist view takes a further step. Not being satisfied to make the observation that personhood is a social and historical construction, we now ask questions about the functions and adequacy of any particular social product. On its face, this latter inquiry would seem to be absurd. After all, if reality is socially constructed, including the standards by which we judge any social construction, then from what position can we stand to judge any societal creation? It would require a reality behind the constructed reality in order for us to talk about such matters. Would this not lead us away from the constructionist paradigm and back towards an objectivist model?

Fortunately, the issue I am addressing has a reasonably long history and thus several guidelines that might help save us from theoretical incoherence. The basic issue is whether any standards exist by which to evaluate the truth claims of a socially constructed reality. The objectivist or exogenic philosophy of science promises a standard beyond time and place, and thus at least the illusion of a firm reality against which any current form can be judged. But once we adopt a constructionist position, we seem to have lost that critical cutting edge and thus can all too easily sink into an uncritical relativism.

Gergen and Habermas: A Sociorational Standard

Gergen's (1985) account recognizes this possibility and offers two suggestions. The first is his correct observation that in challenging the taken-for-granted world of our everyday life, constructionism is inherently critical. That is, rather than viewing current social and psychological forms as eternal verities, constructionism recognizes their situated nature and so opens the door to a critical inquiry about the particular functions such forms currently serve. Although no objective standard is introduced, at least we can call upon different cross-cultural and historical alternatives as one way to evaluate current social and psychological realities. Unfortunately, this kind of critique can itself readily lead to the relativistic stance of merely noting that "we do things this way; they do things differently." Critique may be blunted; even oppressive practices may appear proper.

Gergen's second point joins him especially with Habermas (1971, 1973, 1975; also see McCarthy, 1978) in seeking a socially negotiated theory of truth.

Habermas builds his thesis around what he calls the ideal-speech situation: a dialogic context within which truth claims may be redeemed or judged as redeemable by adopting an idealized communication standard. Without spelling out the full details of his argument, let me simply note that the ideal-speech situation shares many features in common with a psychoanalytic session in which both conscious and unconscious sources of bias are open to examination; the ideal also shares much with a fair argument, in which all sides have equal opportunities to question and challenge and no one version holds sway merely because of matters of unequal power. It is the force of the better argument that Habermas argues can redeem truth claims. Even though his theory remains within the constructionist paradigm, Habermas sees a rational standard—the ideal speech situation—beyond any one time and place that can be applied in evaluating any truth claim.

Nature Resurrected

Other efforts to remain faithful to constructionism while nevertheless seeking a standard against which to judge truth claims have appeared within the critical theories of the pre-Habermasian Frankfurt school, most notably Horkheimer (1974; also Horkheimer & Adorno, 1972), Adorno (1967, 1973) and Marcuse (1960, 1966, 1968). In his excellent work, *Eclipse of Reason* for example, Horkheimer argues on behalf of an objectivity within nature. He argues that subjectivism, the hallmark of modern science and thus exogenic in Gergen's framework, in which truth claims are evaluated by reference to the facts of human experience and experimentation, has led us down sadly distorted pathways; that we need again to discover what the early Greeks knew in joining the objective reason of nature with humanity's subjective capability of apprehending it.

On its face, Horkheimer's view might appear to be exogenic in a slightly altered guise. Yet, I believe that Horkheimer rejects this objectivist view of science and scientism. Horkheimer's argument is a combination of sociohistorical constructionism on the one hand and a concern with its exclusive reliance on the individual, on the other. He sees the latter as a reversion to subjectivism and thereby a denial that nature itself is reasonable.

Horkheimer's position is difficult to maintain. Once we adopt his perspective in surveying what scientific rationality had wrought, however, the basis for his argument becomes clear. Somewhat paradoxically, the exogenic viewpoint, which might appear to provide nature its rightful due, wrenched all reason from nature and placed it within the individual. Horkheimer sought to return to nature what people, in their quest for power and domination, had stolen.

An important, and as yet unanswered question raised by Horkheimer's position is relevant to the constructionist perspective. Has constructionism, in locating the source of reason within the human community, once again stolen reason from nature? One can only surmise that Horkheimer would be displeased with this feature of constructionism; although, as noted, it remains unclear how to tread the delicate line he advocates in his own analysis.

Adorno both joined with Horkheimer and also expanded on a somewhat different critical view in arguing that any given social form, especially psychological forms (e.g., beliefs, attitudes, cognitions about reality) were simultaneously both true and false. They were true insofar as they accurately represented the current state of affairs within a society; they were false insofar as what they represented was not an eternal verity, but a construction usually devised to serve one group's interests in dominating another.

Blaming the victim is illustrative of some of what Adorno means. People tend to hold victims, for example, of unemployment or poverty, somehow responsible for the fate they suffer. On the one hand, because this belief system represents how people actually feel about others and about themselves, it is a true description. On the other hand, insofar as the belief tends to personalize responsibility for occurrences whose roots may better be seen to lie within the social system, the belief is also false: it supports an ongoing system of domination by deflecting attention away from the social causes of personal misfortune and toward personal causation. The latter often renders persons depressed and impotent to act on behalf of social change.

Although no purely objective standard exists against which to evaluate our judgments, Adorno urged us to remain forever vigilant against reifying current realities, transforming them into eternal verities, or submitting to an uncritical relativism. One form which this vigilance took involved his adoption of a kind of constant processural view of the world, revealed for example in his work, *Negative Dialectics*. Somewhat like the early Marcuse (1960, 1968), Adorno maintained that only through an incessant great refusal could one remain critical of any and all ongoing social and psychological forms. Thus, Adorno came to distrust all identities. As with Horkheimer, we can recognize the basis for Adorno's concern and his efforts to find a cure for the modern malaise. His cure was to remain forever sceptical. Naysaying thus was his answer to the relativism of a constructionist view.

Marcuse's work, *Eros and Civilization* adopted a slightly different stance. He was highly critical of the conformism of neoanalytic ego psychology, suggesting that we would have done better to remain with Freud's original instinct theory. For Marcuse, instincts provided the necessary critical cutting edge from which to evaluate the validity of current forms of social and psychological nature. The recent compilation of cross-cultural concepts of the person that Heelas and Lock (1981) edited adopts a somewhat Marcusian stance. They refer to "the natural self" against which cultural constructions are considered. For example, they raise the question of whether the mechanism known as "catharsis" works in nature or is a socially constructed theory that works in culture. While not answering their own question, their stance locates them within the Marcusian camp: both have sought some natural grounding (e.g., in instincts or a so-called natural self) as a protection against the seductions of an uncritical relativism.

Beyond Structuralism

One further effort to establish a critical constructionism is not unrelated to the preceding, but its accent is sufficiently different to warrant separate consideration. This alternative appears most clearly in the current critique of psychoanalysis and individualization developed by Foucault (1979, 1980; also see Dreyfus & Rabinow, 1982) and by Deleuze and Guattari (1983). Precursors to this critique have appeared in process theories of social formation (e.g., Mead, 1934; Whitehead, 1938); the view is also similar to the ideas developed by Lacan (see Lemaire, 1977; Wilden, 1980) and by Derrida (1974, 1978, 1981).

The position exemplified by Deleuze and Guattari's work, for example, similar in certain respects to the process views of Mead and Whitehead, is critical of those theories that emphasize reality as representation rather than as incessant production. Their emphasis is on the ongoing production of social reality rather than on its frozen states of "being." We might say, therefore, that the process of becoming stands always at the ready to remedy our tendency to reify the present forms of being. Distortions in becoming serve as the locus of our critical sense.

While Foucault is clear in his praise of Deleuze and Guattari's position, his own approach to dealing with the relativistic trap of a constructionist position is to adopt what Dreyfus and Rabinow (1982) describe as an interpretive analytics. Without unfolding all the details of this viewpoint, it is sufficient to observe that Foucault is not concerned with stepping outside culture and history (which he too considers an impossibility) in order to discover something firm on which to base his critique; he seeks rather to sustain a Frankfurt-like attitude of suspicion about all constructions while also seeking to uncover their societal role and function. In a somewhat Adornoesque manner, Foucault even mistrusts the "purity" of the knowledge that his own approach uncovers. He worries that like all knowledge, it too might become the servant of powerful interests. Thus, he even subjects his analytics to a critical examination, seeking its role in sustaining ongoing institutions of power and domination.

I will soon return to the poststructuralist formulation; its insights will prove helpful in speculating on how it is that we culturally sustain a concept of personhood that traps us in dangerous contradictions.

THE CURRENT IDEAL AND ITS SOCIAL FUNCTIONS

In this brief overview, I have introduced several ways by which theorists have sought to remain true to a constructionist paradigm while simultaneously adopting a critical perspective. Once the objectivist model is rejected, as I believe it needs to be, then the dilemma of avoiding an uncritical relativism moves to the forefront. As this overview suggests, various ways have been proposed for avoiding such problems, although none has yet been sufficiently developed to permit us to rest comfortably, believing that our task has been completed.

While no clearcut critical constructionist position has emerged which we can simply adopt and follow, the overriding message of the preceding attempts is clear and the guidance to our continuing efforts unequivocal. Social constructions that become frozen in time and taken for granted, especially when they involve constructions that like personhood occupy a strategic position in reproducing societal arrangements, demand our critical scrutiny. These are precisely the kinds of constructions that usually harbor the domination of one group by another, while masking that very feature.

My concern in the second half of this essay is to employ the still emerging insights of critical constructionism to examine the Western concept of the person. Specifically, I will suggest that the Western world's construction of a firmly bounded, self contained, autonomous personhood, held out as the only way to accomplish social harmony and cohesion, when followed, undoes the promises it makes. In my view, the current Western concept is a dangerous construction, helping neither persons nor society to deal with the host of pressing issues we all face. Let us begin with a brief overview of the socially constituted person that dominates the Western world today.

The Self-Contained, Autonomous Individual

Not surprisingly, our society's current view of personhood has been eloquently described by a variety of psychologists: for example, Erikson's (1959) classic analysis of identity; Greenwald's (1980) recent examination of the totalitarian ego; object relations theory of individuation as essential to all human development (e.g., Mahler, et al., 1975).

Erikson tells us in no uncertain terms that the stage of identity, when persons seek to integrate their many prior selves into a coherent unity that clearly marks the boundaries of self as separate from nonself, must occur before any move towards genuine intimacy is possible. We are told that the bonds that unite people cannot be built securely until those people have fully individuated and separated themselves from their environment including other people. First me, then us. This *is* the major thematic of the Western world: the social bond can be built only after the fully self-contained individual has been established.

Listen to recent advocates (Levitz-Jones & Orlofsky, 1985) tell us that:

> True intimacy thus calls for a strong sense of self: one that enables one to be capable of self-abandon and to have experiences approximating fusion without fear of boundary or ego loss. The individual lacking a firm sense of separateness or identity will find the fusion-like experiences of intimacy frightening rather than gratifying, because fusion and closeness become associated with the loss of identity (p. 156).

This passage is fascinating to consider. Observe the use of "or" linking separateness with identity, thus inextricably joining the sense of identity with the requirement of being separate from others. Or, consider how fusion and closeness (why are these linked?) are frightening unless they are preceded by a firmly bounded and separate identity. Again, these passages, which could be repeated in instances so numerous they would fill many volumes, reflect the culturally constructed view. But, does this describe a naturally ordained sequence of human growth or, as the constructionists recommend, a socially constituted version of reality?

Feminist and Crosscultural Alternatives

Feminist materials appear to suggest that alternative views of personhood exist within our own current culture, while crosscultural work suggests significant variations in personhood around the world. I do not intent to survey this literature; a few key references will help to establish the relativism and social constructionism of the Western version and put to rest the presumption that its currently dominant view is naturally ordained.

The contributions of Chodorow (1978) and of Gilligan (1982; also Pollak & Gilligan, 1982) are especially insightful in developing the feminine alternative. These authors suggest a basis for women's greater concern with relationship and connection and men's preference for separation and individuality. Chodorow argues in terms of the near-universal role of women in "mothering" and of the consequences of this both for developing relational interests and a self that is defined through connection rather than separation: because the young girl identifies with the mother, she minimizes differentiations between self and other; the young boy must break this bond (i.e., separate) in order to identify with the father.

Gilligan's revision of Kohlberg's male-centered theory of moral reasoning likewise argues on behalf of women's greater concern with caring (also see Noddings, 1984 on this same theme) and with maintaining connections in their efforts to grapple with moral dilemmas. As Lykes (1985) has recently summarized these distinctions, because women's sense of self is defined in terms of relationship and connection rather than separation and individuation, being defined "with others" (i.e., relationally), is not seen as a threat to autonomy or as a frustration to personal growth and self-development. The latter stem from the male-centered worldview with its more egocentrically separating self-definition. The message from these works is clear in telling us in whose name the cultural ideal has been framed: the name of God-the-father; the male head of the entire patricentric hierarchy.

As I previously noted, Lykes (1985) has also raised some serious questions about the extent to which even some feminist authors have offered a real alternative to the dominant Western view or merely another version of the individualistic male theme. The important point she raises is fundamentally about the meaning of personhood in those for whom a thoroughly different worldview prevails. If the alternative merely adds "attachment" as a force that joins together two otherwise independent entities, then a true alternative has not been proposed. On the other hand, if the very essence of what it means to be a person is fully defined by relationship, caring and embeddedness in both small and larger social networks, then perhaps we are dealing with a genuinely alternative understanding.

The Heelas and Lock volume to which I previously referred contains many illustrations of the rich cultural variety in personhood, lending further support to Geertz's reference to the peculiarity of the still dominant Western form. Work by Shweder and Bourne (1982) and by Miller (1984) offers still further examples of crosscultural differences in the ways by which personhood has been constructed (also see Gergen & Davis, 1985). And the recent volume prepared by Robert Bellah and his many associates (1985) represents both further testimonial to the Western preference for highly individuated ideals for maturity, while raising critical questions about the viability of this kind of person for societal survival and wellbeing.

Critical theorists, ranging from those originally associated with this term (e.g., the Frankfurt group) to more recent varieties (e.g., Foucault, Deleuze, & Guattari among others) have also raised serious questions about the societal function of the Western ideal. Western individualism is seen to be the outcome of a broad social process of individualization.

The demands for a freely contracting labor force joined with concerns over matters of public welfare (e.g., disease control, education, crime and deviance prevention and management) to place an emphasis on the concept of the individual as the fundamental unit of the social order. Not only did the management of this social character become of paramount importance, but these same management issues also contributed to further individualization. That is, once the individual was defined as a unique unit of society and the proper management of these units became a critical social issue, then procedures and disciplines designed to assay this character (e.g., the social and behavioral sciences) emerged, thereby simultaneously extending the reach of individualization as well as enlarging its role in managerial and control functions. To paraphrase Foucault, the individual was constructed out of power, in the name of power, and for the purposes of spreading ever further the reaches of power.

Purposes: Architects Of and For Control

As noted, once we consider persons to be sociohistorical constructions, we next need to inquire about the purposes for which any given version has been designed. In my view, shared in many respects with critical theory and poststructuralism, the Western version combines two contradictory messages, one surface, the other deep. The surface tells of a person who has been designed to be the key architect for accomplishing meaning and security in the world by means of attaining control over the world. This so-called architect, however, is actually constructed less to be the one in control than to be the appliance by which societal control and domination are achieved. Following Foucault on this point, the discourse on personal control masks the critical truth that the actual design is *for* control.

Our culture insists that only individuals can be the locus of meaning in the world; that without individuals, the world would be a meaningless, incoherent and basically insecure place. And so the kind of character that meets this requirement is presented: the separate, self-contained and seemingly autonomous individual.

This character, however, is more a social fiction designed to be the appliance by which societal control is carried and advanced, than a real manifestation of autonomous functioning. The cultural formulation masks the actual power in which the entire system is rooted. The historical project that created the individual as an apparent architect of control was basically to design someone who could fit so tightly into the society's governing apparatus that control over this character could readily be obtained. The historical story is of dual processes, individualization and internalization; the latter describes the internalization of mechanisms designed to make external control take on the quality of internality and hence of personal desire. I will leave until the next section any further comment on this point. I raise it here only in order to summarize the view that the purposes served by the Western concept of the individual involve a combination of an architect *of* control and *for* control, the two terms, *of* and *for,* carrying the burden of a complex sociohistorical process centered around issues of power and domination.

A PECULIAR AND CONTRADICTORY CHARACTER

When Geertz referred to the Western view of personhood as "peculiar," he was referring to the fact that it deviated from the more embedded kind of personhood one finds worldwide. There are other peculiarities in this Western form, however, that suggest a thoroughly contradictory character. Three features are especially important to consider:

1 Constructing a character who is purported to be the source rather than the product of the social order inverts the sequence that actually occurs and establishes a rather shaky foundation on which to build the society.

2 The society promises that social cohesion and the social order can appear only after a firmly formed individuality has been established; it seems more likely that these are the very conditions that interfere with social harmony rather than facilitating it.

3 The ideal of maturity is held to be autonomy, that is, inward rather than external control. A far greater truth tells us both that autonomy masks the underlying reality of a character constructed on behalf of power, and that in-

deed, highly independent characters demand more external control rather than less for the social order itself to be maintained. It would seem that following the ideal advances conditions that facilitate domination.

An Inverted Sequence

One of our first observations is that the culturally prescribed developmental process—I before We—inverts the ordering formulated by the constructionist thesis. The latter emphasizes the role of social and historical processes in the creation of the individual, and locates in the social world those qualities the culture currently views as attributes of the individual. The arguments that have been of growing success in creating a crisis of confidence in the objectivist paradigm should apply with equal force in calling into question the culturally prescribed process which sees the individual as the source of the social order rather than the reverse. One "peculiarity" of the Western view is based on its divergence from the persuasive case that has been made on behalf of the social constructionist argument.

In addition, the constructionist position does not abandon its thesis once social objects (e.g., persons) have been constructed. The process of negotiation continues in order to sustain or transform social objects in a manner much as that described by G. H. Mead (1934) and further clarified in the work of ethnomethodologists (e.g., Cicourel, 1974; Garfinkel, 1967). Thus, the social process remains alive and active even when the person is socially created, in order to sustain or transform the person and other features of social reality.

A Failed Promise

A second, related aspect of the Western view goes one step further than simply observing its inversion of the process of social construction. I believe that the social order is actually undermined by the Western view of the person. Following the culture's main message and those institutions that gave rise to it, carry it and are reproduced by it, undermines the very qualities necessary to sustain the social bond. Persons who are thoroughly self-contained and defined by their separateness from others fail as successful participants in processes that require interconnectedness. At some point, the socially constituted, self-contained individual fails to promote the levels of social cohesion necessary for the collectivity to manage itself without centralized and firm external governance. This is a restatement of the Hobbesian thesis and the tragedy of the commons (e.g., Hardin, 1968). In this case, however, the problem does not stem from something inherent in the nature of persons but rather is inherent within the Western version of persons as self-contained individualists.

Support for this position is by no means easy to come by, although it is clearly an observation shared with de Tocqueville who in visiting the United States years ago expressed his concern over the American brand of individuality. The same view has also been expressed by many recent observers of societal trends (e.g., Lasch, 1978; Sobo, 1975). The recent report of Robert Bellah and his associates (1985) lends further credence to this same view. They argued that the current American character structure seems ill designed to affirm the bonds necessary for the social order to be sustained. A variant on this theme has been recognized by others (e.g., Edney, 1980), whose observations about the commons dilemma led him to worry that essentially anti-democratic rule would be needed in order to govern the otherwise ungovernable masses of modern society.

The field-experimental work reported some years ago by Sherif and Sherif (1953) is also relevant. They suggested the central role of superordinate goals in undermining intergroup conflict by establishing a larger sense of community presumably among persons not constructed to adopt such goals in the normal course of their lives together. Some of Deutsch's (1949a, 1949b, 1969) work on cooperation and competition is also relevant in noting the role of cooperation in cohesive group formation. Deutsch defined cooperation in terms of interpersonal substitutability: that is, in a cooperative social arrangement, one person's goal achievement represents everyone's goal achievement, thus making each person's acts have substitute value for every other person. This definition suggests a kind of personhood that is differently constructed (albeit through experimenter intervention and within the culture of the classroom or laboratory) than the character primarily concerned with her or his own benefit.

All of these works suggest that highly individuated entities may not operate effectively in establishing conditions essential to sustaining the social bond.

DESIRING OPPRESSION

If the social bond and levels of interpersonal connectedness sufficient to manage social problems could not be attained by means of the currently constructed person, then increased external intervention would be required in order to achieve order. And yet, in a culture in which the construction emphasizes autonomy and self-determination, it would seem that increased outside intervention would create strong resistances unless the very system of desire (i.e., personal choice) could be transformed so that people would agree to accept what denies their autonomy.

We have encountered the paradox that is the centerpiece of the current Western world. The society creates a person who is fundamentally at war with the society, which must then intervene on behalf of maintaining the social order that its creation threatens. I believe this peculiar situation is unstable at its core and requires a profound ideology to sustain. What must be sustained is a character who is a willing party to a profound self-deception. This deception lies at the core of the Western frame, within its very conception of the person as a self-contained, autonomous individual. To be the kind of person the Western world recommends is already to be party to a story of power that subjugates the entire cast of characters.

Only a few have sought to address this complex issue. We can see parallels in Bettelheim's (1958) work on identification with the aggressor, Memmi's (1967) writings on the mentality of the colonized, as well as Reich's (1970) work on the inner fascist. Each describes a process by which persons seek to be the very thing that further enslaves them. I find the often ambiguous but invariably provocative writings of Foucault (1979, 1980; also see Dreyfus & Rabinow, 1982) and of Deleuze and Guattari (1983) to be of special value in unfolding one possible scenario for this complex process. Although differing in certain details, both Foucault and Deleuze and Guattari adopt a similar stance in viewing the Western construction of the individual as a construction of power. Foucault places much of his emphasis on the historical processes of this construction, whereas Deleuze and Guattari focus on the transformation of desire that they see at the root of the Western process. Both sets of authors agree in noting the degree to which this form of enslavement is accepted.

Foucault

Although I will not unfold the full details and supportive documentation for Foucault's argument, it is based on a rather thorough historical analysis of institutions involving discipline, confession and sexuality. In addition to the two great forces of Western civilization proposed by Weber (see Gerth & Mills, 1946)—rationalization and bureaucraticization—as previously noted, Foucault emphasizes a third, related force: individualization. Through his historical analysis of key social institutions, Foucault is able to uncover evidence that suggests a clear connection between individualization and social control.

The social forces that disembedded persons from their contexts of living and created the individual as the so-called atom of society, also created a host of problems for the societal management and control of these newly constituted social characters. Foucault argues that in order to manage and control individuals, ways to measure, assess and calculate individual characteristics had to be developed, thereby extending individualization as an aspect of power. Foucault further argued that coinciding with this extension of individualization and its function in governance (i.e., power), we find a growing discourse on individual autonomy that both masked the reality (i.e., that individualization was part of a process of power, management and control) and helped contribute to still further individualization.

It is interesting to note that some recent organizational theorists (e.g., Scott, 1981) advanced a similar argument. Scott, for example, suggests that "differentiation contributes to rationalization and routinization of a field of action and, in this manner, to increased certainty" (p. 176). In other words, differentiation, that is, increased individualization, was part of a process seeking the growing standardization of human action (i.e., management and control) in order to increase the certainty and predictability of human activity.

Deleuze and Guattari

Delueze and Guattari answer the question about why people come to desire their own oppression, by suggesting that the force of desire itself has been transformed. This is another way of specifying the manner by which internalization, which we assume to be the hallmark of mature individuality, carries the seeds of enslavement. They illustrate this with the Oedipal complex.

Adopting aspects of Lacan's distinction between the Real and the Symbolic, Deleuze and Guattari argue that desire is what is Real. They describe desire as a productive force, as a desiring-machine. They contrast production with representation, the Real with the Symbolic. Reality is production rather than the idealist's version of a representational (i.e., symbolic) order. They argue that the Symbolic order (representation) necessarily distorts desire because representation substitutes a world of lack for a world of ongoing productivity: we represent what is not present before us. And so, we come to define desire in terms of lack: we desire what we lack, what is not now before us other than as a representation, a substitute for the real thing. This transforms what to Deleuze and Guattari is the truth of desire, namely that it is not a part of the Symbolic or representational order and thus not a matter of lack, but rather is the force of production itself.

The flavor of their meaning can be gleaned by considering some of the qualities they posit for desire as productive rather than as representational. Desire is not uniform, nor singular, nor arranged in hierarchical structures. Desire involves differences and intensities; it is multiple and characterized by mobile flows and arrangements. Desire is not directed towards anything that lies outside or beyond it. Desire is the force of production itself. "Desire does not lack anything . . . Desire and its object are one and the same thing" (p. 26). It is clear that they have described a process that is very much like the primary process of the unconscious. Yet, unlike the way we have come to consider that process, for Deleuze and Guattari, "The unconscious does not speak, it engineers" (p. 180), thereby continuing to emphasize its productive rather than its representational, symbolic nature.

Deleuze and Guattari next argue that the Western world has managed successfully to implant representation into desire, giving desire a substantive, symbolic quality. In particular, they tell us that the familial triangle (mommy/daddy/me) has come to occupy the territory of desire; people come to desire what they lack and cannot have (i.e., the incestuous Oedipal drama) and therefore come to accept societal institutions as necessary devices designed to govern and control their forbidden appetites.

It is as though people learn that what they really desire is what is forbidden to them; and so they must accept the sanctions designed to keep them from realizing that desire. Deleuze and Guattari tell us that Oedipus is not a state of desire and the drives but an idea that distorts desire and catches us in the social traps designed for our own enslavement. We accept subjugation as valid and necessary because of the forbidden quality of our unconscious desires.

In their view, none of this mythology of Oedipus, of course, is desire, but desire after society has distorted it. Desire knows nothing of mommy, daddy or me. These are positions whose reality is symbolic, not real, that is, not part of the productive process. Deleuze and Guattari argue that within the order of desire, there are no men and women; no mommy, daddy or me; no clearly defined personalities, only vibrations and intensities. A fiction is implanted within the unconscious, interrupting these flows and introducing a theater of characters, laws and prohibitions. These distort the very face of desire. The distortion is conducted in the name of power—the power of the society to impose its structures, laws and rules and so lead us to desire our own enslavement.

Deindividualization

The preceding lays the foundation for the poststructralists' and antistructuralists' call for a process of deindividualization. They view the individual as a product of a system of exploitation, a character designed to desire her or his own domination. The return to reality, to the production of desire, emphasizes a move toward a very different kind of individual, one who is multiple, more fluidly bounded and interconnected, like the force of reality itself. In their terms, this describes vibrations, not definite persons; pantheons, not a monotheistic center; groups of selves, not simple, singular identities (see Sampson, 1985).

The argument is that the Western person-self-ego-identity-individual has been constituted to be self-defeating and socially dangerous, a character who must invariably be at war with society and with itself. The character has been designed to be controlled while masking that feature in the discourse of autonomous self-control. Only by breaking through that character can any hope for civilization be restored.

PSYCHOLOGY'S ROLE

In failing to adopt a constructionist perspective, let alone a critical constructionism, psychology has played a part in perpetuating a social creation in need of serious revision. Foucault and Deleuze and Guattari reserve their particular barbs on this matter for psychoanalysis and its perpetuation of a fundamentally distorted view of the person's unconscious. I believe the case can be extended more broadly into psychology proper, especially those psychologies of the self and identity (see Dreyfus & Rabinow, 1982 on a similar theme).

Nevertheless, it would be absurd to maintain that psychology is either the prime or sole source of this perpetuating social role. Rather, psychology among the other sciences of human behavior participates in constructing the self-understandings that help direct members' views of their behavior and its causes.

Psychology does not create its knowledge out of whole cloth, but in merely reporting the empirical findings it discovers and in treating those findings as though they were eternal verities of human existence rather than sociohistorical constructions, it generates the very kind of knowledge that helps sustain current practices and institutions. At minimum, a constructionist psychology could prove transformative by pointing out the social and historical roots of current psychological "facts," and by suggesting the role of these "psychological facts" in sustaining current social forms.

Psychology by itself did not create the social products nor by itself sustain them; by itself it cannot effect a change. Thus far, however, psychological knowledge has been more effective in sustaining than in transforming forms that are deeply embedded and continually reinforced throughout the society. Needless to say, a psychology of the person that emphasizes our current form of individualism is more likely to gain widespread acceptance because of its congruence with the rest of the culture than a psychology that emphasizes an alternative view of the person.

It seems to me that psychology is reluctant to adopt a more transformative role. This reluctance, however, is not simply based on the field's awareness of the sheer weight of opposing forces and thus its likely inability alone to effect any change. I believe that the problem psychology faces in becoming a more transformative discipline stems from the combination of (a) its own thorough embeddedness in its culture and thus its inability often to perceive that very embeddedness and (b) the reward structure of the larger culture, including the reward structure of psychology itself. A constructionist psychology cannot in and of itself transform the culture, especially in an area like personhood that occupies so central and strategic a position in the social fabric. And yet, if it becomes increasingly clear that current constructions thwart attaining the very promises they make and indeed even are seriously threatening to the survival of the whole, then it seems clear to me which side psychology should be on, whether it proves immediately successful or not.

I have tried to make a case that the currently dominant Western construction of the person, which psychology has more or less dutifully confirmed and held in high esteem, is a very questionable figure on which to pin the hopes of social cohesion and harmony. I believe that it is time now for psychology to expand its efforts in mapping a new direction: asking questions about its own formulations: introducing alternative possibilities. Without visionary thought somewhere in the society, pathways to the future are likely to repeat old formulas rather than striking out in new and potentially more beneficial directions.

REFERENCES

Adorno, T. W. (1967). Sociology and psychology. *New Left Review, 43,* 63–80.
Adorno, T. W. (1973). *Negative dialectics.* New York: Seabury.
Bellah, R., Madsen, R., Sullivan, W. M., Swidler, A., & Tipton, S. M. (1985). *Habits*

of the heart: Individualism and commitment in American life. Berkeley, CA: University of California Press.

Bettelheim, B. (1958). Individual and mass behavior in extreme situation. In E. E. Maccoby, T. M. Newcomb, & E. L. Hartley (Eds.), *Readings in social psychology* (3rd ed.), (pp. 300–310). New York: Henry Holt.

Bhaskar, R. (1979). *The possibility of naturalism.* Atlantic Highlands, NJ: Humanities Press.

Chodorow, N. (1978). *The reproduction of mothering: Psychoanalysis and the sociology of gender.* Berkeley, CA: University of California Press.

Cicourel, A. V. (1974). *Cognitive sociology.* New York: Free Press.

Deleuze, G. & Guattari, F. (1983). *Anti-Oedipus: Capitalism and schizophrenia.* Minneapolis: University of Minnesota Press.

Derrida, J. (1974). *Of grammatology.* Baltimore: Johns Hopkins University Press.

Derrida, J. (1978). *Writing and difference.* Chicago: University of Chicago Press.

Derrida, J. (1981). *Dissemination.* Chicago: University of Chicago Press.

Deutsch, M. (1949a). A theory of cooperation and competition. *Human Relations, 2,* 129–152.

Deutsch, M. (1949b). An experimental study of the effects of cooperation and competition upon group processes. *Human Relations, 2,* 199–232.

Deutsch, M. (1969). Conflicts: Productive and destructive. *Journal of Social Issues, 25,* 7–41.

Dreyfus, H. L. & Rabinow, P. (1982). *Michael Foucault: Beyond structuralism and hermeneutics.* Chicago: University of Chicago Press.

Edney, J. J. (1980). The commons problem: Alternative perspectives. *American Psychologist, 35,* 131–150.

Erikson, E. H. (1959). *Identity and the life cycle.* New York: International Universities Press.

Foucault, M. (1979). *Discipline and punish: The birth of the prison.* New York: Random House.

Foucault, M. (1980). *The history of sexuality. Volume I: An introduction.* New York: Random House.

Franz, C. W. & White, K. M. (1985). Individuation and attachment in personality development: Extending Erikson's theory. *Journal of Personality, 53,* 224–256.

Garfinkel, H. (1967). *Studies in ethnomethodology.* Englewood Cliffs, NJ: Prentice-Hall.

Geertz, C. (1973). *The interpretation of cultures.* New York: Basic Books.

Geertz, C. (1979). From the native's point of view: On the nature of anthropological understanding. In P. Rabinow & W. M. Sullivan (Eds.), *Interpretive social science* (pp. 225–241). Berkeley: University of California Press.

Gergen, K. J. (1982). *Toward transformation in social knowledge.* New York: Springer-Verlag.

Gergen, K. J. (1985). The social constructionist movement in modern psychology. *American Psychologist, 40,* 266–273.

Gergen, K. J. & Davis, K. E. (1985). *The social construction of the person.* New York: Springer-Verlag.

Gerth, H. H. & Mills, C. W. (1946). *From Max Weber: Essays in Sociology.* New York: Oxford University Press.

Giddens, A. (1979). *Central problems in social theory.* Berkeley, CA: University of California Press.

Gilligan, C. (1982). *In a different voice: Psychological theory and women's development.* Cambridge, MA: Harvard University Press.

Greenwald, A. G. (1980). The totalitarian ego: Fabrication and revision of personal history. *American Psychologist, 35,* 603–618.

Habermas, J. (1971). *Knowledge and human interests.* Boston: Beacon Press.

Habermas, J. (1973). *Theory and practice.* Boston: Beacon.

Habermas, J. (1975). *Legitimation crisis.* Boston: Beacon Press.

Hardin, G. J. (1968). The tragedy of the commons. *Science, 162,* 1243–1248.

Heelas, P. & Lock, A. (1981). *Indigenous psychologies: The anthropology of the self.* London: Academic Press.

Horkheimer, M. & Adorno, T. W. (1972). *Dialectic of enlightenment.* New York: Seabury.

Horkheimer, M. (1974). *Eclipse of reason.* New York: Seabury.

Lasch, C. (1978). *The culture of narcissism.* New York: Norton.

Lemaire, A. (1977). *Jaques Lacan.* London: Routledge & Kegan Paul.

Levitz-Jones, E. M. & Orlofsky, J. L. (1985). Separation-individuation and intimacy capacity in college women. *Journal of Personality and Social Psychology, 49,* 156–169.

Lykes, M. B. (1985). Gender and individualistic vs. collectivist bases for notions about the self. *Journal of Personality, 53,* 356–383.

Mahler, M., Pine, F. & Bergman, A. (1975). *The psychological birth of the human infant: Symbiosis and individuation.* New York: Basic Books.

Marcuse, H. (1960). *Reason and revolution.* Boston: Beacon Press.

Marcuse, H. (1966). *Eros and civilization.* Boston: Beacon.

Marcuse, H. (1968). *Negations.* Boston: Beacon Press.

McCarthy, T. A. (1978). *The critical theory of Jurgen Habermas.* Cambridge, MA: MIT Press.

Mead, G. H. (1934). *The social psychology of George Herbart Mead.* Chicago: University of Chicago Press.

Memmi, A. (1967). *The colonizer and the colonized.* Boston: Beacon Press.

Miller, J. G. (1984). Culture and the development of everyday social explanation. *Journal of Personality and Social Psychology, 46,* 961–978.

Noddings, N. (1984). *Caring: A feminine approach to ethics and moral education.* Berkeley, CA: University of California Press.

Pollak, S. & Gilligan, C. (1982). Images of violence in thematic apperception test stories. *Journal of Personality and Social Psychology, 42,* 159–167.

Reich, W. (1970). *The mass psychology of fascism.* New York: Touchstone/Simon & Schuster.

Sampson, E. E. (1977). Psychology and the American ideal. *Journal of Personality and Social Psychology, 35,* 767–782.

Sampson, E. E. (1983a). *Justice and the critique of pure psychology.* New York: Plenum.

Sampson, E. E. (1983b). Deconstructing psychology's subject. *Journal of Mind and Behavior, 4,* 136–164.

Sampson, E. E. (1985). The decentralization of identity: Towards a revised concept of personal and social order. *American Psychologist, 40,* 1203–1211.

Scott, W. R. (1981). *Organizations: Rational, natural and open systems.* Englewood Cliffs, NJ: Prentice-Hall.

Sherif, M. & Sherif, C. W. (1953). *Groups in harmony and tension.* New York: Harper & Row.

Shweder, R. A. & Bourne, E. (1982). Does the concept of the person vary cross-culturally? In A. J. Marsella & G. White (Eds.), *Cultural concepts of mental health and therapy* (pp. 97–137). Boston: Reidel.

Sobo, S. (1975). Narcissism and social disorder. *Yale Review, 64,* 527–543.

Whitehead, A. N. (1938). *Modes of thought.* New York: Free Press/Macmillan.

Wilden, A. (1980). *System and structure.* London: Tavistock.

Chapter 3

The Consumption
of Psychological Knowledge

Warren Thorngate and Louise Plouffe

INTRODUCTION

"Psychology," Glen Davis (1964) once remarked, "is what psychologists do." Research psychologists, of course, do research (almost no one merely searches anymore) and in doing so manage to produce an astonishing amount of putative knowledge. Yet many of us remain skeptical about the nature and quality of this knowledge. Having found its nature suspect and its quality lacking, we have sought to improve the product by suggesting alterations of the production process. As critics of the traditional knowledge production process of our discipline (the scientific method and all that) we have been obliged to offer reasonable alternatives—to "put up or shut up" as it were. Judging from the chapters in this volume, we have. So we have sufficient reason to be proud of our suggestions and examples, and perhaps even optimistic about their chances of widespread adoption by our less insightful colleagues.

Yet, lest we become prematurely smug about our accomplishments, we must not ignore a small but vexing question: What is to become of all the psychological knowledge we have produced, and will presumably continue to produce either by traditional or our decidedly superior methods? Who wants it, and why? Now that we have explored the production of psychological knowledge, let us spend a little time considering its consumption.

To begin, we must define what is meant by psychological knowledge. For convenience, if not great clarity, let us assume that the term represents knowledge about the nature and causes of, or reasons for, human behavior and experience. To be honest, we use the word knowledge as a euphemism for information. And for the time being we shall concentrate on one manifestation of this knowledge: that generated by research psychologists in published or otherwise circulated research reports. Obviously, psychological knowledge is not produced only in research factories, nor is it produced only by psychologists, nor is it manifested only in scholarly reports. Obviously, much of what passes for knowledge, or even information, in our discipline isn't. Indeed, as we hope to show in this chapter, the research productions of Psychology fill only a small part of the domain of psychological knowledge, a territory cluttered with the often competing products of clinicians, clergy, philosophers, novelists, parents, children, advice columnists, politicians and others who have occasion to consider what makes people tick. Whether we, as research psychologists, can produce better knowledge more often than our competitors largely depends on who is judging the products and how.

Despite our differences in judging the quality of psychological knowledge, most of us would agree that we have collectively produced an awful lot of it. In 1927 the first volume of *Psychological Abstracts* was published. It contained 2,730 abstracts of research reports for that year. In 1983, the same journal contained 27,735 abstracts—a tenfold increase over our 1927 production rate. Unlike some disciplines (e.g., computer science), we have not increased our production rate since about 1977—no doubt because of declining research support and an aging population of researchers. But we still manage to generate over 100 abstracted articles per working day. In total, psychologists have published about 800,000 research articles worthy of the *Psychological Abstracts.* Half of these have been published since 1972.

Of course, many other academic disciplines deliver lots of knowledge product too, and in comparison to some of our more established scientific neighbors, our output is rather (some would say mercifully) meager. The *Mathematical Abstracts,* for example, currently lists about 50,000 articles per year, *Physics Abstracts* about 115,000, *Biological Abstracts* about 175,000, *Chemical Abstracts* about 225,000. Nevertheless, we long ago began producing far more than any single individual could consume. And as the years have passed, we have been increasingly hard pressed to cope with the rapidly expanding volume of psychological knowledge.

Notes on the Attentional Economics of Intellectual Abundance

If we could draw a diagram of the growth of psychological knowledge, or claims thereon, it might look something like a cornucopia, expanding in breadth and depth as it increases its length or history. The number of publications in psychology now doubles every 12 years. About 24 years ago it became popular to label such exponential growth in research output as part of the "information explosion," and to worry about coping with the explosion in future years. Since then, the amount of published research in psychology has quadrupled, and by rights our worries should have proportionately increased. But few of us even speak of the explosion now. Perhaps this is because others have developed new technologies for physically condensing publications (e.g., microfilm), and for storing and retrieving them with electronic aids (e.g., computer-aided bibliographic searches). Perhaps it is because so many new journals have recently been established to disseminate all those research manuscripts stored in our drawers. Or perhaps it is because we have chosen to ignore more and more of the old research in our discipline in the somewhat foolish hope that if we are a science, then our knowledge is sure to progress, so what is new must be an improvement over what is not. Thus, like Alfred E. Newman, we may grin at the sheer quantity of our collective output and ask, "What, me worry?" The answer is yes.

Though we are bound by habit, tradition, compulsion or fear to produce even more psychological knowledge, there is no law—natural or otherwise— that compels anyone to consume it. We can, of course, require that students majoring in psychology take our courses and know certain facts and concepts we deem important to their education. But the decision to major in psychology is both voluntary and revocable. And there is no guarantee that what we teach our abecedarians will stay with them forever, or affect anything more profound in their lives than an exam grade. For those who choose not to major in psychology, or the many more who never enter a psychology class, we can exercise virtually no control over the amount or kind of psychology they consume, or eliminate, or even notice.

Like it or not, the products of psychologists must compete for the attentions of almost everyone in the marketplace of ideas. By offering an increasing abundance of products, we at once increase the competitiveness of the marketplace. Each of us must now hawk our scholarly wares in competition with thousands of other psychologists, tens of thousands of other social scientists, hundreds of thousands of other scientific researchers. In twelve years our competition will double. And our marketplace is by no means the only one in town. The entertainment marketplace offers millions of books, films, games, sporting, cultural and artistic events that compete for our customers. The marketplace of news, travel, health, politics, meaningful relationships, and salvation all vie with us for the hearts and minds we claim to study so well. All this competition shows no sign of subsiding.

The marketplace of ideas is a buyers' market, and has been for quite a while. Yet the economy of this market is rather different than that we associate with the shopping mall or town square. What makes it different is the currency of exchange. We demand that people pay *attention* to, or for, our scholarly products; the money they may pay to keep us producing is secondary to the attention they donate to our offerings. We do not produce to be ignored.

As psychologists, we should know that the currency of attention has some very interesting properties. Unlike money, everyone is born with roughly the same amount of attention. Attention cannot be saved or borrowed for a rainy day. Attention does not accumulate interest—indeed, if we may twist a phrase, interest accumulates attention. Most importantly, attention does not expand to accommodate the information available. Because there is almost always more information available than anyone can attend to, one must of necessity be selective about where, or to what or whom, one's attention is paid. The same is true when attending to knowledge. No one can attend to all of it. As a result, the economy of our ideational marketplace is determined almost entirely by the rules that govern how the foci of attention are chosen.

How does one choose the foci of one's attention? The question has no simple answer. Much of our attention is spent for us, or committed to activities that define our jobs, roles, aspirations or worries. A typical academic, for example, must devote a considerable amount of attention to students, lectures, committees, administration and a vast assortment of interruptions; we have no choice. As a result, there are usually only a few hours of discretionary attention available in a typical work week to be spent on matters of preference or taste. The same is true for almost all of those who do not follow academic footsteps. Life is largely a series of attentional obligations.

What little discretionary attention one does have need not, of course, be spent on the consumption of knowledge. The other options of other marketplaces—entertainment, fantasy, travel, salvation, and the like—at present seem to be much more attractive to members of the general public than scientific knowledge, and surely more attractive than our little psychology shops to customers with attention to spend. Also, our attempts to package our knowledge more slickly for public consumption have not greatly improved our share of the attentional market. True, we did draw relatively large crowds in the early 1970's to consume our self-awareness offerings. But they now pass us by to line up at the knowledge shops of small business management and real estate investment. Even our trendy publications no longer sell very well. Far more people now read novels than psychology trade books—the readership ratio is about 10 to 1.

To make matters more tangled, knowledge is not always bought with discretionary attention. People often learn accidently, or while attending to other matters. Thus, one can learn how to do a job on the job, or consume news headlines while waiting for sports scores. There is little conscious choice involved. Similarly, one can consume psychological knowledge packaged in the advice of a friend, or ingest political knowledge by reading cartoons, or swallow moral precepts by watching a film or play or street scene. The knowledge distributed by these means is much like the vitamin supplements that are injected into favorite foods. One consumes both without really paying attention, or choosing to do so. The technique has been known at least since Aesop. And we shall consider it further at the end of this article.

Having duly noted some of the complexities that plague any analysis of the choice of attentional foci and knowledge consumption, let us now attempt to simplify: When given the chance, one tends to attend to matters that matter. In regard to knowledge, this implies that—ceteris paribus—one will prefer to attend to knowledge one judges to be valuable over knowledge one judges to be valueless. More generally, it seems safe to say that the more valuable one judges any given knowledge in relation to other knowledge, the greater the desire to consume it. And just how does one judge the value of any given knowledge? We are glad you asked.

THE VALUATION OF KNOWLEDGE

In order to determine how one comes to assign values to knowledge, and hence to exhibit preferences for consuming various knowledge, it is prudent to begin by assessing what others have said about the topic. As it happens, a lot of people have said a lot of things that have at least indirect relation to knowledge valuation, preference, and consumption. These people include hundreds of philosophers, theologians, sociologists, linguists, economists, politicians, propagandists, and even a few psychologists. Indeed, the topic has been so popular, that we must attend to only a small fraction of the voluminous writings about it, and—true to the first thesis of this paper—be highly selective in which of these writings we choose to consume.

What we have consumed has taught us two lessons. The first lesson is probably obvious to anyone who is not a scientist: The scientific criteria for evaluating knowledge (e.g., logical consistency, observability, refutability, parsimony, elegance) have never been very popular in evaluating most knowledge, and probably never will be. Most of us have undergone years of training in order to learn to use these criteria; most people lack the ability, motivation or patience to do the same. Even those of us who attempt to employ scientific criteria religiously in our work .e prone to revert to other criteria when judging, say, the value of a news report, or an advertising claim, or a novel, or excuse. Science, like opera, is an unnatural act.

The second lesson we have learned from perusing the epistemological and related literature has been more constructive. The value one assigns to any given knowledge seems to be based on a combination of four assessments, one for each of four generic criteria. These criteria we shall label (1) comprehensibility, (2) credibility, (3) importance, and (4) interest. Let us consider these in turn.

Comprehensibility

It is difficult for one to evaluate any knowledge that one cannot comprehend, and more difficult to consume it. This is one reason why few people in North America buy books written in Polish, or why few buy books about abstract algebra, sorting algorithms, or inferential statistics. It seems that most people will eschew the knowledge they cannot comprehend, and by their action we may infer they devalue it. However, many people seem to place a rather high value on knowledge they can partially comprehend, sometimes because it whets their curiosity (see Interest, below), sometimes because they can use the knowledge to impress their even more ignorant friends (see Importance, below). Curiously, the ability to appear knowledgable about subjects incomprehensible to others can have numerous indirect benefits. Professionals of all kinds guard their status, and their fees, by speaking in ways that few outside their respective professions can understand (see Bakan, 1967). The same is true of most prophets, charismatic religious leaders, and academics. It is at first rather paradoxical that people such as these could attract large numbers of consumers who haven't any idea about what, if anything, the producers know. But any good social psychologist should know that the followers will at least comprehend the style of their chosen leaders, and if the producer's style is knowledgable the consumers will likely infer that so too is the substance. As any good advertiser can tell us, the secret of selling the incomprehensible in the marketplace of ideas can be stated in one word: packaging.

Credibility

The comprehension of any given knowledge does not guarantee that it will be valued. The knowledge must meet three more criteria in the valuation process, one of which is credibility, sometimes called degree of belief. We think it safe to say that, in general, people place a higher value on credible knowledge than on incredible knowledge. Of course, people often disagree about just what knowledge is credible and what is not. These disagreements often reflect variances in the epistemologies invoked to assess credibility. There seems to be a healthy assortment of different epistemologies that one can use to assess the credibility of knowledge. For the sake of brevity, we shall consider only mysticism, rationalism, empiricism, analogy, authority, and epistemological preference.

Mysticism Those who claim that certain knowledge is credible, believable, or true, incredible, unbelievable or false by virtue of divine revelation, inner voices, rare coincidental events, dreams, visions, altered states of consciousness, or sudden inspiration are said to invoke a mystical epistemology in making their assessment. Mysticism has been, and continues to be, a highly popular means of assessing credibility, and highly resistant to scientific scrutiny. Ironically, most scientific knowledge has its origin in mysticism; astronomy, chemistry, mathematics, and psychology were originally the domains of mystics, and many of those who presently claim these fields as their own maintain strong mystical inclinations. In modern dress, mysticism comes to us whenever we trust a gut-level feeling, a vague sense that something is true or false, an unexplainable hunch, a sudden burst of insight or inspiration. Some would claim that these are mere processes, and point to a part of our brain (usually somewhere in the right hemisphere) in which they are likely to occur. Yet such claims do not explain how or why the processes occur.

It is difficult for us to say much more about mysticism without sounding foolish, so we shall retreat from the challenge. Perhaps we should only mention that, contrary to popular belief, it is probably not the favored epistemology of "primitive" societies (see Levi-Strauss, 1966), nor is it necessarily primitive in function or form. It does, however, lack a high degree of intra- and inter-judge reliability. The high degree of consensus shown within (but not between) various mystical groups, cults, or religious orders concerning the truth or credibility of assorted knowledge is likely to be more the result of social comparison, conformity and habit than of common mystical experience. Mysticism, it seems, requires a high degree of symbolic, rather than sensory, ability and experience. Few people have both, but most people are quite willing to trust the words or deeds of those who claim they do, as long as the claimants are judged to be credible. Mysticism and authority (see below) thus tend to be closely linked epistemologies.

Rationalism   Whenever one assesses the credibility of some claim to knowledge by testing it against logical derivations of knowledge previously assessed as credible or incredible, one is said to be indulging in rationalism. In its ideal form, the epistemology of rationalism gives us theorems where once only axioms bloomed. It is typified by Euclid's geometry. It was once taught in rhetoric courses as a preferred epistemological habit. It forms the basis for most courtroom procedure. It is the essence of mathematics and a large part of scientific reasoning.

The rationalist principle of credibility assessment is quite simple: conclusions that can be logically derived from credible premises or axioms are credible; otherwise they are not. Finding credible premises, however, can be far from simple, and the epistemologies for assessing them can vary enormously. Mathematicians, for example, are prone to assess a premise as credible if it is "intuitively obvious," a technique that works well for such claims to knowledge as "four is greater than two," or "the sun is brighter than the moon," but less well for such claims as "Russia wants to control the world," or "There is only one god." Scientists, in contrast, are prone to assess premises by careful—often tedious—observation and measurement. This seems defensible when assessing such premises as "women are more intelligent then men," but downright silly when assessing such premises as "it is painful to be hit by a train." Many times, premises are neither intuitively obvious nor verifiable by observation and measurement. Two examples are "Robert Stanfield would have been a better Prime Minister than Pierre Trudeau," and "the mind will always be a mystery."

Rationalism has been aided in no small way by the development of the predicate calculus and two-valued logic. Some might claim that it has also been aided by alternatives to both: modal logic, fuzzy calculi, and a variety of statistical philosophies that attempt to solve the classic problems of indication by deductive means. However, as the sophistication and rigour of rationalism has increased, so too have the mental requirements necessary to use it in credibility assessment. Long ago, Boolean algebra became popular as a means of simplifying complex logical statements to render them comprehensible to the average mathematical mind. But most of us either lack such a mind or have no time or desire to develop one.

We instead tend to resort to a less formal and rigorous, but more manageable, form of logic in our rationalist pursuits. Abelson and Rosenberg (1962) have labeled this form psycho-logic; it is quasi-rationalism that often deviates in its rules from formal logic (e.g., see Heider, 1958; McGuire, 1960; Nisbett & Ross, 1980), and often shows inconsistency and context dependency. This psycho-logic gives us reason to conclude that if John likes George and George likes Fred, then John should like Fred. It also gives scientists reason to conclude that if theory T predicts observation M and M is observed, then T is credible. Popper (1959) became famous for demonstrating why this scientific reasoning is formally illogical. But scientists have shown scant desire to recant.

Empiricism If one assesses the credibility of knowledge by checking it against what one sees, hears, touches, tastes or smells, then one is said to be engaging in empiricism. Like all other epistemologies, empiricism comes in several different flavors. Perhaps the best known of these is found in science. Scientific empiricism is noted for its rigour. Sensory experience is supposed to be augmented by instruments of measurement that will reliably convert raw sensations into numbers. The means by which this conversion occurs are supposed to be public, that is, repeatable by anyone who has the same sensory experience. These sensory experiences, or observations, are supposed to be obtained under well-defined conditions. By comparing changes in observations that accompany changes in conditions to the changes predicted by various knowledge claims, one can in principle assess the credibility of these claims— the closer the claims match the observations, the more credible they are.

Scientific empiricism has, of course, become a very powerful technique for assessing the credibility of many claims to knowledge, and has increased its power greatly as measurement instruments (e.g., the transit, microscope, telescope, polygraph) and means of manipulating and controlling conditions (e.g., factorial designs, randomization) have improved. It is without doubt the most popular epistemology in psychological research, even though—as we so well know from this volume—it has met with far less than wild success in validating or invalidating the credibility of countless claims to knowledge of the mind. What it has done is provide researchers with 100 years of partial reinforcements—a significant difference here, a partial insight there, lots of publications, and occasional support for almost every thesis and antithesis imaginable. Partial reinforcements have a way of sustaining behavior, including superstitious behavior, longer than rationalism would prescribe. So despite our rational arguments for terminating the exclusive use of scientific empiricism in this discipline, we can probably rest assured that it will continue to dominate psychological enquiry for several years to come.

But one does not have to engage in scientific empiricism to be empirical, and most people find other flavors of empiricism far more suited to their tastes. Perhaps the most popular of these is what we shall call anecdotal empiricism, a flavor of empiricism that is concocted from memory of personal anecdotes or experiences. The major principle of anecdotal empiricism can be easily stated: a claim to knowledge is assessed as credible if it is similar to, or congruent with, recalled anecdotes from personal experience; otherwise it is deemed incredible. Many scientific empiricists are prone to dismiss anecdotal empiricism as unscientific (which it is) and hence inferior (which it probably is not). Clearly anecdotal empiricism lacks the usual rigor of measurement, public accessibility, and experimental control of the best scientific empiricism. But it is also far easier to invoke, and takes much less time to learn, than its scientific counterpart. In addition, anecdotal empiricism is immensely useful in functioning in an imperfect world, a world full of singular events, few opportunities for careful measurement, and very little control. Though anecdotal empiricism may be more prone to various errors than scientific empiricism, the actual increase in errors may be barely noticeable (cf. Thorngate, 1980). After all, it doesn't take a scale, ruler or experiment to conclude that a mouse is smaller than an elephant, that one cannot burn an ice cube, or that most people get mad when insulted. To quantify, qualify or confirm such knowledge by scientific means is quite often an incredible waste of time.

Anecdotal empiricism is, of course, not without its drawbacks. Single but memorable anecdotes, for example, tend to become far more salient in assessing credibility than they often should. Thus, one bad experience with one Peruvian may result in condemnation of all Peruvians, even though the one experience may be quite unrepresentative of those which other Peruvians may provide. In addition, many anecdotes are not directly experienced, but instead are indirectly experienced in communication with others. The vast majority of one's anecdotes about government, international events, movie stars, and science are obtained indirectly, and are thus subject to whatever distortions occur in the communication process. People who have no previous anecdotes of their own with which to judge those obtained indirectly usually swallow the indirect ones whole. (How many of us, for example, did not once believe that Jack really did meet a giant when he climbed the bean stalk?) As a result, these original anecdotes become the basis of assessing the credibility of subsequent anecdotes, even though the originals may actually be incredible (Thorngate, 1979). Replacing the original anecdotes with more credible ones may take large doses of rationalism or therapy.

Analogy   Whenever one assesses the credibility of some given claim to knowledge by noting how well the structure or form, rather than the content, of the claim matches knowledge previously assessed as credible or incredible, one is said to be employing an analogical epistemology. Analogies are difficult to describe with any precision, in part because there are so many variants of them. Included are the literary variants of simile and metaphor, the comic variant of caricature, the artistic variant of symbolism, and the scientific variants of verbal and mathematical models. Despite the problems in defining analogical epistemology in any precise way (or perhaps because of it), analogies and their variants are very common methods of assigning credibility to knowledge. The high frequency of indicant phrases such as "equivalent to," "akin to," "as though," or "is like," heard in everyday speech attests to the popularity of analogies. So too does our common use of anthropormorphism (e.g., "a computer is like a dumb clerk"), animism ("a pretentious little wine"), mechanism ("our committee performs with clockwork precision"), physicalism ("she has the personality of a fire hydrant"), and teleology ("my car wants to veer to the left"). Indeed, the use of analogy and its variants seems to infuse the thinking of almost everyone, and form the basis for much accepted knowledge. Consider, for example, the following clichés, all of which are as analogical or metaphorical as they are accepted as credible descriptions: the dead of night; lady luck; black moods; heavy hearts; naked truths; golden opportunities; a fly in the ointment; the salt of the earth, the heartbreak of psoriasis.

In order to accept a claim to knowledge as credible by analogy, the analogy itself must be accepted as credible. The means by which analogies are so accepted, or rejected, are not well understood. Acceptable analogies, metaphors, etc. seem to have large number of structural correspondences; for example, the widely acceptable metaphor of "the seasons of life" seems to have correspondences in relation to time, growth, activity, decay, and even color (white hair and the snow of winter). In contrast, metaphors such as "the fingernails of life" or "leaves of the economy" have never been acceptable to more than a few misguided connoisseurs, largely because their correspondences are at best very obscure.

Correspondence does not appear to be the only criterion by which analogies and their variants are assessed. Many analogies appear to be learned early in life, or borrowed from others, and accepted as credible despite the absence of multifarious or close correspondence. Many Americans, for example, consider the arms race to be analogous to a gunfight at the OK corral, or believe Central and South America to lie within their "back yard." The emotional and social contortions of soap operas often become metaphors for normal human relationships. And one's success is often judged by the age of one's scotch.

The dearth of formal rules for assessing correspondence, and the resulting problems of over-extending sloppy analogies, have caused many rationalists and empiricists to consider analogy as a rather loose epistemology. Analogies often do lack sufficient precision for some persons or topics of discourse, but the epistemology does have several advantages over its competition. For example, analogies and their variants may be the only means of approximating some comprehension or understanding of new things, events or ideas. Because analogies are normally rich in imagery (imagery borrowed from the previously known analogous object), it is generally easier to convey meaning by using them than by using any possible alternative. For example, telling someone that the eyeball works something like a camera will probably convey more understanding than telling someone the proper names and behaviors of all the eyeball parts—except, of course, if the person has no idea of how a camera works. Even when later knowledge reveals the limitations of an analogy, it may still be useful as a shorthand method of organizing facts and ideas about its subject. Biologists, for example, are quite aware of the limits of teleology as a metaphor of evolution, but they still resort to it often as a useful conceptual device. If we may pull our metaphorical bootstraps, we would say that analogies are to thought what acronyms are to writing.

Authority The four epistemologies discussed so far have at least one thing in common: they are all used to evaluate the credibility of knowledge derived from first-hand or direct experience. Not all knowledge, of course, comes to us this way; a large portion of knowledge comes to us second-hand or indirectly, and when it does, the source of the knowledge may become at least as important as the knowledge itself in any evaluation of its credibility. Whenever one assesses the credibility of knowledge by assessing the credibility of its source, one is said to be invoking the epistemology of authority. The underlying rule of this epistemology is quite simple: if the source of a knowledge claim is credible, then consider the knowledge as credible; otherwise, consider it incredible.

Potential authorities come in a wide variety of shapes and sizes, and their credibility can be assessed in several different ways. Authority, for example, is often assigned to persons. Early in life, children often ascribe authority to their parents; later they may change their minds and shift their ascription to rock or movie starts, selected peers, or even teachers. Adults often add news reporters, advice columnists, members of the clergy, politicians, doctors, lawyers and other professionals to the list. The domains of authority ascribed to these people range from rather small (e.g., the authority of a plumber) to quite large (e.g., the authority of the Pope). In principle, anyone can be judged an authority on at least some small knowledge niche (e.g., an authority on curling brooms, antique hubcap design, or camel grooming), and many people attempt to cultivate such specialized authority as an aspect of personal identity or status. In practice, errors in the ascription of authority are common; many people are judged as authorities on matters about which they have no credible knowledge; others are overlooked as authorities on matters about which they may have much credible knowledge. Pierre Trudeau and Ronald Reagan exemplify the former; many elderly persons exemplify the latter; academics seem to be equally divided between the two.

Sometimes the authority of an individual regarding some claim to knowledge can be assessed by checking the claim with one of the other epistemologies. Thus, when a politician claims that wages must be diminished, then votes to boost his/her own salary by 50%, one may resort to rationalism, empiricism or analogy to test the credibility of the claim and adjust one's judgement of the authority of the politician accordingly. The authority of science is predicated on this technique of verification. According to the classic rules of the scientific game, anyone who wishes to challenge the knowledge of a scientist can attempt to undertake or replicate relevant research, or attempt to find logical flaws in the scientist's argument. Alas, such rules are now almost impossible to follow. Few of us can afford the time, money, or organization necessary to challenge knowledge of particle physics, radio astronomy, genetics, neurochemistry, or other results of large scale scientific enquiry. As more science is sponsored by private corporations, more scientific research becomes proprietory, and thus cannot be challenged in the manner of public research. Increasingly, scientists are called upon to check the credibility of each other's works. But it is increasingly difficult to do so. Not only has the checking become more difficult, but the amount to be checked has increased exponentially. At the same time, the scholarly rewards for checking have diminished, at least in disciplines such as psychology. Those of us who strive to keep the discipline honest are generally regarded by our colleagues as reactionaries, whiners, or nabobs of negativism. We may righteously, if not gleefully, note that these are the same colleagues who never bother to fathom the differences between knowledge and understanding, motion and progress.

The authority of an individual is not, of course, judged only by checking the individual's claims with alternative epistemologies. As both casual observation and attitude change research have shown, authority may be ascribed on the basis of all manner of cues or characteristics, most of which have blemished reputations richly deserved (at least from an empirical point of view). Height (tall), sex (male), voice (low), speech (fast), clothing (expensive), age (50), hair (grey), posture (upright), gaze (straight), and looks (good) all contribute to many persons' judgements of authority, usually without the slightest evidence for their validity. So too do such artifactual variables as size of desk, salary or crucifix, number of secretaries or degrees, length of vita or wait for appointment, and hourly charges for consultation. In short, a lot of people are gullible.

Gullibility has never had a high reputation as a component of any epistemology, and its reputation is especially tarnished amongst members of intellectual communities. But gullibility does serve some important functions, and should not be dismissed without consideration of its merits, however few. Gullibility, for example, is predicated upon a certain optimism about our species; to be gullible, one must usually assume that most people who pass along claims to knowledge are right until proven wrong, innocent until proven guilty. Gullibility also allows one to accept much knowledge as entertainment (see Interest below), and to avoid wasting valuable time checking out knowledge claims that have little bearing upon one's existence (see Importance below). Thus, if Henry Higgins tells us that the rain in Spain falls mainly on the plain, we might as well take his word for it. Unless, perhaps, we are going to Spain, accepting his claim will cause us no pain, and may actually prove useful in speech therapy. In addition, he may return the favor by believing us even when he has no other reason for doing so. We would not call this gullibility. We would call it sagacity.

Authority is not only ascribed to people; it is equally common to ascribe authority to institutions, laws, traditions, norms, and habits. Thus, a Bible passage may be judged as credible because the Bible is judged authoritative; allegations of royal Canadian Mounted Police misconduct may be judged incredible because the misconduct is against the law; we may pronounce the common suffix of the words tough, though, and through in three different ways because people have traditionally done so, people do so now, and we are in the habit of doing so too.

Science as an institution has accrued considerable authority by virtue of past accomplishments of scientists, generally favorable—if distorted—press coverage, and a dearth of challenges to its intellectual products. But science is probably not the most authoritative institution in most cultures, and it holds no popular claim to authority regarding matters of morals, taste, or the heart. In many cultures, of course, religious authority is dominant and pervasive. Other cultures assign great authority to the whims of the majority, or to displays of power. If knowledge christened with the adjective "scientific" does not compete against that generated by other authorities, then the authority vested in science is likely to be accepted, and the knowledge deemed credible. But if scientific knowledge runs contrary to that of other authorities, the latter stand a better than even chance of domination. When science competes with Genesis, it usually loses. When knowledge from psychology runs contrary to public consensus, it is the authority of psychology, not the authority of consensus, that is likely to be diminished.

Epistemological Preference   The variety of epistemologies that can be used to assess the credibility of knowledge is matched by the variety of preferences people exhibit for these epistemologies. It is likely that everyone uses each of them some of the time and no one uses only one all of the time. But between these extremes different people are likely to exhibit all sorts of interesting preferences for using one or more epistemologies in given situations. Royce (1964) has followed the lead of Sorokin (1941) in exploring individual differences in preferences for three of the epistemologies listed above: rationalism, empiricism, and analogy (he calls it metaphor). He has even developed a simple questionnaire to determine the extent to which one exhibits these epistemologies as traits. The questionnaire attempts to measure a bit of what all of us have undoubtedly noticed: Some people just seem to be more "logical" or "mathematical" than others; some seem to enjoy keeping records and taking things apart; some seem to write poetry and find symbols in everything. In addition, some people seem to rely a lot on inspiration, intuition and gut feelings; and some people read the Bible for all their beliefs, or believe anything they hear on television. Such individual differences are likely the result of variance in learning, ability, and taste.

But individual differences do not exclusively determine epistemological preference. Some epistemologies are simply incapable of assessing the credibility of certain knowledge. For example, it is difficult to determine if the claim that you have five fingers on your right hand is credible by means of rationalism, metaphor, or mysticism. Similarly, one cannot make great use of empiricism to determine the credibility of the claim that Odysseus visited Pylos, that life is like a river, or that it is better to give than to receive. Even though it may be possible to employ a given epistemology in assessing the credibility of a given knowledge claim, it may be awfully awkward or tedious to do so. Thus, one might prefer the simplicity of invoking the authority of an encyclopedia, rather than the agony and expense of invoking empiricism, in order to determine whether lead is more poisonous than mercury, Venus is closer than Mars, or the Bay of Fundy has the world's highest tides. And it might be more convenient to invoke mysticism than rationalism to assess the credibility of the claim that Bach wrote more beautiful music than did Sousa, or any claim for or against the existence of any god.

It is also possible to invoke more than one epistemology in assessing a given knowledge claim. We have previously noted how one can sometimes check someone else's knowledge claim by rational, empirical or other means in order to assess the other's credibility; when this is done one is essentially pitting authority against one or more of the other epistemologies. Other combinations frequently occur, and are usually noted when they generate opposing assessments. For example, conflicts between one's head and heart seem to be caused by differences between the results of invoking mysticism and rationalism (or empiricism). If what one sees "just doesn't make sense," a conflict between empiricism and rationalism is likely to be causing it. Metaphor and authority often produce a sense of conflict when judging the credibility of Bible stories. Great literature becomes great only when one ceases to interpret it literally.

When the credibility assessments afforded by differing epistemologies conflict, one is often impelled to choose between them. There is probably no natural order of preference, and preferences for conflicting epistemologies are as likely to be social context, cultural tradition, or sheer whimsy as any other preferences. However, it is surprising how often people report distinct preferences for some variant of mysticism in resolving epistemological conflict, especially when one considers how many "civilized" attempts are made to discourage its use. Consider, for example, business executives or government leaders who report that they rely on gut feelings to make complex decisions or resolve difficult conflicts; consider the number of scientists who pray for inspiration and insight rather than perspiration or foresight to guide them through the paradoxes of their work. Authority, as well, has not lost much ground as the epistemology to which people defer in resolving epistemological conflicts. Even at the height of the "me" generation in the mid-1970s, most narcissists were quite willing to trust the authority of popular psychology and self-help books, rather than their own sensibilities, in resolving conflicts about how they should develop their limited potentials.

Intellectual life would be sufficiently complex if credibility conflicts could exist only between epistemologies, but to confuse almost everything, such conflicts can exist within epistemologies as well. Even formal rationalism can lead to conflicting assessments; we call these paradoxes or dilemmas. Empiricism can result in contrary observations; we call some of these illusions, others we ascribe to different points of view. The same authority can render opposing assessments; that is why we have courts of appeal. Mysticism can leave us ambivalent. And metaphors can not only be mixed, but also purposely concocted to elicit several contradictory messages or levels of meaning—indeed, it is just these metaphors we celebrate as art. In addition, the potential for conflicts between a formal version of some epistemology and its informal counterpart is enormous. Psychologic often mismatches formal logic; anecdotal empiricism often contradicts scientific empiricism; children and developmental psychologists frequently disagree.

Perhaps it should be surprising, therefore, that different epistemologies occasionally reach the same conclusions or converge upon the same assessments of credibility. It is tempting to speculate that when this occurs, the result is a universal truth, and to seek such truths in hopes of avoiding incessant epistemological conflict. Yet the nature and importance of such truths may dash our hopes of epistemological repose. It is known, for example, that vague ideas last longer than precise ideas because, by definition, they can be reconstrued in many different ways to suit many different epistemologies. This is particularly true of ideas regarding human behavior and experience. It is also known that some truths, while compatible with numerous epistemologies, are utterly trivial. We doubt, for example, that any epistemology would challenge the claim that there are no golf courses in Antarctica, or that Markov models sometimes do not accurately predict learning curves. But we are hard pressed to defend these universal truths as important ones.

Importance

We have so far tried to show some ways in which comprehensibility and credibility can affect the valuation of knowledge, and to show how each can in turn be influenced by a wide assortment of personal, social, and circumstantial factors. Yet comprehension and credibility do not by themselves dictate the value of knowledge; indeed, they may not even be necessary for valuation. To illustrate this point, consider the following: Is it more valuable to know that acid rain is killing eastern forests, or that Bobby Orr once played for the Boston Bruins? Is it more valuable to believe there is life after death, or that infants can rarely fathom Fourier Analysis? In the first case, two equally comprehensible and credible morsels of knowledge may not have equal value (we hope you picked acid rain). In the second case an arguably incomprehensible incredible myth may be preferred to a comprehensible and credible truth. So in both cases, something other than comprehension and credibility must be governing preference. Following the lead of Whitehead (1938) we shall refer to this extra ingredient as *importance,* or a synonym such as relevance, usefulness, or centrality.

Almost all comprehensible knowledge, and a good deal of incomprehensible knowledge, can be assessed according to its importance, and in general the more important the knowledge, the more highly valued it will be. One's assessments of importance seem to be largely independent of one's assessments of credibility. Thus, incredible knowledge can be either important, trivial or somewhere in between, as can knowledge deemed credible to varying degrees. For example, one does not have to believe in God, communism, free enterprise or Santa Claus to conclude that knowledge about them is important. And one can believe in serial-position effects, number theory, élan vital, or the tooth fairy yet readily admit that such beliefs are generally less than central to one's life or the trajectory of world events. What does affect one's life and world events is a curious mixture of the credible and incredible, of truth and myth. For important myths are probably more valuable than trivial truths, just as important truths are more valuable than trivial myths.

As is true of comprehension and credibility, there are wide individual, social and circumstantial differences in the assessment of importance. Knowledge of the inner workings of SPSS, for example, may be important to a social scientist and utterly useless to a sales clerk. Indeed, even a social scientist may consider knowledge of SPSS to be useful only at work or when talking shop to colleagues and otherwise far less important than knowledge of local but routes. Contrary to the assumption of many Americans, knowledge of U.S. government is not especially important to Canadians, ranking noticeably below knowledge of hockey and French. In contrast, knowledge of Canada seems far more important to Canadians than to Americans who are usually content to know only that this country is North America's largest producer of winter.

Despite the highly personal and contextual nature of one's assessment of the importance of any given knowledge, it is possible to derive a few generalizations about importance and the means by which importance is ascribed. In part, this is because some contexts are much more common than others. For example, it is generally more important to know how to cook than to know how to conjugate Latin verbs because more people eat than speak Latin. Knowledge of cooking is also generally more important because the usual consequence of cooking-eating is a human need as well as a desire, while knowledge of Latin is almost never needed and desirable only to punctuate the mundane with the arcane.

In order to discuss the generalizations that may be made about judging importance, let us first anticipate a typical philosopher's remarks about the topic: There are several different types of kinds of importance, and generalizations about one type or kind may not transfer to others. For reasons of space, if not naiveté, we shall limit our discussion to two kinds of importance: pragmatic and psychological. The terms are sufficiently vague to cover most of the importance domain, and sufficiently abstract to give the impression we have derived them only after considerable thought. They should at least suffice for our limited purpose.

Pragmatic Importance A sizable proportion of available knowledge concerns means to accomplish various ends. It is sometimes called tactical knowledge or "how to" knowledge, and the importance one assigns to bits of it we term pragmatic importance. Every art, craft and profession has its own set of tactical knowledge, and the knowledge therein is generally considered pragmatically important by corresponding artists, crafts people, or professionals. Thus, it is pragmatically important for a composer to know about techniques of orchestration, for a bricklayer to know about the use of a plumb bob, for the physician to know about symptom-disease relations. Most of this occupation related knowledge is considered to be sufficiently important that those who wish to pursue a profession must purchase the right to learn it (via tuition), spend months or years attempting to learn it (via apprenticeships), pass examinations on their progress in learning it, and usually agree to keep at least some of it secret. Someone who wishes to become a luthier, for example, must learn a host of pragmatically important rules and skills ranging from the rule of eighteen and the judgement of wood quality to the construction of jigs, the bending of ribs, the application of glue, the tapering of braces, and the esthetics of purfling. Many luthiers are reluctant to share this knowledge freely with anyone who asks because their secrets may help to insure their livelihood. On a larger scale, some tactical or "how to" knowledge is so important that very large corporations can gain considerable market advantage by having it to themselves. The result is a host of trade secrets, and a bullish business in stealing them.

But pragmatically important knowledge is not limited to the marketplace, nor is all of it only available to those who can pay. Most pragmatically important knowledge is free and is used everyday by everyone alive. Knowledge of how to tie one's shoes, how to brush one's teeth, how to use a phone, or find a drugstore, or ask a favor, or intimidate a colleague, or lie convincingly are all examples of knowledge judged pragmatically important by most people and freely available. In contrast, knowledge of frog dissection techniques, the Dewey Decimal System, elevator repair, or how to reach Flin Flon, Manitoba does not usually qualify as pragmatically important because few people either need or desire it to lead or improve their lives.

Judgments of pragmatic importance seem almost entirely dependent upon the pragmatic needs of individuals. As a result, it is often possible to determine the pragmatic needs of individuals by examining what pragmatic information they desire. One interesting, though indirect, method of examining pragmatic information desires is to observe the kinds of books, magazines and other printed knowledge that people purchase or borrow. Consider, for example, a bookstore. Booksellers tend to stock books that sell, and if one peruses the stacks one can see that books on auto repair outnumber books on violin repair, that books on computer programming outnumber books on creative writing, that books on training dogs outnumber books on learning esperanto. Now examine the psychology section. Books on child rearing, IQ testing, management and other techniques of manipulation will likely outnumber books on research methods, statistical techniques, and problems of program evaluation. Books on the latter topics are more likely to be found in the required text sections of university bookstores, or in used bookstores (a sad misnomer; most books come to these stores because they are unused). The observation supports a common claim that most people are far more concerned with the products of psychological research than with the process of psychological research. Indeed, it may be foolish to publicize widely the tactical knowledge of our research processes. Often this knowledge exposes the limitations of research processes, and casts doubt on almost all popular research products. The effect is to impugn the credibility of almost all pragmatically important popular psychology. But lacking a credible alternative, most members of the public will continue to consume the incredible stuff and begin to resent our critical interjections.

Psychology is by no means the only science that survives largely on the pragmatic importance of its products, promised or otherwise. Public and governmental support for almost all sciences are predicated on the technology that can be derived from them, and though scientists may be quick to distinguish themselves from mere producers of technique, the distinction is often conveniently blurred when applying for research funding. Social science has grown in proportion to public and governmental desires for social scientists to provide techniques for solving social problems. Until recently, few social scientists publicly admitted that the desires were misplaced or unrealistic, in part because most believed the techniques could eventually be provided, and in part because one does not bite hands that feed research empires. Among these social scientists are many psychologists who have invested great amounts of time, money and effort looking for ways to cure the mentally ill, educate the mentally retarded, eliminate prejudice and violence, promote cooperation and health, sway the opinions of the masses, or otherwise accomplish the goals of their sponsors. Of course, far less practical knowledge has come from these investments than most psychologists or their sponsors would desire, and much of what has come has been too costly or controversial to employ (see Lindblom & Cohen, 1979).

The failure of social science to produce many pragmatically important products would perhaps be tragic were it not for the fact that the world has survived, and will likely continue to survive, without them. Trial and error continues to be a powerful substitute for scientifically based technology, and will probably continue to be widely used in developing tricks of the social trades unless and until social science can replace the technique with something better. In theory, more errors of judgment and action will be made without good technological contributions of social science than with them. But one can accommodate to this deficit by arranging more avenues of appeal, and more social structures for compensating those who must suffer the mistakes that develop from pragmatic ignorance. Most societies have a considerable amount of legal and legislative knowledge that is pragmatically important for securing such arrangements. In addition, a wealth of informal but very practical knowledge exists in most societies for increasing the chances that the mistakes of others will benefit oneself. In the vernacular, this is knowledge about "beating the system." And we hazard a guess that most people judge this knowledge to be far more pragmatically important than knowledge of how to make the system fair or perfect.

Psychological Importance Not all knowledge is important because its use can make money, cure disease, or afford us the luxury of changing people or things to suit our fancies. Knowledge can also be important because it promotes understanding, provides a sense of order, continuity, elation or peace, establishes a focus for the expression of emotion, inflates or guards the ego, develops or maintains a favored (usually positive) self-image. If knowledge serves any of these or similar functions, it is said to be psychologically important, and consequently valuable. Otherwise it is said to be psychologically unimportant, though it may still be valuable for other reasons (credibility, pragmatic, importance, or interest).

There are many common examples of knowledge that is psychologically, rather than pragmatically, important. Familiar quotations such as "To everything there is a season," "Anything that can go wrong will," "It is better to give than to receive," or "Winning isn't everything, it's the only thing" are often highly valued, not for their pragmatic importance, but for the psychological support or relief they provide. People who listen to sermons do not generally do so for practical advice; instead they listen for hope or encouragement. Knowledge of archeology or astronomy will not make not make one rich, but many value it as a source of perspective or wonder. Large sums of time and money are often spent to gain knowledge of one's family history not to gain power, but to gain a sense of continuity and self. Novels, biographies, and humor are read much more often than accounting texts not only because they are more interesting (see next section), but because they provide escape, relief, catharsis, entertainment, and possibilities for interpersonal comparisons.

Much of what can be said about psychological importance already has been said. Katz, Sarnoff and McClintock (1956), for example, have noted that many attitudes have functional significance for individuals by serving psychological (and largely Freudian) needs. Allport and Postman (1947) have noted a similar function for prejudicial beliefs. The need for knowledge posited by Heider (1958) and Festinger (1954) is almost entirely a psychological rather than pragmatic one; they consider important knowledge to be that which makes the world and events therein connected and predictable, or that which allows one to assess one's ability, skill, or accomplishment.

It seems reasonable to expect that knowledge from psychology would be dripping with psychological importance; after all, the discipline is founded on hopes that psychologists can provide credible accounts of human behavior and experience, and such accounts are psychologically important almost by definition. Sure enough, a considerable amount of psychology has, by all appearances, become quite psychologically important not only to psychologists but also to people untrained, and usually uninterested, in the discipline. Two types of knowledge generated by psychologists seem to attain noticeable psychological importance amongst members of the general public: statistics and conjectures. Because these roughly correspond to the facts and theories that psychologists compulsively generate according to their scientific mandate, it is tempting to conclude that the products of psychology are important to society by virtue of the needs for understanding they fulfill. This conclusion, however, is somewhat spurious.

There is good evidence to suggest that many of the public's needs fulfilled by psychological knowledge are not those which psychologists believe are, or should be, fulfilled by consumption of their works. Psychology, in short, may be psychologically important for the wrong reasons, or at least for reasons not shared by psychologists. This is not uncommon in the world of mass consumption. The demand for cigarette paper grew rapidly in the late 1960's, not because people suddenly needed to roll their own cigarettes but because they needed to roll more stimulating substances. Work boots, safety pins, slide rules, surf boards, guns and guitars have all been purchased as items of fashion at some time in the recent past, often to the great (and pleasant) surprise of their producers. Indeed, the automobile industry has gained no small measure of notoriety, and profit, by exploiting the realization that cars are purchased as much for status as for transportation.

What are the psychological needs fulfilled by psychological knowledge? Consider, first, public consumption of psychological statistics. Psychologists who produce such statistics usually consider them to be important to the extent that they can illuminate or test some hypothesis about behavior or experience; they are "facts" which have almost no meaning until they are incorporated into some larger theoretical system. But the statistics themselves often provide members of the public with important opportunities for social comparison, for measuring their own behavior and experience against that of others, for indulging in vanity. For better or worse, there is a pervasive public concern about personal normality and abnormality. The concern is probably sustained by a fear of being abnormally deficient, a desire to be abnormally proficient, and a need to be accepted as a "regular" member of personally important groups. To the extent that psychological statistics placate or stimulate this concern, psychological knowledge becomes psychologically important.

The need or desire to evaluate oneself in comparison to others is often fulfilled in everyday interaction. Thus, one can usually determine one's relative popularity, credibility, status, or agreement on matters of discussion in groups by simple informal observation. But many behaviors and experiences are not so easy to compare. For example, comparisons of childhood traumas, suicide attempts, legal misdeeds, or sexual fantasies and practices are usually not made in polite company, sometimes because of embarrassment and sometimes because of fears that such personal knowledge will be exploited by those with whom it is shared. The experiences that are shared are often inflated or otherwise distorted and, when heard, can lead many to doubt their own capabilities or sanity. Daily gossip, for example, is regularly filled with claims of highly intelligent children, astonishing sexual performances, extraordinary feats of skill, heroism or vengeance. One is thus forced by circumstance to compare oneself to the boasts, rather than the behaviors, of others. As a result, one may constantly fall short of the abnormal norms perpetrated by braggarts.

Enter the psychologist. In the name of science, its claims of objectivity, and its promotion of understanding, psychologists have been able to extract a remarkable amount of private or unnoticed information from people regarding their behavior and experience. Judging from the popularity of psychological surveys, polls, and other studies conducted by psychologists that gather related data, the public maintains a large appetite for the statistics they provide. If a psychologist discovers that 60% of married persons have had at least one affair, then 60% of married persons may be comforted to know they are not alone. If a psychologist estimates that 20% of the public have had at least one homosexual experience, then 20% of the public may cease to worry. And if a psychologist reports that 30% of all women have experienced at least one attempted rape, the statistic alone may prompt a public retting of the problem. Publicity about such statistics has often contributed to the establishment of self-help groups devoted to individuals who share a common psychological problem (e.g., alcoholism, stress, phobias, violence).

As any good psychologist or reasonable person should know, not all statistics are valid; many are based on highly biased samples of people, situations and responses, and are as likely to distort the truth as approximate it. But members of the public often ignore the source or validity of statistics, particularly when the statistics are of great psychological importance. Thus, a parent may accept as valid and important the dubious claim that most children are cruel if it allows the parent to conclude that when little Bruce teases his sisters without mercy it is perfectly normal. Occasionally, publicity about just one example of a rare behavior or condition can serve the same psychological end. A case history of dyslexia may provide worried parents with a moot but socially acceptable label for their child's reading difficulties; after all, brain damage elicits much more social tolerance than does mere stupidity.

Most psychologists are quick to caution others about the limitations of their statistics, especially the statistics that have some potential for psychological importance. It is part of the tradition of intellectual honesty in science to do so, a tradition founded on the avoidance of spurious results. Alas, this tradition often conflicts with the traditions of those who earn their living by spreading the word. News reporters, in particular, have long recognized that caution does not sell. As a result, their reports of psychological research are usually selective, and biased toward the sensational. Such a bias was graphically demonstrated several years ago when one of us (WT) was interviewed by a news reporter about some statistics concerning community reactions to sexually explicit publications gathered for a local obscenity trial. After listening impatiently to a discourse on the tactical and ethical difficulties of gathering such data and the caution needed to interpret the results, the reporter interrupted. "Listen," he said, "people don't give a damn about your problems, they just want your facts."

As mentioned previously, psychological statistics are not the only products of psychology that can accrue psychological importance. The conjectures of psychologists regarding the causes of selected behavior (or misbehavior) or the effects of selected experience are also candidates for psychological importance and for the public allegiance that so often follows the fulfillment of psychological needs. Of course, not all scientific conjectures about the causes of behavior or consequences of experiences are judged to be psychologically important, even though they may be quite valid and even interesting. Markov learning models, for example, will probably never rank among the important ideas of civilization, nor will stage theories of group development, algebraic accounts of attitude change, or schematic explanations of cognitive processes. In contrast, theories that posit unconscious desires, personal, social and higher level needs, conflicts of beliefs or values, intellectual or moral development, or circumstantial determinants of behavior will probably always rank among the most psychologically important products of psychology, even though their validity may be far less than perfect. The degree of psychological importance ascribed to any given conjecture in psychology does not seem to be highly related to its scientific merit. Instead, the importance of a psychological conjecture seems to be largely dependent upon its potential to condone, condemn or clarify images of humanity.

There are, of course, several different images of humanity, each with its own set of adherents and detractors. These images vary along several dimensions, for example, the extent to which people are basically good or evil, active or reactive, cooperative or competitive, flexible or rigid, lazy or industrious, thoughtful or thoughtless, masters or victims of circumstance, perfectable or not (see Wrightsman, 1964). Almost all combinations of such dimensions are possible, and together they provide a rich source of confusion and debate about the nature and fate of the species. Many conjectures of psychologists address themselves to the confusion and debate. The images of humanity perpetrated by these conjectures are sometimes explicit but more often implicit, sometimes denoted but more often connoted. This allows psychologists to maintain an aura of scientific objectivity in generating and expressing their conjectures while following their own (or their mentors') instincts about the nature and fate of others, if not themselves. The result is a set of theoretical statements, scientifically packaged, that can be injected into philosophical disagreements. Those statements that support one's favorite philosophical thesis, or refute its antithesis, or even inject some new life into stale syntheses, are normally judged to be psychologically important. Those statements that do none of these things are normally judged to be psychologically trivial.

Some examples are in order. Many people today are enamored with the notion that humans are basically good, and that what evil they do is largely the result of ignorance or circumstance. A good deal of conjecture generated by humanistic psychologists supports this notion, largely because humanistic psychology is predicated upon it. In contrast, a good deal of Freudian psychology is defined by the conjectures that people are basically nasty and brutish (if not short) and that what good they do is largely the result of sublimation and the fear of agents of civilization. The empirical support for both positions is distinctly equivocal. But it is no coincidence that today's optimists dismiss Freud as passé and read a lot of humanistic psychology.

Topics of philosophical speculation come and go, but one that never ceases to engage interest and debate is the topic of personal suffering. Some people believe that personal suffering is largely a matter of personal failure. Individuals are assumed to be free agents entirely responsible for the consequences of their own decisions. Smart people with lots of knowledge deserve to succeed; the dumb and the ignorant deserve to fail. Many people in business and prison hold these beliefs. One will rarely catch them reading Maslow, Rogers, Horney, or Laing. If they read any psychology at all, it will likely be written by Sartre, Galton, Jensen, or Burt. In contrast, others believe that personal suffering is largely the result of one's environment. They would likely enjoy the works of Skinner, Lewin, or Harlow. They would probably not enjoy recent work on cognitive limitations of rational choice (e.g., see Nisbett & Ross, 1980).

In sum, psychological conjectures that do not mesh with the beliefs or ideologies of individuals, however loosely defined, will likely not be judged by them as psychologically important. Sampson (1977) has reached the equivalent conclusion with respect to western ideology, and Strickland (1984) has noted the same phenomenon in Soviet psychology. Sociologists have been discussing related phenomena for almost 50 years (see Garfinkel, 1981; Holzner, 1986; Mannheim, 1936). Beliefs and ideologies, however, sometimes change, and there is some evidence to suggest the conjectures of psychologists are occasionally instrumental in promoting such change. How is it that a conjecture at odds with a contemporary ideology can stimulate a change in the ideology when most people reject the conjecture as irrelevant? The answer to this apparent paradox is still hidden in the tomes of intellectual history. We can only speculate that no ideology is completely satisfying to all people, and that aberrant psychological conjectures, like genetic mutants, can evolve very rapidly under unsatisfactory conditions. We can also speculate that people often become bored with the same old explanations, valid or not, and that some of these people will seek excitement by embracing currently trivial alternatives. Interest, it seems, plays a subtle but central role in one's valuation of knowledge. And it is to this topic we now turn.

Interest

The consumption of knowledge is much like the consumption of food. Valuable knowledge should be digestible (comprehensible), edible (credible) and nutritious (important). But many people eschew foods with these features. Spinach, rutabagas, liver, squid, and powdered milk are often greeted with turned-up noses even though they are not poisonous, can be easily chewed and swallowed, and contain valuable nutrients. Similarly, many people eschew seemingly valuable knowledge. People regularly skip over newspaper articles on the advantages of seat belts, studies of environmental pollution, or historical trends in trade union movements. In addition, a considerable number of decision makers regularly ignore thoughtful academic research or advice. There are doubtless many reasons for eschewing such valuable knowledge. But some of the most popular reasons concern matters of taste. One's tastes for knowledge is reflected in one's interests. As a result, the value of knowledge is as much a function of its interest as its comprehensibility, credibility, and importance. Other things being equal, the greater the interest stimulated by knowledge, the greater will be its value.

Just as many people prefer sweet to sour, cooked to raw, salty to bland, and frequent changes of menu, so too do many people appear to prefer excitement to boredom, whimsy to ponderosity, entertainment to pedantry, and frequent shifts in attentional focus. Of course, not all people share these preferential criteria; the world is sprinkled with health food converts and intellectuals. But we live in an age of the Big Mac and the Twinkie, of Believe It or Not and the 30-second news clip. Most people have come to expect the food they consume to be quickly prepared, mildly seasoned, and tasty. Most people have come to expect the knowledge they consume to be preprocessed, easily understood, and interesting. Profundity is a punch line. Today's great truth is tomorrow's new item in Trivial Pursuit. Advances in psychological knowledge are the stuff read by Barbiedoll blonds between weather and sports. When given a choice between understanding and entertainment, most people choose the latter. That is why most people do not read the London Times, or listen to CBC radio. It is a venial sin to be trivial. It is a mortal sin to be dull. Interest accrues attention. Without interest, the knowledge one produces will never be consumed.

Interest, like the other three parameters of knowledge valuation, is stimulated by a variety of knowledge features. These can be divided into two generic categories: features of *content* and features of *form*. The interest generated by the content of knowledge is often called intrinsic interest, though it is often affected by social conditions that are extrinsic to the knowledge itself. Intrinsic interest seems to bear a strong relationship to pragmatic or psychological importance—people tend to show more interest in knowledge of things, events or ideas that are important to them than in knowledge of matters deemed unimportant. Stock brokers, for example, often claim to read the *Wall Street Journal* or *Financial Post* with great interest; lighthouse keepers usually do not. Expectant parents often show greater interest in developmental psychology than in Spanish literature for reasons we hope are obvious.

Yet the intrinsic interest of knowledge is not necessarily tied to current or pressing concerns. Indeed, the intrinsic interest of knowledge can occasionally lead to radical shifts in one's assessment of importance. A student who happens to hear a Bartok string quartet, for example, may become sufficiently fascinated by it to change majors and pursue the impoverished life of a composer. Someone who learns that the world's population is doubling every 40 years, or learns of the work of Sister Teresa, may be so taken by the knowledge that he or she will quit a career in computing for one in third world development. These kinds of radical changes are rare, but they do inspire many academics and clerics to continue their pursuit and teaching of intrinsically interesting knowledge in the face of stultifying student and public apathy.

Even when knowledge does not alter importance, it can still be intrinsically interesting. Many people are fascinated by knowledge about animals, others enjoy popular accounts of particle physics, high technology, or brain research. Knowledge collection forms the basis of several hobbies pursued for largely intrinsic rewards. Amateur experts on coins, stamps, local history, computer programming, or cultural trivia abound. Though the interest indicated by these recreational knowledge pursuits may serve some forms of psychological importance (e.g., personal identity, social status, escape from stress), it is difficult to stretch the point. Areas of knowledge often appear to be interchangeable in the psychological functions they serve. Many people flit from one interest to another according to their mood or curiosity. It is the content, and not the function, of knowledge that determines what they will seek or abandon.

Psychological knowledge surely has much intrinsic interest to some people and some intrinsic interest to most. A small number of topics studied by psychologists have almost universal appeal. Abnormal behavior, impression formation, personality, conformity, intelligence, consciousness, and personal development can usually attract large and curious audiences by their titles alone. Sensation, perception, classical conditioning, verbal learning, physiological processes, and research methods attract much smaller and selective audiences, though their numbers often become fiercely dedicated to the topics and pursue them almost entirely for the intrinsic interest they stimulate. Graduate schools are packed with such people, and all of them can readily attest to the numerous sacrifices that must be made in order to pursue their intellectual passions.

Alas, interest in the content of psychological knowledge is regularly vitiated by its form. Psychologists, as scientists, strive to be abstract, precise and logically consistent in the production and communication of their knowledge. The result is a form of psychological knowledge that almost no one enjoys. It is dry, partite, ponderous, and bland. It is the oyster that covers the pearl. It is often incomprehensible. Above all it is boring. So it is little wonder that most people go elsewhere to satisfy their tastes for psychological knowledge.

Much of the boredom that characterizes the form or packaging of psychological knowledge can be traced to the incompetence of psychologists. Most psychologists can barely write, and almost none can write well. Most cannot speak coherently, and almost none acquire training in the rhetorical or pedagogical arts. Some rather pathological norms govern communication in psychology. One is supposed to let facts speak for themselves, avoid anecdotes or speculations, document even the most harmless statements, and follow logical progressions from one idea to the next. The preferred style is concise, orderly and prosaic. It can be mastered in about two months. It can be fathomed by colleagues who have intrinsic interests in the content it attempts to convey. It can quickly expose bad ideas. And it can knock the life out of good ones.

Changes in the style of psychologists' scientific prose may alleviate some of the boredom that it now so consistently engenders. But the possibilities for change are very much constrained by the tenets and traditions of science.

Science is not only a style of discovery, it is also a style of communication, one which prescribes abstraction, precision and logical consistency, and proscribes their opposites. Yet any good novelist, playwrite or poet knows that the best way to capture and sustain the interests of an audience is to adopt a style that scientists are supposed to eschew. Consider a concrete example. Research in social psychology has tended to support the proposition that if an individual delivers positive verbal reinforcements to disliked others, then the others will, on average, deliver more positive reinforcements in return than they will if the individual delivers negative verbal reinforcements to them. In other words, you catch more flies with honey than vinegar. These "other words" are decidedly unscientific. They are also, we submit, far more interesting and memorable.

Psychological content conveyed in scientific forms is rather analogous to a vitamin pill: Few people doubt its nutritive value, but most people find it hard to swallow. The craving for knowledge of human behavior and experience is a craving for tastes, smells, textures, for sensations as well as perceptions, for excitement as well as insight. These qualities are as alien to science as they are integral to art. That is why most people prefer Shakespeare to Skinner, Tolstoy to Tolman, Henry to William James. Psychologists may have good intentions, good methods and good results, but they do not tell good stories.

A SUMMARY AND SOME DANGEROUS CONCLUSIONS

We have so far tried to show that as the amount and variety of human knowledge has grown, the potential consumers of this knowledge have acquired increasing degrees of freedom to choose the knowledge they consume or ignore. Their choices are presumably governed by the values they ascribe to the knowledge available, and these values are in turn determined by their assessments of four general features of knowledge: comprehensibility, credibility, importance, and interest. Each of these features has several variants and the salience of each feature and variant can differ from time to time, circumstance to circumstance, consumer to consumer.

Only a cynic would deny that the most valuable knowledge is that which is comprehensible, credible, important, and interesting according to every variant and method of assessment. Alas, such knowledge appears to be rare, if it appears at all. It is not unreasonable to assume that all knowledge is deficient in at least one way to at least one person—with sufficient tenacity one can always uncover, or stimulate, disagreement. But even if all knowledge is a compromise, preferences for knowledge can still be clearly established. Two questions remain: How much value do consumers ascribe to the knowledge produced by psychologists? and, If there is knowledge of greater value, what is it? There is one safe answer to both questions: It all depends. The answer can hardly be wrong, but it is trite and unsatisfying. Let us therefore review our speculations about the comprehensibility, credibility, importance and interest of knowledge produced by psychologists, then attempt some dangerous conclusions about the value of these products and their competitors.

To be comprehensible, knowledge must relate to familiar experiences and be expressed in familiar language. The experiences and language familiar to psychologists are often alien to the remainder of humanity. Psychologists are prone to experience psychology as theory and measurement and to speak of psychology in professional tongues. It is therefore not surprising that a large number of potential consumers of psychological knowledge cannot comprehend what psychologists offer.

To be credible, knowledge must pass at least one epistemological test of mysticism, rationalism, empiricism, analogy, or authority. Psychologists tend to invoke rather formal and stringent tests of rationalism and empiricism in their assessments of the credibility of psychological knowledge. This choice of tests is largely motivated by the fear of producing falsehoods. In contrast, most consumers of psychological knowledge are prone to test its credibility by almost any epistemology that will get the job done. They do not always do so because they are ignorant, lazy, or dumb. More often they do so because they do not wish to overlook the truth. Stated somewhat differently, psychologists and other scientists strive to avoid errors of commission in the production of knowledge; other people strive to avoid errors of omission in the consumption of knowledge. As a result, psychologists are much more likely to reject knowledge claims that others accept than to accept knowledge claims that others reject. Yet few people enjoy being told they are wrong or misguided, and few people embrace those who tell them so. That is why psychology, as a skeptical science, will probably never gain a large and fanatical following.

To be important, knowledge must possess some pragmatic or psychological significance. In general, the knowledge produced by psychologists has only marginal and indirect practical consequences. Sometimes this is because psychologists do not desire to produce practical knowledge. More often, however, it is because psychologists cannot produce such knowledge. Constraints of time, money, ethics, politics, and vested interests in suffering often conspire to spoil most attempts to produce knowledge of pragmatic significance. So too does the sheer complexity of the causes and consequences of practical matters. For these reasons we must look to the psychological significance of psychological knowledge as the major source of its importance. Here there is great potential—the facts and conjectures produced by psychologists can, in theory, be of central importance in transferring people's conceptions of themselves and their notions of the structures and functions of society (see Gergen, 1982). Yet it is likely that most people do not wish to change their conceptions—complacency abounds. Psychological knowledge need not be a threat to the philosophies of the smug majority; if it appears threatening, it can simply be dismissed or ignored. Most of the time it is. Apathy is a popular defense against anxiety.

To be interesting, knowledge must somehow excite the imagination, pique curiosity, arouse the senses. In principle, the content of most psychological knowledge can do all these things; the psyche is inherently interesting. In practice, however, most of the knowledge produced by psychologists does none of these things; it is tasteless, colorless and dull. The fault seems to lie in its form or packaging. As a product of science, psychological knowledge is by tradition, if not necessity, stripped of its wonder, ground to an emotional pulp, and distributed in plain brown envelopes. It is food for the cortex, not the soul. It is meant to bypass the senses and the passions. It has the subtlety and all the excitement of weak tea.

We are thus drawn to some dangerous conclusions. Though psychologists may exercise some control over the knowledge they produce, they exercise almost no control over the knowledge others consume. At the moment, psychology does not seem to produce much of what its potential consumers seem to value. To become more attractive to consumers, psychology will likely be increasingly obliged to set its research agenda according to desires for comprehensible, credible, important, and interesting knowledge defined by consumers, not by research psychologists. This may stimulate psychologists to explore new topics and research methods based upon an expanded epistemological foundation. But it will also confront us with the very real danger of becoming sycophants to an often fickle audience.

Of course, several authors in this volume have argued that psychology has already become sycophantic by accepting rather than challenging popular ideologies. There is scant reason to expect, however, that by becoming a critical discipline psychology will soon accrue a larger and more appreciative following. On the contrary, we can expect that psychology as a critical discipline will become far more insular than it is now. Abstract art, experimental music, and academic philosophy all began as critical endeavors and soon became elitist and incestuous. The same fate is likely to await those of us anxious to transform Western thought by publishing clever dialectic arguments in the Journal of Critical Psychology.

What, then, should we do? In the extremes, we can abandon psychology as a discipline, become folk psychologists, and pander to consumers in exchange for their attention. Alternatively, we can recognize our discipline, become critical psychologists, and attack the assumptions of consumers in exchange for the attention of our peers. Neither solution seems satisfactory. A compromise may thus be in order.

Fortunately, epistemology is not the same as ideology, so we need not adopt versions of both as a package deal. If our goal as psychologists is to create and popularize new conceptions of humanity, and thus to challenge existing ideologies, then we should make use of consumers' epistemologies to do so. We should argue concretely, not abstractly. We should speak of anecdotes, not statistics. We should use simple language and the best metaphors we can find. We should address ourselves to issues of emotional, moral, and political importance. And we should tell good stories.

The result would scarcely resemble psychology as we now know it. Our methods of communication would be more akin to those of the novelist, dramatist, or satirist than to those who parade in white lab coats. We would be forced to master the art of careful observation and elegant description, and to live more by our wits than our grants. But we should then be rewarded with the attention so many now covet, and thus a chance to influence persons other than ourselves.

It has often been said that the last thirty years have been cursed by the triumph of style over substance. If that is the new reality, then psychologists are clearly at a disadvantage in the marketplace of ideas. We stand a chance of regaining some advantage by changing our style to better match the epistemologies of those not trained in our ways. If what we offer is truly substantial, it will easily survive a change in our style. If what we offer is not substantial, we have no business as a discipline.

REFERENCES

Abelson, R. & Rosenberg, M. (1958). Symbolic psycho-logic: A model of attitudinal cognition. *Behavioral Science, 3,* 1–8.

Allport, G. & Postman, L. (1947). *The psychology of rumor.* New York: Holt.

Bakan, D. (1967). The mystery-mastery complex in contemporary psychology. In D. Bakan (Ed.), *On method.* San Francisco: Jossey Bass, 37–49.

Davis, G. (1964). Personal communication.

Festinger, L. (1954). A theory of social comparison processes. *Human Relations, 7,* 117–140.

Garfinkel, A. (1981). *Forms of explanation.* New Haven: Yale University Press.

Gergen, K. (1982). *Toward transformation in social knowledge.* New York: Springer-Verlag.

Heider, F. (1958). *The psychology of interpersonal relations.* New York: Wiley.

Holzner, B. (1968). *Reality construction in society.* Cambridge, MA: Schenkman.

Katz, D., Sarnoff, I., & McClintock, C. (1956). Ego-defense and attitude change. *Human Relations, 9,* 27–45.

Lévi-Strauss, C. (1966). *The savage mind.* Chicago: University of Chicago Press.

Lindblom, C. & Cohen, D. (1979). *Usable knowledge.* New Haven: Yale University Press.

Mannheim, K. (1936). *Ideology and utopia.* New York: Harcourt, Brace and World.

McGuire, W. (1960). Cognitive consistency and attitude change. *Journal of Abnormal and Social Psychology, 60,* 345–353.

Nisbett, R. & Ross, L. 1980). *Human inference: Strategies and shortcomings of social judgment.* Englewood Cliffs, New Jersey: Prentice-Hall.

Popper, K. (1959). *The logic of scientific discovery.* New York: Harper.

Royce, J. (1964). *The encapsulated man.* Princeton: Van Nostrand.

Sampson, E. (1977). Psychology and the American ideal. *Journal of Personality and Social Psychology, 35,* 767–782.

Sorokin, P. (1941). *The crisis of our age*. New York: Dutton.

Strickland, L. (Ed.) (1984). *Directions in Soviet social psychology.* New York: Springer-Verlag.

Thorngate, W. (1979). Memory, cognition and social performance. In L. Strickland (Ed.), *Soviet and western perspectives in social psychology.* Oxford: Pergamon.

Thorngate, W. (1980). Efficient decision heuristics. *Behavioral Science, 25,* 219–225.

Tiger, L. (1979). *Optimism: The biology of hope.* New York: Simon and Schuster.

Whitehead, A. (1938). *Modes of thought.* New York: Macmillan.

Writghtsman, L. (1964). Measurement of philosophies of human nature. *Psychological Reports, 14,* 743–751.

Chapter 4

An Appeal for Objectivism in Psychological Metatheory

James Foster

Ho-gen, a Chinese Zen teacher, lived alone in a small temple in the country. One day four travelling monks appeared and asked if they might make a fire in his yard to warm themselves.

While they were building the fire, Ho-gen heard them arguing about subjectivity and objectivity. He joined them and said: "There is a big stone. Do you consider it to be inside or outside your mind?"

One of the monks replied: "From the Buddhist viewpoint everything is an objectification of mind, so I would say that the stone is inside my mind."

"Your head must feel very heavy," observed Ho-gen, "if you are carrying around a stone like that in your mind." (Zen parable)

Like the monks in our story, and like the relativist position which is becoming increasingly popular in recent psychological metatheory literature, let us assume that the human understanding is truly not capable of direct access to the actual nature of any given object or event. In other words, that due to various mitigating linguistic, historical, cultural or similar "frames of reference," it would be expected that the *validity* of any given theory about an object or event cannot possibly be tested against its ability to explain the object or event which the focus of that theory. This is what amounts to the radical import of relativism: that in deciding whether or not a theory is true, its material relation to the object or event (hereafter referred to conjointly as "the object") would be judged as completely irrelevant—indeed, must necessarily be deemed irrelevant given relativism's premise that the mind does not have direct access to the objective domain.

This sort of conclusion is more than disturbing to the average scientist; for it is well known that the sciences, including social sciences such as psychology, tend to ignore the existence of relativistic effects. While there is no doubt that scientific judgment is "relativized" by extra-scientific effects, the daily world around us or the scientist's place within the limits of knowledge gained up to that scientist's point in history, but the relativist appears to assess the impact of these extra-scientific effects as the primary force in science. The relativist's slogan is that "we'll see what we expect to see" and our scientific expectations are shaped by whichever theory is most popular at the time. But there is a very serious problem with this proposition; for how do some scientific theories eventually come to be recognized as invalid, or at least, as less adequate than another competing theory?

The question as to how competing theories are decided is crucial; for it decides whether or not psychology is essentialy based on scientific or merely ideological grounds and, in general, whether or not objectivism or relativism prevails in the sciences.

Relativists do not argue that all theoretical claims are necessarily invalid, only that their validity (or invalidity) is impossible to determine. Thus, any theory may be true or it may be false, but we can never know with certainty since it has been accepted that the observer is incapable of direct access to the true nature of that which the theory claims to entail. Accordingly, a critical analysis of how competing theories are decided cannot involve the weighing of one theory against another in terms of their correspondence to the object under question. Standard marks of explanatory power such as accuracy in measurement and prediction or any other similar tests of reliability are summarily dismissed by the relativists on the ground that such checks operate *within* the assumptions set by the theory in question. What is therefore required is criticism which steps outside of the theory under scrutiny. While such "meta"-criticism would have to flow from yet another theoretical perspective, this hardly bothers the relativist; since all knowledge is based on theory and nothing more, an infinite plurality of theories has really always been our lot. For some, this conclusion may appear to be somewhat disappointing in that it implies a chaotic scenario where science should be viewed as nothing less than an unlimited number of competing theories none of which can be said to be any more valid than the next. For others, relativism invites a new sense of freedom which more readily allows the opportunity to challenge prevailing paradigms and question the apparently arrogant stoicism of scientific practice. Thus, the relativist claims to stand on the side of tolerance for the opinions of others, holism and a healthy, anti-authoritarian liberalism:

> Non-positivist readers will agree with me that theories cannot be evaluated without values and without theories. They will accept my relationism, namely that any given theory is better or worse than other theories only in relation to some frame of reference (Brandt, 1982, p. 109):

> It may be useful, then, to consider competing theoretical accounts in terms of their generative capacity, that is, the capacity to challenge the guiding assumptions of the culture, to raise fundamental questions regarding contemporary social life, to foster reconsideration of that which is "taken for granted," and thereby to furnish new alternatives for social action. It is the generative theory that can provoke debate, transform social reality, and ultimately serve to reorder social conduct (Gergen, 1978, p. 1344).

REACTIONARY ASPECTS OF RELATIVISM

Few would doubt that any given culture or subculture carries its share of "hidden," yet pervasive, assumptions. Furthermore, there is no reason to suppose that the sciences, especially the social sciences, are immune from such assumptions. However, one can be equally certain that none of these assumptions will be alleviated by relativism. The general counter-argument is this: that if all knowledge is essentially independent of any objective content, then those who desire change can only point to their own subjectivist arguments in order to bring others around to adopt their preferred point of view. Various writers have waxed poetic in describing their visions of an ideal society where everyone follows a relativistic epistemology and a time when there are no deep divisions over competing positions, but only an open-minded and liberal attitude toward one another's views despite all individual differences. The relativist philosopher Ian Hacking hopes that everyone will someday adopt his brand of epistemology, a view which follows along the lines of Paul Feyerabend's "epistemological anarchism" (Feyerabend, 1975). Hacking wrote that: "Anarcho-rationalism is tolerance for other people combined with the discipline of one's own standard of truth and reason" (1982, p. 66).

However, history tells another story. Given that any society entails some sort of order, by definition, what policy should it follow and how is it to be implemented? Although the Italian intelligentsia of the 1930's and Benito Mussolini were agreed upon relativism, they could not have been too pleased by the manner in which the fascist leader used relativism to assert his own social visions over any other views, and thus, Mussolini was perfectly correct when he wrote that, "Fascism is relativism" (Cunningham, unpubl.). This identity follows from the argument that if all theories are of equal truth value, or as Brandt put it above that "any given theory is better or worse than other theories only in relation to some frame of reference," Mussolini should, thereby, be compelled only to entertain an open hearing of alternatives according to his own standard of truth and reason. History has noted that in other fascist regimes, when it is generally accepted that an authority has access to objectivity, then Pilate's question "what is truth?" must be a matter somehow decided upon subjectivist grounds.

Now, where the question turns to an examination of those subjectivist factors which must ultimately be responsible for mental judgment, perhaps the ultimate "answer" was discovered by nineteenth-century German romantic romantic idealists such as Schopenhauer in his lofty appraisal of "the will." Accepting the assumption that thoughts about the world and our place in it are embedded within our own subjectivity, it would follow that consciousness itself must be influenced by something greater than itself, and if that something is *not* the material world, what else is there other than some inner drive behind our perception, behind consciousness: "Consciousness is the mere surface of our mind of which, as of the earth, we do not know the inside but only the crust" (Schopenhauer, 1844/1969).

The same position may be found in Neitzsche's theory of the "power to will." Almost a century ago, Neitzsche put forward the same basic arguments frequently heard from contemporary proponents of relativism:

> Granted that nothing is 'given' as real except our world of desires and passions, that we can rise or sink to no other 'reality' than the reality of our drives—for thinking is only the relationship of these drives to one another—. . . (1866/1973, p. 48).

It is more than likely that contemporary proponents of relativism are not in favor of dismissing all rational discourse from society and substituting the blind imposition of the will of any individual or group. Nevertheless, it must be emphasized that, contrary to the romantic visions of intellectual tolerance, there is absolutely nothing in relativism which prevents the possibility of the most oppressive social order from arbitrarily controlling the social conduct of its citizens. Thus, far from presenting itself on the side of progressive and liberal thinking, relativism *invites* reactionary attitudes to take hold and preserve the *status quo* while holding behind a sophisticated epistemological argument.

RELATIVISM AND THE HISTORY OF SCIENCE: ON THOMAS KUHN

In looking over the history of humankind, it is not always easy to recognize where progress has been made. The exception to this observation is the history of science, of which psychology is certainly a part. Granted, science has its share of amusing examples of regressive thinking. For example, an atavistic fascination with pythagorean numerology inspired Kepler's "not quite right" model of the solar system. Numerology also moved Newton to delineate the spectrum of sunlight in seven, rather than six, colors: "indigo" is hardy distinguishable from the supposedly neighboring colors of blue and violet (Sagan, 1980). However, one could safely argue that most laypersons and scientists alike would regard scientific knowledge as essentially cumulative in character and some would cite achievements such as reaching the moon, heart transplants and personal computers as a direct result of an increasingly larger store of scientific knowledge.

For the relativist, such progress presents a challenging problem; for if there is to be a barrier between human understanding and the objective world, then there can be no such thing as an advance in knowledge about the world. Thus, contrary to popular scientific belief, intellectual history does not describe a series of discoveries about the actual nature of the world and ourselves. This would be impossible since according to relativism, human knowledge cannot reflect the actual state of the world, rather the objective world is as a *tabula rasa* upon which the understanding imposes its "constructions" (Royce and Powell, 1983). As Kuhn put it in his immensely popular thesis, *The Structure of Scientific Revolutions* (1970):

> Why should progress . . . be the apparently universal concomitant of scientific revolutions? (. . .) Revolutions close with a total victory for one of the two opposing camps. Will that group ever say that the result of its victory has been something less than progress? . . . Scientific education makes use of no equivalent for the art museum of the library of classics, and the result is a sometimes drastic distortion in scientist's perception of his discipline's past . . . In short, he comes to see it as progress. No alternative is available to him while he remains in the field.

If, contrary to the central assumption posited by objectivism, the scientist has no access to the nature of the object itself, then it would necessarily follow that to speak of gaining a greater knowledge of the object, that is, of a progress in scientific knowledge, would be meaningless. The scientist's investigations are not guided by the nature of the object, but rather by the scientist's preconceived idea of the object. This conclusion is to be expected from an epistemology which asserts the primacy of a cognitive understanding of "external" stimuli before its perception; a reversal of sorts suggesting that one must believe it to see it. Indeed, Kuhn argued that science could be neatly divided into two parts: the creative moment when a new large-scale theory or "paradigm" somehow appears on the scene and the remainder of scientific history which consists of the comparatively dull task of providing substantial support for the paradigm. This latter activity was referred to as "normal science," described as:

> an attempt to force nature into the preformed and relatively inflexible box the paradigm supplies. Nor part of the aim of normal science is to call forth new sorts of phenomena; indeed those that will not fit the box are *not seen at all* (1970, p. 24, emphasis added).

It bears repeating that in following this position consistently, the notion of scientific progress *must* be regarded as meaningless. With this in mind, let us now accept Kuhn's scenario: All access to the object under scientific scrutiny is said to be distorted to the degree that an observer could perceive *only* that which the scientific community collectively would expect to perceive within the limits of the prevailing paradigm. Now, let us return to the question posed at the beginning of this discussion: how would Kuhn account for the undeniable fact that the history of science is marked by changes in the paradigms. Kuhn answers that:

> the transition from a paradigm in crisis to a new one, from which a new tradition of normal science can emerge is far from cumulative process, one achieved by an articulation or extension of the old paradigm. Rather it is a reconstruction of the field from new fundamentals. . . . When the transition is complete, the profession will have changed its view of the field. . . . Scientists do not see something as something else; instead they simply see it (1970, p. 85).

Those familiar with this sort of claim will quickly recognize the neo-Kantian language of this passage. Before entering upon a particular critique of Kuhn's epistemology, and, by implication, of relativism in general, it would be valuable to briefly review Kant's position.

SOME OF THE HISTORICAL ROOTS OF RELATIVISM

Kant had inherited the absurdity of classical empiricism bequeathed by Hume. It was Hume who had demonstrated that by beginning from the premise that if all knowledge is derived from sensory experience, then any awareness of whatever may lie beyond pure sensation (e.g., knowledge of causal connections) can never be justified. As Hume put it:

> The mind can never possibly find the effect in the supposed cause, even by the most accurate scrutiny and examination. For the effect is totally different from the cause, and consequently can never be discovered in it (1777/1975, p. 29).

Hume neatly summed up this position in this way: "One event follows another; but we never can observe any tie between them" (p. 74). Thus, without being able to refer to the perpetually consistent action of some objects as anything more than sequences which appear to be regular on the basis of our "customs" or "habits," empiricism denied the possibility of scientific knowledge. But where empiricism argued against the temporal and spatial coordination of the object, it also argued against the possibility of an individual existing in the world. Indeed, one conclusion which Hume logically drew from this position is the denial of self-identity; for if there is no observable *connection* between the individual's state of being from one moment to the next, then there is, for the empiricist, no epistemological justification for self-identity. Hume often relegated self-identity to a mere "feeling" or "sentiment." But from whence this sentiment?

How does the mind come by this conviction that objects and ourselves exist as continuous forms within time and space. Kant provided the answer to this question by arguing that all knowledge is as it is because of certain a priori categories of the understanding. Accordingly, all that is perceived is first "filtered" through the understanding before it gains any meaningful comprehension in the mind. Kant states:

> Our knowledge springs from two fundamental sources of the mind; the first is the capacity of receiving representations . . . the second is the power of knowing an object as given to us, through the second the object is thought in relation to that (given) representation . . . (1781/1929, p. 92).

On the basis of this major assumption, which bears a strong resemblance to the last excerpt taken from Kuhn's book, Kant further claimed that:

> . . . these two powers . . . cannot exchange their functions. The understanding can intuit nothing, the senses can think nothing. Only through their union can knowledge arise (*Kant,* p. 93).

This, then, was to be the meeting point between the subjective and objective domains. However, their union could hardly be called a happy one; for Kant's answer to strict empiricism entailed *including* the mind itself as an integral part of knowledge. Thus, a priori cognitive structures provide form to the otherwise insensible myriad of sensory stimuli. If that is the case, then it is the nature of the mind itself which becomes the sole ground for determining our knowledge about the world. Kant concludes:

> All appearances, as possible experiences, thus lie *a priori* in the understanding, and receive from it their formal possibility. . . . However exaggerated and absurd it may sound, to say that the understanding is itself the source of the laws of nature, and so of its formal unity, such an assertion is none the less correct (*Kant,* p. 148).

In sum, for all of Kant's cautionary measures to avoid a pendulum swing from Hume's strict empiricism toward a subjective idealism, his work clearly indicated that priority be given to the subject end in the subject-object relation.

TWENTIETH-CENTURY SOPHISM

Let us now follow the pattern of almost all historical accounts provided by Western philosophers by blithely passing over the nineteenth-century materialist response to Kant's idealism and we go directly to the logical positivism of Russell and Whitehead. Logical positivism is the bane of the contemporary relativist; it stands for a pendulum swing back to basing knowledge on the object end of the subject-object relation.

The position which is proposed by the author is "objectivism" which will now be distinguished from logical positivism. Objectivism does not call for the imposition of a particular philosophy upon ordinary scientific practice, but only asserts that (1) objects exist independently of mind and that, as such, (2) objects present the capacity to correct subjective judgement. These same assumptions have also been argued in the "dialectical materialism" of Marx and Engels (1963), Cunningham's "objectivism" (1973) and Ruben's "realism" (1979). Positivism lies in contradiction to objectivism where it emphasizes the need for a value-free observation language and stresses the problem of verifiability even under very stringent observation conditions. Of the many problems which finally brought about the dismissal of positivism, one was the assumption that the act of knowing is an essentially passive process. From this assumption, positivism leads to what Ruben aptly called "a pictorial version of correspondence" (p. 184); that is, the perception of an object implies a mental image of the object. Thus, *again,* the mind deals not with the object directly, but only with its mental representation. If that is so, then how do we know for certain that our mental representation inside our heads truly reflects the nature of the object itself? In this way, positivism also implies an incommensurable, to borrow from Kuhn's language, separation between the mind and the object. Positivism and relativism stand on the same side against objectivism.

For the objectivist, perception is an intrinsic element within the process of coming to know the object. That process is by its very nature an active one. In direct contrast to the positivist's view, objectivism argues that sensing involves the active "feeling-out" (Leontiev, 1981) of the object, a term which connotes the truly active and exploratory character of perception. In describing the *process* of knowing, objectivism, contrary to Kant and a priori relativism, does not hold that it is the mind which activates or completely directs the activity of coming to know an object. Kuhn's view is that perception is constantly initiated and guided by the mind and prior knowledge; for the mind cannot comprehend without the guidance of the prevailing paradigm. Again, it must be stressed that this view is based on the completely abstract notion that the process of perception is a passive one.

What is called for is a recognition of the mind as actively participating "*in* the world" (Vygotsky, 1978). Here objectivism radically opposes the relativist's argument that we cannot discuss the true nature of the object because its ontological status lies on a fundamentally different plane than our world of mental representations, ideas, models and paradigms. For Kuhn, knowing does not necessarily entail active participation in the world, but rather the beginning and end of knowing is always in the mind. Kuhn states: "They (the paradigms) are the source of the methods, problem-field, and standards of solution accepted by any mature scientific community at any given time" (p. 103). Accordingly theory does not aid perception, it supplants perception.

ABSURDITY IN ITS PLACE

In spite of the increasing interest in relativism since Kant, it still sounds "exaggerated and absurd . . . to say that the understanding is itself the source of the laws of nature." If all knowledge about the object, including the object of human behavior, is merely a determination of our own mind, then the theoretical psychologists who claim that science is an exercise which begins and ends in the mind are absolutely correct. Neil Agnew and Sandra Pyke (1969) defined science as "the game and art of describing a pattern within a system of sensing and conceptual biases" (p. 257). Since Agnew and Pyke have further argued that all "sensing" is based on our concepts, then they are really asserting that all sensory knowledge can only be understood within a system of concepts. Perhaps Brandt's definition of psychology as simply "a beautiful game" (1982, p. 257) would be more appropriate.

Accepting that the actual status of the object is a matter exclusively beyond the mind, then it must follow that all scientific knowledge represents nothing more than the collective whim of the scientific community. The relativist, though, is somehow above it all and can somehow observe the true reality of what scientists are doing. Thus, the relativist sees the scientist as a puppet playing a role in a very large game. There's an attractive radical chic to this position which invites us to put Mickey Mouse ears on our vision of the sober and resolute scientist at work.

However, in order to provide a modicum of plausibility to relativism, it must be demonstrated that there is absolutely no situation where the actual nature of the object asserts itself as more meaningful than any interpretation of it. Should it ever occur that the object itself directs our interpretation of it, then we must accept the fact that interpretation, our understanding, is subject to correction by the actual nature of the object. This necessarily implies an acceptance of objectivism and, by the same stroke, a denial of relativism. The relativist cannot have it both ways; because it is essential to the legitimacy of relativism that the subject does not have direct access to the object. If all knowledge about the world is true only in relation to the claimant's "frame of reference," then that is all there is to say. The relativist cannot also say that the object itself, to a degree, contributes to our knowledge of the world since that would imply *two* frames of reference, that is, contributions from both the object and the subject. If this is what relativism truly stands for, then relativism is a banality. The interesting aspect of relativism is that it proposes a primacy of the mind over matter; that it is the paradigm which shapes our view of the object, not the other way round. To say that the object itself also contributes to our knowledge admits that the object can influence our understanding, can correct our prior knowledge, and most importantly, can lead to the formation of theories about the nature of the object; in short, objectivism.

Do we have the makings for yet another perpetually irreconcilable dualism? No, because in so far as all relativist accounts purport a primacy of the subject over the object also *inevitably* admit that there is some access to the object, all relativist accounts suffer from logical inconsistency. A strong claim, but let us return to Kuhn's writings to measure its validity.

The thrust of Kuhn's position is that the epistemological relations which exist between the scientist and the object will change as paradigms change:

> Paradigm changes . . . cause scientists to see the world of research-engagement differently. In so far as their only recourse to that world is through what they see and do, we may want to say that after a revolution scientists are responding to a different world (1970, p. 111).

This excerpt is followed by the inevitable mixing of objectivism and relativism where Kuhn further explains that the scientist's perception is:

> "determined jointly by the environment and his particular normal-scientific tradition . . . at times of (scientific) revolution, when the normal-scientific tradition changes, the scientist's perception of his environment must be re-educated—in some familiar situations he must learn to see a new gestalt"(*Kuhn,* p. 112).

Conceding the possibility of educating another to see the object in a different way assumes that perception is not as rigid as Kuhn's paradigm-fixed portrayal of perception suggests. Indeed, by allowing that one could "learn to see" things differently, it is assumed that the mind is able to make objective comparisons between the old "world-view" and the object itself, between the new "world-view" and the object itself, and between both "world-views" and the object itself. Without making such comparisons it is unclear what else Kuhn could have meant by the phrase "learn to see." Such comparisons imply, as Kuhn himself said, that perception is "determined jointly by the environment and . . . normal-scientific tradition."

Again, relativists cannot have it both ways: *either* the object exists independently of thought and, thus, has the capacity to resist change when thoughts about the object change—the capacity which sets up the possibility of the object itself influencing, correcting and provoking the mind, *or* the object exists in a dependent relation with the mind so that the object changes as our thoughts about the object change. If we speak of having *some* access to the true nature of the object itself, but it is distorted by prior knowledge, then we have admitted that we can observe a distortion, implying a comparative understanding of the objects true nature, its distortion and the possibility of correcting the distortion. Thus, objectivism is able to supercede relativism. The possibility of an irreconciable dualism between the two positions really never exists. It is not a question of emphasis or even persuasive argument; necessity dictates that objectivism, that is, the position that objects exist independently of mind, is accepted once it is also accepted that *some* access to the object is possible.

Let us now suppose that Kuhn is absolutely correct and that all scientific knowledge is dependent upon that which is allowed by the prevailing paradigm. Like Kuhn, we will assume that scientists are engaged in "an attempt to force nature into the preformed and relatively inflexible box that the paradigm supplies . . . indeed, those (phenomena) that will not fit the box are often not seen at all" (p. 24). But if we cannot even see a discrepancy between the object and the paradigm, how is it possible to have the knowledge that paradigms exist at all? Against what background could such knowledge emerge? The identity proposed here between the object and our thoughts about the object should really work to prevent Kuhn from providing such remarkably detailed accounts of the nature of paradigms. How can Kuhn and other relativists, without making comparisons to the object itself, explain the distortions caused by the paradigm and expose the *errors* which inundated scientific thinking under other paradigms? Philosopher Donald Davidson caught this inconsistency when he wrote that "Kuhn is brilliant at saying what things were like before the revolution using— what else?—our post-revolutionary idiom" (1982, p. 67).

The incommensurability of "paradigms" or "world-views" is not only logically inconsistent in explaining different historical periods, but is also unsuccessful in its attempt to explain differences between cultures. The application of relativism leads to what critical anthropologists refer to as the "translation problem;" for example, if another culture lives according to a world-view which differs from that held by the anthropologist observing that culture, then it should be impossible for the anthropologist to say, on the one hand, "yes, those Herns (to use W. Newton-Smith's fictitious culture) have a different world-view" and then go on to describe just how different that world-view really is in terms that are quite comprehensible. W. Newton-Smith (1982) argued that "the possibility of translation entails the falsehood of relativism" (p. 115). She also exposes the implicit egocentrism inherent in relativism, a character which evolves from the proposition of world-views. A cultural disparity sufficient to suggest the existence of a different world-view would require a cultural and communication gap so wide that it would not be bridged by even the simplest logic. Thus, Newton-Smith concludes:

> Not only is relativism not explanatory, it is not charitable either. It started off with the aim of giving a charitable construal of the diversity of belief and in the end deprives the Herns of any beliefs at all. The relativist wants to stop using "philosophical B-52's" (Hacking's phrase) to read our truth, logic and rationality on to the Herns. In the end we cannot give them any truth, logic or rationality at all (p. 115).

Can it be reasonably argued that those scientists who upheld a general theory which differs from what may be presently maintained in science actually lived according to a world-view "incommensurable" with our own? If past scientific theories are logically incompatible with each other, then history should be totally inaccessible. The application of relativism in psychology has produced the view that the conflicting diversity of psychological theories is a result of different psychologists looking at the object from different "world-views." If this is accepted, then it follows that there is no standard by which any psychological theory can be said to be more correct than another. Just one example from the history of psychology is all that is necessary in order to contradict a claim of this kind.

THE RISE AND FALL OF RECAPITULATION THEORY

Many psychological journals published near the turn of this century contained at least one article which directly or indirectly touched upon the once strictly biological theory of recapitulation; it had all the qualities of a Kuhnian paradigm. Even today, while most people are likely to be unfamiliar with the term "recapitulation," they are likely to recognize the general concept: that over the course of its individual development, an organism is expected to pass through a series of stages which resemble the adult appearance of those species which contributed the evolutionary history of the organism. While the comparative biologist Ernst Haeckel cannot be credited with being the first to propose this idea (Foster, 1984; Gould 1977; Mayr, 1982), his energetic efforts to popularize recapitulation theory must be recognized. Haeckel believed that recapitulation was a logical consequence of Darwin's theory of evolution, but as will be explained, Haeckel's recapitulation theory denies the possibility of evolution.

Through his many speaking tours throughout continental Europe, Haeckel popularized recapitulation with the result that many scientists came to regard each species as if they were set along a single vertical track. They believed that a given species embodied a culmination of all of its ancestral species plus the new distinctive feature which appeared at the end of its individual development. The model was the evolutionary tree; Haeckel drew an amoeba-like creature at the bottom of the tree and, in supposedly increasing complexity, other species filled the higher branches with the human species at the top. Embryology was simply energized by the notion that the history of the biological world could be observed in the first stages of development.

Now, the rejection of recapitulation theory could not be described as a scientific revolution; but, then, since knowledge is a cumulative process rather than a series of incommensurable gestalt-like shifts, this is hardly surprising. As early as 1828, criticism of recapitulation theory, largely based on observation, was put forward by the embryologist Karl Ernst Von Baer (Gould, 1977). Von Baer found that the individual development of an organism is best described as a process involving a gradual development from a general, almost undifferentiated form growing more differentiated as it approached its species' adult appearance. At *no* time would the developing organism resemble the adult appearance of any other species. This empirical data was confirmed during embryology's boom era following on the hopes and expectations raised by recapitulation theory. Then, later genetic studies provided the missing material link in Darwin's theory, that is, that the *cause* of the variations upon which natural selection worked its evolutionary effects lay in the genes. One need not be a biologist to understand that if genetic variation can affect the development of an individual organism right from the beginning of its embryonic life, then recapitulation, with its notion that the final development of the individual is the culmination of the steady, well-ordered contribution of one species after the next, is an impossibility.

However, before recapitulation theory had been generally dismissed within biology, a number of prominent psychologists had adopted its theme of cumulative development to explain psychological development. They relied upon the theory to provide a sound, biological foundation for their accounts which described the development of the child as a series of stages which reflect the contribution of significant psycho-social turning points in the history of the human species. This notion of psychological recapitulation created a vast amount of theory (Foster, 1984) before the fundamental flaws underlying the biological "principle" became general knowledge.

Exactly how this extension from the original biological formula was implemented may best be explained by referring to passages from some of these recapitulations writings. First, from G. Stanley Halls's curious views on the appearance of independent, individualistic behavior in early adolescence:

> Everything in short, suggests the culmination of one stage of life as if it thus represented what was once, . . . the age of maturity in some remote, perhaps pigmoid stage of human evolution, when in a warm climate the young of our species once shifted for themselves independently of further parental aid. The qualities now developed are phyletically vastly older than all the neo-atavistic traits of body and

soul, later to superposed like a new and higher story built on to our primal nature (1904, v. 1, pp. ix–x).

From Sigmund Freud:

> In a certain sense he [primitive man] is still our contemporary: there are people whom we still consider more closely related to primitive man than to ourselves, in whom we therefore recognize the direct descendants and representatives of earlier man. We can thus judge the so-called savage and semi-savage races; their psychic life assumes a peculiar interest for us, for we can recognize in their psychic life a well-preserved, early stage of our own development (1918, p. 3).

And, finally, from Carl Jung:

> These considerations tempt us to draw a parallel between the mythological thinking of ancient man and the similar thinking found in children, primitives, and in dreams. This idea is not at all strange; we know it quite well from comparative anatomy and from evolution, which show that the structure and function of the human body are the result of a series of embryonic mutations corresponding to similar mutations in our racial history. The supposition that there may also be in psychology a correspondence between ontogenesis and phylogenesis therefore seems justified. If this is so, it would mean that infantile thinking and dream thinking are simply a recapitulation of earlier evolutionary stages (1959, pp. 26–27).

There are three major difficulties with the notion of psychological recapitulation: First, the biological principle upon which this notion is based has been shown to be, at the least, highly implausible. Over the course of its biological development no species, including our own, undergoes a recapitulation of the adult appearance of any other species. Therefore, the extension of this concept into the psychological domain amounts to nothing more than making a large falsehood even larger. Secondly, there is no clear justification for making the leap from biological to psychological development, nor did the proponents of this extension ever fully argue one. Instead, somewhere in their texts, one finds the insidious introduction of the empty analogy, as in biology, so in psychology. The quote above from Jung is a good example of how this centrally important assumption is casually slipped in. Finally, there is an outstanding lack of any anthropological support for this notion which assumes that the thinking of prehistoric adults must have been fundamentally different from that of modern adults. It was the aim of psychological recapitulation theory to map the mental landscape of the modern child by referring to points in our cultural past (actually in the past or as preserved in remote areas of the present world) and, thereby, explain the foundations of everyday psychic functioning. An abundance of evidence which clearly attest to a high level of social and intellectual sophistication on the part of nonindustrial societies strongly suggests a contrary conclusion: for example, Jim Freedman's account of the collision which occurs when overseas capital interests attempt to fit within East African peasant communities (in Turner and Smith, 1979). Challenging counter-evidence is also found in G. P. Murdock's article "The Common Denominator of Cultures" (in Linton, 1945) where he lists over one hundred social characteristics common to every ethnographically and historically known culture.

Under the weight of such contrary evidence, it is not surprising that the notion of psychological recapitulation is no longer at the leading edge of contemporary psychology. Despite the fact that Hall's major work on the subject *Adolescence* (1904) sold over 25,000 copies shortly after its publication, a record at that time for a book of its category, and that Hall went on to influence the construction of the elementary school curriculum (Ross, 1972), few psychologists today refer to Hall's work on recapitulation. Since its moment of glory at the Clark Conference of 1909, Freud's work has waned to the point that at present writing there is no faculty of psychology in North America which offers graduate training in psychoanalysis. Equally, Jungian psychology is more likely to be found in contemporary novels than in the classroom. Would these results have occurred if the biological principle of recapitulation was an actual fact and its effects on psychological development was a *fact* that psychologists could study? The relativist answers, "What is fact?"

AS TO THE LAST WORD FROM THE RELATIVISTS AND POSITIVISTS

Following Kuhn, it could be argued that all the objections raised toward the theory of psychological recapitulation merely indicate that there is a new paradigm in place in psychology. Objectivism, too, is merely another paradigm which can blind one to understanding another epistemological frame of reference. After all that has been argued, the best counter-argument is no argument. In the middle of a world filled with real suffering, one can only argue about objectivity for so long before the exercise approaches immoral conduct. As the objectivist writer Ruben pointed out, there really is no philosophical justification for the claim that objects really do exist independently of mind, *but objectivity has no need for an intellectual justification.*

In our everyday life, we practice objectivism: we can argue different points of view and work at understanding one another's argument, and every day we gain new knowledge about our environment, about others and all that exists independently of our thoughts stands ready to provoke new thought and correct our old knowledge. And what of past lives, are we incommensurably separated from the scientists of the past and their points of view? Are we separated from the knowledge gained in the past by a radically different frame of reference? The relativist and the positivist are agreed that all historical knowledge is, at best, speculative. Hume said:

A man, who should find in a desert country the remains of pompous buildings, would conclude that the country had, in ancient times, been cultivated by civilized inhabitants; but did nothing of this nature occur *to him,* he could never form such an inference . . . (1777/1975, p. 46; emphasis added).

Here, again, the conclusion rests on the assumption that all knowledge is dependent upon one's own personal epistemological frame of reference; the clock turns back two thousand years to the solipsism of the Greek sophists.

CONCLUSION

It has been argued that any line of reasoning which leads to relativism also lends to political anarchism, itself the most fertile intellectual soil for totalitarianism, as Mussolini well knew. It has also been argued that at its core relativism is logically inconsistent. This serious criticism stems largely from the writings of its proponents and their "contention that assertions cannot be judged true or false in themselves, but must be so judged with reference to one or more aspects of the total situation in which they have been made" (Mandelbaum, 1982, p. 35). The statement is typical of the mixing of objectivism and relativism where it assumes that the observer does have access to the situation—to the object itself. Once some access to the object is allowed, then a denial of relativism follows as a matter of necessity, since perception would be subject to the correcting capacity of the object and it would be the object, not the paradigm, which would shape our interpretation. Furthermore, the term "total situation," synonymous with frame of reference, presumably consists of practically anything at all which might contribute or any way affect a truth claim—for relativists, this means everything from the language in which the claim was couched to the cultural/historical milieu in which the claimant was born. Thus, there is nothing to prevent the claims that extremely fringe extrascientific effects, from astrological arrangements to the waning popularity of antiquarianism in the twentieth century, are the "real reasons" behind the entry of a scientific discovery. Why not? To suggest otherwise would be to assert that there are some standards which are better than others for measuring the objective value of a claim; a position which is contrary to the tenets of relativism.

What would be the value of criticism from a relativist stand-point? If all truth claims are true only within the particular frame of reference in which the claim is presented, then all claims which assert to be concerned with what is *in truth* accounts for the rise and fall of a scientific theory must be naive realism. Of course, these consequences have yet to abate the tendency for relativists to criticize objectivist literature. Thus, the supreme contradiction lies in relativist writings where one can almost hear the critical author saying, "No, no. The objectivist does not have a true understanding of the way things really are in (science, psychology, etc.), but I do and I will explain the true picture in my critique."

Let us at least try to work within a theoretical framework that is not logically inconsistent. The author proposes a more constructive approach which asserts that the active process of knowing entails the accessibility of the object which exists independently of the mind such that it is able to initiate and correct knowledge. It would follow that no matter how "theory-laden" (Royce and Powell, 1983) a particular truth-claim may be, there exists an independent standard by which the claim may be validated. Objectivism does not deny that observation statements or other types of truth claims will be affected by theory, perhaps completely erroneous theory, but it recognizes, where relativism does not, that theory can eventually be corrected by comparison to the object itself which stands independently of thought.

From the historical example of the fall of psychological recapitulation theory in psychology, two implications were drawn: first, that, contrary to Kuhn's proposition, scientific history *is* cumulative, rather than a series of irrational, gestalt-like shifts in perception and, second, that psychology, the most subjective of the sciences, *is* amenable to the practice of objectivism. Finally, it should be clear that objectivism does not propose that simplistic view that direct access to the object means absolute knowledge on "first sight." This follows from objectivism's emphasis upon the active nature of knowing. Knowledge about the object is never fully complete, from which it does *not* follow that knowledge of the object must be erroneous; what follows is an increasingly greater and more correct understanding of the object with every increase in interaction with the object. If it is not accepted that knowledge which reflects the actual nature of the object can be gained through this interaction, then the relativists are right and we should all "heed the 'principle of anything goes'" (Brandt, 1982, p. 257).

As a last word on the subject: It is disturbing to find relativism still seriously being argued as being on the side of liberal tolerance, happy eclecticism and a new dawn for the sciences, whereas, objectivism is thought to support an intolerant, close-minded, *status quo* view of the world. It is precisely the converse; for by denying the possibility of direct access to the object, the relativist allows one to only point to beliefs and if one belief is as equally true as another, then why not impose one world-view over the many others. George Orwell warned of the implications of relativism through the character O'Brien, who played the cunning ideologist in *1984*. In the following excerpt from the book, O'Brien is depicted "re-educating," to borrow from Kuhn's language, the dissident Winston Smith, on the matter of objectivity:

The second thing for you to realize is that power is power over human beings. Over the body—but, above all, over the mind. Power over matter—external reality, as you would call it—is not important. Already our control over matter is absolute. . . . We control matter because we control the mind. Reality is inside the skull. You will learn by degrees, Winston. There is nothing that we could not do.

Invisibility, levitation—anything. I could float off this floor like a soap bubble if I wish to. I do not wish to, because the Party does not wish it. You must get rid of those nineteenth-century ideas about the laws of Nature. We make the laws of Nature (1983, p. 897).

REFERENCES

Agnew, N. Mck., & Pyke S. W. (1969). *The science game: An introduction to research in the behavioral sciences.* Englewood Cliffs, NJ: Prentice-Hall.

Brandt, L. W. (1982). *Psychologists caught: A psycho-logic of psychology.* Toronto: University of Toronto Press.

Cunningham, F. *Relativism.* Unpublished manuscript.

Cunningham, F. (1973). *Objectivity in social sciences.* Toronto: University of Toronto Press.

Davidson, D. (1982). On the very idea of a conceptual scheme. In M. Krauz & J. W. Meiland (Ed.), *Relativism, cognitive and moral.* Notre Dame, IN: Notre Dame University Press.

Engels, F. (1976). *Anti-Duhring.* Peking: Foreign Languages Press. (Originally published in 1894).

Feyerabend, P. K. (1975). *Against method.* London: New Left Books.

Foster, J. (1984). *The history of recapitulation theory in psychology.* Unpublished master's thesis, University of Victoria, Victoria, B.C.

Freedman, J. (1979). East African peasants and capitalist development: The Kiga of Northern Ruanda. In D. H. Turner & G. A. Smith (Ed.), *Challenging anthropology* (pp. 245–260). Toronto: McGraw-Hill.

Freud, S. (1918). *Totem and taboo: Resemblances between the psychic lives of savages and neurotics* (A. A. Brill, Trans.). New York: Vintage Books.

Gergen, K. J. (1978). Toward generative theory. *Journal of Personality and Social Psychology, 36,* 1344–1360.

Gould, S. J. (1977). *Ontogeny and phylogeny.* Cambridge, MA: Belknap/Harvard University Press.

Hacking, I. (1982). Language, truth and reason. In M. Hollis & S. Lukes (Eds.), *Rationality and relativism* (pp. 48–66). Cambridge, MA: MIT Press.

Hall, G. S. (1904). *Adolescence.* Englewood Cliffs, NJ: Prentice Hall.

Hume, D. (1975). *Enquiries concerning human understanding and concerning the principles of morals* (3rd ed.). Oxford: Oxford University Press. (Original work published in 1777).

Jung, C. G. (1959). *The basic writings of C. G. Jung* (V. S. de Laszlo, Ed. and Trans.). New York: Random House.

Kant, I. (1929). *Critique of pure reason.* (N. K. Smith, Trans.). New York: St. Martin's Press. (Original work published in 1781).

Kuhn, T. S. (1970). *The structure of scientific revolutions* (2nd ed.). Chicago: University of Chicago Press.

Leontiev, A. N. (1981). *Problems of the development of the mind.* Moscow: Progress Publishers.

Marx, K. & Engels, F. (1963). *Reader in Marxist philosophy.* New York: International Publishers.

Mayr, E. (1982). *The growth of biological thought: Diversity, evolution and inheritance.* Cambridge, MA: Belknap/Harvard University Press.

Murdock, G. P. (1945). The common denominator of cultures. In R. Linton (Ed.), *The science of man in the world crises.* New York: Columbia University.

Neitzsche, F. (1973). *Beyond good and evil* (R. J., Hollingdale, Trans.). Harmondsworth, Eng.: Penguin Books. (Originally published in 1886).

Newton-Smith, W. (1982). Relativism and the possibility of interpretation. In M. Hollins & S. Lukes (Eds.), *Rationality and relativism* (pp. 106–122). Cambridge, MA: MIT Press.

Orwell, G. (1976). 1984. In *George Orwell* (compendium). London: Secker & Warburg/Octopus Books.

Ross, D. (1972). *G. Stanley Hall: The psychologist as prophet.* Chicago: University of Chicago Press.

Royce, J. R., & Powell, A. (1983). *Theory of personality and individual differences.* Englewood Cliffs, NJ: Prentice-Hall.

Ruben, David-Hillel (1979). *Marxism and materialism: A study in Marxist theory of knowledge* (2nd ed.). Sussex: Harvester.

Sagan, C. (1980). *Cosmos.* New York: Random House.

Schopenhauer, A. (1969). The will as thing-in-itself. In P. Gardiner (Ed.), *Nineteenth-Century Philosophy.* New York: Free Press. (Originally published in 1844).

Vygotsky, V. S. (1978). *Mind in society: The development of higher psychological processes* (M. Cole, V. John-Steiner, S. Scribner, & E. Souberman, Eds. and Trans.). Cambridge, MA: Harvard University Press.

Part Two

Studies in Metatheory

Chapter 5

The Language
of Psychological
Understanding

Kenneth J. Gergen

INTRODUCTION

Throughout the social sciences and humanities there has been a steadily grow-ing awareness that the empiricist promise for cumulative behavioral science is largely empty. The empiricist foundations on which psychological study have long rested have been all but abandoned by philosophers of science. No longer are there compelling rationale for assumptions of verification, falsification, and the accumulation of knowledge through empirical research. Social thinkers have also convincingly demonstrated that the traditional scientific claim to value free description is wholly misleading. Further analysis reveals that the tradi-tional attempt to buttress knowledge claims by an appeal to observable behavior is largely unwarranted; propositions about human action rely not on observation but interpretation of underlying dispositions (see Gergen, Chap. 1; Shames, Chap. 2 in this volume). Yet, while recent analysis throws most traditional pursuits into critical relief, the question of alternatives looms ominously on the horizon. How are we now to envision the nature of psychological knowledge, its acquisition and its utility? If the ship is abandoned, is there to be a new fleet—and if so, how is it to be designed?

CRITIQUE AND THE GROUNDS FOR METATHEORY

In my view the metapsychological inquiry that has sprung to life over the past decade possess three moments of special productivity. The first is in the generation of professional self-reflexivity—an acute self-consciousness of what we are doing and why. As assessment and criticism of the traditional investments have been advanced, and fresh questions have been asked about the potentials and functions of psychological study, an enhanced awareness of the past century's accomplishments (and failings) has begun to emerge. No longer is there an unquestioning acceptance of presentist history with its self-congratulatory celebration of accumulated accomplishments. Second, this critical dialogue has begun to generate a structure of metatheoretical discourse of far greater weight and sophistication than anything previously extant within the field. Traditional attempts to evaluate theoretical constructions in psychology typically employed criteria that were either misleading (as in the criterion of empirical validity) or banal (as in the criterion of parsimony). In contrast, from the controversies of the past decade have emerged new and challenging forms of metatheoretical discourse. Theories may now be properly examined in terms of their placement within the historical context, their ideological underpinnings, the forms of society which they foster or sustain, the root metaphors on which they draw, the literary tropes that inform their construction, epistemological assumptions to which they are implicitly committed, and so on. In effect, the discipline's means for sustaining self-conscious direction have been vitally enriched.

It is metapsychology's third special moment of productivity that most concerns me in the present paper. Like Simple Simon, the profession continuously asks of the critical movement, "Let me taste your wares." There is strong inhibition against relinquishing the old, (even fully apprised of the costs), without the availability of new and effective modes of inquiry. It is my contention that the seeds for such alternatives have already been planted. Specifically, they are contained within the largely unexplicated assumptions underlying the forms of critical assessment that have thus far been advanced. Although such assessment appears to be "about traditional psychology" indirectly it also illuminates its own forestructure of understanding. As we proceed to explicate this forestructure, we shall increasingly find that it presages an array of positive programs of inquiry.

These new programs of inquiry are already beginning to emerge, and indeed, are represented in many of the papers for this volume. To illustrate, Harre and Secord's (1972) attacks on the traditional empirical model were based, in part, on a humanist (voluntarist) conception of human functioning. Such assumptions have since been played out in variety of ethogenic-dramaturgic inquiries. The criticisms of normal science ideology, so well honed within the Frank-furt school, have fueled many of the contemporary attacks on empirical psychology. At the same time, as the assumptions underlying these attacks have become more fully framed, they have given rise to a school of critical psychol-ogy (cf. Wexler, 1982). This latter school has come to see itself as an essential implement in the process of social transformation. Similarly, active criticism has been waged against traditional psychology for its arrogant insensitivity to the historical dependency of its theories and findings. When the assumptions underlying this line of critique are more fully unpacked, they form the basis for developing an historical or diachronic psychology (see Gergen & Gergen, 1984). Finally, criticism of traditional psychology has demonstrated the extent to which its generalizations are dependent not upon empirical observation but interpretive or hermeneutic processes. When the hidden presumptions are eluci-dated, this line of attack provides the basis for the social constructionist move-ment in psychology (Gergen, 1985). Similar cases could be made for the emer-gence of dialectic theorizing (Georgoudi, 1984), and new forms of historical writing in social psychology (Morawski, 1982).

Although most of these enterprises are in their fledgling state, not yet elaborated sufficiently to furnish clear and compelling models, it is not to fur-ther elaboration that I wish to devote the remainder of my present offering. Rather, it is my intent to develop the grounds for an additional form of inquiry, one I find particularly intriguing in implication and promise. This inquiry is into the forms, origins and functions of psychological discourse. We possess an immense vocabulary for speaking of mental life. We can discourse at length about the state of our emotions, ambitions, values, memories, plans, hopes, motives, intentions and the like. Yet, how are we to understand the emergence of this vocabulary and the conventions in which it is embedded? What are its functions in the culture, its potentials for growth and change, and its particular forms in other historical or cultural climes?

FROM HISTORICAL CONTINGENCY
TO THEORETICAL AUTONOMY

Before touching on these issues at greater length, it is important to explore the grounding rationale for such study. For this exploration nicely illustrates the preceding contention that when the grounds of critique are illuminated they form the basis for alternative forms of inquiry. To turn the clock back, one of the most challenging rebuttals to my earlier argument for social psychology as history (Gergen, 1973) was that many theories did seem to weather the ravages of time. Aristotle's views on social influence, or La Rochefoucauld's maxims, for example, are echoed in contemporary psychological formulations. Problems in aggression, power and social attraction seem universal. As it happens, this line of rebuttal proves problematic on a variety of counts (Gergen, 1982). However, it is intriguing nevertheless that theories of human behavior can persist for seemingly indefinite periods without serious empirical challenge. How are we to account for this special elasticity?

Upon examining this issue more carefully, it becomes increasingly clear that the language for describing or accounting for human activity does not itself refer to observable actions. Rather, in most instances it refers to the intention, disposition, or motivation believed to underlie the activity. Consider the descriptive term, aggression, for example. After much debate about the definition of this term it has generally come to designate those instances in which an individual *intends* to bring harm to another. Thus, virtually any observable movement of the body could count as aggression; by the same token, the identical posture, hand movement, or vocal utterance could also be viewed as altruism, domination, submissiveness, loving, or nurturing, depending on the motives attributed to the actor. In effect, the entire literature on aggression thus depends not on the accumulated observations from experiments, field studies, longitudinal research and the like. Rather, theories of aggression are sustained by the manner in which investigators attribute motives to the subjects in such research. It is in this way that most theories of psychology can be maintained over long periods of time without real risk of falsification. The theories do not rest on evidential grounds but on suppositions about the minds of human actors. In other terms, we find the language for speaking of human activity is not grounded in or derived from the spatio-temporal coordinates of human activity. Thus, semantically speaking, the language of human action is virtually freefloating.

Yet, there is one further link in the argument that must be made to secure a major place for the study of psychological discourse. The central question is whether there is any empirical means of grounding discourse about the realm of psychological dispositions to which the language of human activity putatively refers? If descriptive terms cannot be linked directly to observations of human conduct, can they be linked to underlying psychological states? (In another sense this is to ask whether we can empirically assess states of mind, including intentions, motives, needs, cognitions, morally principled thinking, psychological defenses, emotions, and so on.) Although this question deserves far more attention than we can afford at this juncture, the arguments thus far developed strongly suggest a negative answer. Attempts to assess psychological states principally depend on publicly observed acts of the person (as in answers to test items, the pressing of buttons, language use, recognition of nonsense syllables, and the like). Yet, the definition of each of these actions must also be made in psychological terms. For example, the investigator is not concerned with the physical character of the check-mark in a response to a personality test item. Rather, the check-mark is only interesting and meaningful once it has been interpreted or defined psychologically. The check-mark is thus defined as an indicator of need for approval, perception of external control, self-esteem, and the like. In effect, any measure of a psychological state suffers the same problem confronted in measuring human behavior. In both cases the definition of the behavior or measure is itself stated in psychological terms. In testing whether an action was motivated by aggression as opposed to some other disposition requires selecting another action which must itself be defined psychologically. Each activity used for the inferential triangulation of a mental condition, must itself be indexed by terms not referring to the activity itself but to suppositions about underlying psychological dispositions. Thus, every attempt to assess a psychological condition would itself rely upon an empirically unwarranted commitment to the existence of yet another (and perhaps many other) psychological conditions.

To illustrate, if one wishes to determine whether an individual were in a state of depression, it might be reasonable to question him. The verbal report, "I feel depressed" might be viewed as reasonable evidence in favor of a diagnosis of depression. Yet, drawing this seemingly simple inference is no trivial matter. How does one know what is intended by the words? Is the individual, in fact, trying to solicit sympathy, expressing self-pity, attempting to gain control of the situation, showing signs of suppressed anger, trying to avoid responsibility, or is some other more complex motive at stake (e.g., is depression a superficial defense mechanism against some deeper, but undesirable motive)? To explore which, if any, of these motives or dynamics (if any) furnish the proper reading of the verbal proclamation, one turns to other actions—perhaps to facial expressions, rapidity of body movements, posture and the like. Yet, each of these actions is again opaque; each can be read in a multiplicity of ways (perhaps the same ways as the verbal expression). Indeed, attempts to read subsequent actions may only enrich the possible vocabulary for understanding the original proclamation (e.g., the faint smile suggests that the statement of depression might have been a form of self-criticism or derision). The attempt to "triangulate" the correct psychological underpinning or meaning can thus lead not to a narrowing but to an expansion of potentials.

Again, there are additional steps in the argument that deserve more extended treatment (see Gergen, 1982). However, the present should be sufficient to establish the necessary context for what follows. Essentially we now find ourselves at the present juncture: We possess an immense and highly variegated language concerning mental events, processes, structures, and the like, and such discourse seems to have little in the way of empirical anchor. Accounts of human psychology may thus proceed in relative autonomy from the world envisioned by these accounts. Drawing from a traditional (though not unchallenged) philosophical distinction, this is to say that language about the mind appears to be more analytic than synthetic in character. That is, the warrant for its usage appears to depend on the conventions governing its use within the linguistic domain rather than on its relationship to an independent world. Language about the mind thus bears strong kinship to mathematics, where the use of any symbol depends on the rules governing its use within the system. Although talk about an independent reality (about cats, rats, and mats) is also dependent on linguistic rules, that talk can be favored or inhibited by what is commonly observed to be the state of things. In effect, whether I am depressed or not depends primarily on what else is said about me, "I had lost hope," "I felt there was no future," "I felt helpless," etc.—all statements referring to my state of mind. In contrast, the verity of my reports of the weather may be vitally dependent on my looking from the window. By common standards of language usage, my announcement that it is a sunny day could be discredited by a pelting rain.

TOWARD THE STUDY OF PSYCHOLOGICAL DISCOURSE

Given this state of affairs we find ourselves positioned to examine the structure and functions of psychological discourse without concern for its ontological warrants. We may inquire into the structure of this discourse, how it is organized, its constraints—both inherent and conventional, its guiding metaphors, its limits and potentials. We may consider ways in which such discourse is fashioned by, embedded in, and serves to influence the culture of which it is a part. We may consider the functions of such discourse within human relations, what it enables us to do, what it inhibits, how it serves human ends and how it obfuscates. And we are invited to consider contemporary discourse in light of other historical eras and other cultural settings.

Such explorations as these would seem of no small consequence. Psychological discourse is, for one, a critical feature of social life. What people say about their intentions, feelings, motives, memories and so on may be of vital (even lethal) consequence. To attribute malevolent intentions to the Russian government is to have different—and possibly disastrous—consequences for international policy than is the attribution of ambivalence or fear. Further, such discourse seems woven intricately into the social fabric, so that creating self-consciousness about its nature and functions may have an emancipating effect on the culture. For example, contemporary discourse about the psychological underpinnings of homosexuality, performance on aptitude tests, gender, and political decision making render support for certain problematic institutions. To throw such discourse into critical relief is to threaten the warrant for such institutions. The belief that homosexuality is a form of mental inbalance is to promote discriminatory practices; to suppose that IQ tests measure inherited mental abilities lends itself to creating prejudicial hierarchies, and so on. Finally, inquiry into such discourse begins to demonstrate the limits and potentials of what we take to be knowledge of human beings. As commonly considered, such knowledge is largely recorded and sustained through linguistic means. Knowledge is thus largely that which can be expressed in the written and spoken word. Yet, if the rendering of psychological accounts is constrained or fashioned by the structure of linguistic practice, then little can be known that is not already determined by the existing conventions. To elucidate the conventions is thus to foreshadow virtually all that "can be known." In this sense the study of theoretical language should occupy a critical position in a field of metapsychological inquiry.

This charting of possibilities is not simply to offer a set of promisory notes. In fact, significant headway has been made in many of the above domains. Ground breaking attempts to elucidate the structure and potentials of psychological discourse have long been carried out by philosophers within the ordinary language and analytic domains. Wittgenstein's later writings are seminal in this regard, as are the subsequent work of Ryle, Austin, Anscombe, Peters, and others. More recently psychologists have turned their attentions to such problems. The work of Smedslund (1978) and those in the area of descriptive psychology (Ossorio, Davis, and others) are notable in this respect. In these cases the attempt has been to locate basic suppositions that underlie cultural (and scientific) knowledge about the mind. Investigators such as Shweder (Shweder & D'Andrade, 1980) and Semin & Chassein (in press) have begun analysis on the extent to which scientific conceptions of mind represent by-products of the implicit personality theories of the culture. Still others, influenced by movements in literary theory and historiography, have centered on the various metaphors, literary figures, or tropes guiding contemporary understanding of the mind (cf. Ortony, 1979). Anthropologists have come to share these concerns in their development of ethnopsychology, where the special concern is with cross-cultural similarities and differences in concepts of mental functioning (cf. Heelas & Locke, 1981; Shweder & Miller, 1985). And finally, historically oriented investigators have focused on such concepts as they have developed and changed over the course of history.

During the past several years much of my own attention has been given to the study of psychological language. In particular I have been concerned with the structure, origins, functions, and potential malleability of such discourse. At the outset the attempt was to explore various forms of psychological explanation—to take systematic account of the means by which people (including professional psychologists) explain human actions (Gergen & Gergen, 1982), and to ask about the pragmatic and ideological implications of competing explanatory forms. This interest was later expanded to include the study of narrative explanations—both of self and others (Gergen & Gergen, 1983). In this case the concern was with the kinds of stories that can be used to inject coherence into isolated events across time. Additional work has centered on the constraints placed over the existing ontology of mind by the pragmatic aspects of human interchange; here the attempt has been to show that major features of existing theories of mind are necessary byproducts of using a verbal language (Gergen, 1985). Finally, attention has been given to both the structure and flexibility of existing ethnopsychologies. In the case of structure, the attempt has been to demonstrate how most of what we take to be the knowledge about the mind is revealed by unpacking the existing language conventions (Gergen,

1984). In the case of process we have tried to show how mental testing approximates a blank slate upon which the agency of science may inscribe its wishes (Gergen, Hepburn, & Comer, 1986).

THE PRINCIPLE OF FUNCTIONAL CIRCULARITY

It would be appropriate in the present context to review work within one or more of these domains; in this way some substantive meat could be placed on the seemingly bare bones of language analysis. However, rather than recapitulating the earlier work, I would like to render the necessary illustration by breaking new conceptual ground. Specifically I would like to put forward a single proposition, one of some implication both for the study of psychological discourse and for the field of psychology. Then I would like to carry out the conceptual work necessary to give the proposition a cutting edge. My proposal, which I shall call the principle of *functional circularity,* can be stated in both a general and a restricted form. The general form is also the stronger of the two: *All reasonable propositions declaring a functional linkage between mental terms and observable events are analytically true;* that is their truth is derived from the structure of the language as opposed to their relationship to observables. Propositions of this sort might include such statements as "Whenever the volume on my stereo is high my neighbors become irritated," "When people are angry they are likely to become aggressive," or "Whenever Lorna enters the room I am overcome with emotion." The more specific rendering of the functional circularity proposal has specific application to psychological study: *All reasonable propositions declaring a functional relationship between the stimulus world and the psychological domain, or between the latter domain and subsequent action, are true by definition.* Should such a proposition prove viable we would find that theories and research in psychology which purport to describe processes of perception, language learning, information processing, emotional expression, the relation between attitudes and behavior, the relation between thought and action, and so on are essentially products or extensions of existing language conventions. When these conventions are examined in detail, we would discover that such statements are necessary derivatives of the definitional structure. In effect, propositions within the S–O–R framework may not be fundamentally empirical, but by-products of a linguistic forestructure.

I can understand why the proposal for functional circularity may not be greeted with lusty enthusiasm. Many readers may feel a certain trepidation at this point. The remainder of this chapter will be insufficient to win approval. However, there are three strokes that can be more ably made, and if these prove palatable, then one might agree that the general formulation merits more serious consideration.

The first of these supporting proposals is that *the definitional system for psychological terms is essentially self-contained.* As we established earlier, there is no obvious way by which the definition of a psychological term can be established ostensibly, that is, by a process of pointing to a set of observable particulars. With this manner of definition abandoned, we have the remaining possibility of defining mental predicates in terms of other mental predicates. As suggested earlier, mental terms are much like mathematical integers; their meaning is principally derived from the way in which they figure within a set of conventional rules governing the system in which they are a part. If each mental term is defined by yet other mental terms, we are confronted by a full definitional circularity with respect to such terms. For example, if we examine the definition of a mental term such as "purpose," we find (using a standard *Random House Dictionary*) that it is chiefly defined as a "reason." A reason, in turn is defined as a "mental power" or "power of mind;" and, mind in turn is defined as an agency that, among other things, has the power to reason. The system of definition is essentially closed. In other instances this circularity is more extended. For example, an "attitude" is traditionally defined as a "manner of feeling," which in turn is defined as an "affective state of consciousness." The latter in turn, is distinguished by its *not* being a "cognitive state." Cognitive states of mind are essentially those in which reason plays a major role. A reason is in turn a mental power or power of mind, and mind is defined as an agency that, among other things, experiences affective states. It should also be noted that although dictionary definitions of ostensively defined entities are also linguistic, they are not, as in the case of psychological terms, circular. A "bird," for example, is defined as a "warm blooded vertebrate covered with feathers and forelimbs modified into wings." However "wings" are defined in turn as "anterior extremities or appendages of the scapular arch." If one then searches for the meaning of such terms as "extremities," "appendages," or "scapular arch" one never returns to the word "bird."

In this light let us consider now the problem of specifying functional relationships among mental entities. It is often said that our thoughts are biased by our emotions or values, that our reason informs our intention, that our moral beliefs inhibit our instinctive drives for pleasure, and so on. Why are such functional relationships perfectly plausible? As we have seen, they are not grounded in observation. So how are we to account for this compelling validity? And too, other causal relationships among mental entities can be specified which seem less plausible or compelling. Linguistic convention permits one to say that the death instinct influences our moral beliefs, our intentions influence our dreams, or hopes inhibit happiness. Yet, such propositions either fail to "ring true" or generate resistance. If there is no objective reason to suppose such propositions are invalid how are we to account for their impotence?

It is my proposal that the degree of apparent validity attached to propositions connecting one mental state to another is dependent on the extent of their definitional circularity (up to the point of simple redundancy). That is, the more closely the causal agent is defined by that entity upon which it acts, the more plausible will be the functional proposition. To be more precise, as term A increasingly shares definitional space with term B, it becomes increasingly plausible to say that A causes B (or vice versa). To the extent that A is defined by the absence of B, it becomes increasingly plausible to say that A inhibits or has a negative effect on B. To illustrate, in the former case it is above suspicion to say that concentration will generally improve one's ability to think logically. Concentration is by definition a constituent part of thought. Thinking is a concentrated effort. By the same token, it is perfectly plausible to say that mental distraction (or failure to concentrate) will decrease one's ability to think logically. The absence of concentration is, by definition, the absence of thought.

For purposes of clarity let us consider a contrasting case. We commonly say: "It is difficult for me to think when I am so emotional." However, emotion is by definition the absence of cognition (or thought); the redundancy of the statement contributes to its plausibility. This common belief is also reflected in the psychological literature in the hypothesis that high states of arousal interfere with problem solving. Yet if problem solving is defined as the exercise of reasoning powers, reason is the absence of emotion, and emotion is a state of arousal, then it is true by definitional extension that high arousal and problem solving are mutually exclusive. By conventional standards it would border on cultural nonsense to assert the contrary of such propositions (e.g., I am most logical when I am very emotional, excited, or aroused). More complex propositions could and should be considered. However, given the basic self-containment of psychological terminology, thorough examination should reveal that they are fundamentally circular.

We may now turn to the second supporting proposal, one that is perhaps more succinctly stated than the first. However, its efficiency should not be mistaken for triviality. Indeed, the implications of this second proposal are broadly substantial, and it is only a single implication that we shall examine within the present context. The proposal in this case is that *propositions about the external world may generally be converted or reduced to statements about mental conditions*. The wisdom behind this proposition is amply demonstrated in our common folk wisdom. As we say, "beauty is in the eye of the beholder," or "you *think* I am . . . angry . . . or in love, etc., but it's all in your head." Although a good deal of psychological theory has been based on such reduction, the ultimate implications of doing so have yet to be examined. For example, it has become commonplace at this juncture, to say that behavior is a joint function of situation and personality (Magnusson & Endler, 1977). Yet, for those who take this stance, the "situation" is essentially "that which the individual perceives." The "real" situation is thus reduced to perception. At this point one begins to develop an uneasy sense of incoherence, for perceptions of situations are meat and potatoes for a personality psychologist. Thus the concept of a situation, independent of an observer, can (and one might argue, should) be abandoned. As a result interactionism is an unwarranted conclusion; all could be reduced to personality study.

Similar problems emerge in Bandura's (1977) attempt to integrate behaviorist and cognitive approaches to the acquisition of aggressive tendencies. Bandura first endorses the behaviorist tradition; he argues:

> The influential role of antecedent events in regulating aggressive behavior is most clearly revealed in experiments that arrange the necessary learning conditions. When aggression is rewarded in certain contexts . . . the level of aggressive responding can be altered simply by changing the contextual events that signal probable outcomes (p. 63).

This account primarily employs the language of the stimulus world; it reifies environmental events and little reference is made to a psychological world. Yet, later in his analysis Bandura shifts the focus and adopts the language of internal representation. He argues:

> People do not respond to each momentary item of feedback as an isolated experience. Rather, they proceed and synthesize feedback information from sequences of events over long periods of time regarding the conditions necessary for reinforcement, and the pattern and rate with which actions produce the outcomes. It is for this reason that vast amounts of behavior can be maintained with only infrequent immediate reinforcement. Because outcomes affect behavior through integrative thought, knowledge about schedules of reinforcement can exert greater influence upon behavior than does the reinforcement itself (p. 97).

Here the external world becomes transformed into a psychological world and this latter domain has the capacity to construct its own ontology. The language of external events has been transformed into a language of internal events. If the implications are pressed, Bandura could abandon the former language in favor of the latter. There is nothing in the former that cannot be translated into the latter.

At this point one may wish to offer rebuttal: Earlier the distinction was made between analytic and synthetic definitions—the former dependent on linguistic structure and the later on the extension to a range of observables. Yet, it has now been proposed that the language of observables can be reduced to psychological language. Does this not challenge the distinction between the synthetic and the analytic, and if so, are we to conclude that all propositions describing a functional relationship among events are true by definition? Such conclusions possess only an apparent validity. It has been proposed that "real world descriptors" *can be* reduced to psychological equivalents, not that they must be. They may retain their synthetic character so long as the definition remains ostensive, that is, unconverted to linguistic description. If the definitional process is itself described, the resulting definition lapses into an analytic circularity. Thus, to say that the moon is the earth's natural satellite orbiting the earth at a distance of 238,857 miles is itself uninformative until these definitional terms are linked to actions or ostensive "objects" outside the definitional system itself. One must understand what "orbit" and "miles" are outside the confines of the language. The difference here is between the information contained in the proposition "Let A equal 7" and "Let A equal that to which I am pointing." It is the latter that enables one to use language for pragmatic purposes outside of language use itself.

The third proposal need detain us only briefly, as the groundwork has already been laid. To recapitulate an earlier argument, *most reasonable propositions about human conduct may be converted or reduced to statements about mental conditions.* As will be recalled, there are manifest difficulties attendant upon using language to index the ongoing actions of persons. While that language gives the appearance of referring to observable behavior, in fact, it refers to the intentions, motives or dispositions underlying the action. The term aggression refers to the intent to agress, altruism to the intent to help, conformity to the motive to conform and so on. In effect one cannot behave in any of these ways without intending to do so and any configuration of the body may count as an instance of the action if the person is intending, trying or motivated to reach such ends. Rather than retracing the earlier steps once again, let us move over the threshold upon which we are now poised.

If all propositions about reality can be reduced to propositions about mental states, and propositions about human action are also used to index mental states, then it follows that all S–O–R propositions are essentially propositions about mental states. Yet, following our initial argument, mental state language is essentially a closed system of definition; all states are defined in terms of each other. As we have also seen, propositions about relations among mental states generally rely on a definitional unpacking; the more common the definitional space the greater the plausibility of a causal link. It follows ineluctably that S–O–R propositions are true by virtue of linguistic convention. Further, and more generally, all reasonable propositions relating mental predicates to observable events should be equally circular.

Illustrations may be useful at this juncture. Let us consider first the case of relating psychological concepts to overt behavior. For example, traditional research on the relationship between attitudes and behavior maintains that there is a strong functional relationship between one's attitudes and one's behavior toward a given object, person or issue (cf. Ajzen & Fishbein, 1980). Yet, one becomes suspicious of underlying problems when it becomes apparent that the only means of assessing attitudes is through behavior. Thus, the proposition can be read out as a description about relationships among forms of conduct. People's statements about their behavior are, on this account, related to their behavior. Yet, we have also seen that our language for behavior (including people's statements) is an intentional one; that is, it indexes motivational states.

One is not interested in the overt sounds of a person's statements, but their underlying intent. It is not people's bodily movements that are important in their joining a protest or using prophylactics, but their intentions in doing so. As a result, we find that what appears to be a proposition about the functional relationship between behaviors is a proposition about the relationship among mental entities. Thus, for example, when a measure of attitudes toward nuclear arms is correlated with voting for or against Reagan, one has a verbal indicator of affect (or attitude) toward nuclear arms (the attitude measure), and a behavioral indicator (voting) of affect toward the same issue. In effect, one is essentially trying to establish that positive sentiments toward X are related to positive sentiments toward X. The relationship is fully circular.

One might wish to rebut this argument by pointing to imperfect correlations at the empirical level. Do not such irregularities suggest that the research is not circular? Such a rebuttal is of little consequence. Any deviation must be explained, and from the present perspective such explanation will again fall back on circular reasoning. One would in this case have to specify another psychological basis or meaning for a Reagan vote, (e.g., improved economy, national pride). With such specification one commits oneself to a new proposition, for example positive sentiments toward nuclear arms are related to positive sentiments toward a strong economy, and a supporting explanation such as "nuclear arms programs bolster the economy." Yet, as we see, this new explanation once again reinstates functional circularity. One is essentially arguing once again that positive attitudes toward the economy are related to positive attitudes toward the economy. In effect, the sense we make of "if-then" propositions seems to depend on their inherent circularity.

We confront much the same situation in the case of propositions about the effects of stimuli on psychological states. To propose, for example, that physical beauty engenders attraction is to say little more than attractive persons are attractive. In the same way, the proposition that similarity breeds attraction becomes circular as soon as an explanation is given for the functional linkage. If one argues that similarity breeds attraction because similar people boost one's esteem, and enhanced self-esteem is considered an attractive or desirable state of mind, then the proposition again reverts to the redundant form: attractiveness is attractive. There is little reason to suppose that the full range of functional propositions from the domain of psychophysics, cognition and learning are not subject to the same problem. The notorious circularity of the law of effect furnishes good reason to suspect that it is so. The present conceptual analysis furnishes the rationale for why it must be so.

Can the chain of functional circularity be broken through physiological reductionism? For many the prospects of reducing or translating psychological terms into material terms has been an attractive one, and the dissolution of the present conundrum would only add impetus to such a venture. Yet, by extending the implications of the present analysis we find this option proscribed. In particular, we find that the vocabulary of the mental world is without empirical anchor. If so, there is no means of developing reductionist linkages. There are no entities to be reduced. Consider the search for a physiological basis for depression. In order to determine the physiological correlates one must isolate the existence of depression independent of physiology itself. (If one is limited only to a language of physiology there is simply nothing to reduce.) Yet, locating depression independent of physiology confronts us with the same interpretive problem with which our analysis began. One's declaration, "I am depressed" must be interpreted—whether it truly reflects depression or not is opaque. There is virtually no motive state, including joy, that cannot serve as the instigator for proclaiming one's depression. Each further indicator is subject to the same relativity of interpretation. In effect, depression is not a state of mind, but an historically situated construction.

CONCLUSION

If the functional circularity argument can be sustained, a radical reorientation toward research and theory in psychology is invited. Empirical research would be thrown into serious question both as a means of building knowledge and of warranting theoretical conclusions. Rather, attention would properly shift to the structure of psychological language—what is permitted and what denied in the way of propositions. A different order of theoretical question would also emerge. For example, if propositions of the kind described here are both pervasive in social life and circular, what is their function within social interchange? If they do not inform us of the world, what role do they serve in personal affairs? And, how is it possible to alter the structure of psychological understanding? If the system is self-referring, self-contained, and circular, how can new understandings ever emerge? It is to just such questions that I would hope a mature discipline of metapsychology would address itself.

REFERENCES

Ajzen, I. & Fishbein, M. (1980). *Understanding attitudes and predicting social behavior.* Englewood Cliffs, NJ: Prentice-Hall.
Bandura, A. (1977). *Social learning theory.* Englewood Cliffs, NJ: Prentice-Hall.
Georgoudi, M. (1984). Modern dialectics in social psychology. In K. J. Gergen & M. M. Gergen (Eds), *Historical social psychology.* Hillsdale, NJ: Lawrence Erlbaum.
Gergen, K. J. (1982). *Toward transformation in social knowledge.* New York: Springer-Verlag.
Gergen, K. J. (1973). Social psychology as history. *Journal of Personality and Social Psychology, 26,* 309–320.
Gergen, K. J. (1984). Aggression as discourse. In A. Mummendey (Ed.), *Aggression: From individual behavior to social interaction.* Berlin: Springer-Verlag.
Gergen, K. J. (1985). Social pragmatics and the origins of psychological discourse. In

K. J. Gergen & K. E. Davis (Eds.), *The social construction of the person*. New York: Springer-Verlag.

Gergen, K. J. & Gergen, M. M. (1982). Form and function in the explanation of human conduct. In P. Secord (Ed.), *Explaining human behavior*. Beverly Hills: Sage.

Gergen, K. J. & Gergen, M. M. (1983). Narratives of the self. In K. Scheibe & T. Sarbin (Eds.), *Studies in social identity*. New York: Praeger.

Gergen, K. J. & Gergen, M. M. (Eds.). (1984). *Historical social psychology*. Hillsdale, NJ: Lawrence Erlbaum.

Gergen, K. J., Hepburn, A. & Comer, D. (1986). The hermeneutics of personality description. *Journal of Personality and Social Psychology*.

Harre, R. & Secord, P. F. (1972). *The explanation of social behavior*. Oxford: Blackwell.

Heelas, P. & Locke, A. (1981). *Indigenous psychologies*. London: Academic Press.

Magnusson, D., & Endler, N. S. (Eds.). (1977). *Personality at the crossroads: Current issues in interactional psychology*. Hillsdale, NJ: Lawrence Erlbaum.

Morawski, J. G. (1982). Assessing psychology's moral heritage through our neglected utopias. *American Psychologist, 37*, 1082–1095.

Semin, G. R. & Chassein, J. (1985). The relationship between higher order models and everyday conceptions of personality. *European Journal of Social Psychology, 15*, 1–16.

Shweder, R. A. & D'Andrade, R. G. (1980). The systematic distortion hypothesis. In R. A. Shweder (Ed.), *Fallible judgment in behavior research*. San Francisco: Jossey Bass.

Shweder, R. A. & Miller, J. (1985). The social construction of the person: How is it possible. In K. J. Gergen & K. E. Davis (Eds.), *The social construction of person*. New York: Springer-Verlag.

Smedslund, J. (1978). Bandura's theory of self-efficacy; a set of common sense theorems. *Scandinavian Journal of Psychology, 19*, 1–14.

Van den Berg, J. H. (1961). *The changing nature of man*. New York: Norton.

Wexler, P. (1982). *Critical social psychology*. Boston: Routledge & Kegan Paul.

Chapter 6

The Psychology of Control: A Textual Critique

Henderikus J. Stam

INTRODUCTION

Metascientific analysis generally does not concern itself with the internal or substantive questions of theories but, rather, with those questions broadly conceived of as metaphysical and socio-historical. Metapsychological questions then can be conceived of as questions that address certain assumptions in psychological writing from a self-consciously "critical" perspective, where critical refers to extradisciplinary (e.g., social, historical, philosophical) and not the original absence of substantive criticism in theory itself.

Being essentially backward looking, metapsychology cannot prescribe new theory but it can make a case for abandoning certain theoretical routes that may

I thank Kenneth Gergen, Lorraine Radtke, Tim Rogers, and Philip Wexler for their critical comments on earlier drafts of this chapter. I am also grateful for the comments of participants in the Theory Seminar of the Center for Advanced Study in Theoretical Psychology at the University of Alberta.

not be useful in theory construction. It can also point the way to strategies for developing new theory that are implicit in its critiques. It could be argued for example that behaviorism was widely adopted over such positions as functionalism and pragmatism because its early practitioners believed in its *promise* as a "scientific" theory with more clearly articulated methods and quantitative analyses. This is a metapsychological reason. It would not be considered such if the final dissolution of either pragmatism or functionalism had come through some critical scientific evidence or telling internal critique. Thus, in their criticism of earlier theories as nonscientific, behaviorists made clear their lasting commitment to a scientific psychology before they knew what forms such a psychology might eventually assume.

This paper is concerned with a metapsychological critique of self-control theories. Psychological work within the tradition of logical positivism has long been concerned with the notion of control (see Morawski, chap. 7, this volume). With the advent of cognitive formulations in recent decades, however, there has also emerged a concern with the "perception" of control and its effect on behavior. From areas in sociology through social psychology to health psychology there is a concerted effort to discover how people experience their autonomy and how their perceptions of autonomy or control are necessary to their daily lives.* As one recent work on the subject declared, "the psychology of control is about the control of oneself and one's perceptions of reality" (Langer, 1983, p. 13).

Here I will examine this literature by viewing it as both a cultural and theoretical production. Reading psychology as a cultural production means treating this literature as one treats other products of culture in order to bring to light some otherwise hidden or unstated assumptions about the character of social reality (Wexler, 1983). Mainstream psychology often serves to reproduce the culture of which it is a part (Sampson, 1983). That is, mainstream psychology, has uncritically accepted advanced industrial civilization as the backdrop against which to study mind, behavior, personality, and social interaction. Because of this, psychology often generates the self-understandings that help sustain the dominant culture. But psychology is a specific kind of cultural product, it is above all theoretical. By reading the psychological literature as a theoretical production, it is possible to describe how the unstated assumptions of social reality are translated into the final product of a psychological literature.

I will attempt a textual critique of the literature on control by focussing on four interpretive practices derived from Philip Wexler's (1983) critique of equity theory. These are (a) desocialization, (b) deproblematization, (c) deinstitutionalization, and (d) dehistoricization. Each of these practices serves to con-

---

*Witness, for example, the recent pronouncement that the construct of perceived control is "central to many discussions in the new field of health psychology" (Peterson, 1982, p. 153. See also Krause & Stryker, 1984; Langer, 1983; Seeman & Seeman, 1983; Taylor, 1983).

struct a particular view of the world that is ideologically loaded in favor of the dominant culture.

There is more at stake here, however, than documenting the ideological nature of psychological discourse. Emphasizing the role of such discourse in a broader social context neglects the nature of its own making, namely, its production by human activity through a series of transformative activities (Wexler, 1982). Simply documenting the cultural reproduction of psychological knowledge can not help us construct emancipatory knowledge or psychological knowledge that changes individual perception and action. Rather it narrowly focuses strategies for social change on demands for systemic change. Therefore, I will finish by discussing a proposal that uses the concept of power relations to rewrite this literature. Specifically, I will argue that self-control is the discourse of the relationship between identity and power as produced within narrow ideological boundaries.

The Need for a Textual Critique

Why should we be concerned with textual critiques as opposed to more broadly conceived cultural critiques? Within the context of "textual criticism" or "textual theory," *text* typically refers to whatever is articulated by language (e.g., Culler, 1982). The concept of text is interdisciplinary in the sense that it is used to treat objects or "realities" as discourse—realities such as social class and institutions. According to Jameson (1981):

> When properly used, the concept of "text" does not . . . "reduce" these realities to small and manageable written documents of one kind or another, but rather liberates us from the empirical object—whether institution, event, or individual work—by displacing our attention to its *constitution* as an object and its *relationship* to other objects thus constituted (p. 297).

Likewise Barthes (1979) argues that the text is a "methodological field" that exists only as discourse. The text "is experienced only in an activity, a production" (p. 75). And Ricouer (1971) argues that objects of analysis in the social sciences display textual features.

It is not possible to detail here the implications for psychology of the adoption of the textual metaphor, save that it situates psychological theorizing as a historical practice that discloses "not a determinate world of social facts, but an indeterminate production of artifacts, itself included" (Pfohl, 1985, p. 231). This does not imply that there exists a unified theoretical body of work that can now be applied, willy-nilly, to psychology. Rather, it places within our grasp tools that are reflexive and deny the claim that theory itself is not a component of the texts of social practices into which it inserts itself.

The practice of textual criticism is more than the elaboration of a text for the reader. Rather, the task of criticism is, following Eagleton, "to show the text as it cannot know itself, to manifest those conditions of its making about which it is necessarily silent" (Eagleton, 1976, p. 43). In other words, we can treat text as a production of ideology. A text usually carries within it certain contradictions or absences which can be termed the "not-said" of the work. Ideology is present in the text precisely in "the form of its eloquent silences" (Eagleton, 1976, p. 89). Thus, when we speak of criticism, we mean the work of explicating the unconsciousness of the text—"that of which it is not, and cannot be, aware" (Eagleton, 1976, p. 89; see also Coward & Ellis, 1977; Mannheim, 1936; Sampson, 1981). This does not mean situating criticism at the same level as the text and completing what it is the text does not say. Rather, the task of criticism is "to install itself in the very incompleteness of the work in order to *theorize* it—to explain the ideological necessity of those 'not-saids' which constitute the very principle of its identity" (p. 89). Thus, if we view psychology as generating the self-understandings that help sustain the dominant culture, then a textual critique can be viewed as a self-conscious undoing of these self-understandings.*

THE PROBLEM OF CONTROL

I will begin by describing some major works that address the problem of control. For the moment, the question of *why* the social sciences might be so concerned with control is left aside to be addressed in the conclusion. Furthermore, this is not a comprehensive review of the literature. Rather, what follows is an appraisal of the major theories and trends found in this research as it is represented in sociological and psychological texts. Sociological conceptions of control appear to be mirror-images of those in psychology. Where psychology treats society as a unitary monolith composed of complex persons, sociology treats persons as passive players in complex social structures. This is especially evident in control theories.

Social Control

In sociology, the concept of social control has had a long and varied history. It became popular at the turn of the century, partly as a solution to the Hobbesian problem of individual and uncontrolled egoism. Sociologists argued that with the advance of capitalism there were no longer any institutions of social control to harness unrestricted individualism. Edward Ross (1901) was the most influential proponent of the notion of social control. He argued that there were two types: internal and external. Internal controls were social ideals that appealed to reason whereas external controls such as punishment appealed directly to the will and passions (see Schwendinger & Schwendinger, 1974, for a historical

---

*There are several critiques within the social sciences that are more or less explicitly "textual" critiques, beginning with Mills' (1943) extensive critique of the sociological literature on social disorganization. (See also Dorfman & Mattelart, 1975; Fitzgerald, 1979; Potter, Stringer & Wetherell, 1984; Sampson, 1977; Stam & Spanos, 1982; Wexler, 1983).

perspective). By the 1920's "social control" had become a central tenet of the new North American sociology. At this time social control referred to, not conformity, but the rational and moral grounds for collective problem solving in society (Janowitz, 1978). By the 1940's however social control had become synonymous with social conformity (e.g., Roucek, 1947) and its use was often restricted to this meaning (see Janowitz, 1978, however for an argument for conceptual continuity).

Although a number of recent sociological papers have addressed the issue of social control (see Gibbs, 1982), I will limit myself to a few brief remarks about a recent work by Morris Janowitz (1978). In *The Last Half-Century* Janowitz argues that the "core element in the idea of social control is that of self-regulation; therefore social control implies effective self-regulation" (p. 50). Janowitz eschews the coercive implications of social control but, instead, argues that social control "refers to the capacity of a social group, including a whole society, to regulate itself. Self-regulation must imply a set of 'higher moral principles' beyond those of self-interest" (p. 3). Thus Janowitz has returned some of the original connotations to his usage of social control. He argues that social control refers to both a mode of analysis and a value orientation.

> Self-regulation is a moral aspiration and is multivalued in orientation. There is in fact a hierarchy of values, one that requires continual clarification. As a moral aspiration, social control assigns the highest importance to the reduction of coercion. But at the same time it assumes that the pursuit of effective social control both depends on and will enhance personal and political freedom. As a strategy of directed societal change, social control emphasizes the centrality of rationality and rational inquiry. (p. 551).

Although rational inquiry is never explicitly defined, it is implicitly equated with social science research.

Janowitz also sees the necessity of coercion in any system of social control, although it is circumscribed by legitimate norms. The greater the social control, the less need for coercion. In other words, for Janowitz, the effectively functioning society is the one which is self-regulating and therefore autonomous. But more important, Janowitz draws little distinction between social and personal control.

> Personal control is the psychological and personality counterpart of social control. Personal control focuses on the capacity of the person to channel his energies and to satisfy his needs while minimizing disruption and damage to himself or others. Personal control implies mastery over one's psychological environment and encompasses psychological conditions that enhance rationality (p. 29).

In other words, personality and society are organized in similar ways and thus ought to be controlled in similar ways; they are mirror images of one another.*

Psychology of Control

Three areas in psychology where notions of control are primary, are the literatures of (a) the locus of control construct (e.g., Rotter, 1966), (b) learned helplessness theory (e.g., Abramson, Seligman, & Teasdale, 1978), and (c) self-efficacy theory (e.g., Bandura, 1982).** As will become apparent, each of these theoretical statements revolves around the core construct of *expectancy.* As such, they are statements about highly individualized cognitive events.

The focus here will primarily be on the applications of these constructs by their authors and not on the substantive elements of these theories. It is in their applications that they are most transparent—we are privy to views of the social sphere that is implicit in the constructs themselves. This social sphere is treated as a monolith. My argument is that this is not accidental but in fact written into these theories by necessity. Only a sterile conception of "society" could support the cognitivist tenets of these propositions.

Defining Control   In psychology there are multiple uses of the terms "control" and "perceived control." To complicate matters, there are terms that are related but at the same time not mutually substitutable (see Arnkoff &

---

*A second area of concern in sociology that is explicitly concerned with control is that of labor. Melvin Kohn (1976) has argued that working at jobs of little substantive complexity causes feelings of powerlessness where powerlessness is defined (from Seeman, 1959, p. 784) as "the expectancy or probability held by the individual that his own behavior cannot determine the occurrence of the outcomes . . . he seeks." The distinct similarity to the construct of "locus of control" (Rotter, 1966) is purposeful, not accidental. In a later paper Kohn and Schooler (1981) bring the construct of self-directedness to bear on the relationship between job conditions and personality. Self-directedness refers to "the beliefs that one has the personal capacity to take responsibility for one's actions and that society is so constituted as to make self-direction possible" (p. 1276). This is a central explanatory concept for several large studies conducted by Kohn and his colleagues where self-direction proves to be pivotal in establishing and maintaining one's place in the job structure.

In a related vein, the notion of alienation has been increasingly subjectified (e.g., Baxter, 1982; Kanungo, 1982). For example, a recent work by Kanungo (1982) defined alienation as a "generalized cognitive (or belief) state of psychological separation from work, insofar as work is perceived to lack the potential for satisfying one's salient needs and expectations" (p. 80). What might those needs be? Kanungo (1982) argues that managers may value autonomy and control in their jobs, as opposed to workers who may value security and a sense of belonging. This leads the two groups to different levels of alienation and job involvement. The entire process is psychologized and individualized.

**A large number of studies have also been conducted in recent years on the control of aversive events (see reviews by Averill, 1973; Miller, 1979; Thompson, 1981). This literature is theoretically disjointed however and is thus more difficult to summarize in a short space. Nevertheless, despite its empirical bent, its overriding themes are very supportive of the conceptions of control discussed in these three literatures. For example, a recent study by Taylor, Lichtman, and Wood (1984) that used breast cancer patients as subjects, concluded that "the ubiquitous appearance of attributions in this population and the strong relation between control and adjustment clearly indicate that social psychological emphasis on attributions and control is well-placed." (p. 500).

Mahoney, 1979; Seligman & Miller, 1979; Singer, 1979). For example, in addition to those outlined below, one can also find discussions of perceived freedom, choice, competence, skill, origin, mindfulness, causal agent, direction, regulation, restraint, personal causation, engagement style, and so on. It is not necessary however to focus on the fine gradations in order to make the statement that they are highly individualized and noncontextual. They all belong to the domain of perceptions, beliefs, or cognitions. For example, locus of control typically refers to beliefs people hold regarding the likelihood that outcomes are under their control; learned helplessness depends on an expectancy which depends on an attribution which depends on the perception of noncontingency; self-efficacy refers to expectations of mastery. Both learned helplessness and self-efficacy theories are concerned with the role of expectancy in performance on tasks that lead to success or failure.

Locus of Control   The locus of control construct has proven to be a popular and enduring one in psychology. Over ten years ago Rotter (1975) had already noted well over 600 studies that concerned themselves with some aspect of internal versus external control and there are no signs of abatement. Reviews of this literature are numerous (e.g., Lefcourt, 1982; Phares, 1976; Strickland, 1977), as are the critiques (e.g., Furby, 1979; Gurin, Gurin, & Morrison, 1978).

Originally, locus of control referred to an expectancy or belief. As Rotter (1966, p. 1) defined it:

> When a reinforcement is perceived by the subject as following some action of his own but not being entirely contingent upon his action, then, in our culture, it is typically perceived as the result of luck, chance, fate, as under the control of powerful others, or as unpredictable because of the great complexity of the forces surrounding him. When the event is interpreted in this way by an individual, we have labeled this a belief in *external control.* If the person perceives that the event is contingent upon his own relatively permanent characteristics, we have termed this a belief in *internal control.*

Because of its widespread use, the construct has come to be used in ways not always intended by Rotter and most critiques have focussed on these conceptual and methodological issues (e.g., Brewin & Shapiro, 1984; Collins, 1974; Lefcourt, 1981, Palenzuela, 1984; Rotter, 1975; Strickland, 1982). Nevertheless, the idea that individuals hold pervasive and stable beliefs that outcomes are or are not under their control is what is generally meant by this construct; hence, the description of people as "internals" or "externals." Investigators using this construct also argue that people classified according to these expectancies behave in ways consistent with these descriptions (e.g., Lefcourt, 1982).* In other words, one's behavior is dependent, at least in part, on one's perception of whether there is a relationship between one's actions and changes in the environment.

In a recent critique of this construct, Lita Furby (1979) argued that much of the locus of control research suffers from an individualistic bias insofar as it promotes the ideal of an internal locus of control. Likewise, Sampson (1983) has cogently argued that the locus of control construct neatly captures the protestant ethic in its affirmation of the internal ideal. One is capable of achievement by being in control of one's destiny and by virtue of hard work. And, in a series of papers, the Gurins (e.g., Gurin, Gurin, & Morrison, 1978) presented evidence for the separation of personal control from an ideology about control where the latter refers to people's beliefs about the role of internal and external forces in the distribution of rewards in society.

My purpose here is not to duplicate these critiques but rather to highlight one implication drawn from this literature by one of its primary spokespersons, Herbert Lefcourt. Lefcourt (1982) began his recent book with the statement that the current world situation is one that poses a threat to survival. What is Lefcourt's solution to problems of overcrowding, pollution, crime, cruelty, and so on?

> "Man [sic] must come to be more effective and more able to perceive himself as the determiner of his fate if he is to live comfortably with himself. It is through the very abnegation of self-direction and the surrender to indomitable forces that man commits horrendous acts upon dissimilar others" (p. 3).

For Lefcourt, deprived social position can create a sense of fatalism that engenders infantile and regressive behavior. This deprivation of the sense of self-determination leads people to be less able to learn about themselves and thus less able to develop a definite measure of their own worth. Says Lefcourt "it should come as no surprise, therefore, to discover that Negroes, whose socialization encourages a fatalistic outlook on life, have often been found to hold aberrant self-assessments" (p. 21).

Lefcourt also maintains that this construct is essential for the maintenance of moral order. Following a discussion of the holocaust, Eichmann, and Lieutenant Calley, Lefcourt argues that maintaining an internal control orientation can be a bulwark against unquestioning submission to authority. Thus, an internal locus of control by those involved could have prevented the holocaust and the massacre at My Lai. How? An internal orientation is a correlate of the kinds

---

*The locus of control construct has also spawned, or been associated with, a host of related constructs such as "personal causation" and "engagement style" (e.g., Gregory, 1981; de Charms, 1981; McKinney, 1981). Although it is possible to draw a number of conceptual and methodological distinctions between these constructs, they all share the emphasis on autonomy and control.

of cognitive activity that, according to Lefcourt, facilitates the maintenance of personal causation. Therefore:

> if Eichmann had been more able to ponder the ramifications of Nazi requests for complicity, perhaps he would have looked more askance at the enthusiasm exhibited by his fellow bureaucrats for participating in the execution of the "Final Solution" (p. 61).

The essential point is clear. The notion of internal control orientation serves to explain much of social reality and especially morality. The extrapolation of the psychological to the social is accomplished with no apparent difficulty. As will become clear below however, the "social" that is presented here is merely a caricature that serves as a homogenous backdrop to prop up the theory. Such understandings of human functioning require artifactual social contexts to hide their ideological underpinnings.

Learned Helplessness   This discussion of learned helplessness theory will focus on the human literature and specifically on the cognitive or attributional reformulation of this theory (Abramson, Seligman, & Teasdale, 1978). As with the locus of control literature, the learned helplessness literature appears to have grown exponentially over the last decade. Naturally, there are a large number of reviews and critiques of this literature but, again, they are almost all at the conceptual and methodological level (e.g., Huesmann, 1978).

"Learned helplessness" was first used to describe the impaired escape-avoidance response of dogs following their exposure to uncontrollable shocks (Seligman & Maier, 1967). It referred to the motivational, cognitive, and emotional deficits that resulted from the learned expectations that outcomes were uncontrollable. This explanation was readily applied to human problems. Studies with human subjects however made obvious certain problems with the original hypothesis. The reformulation of learned helplessness theory utilizes attribution theory to specify more accurately the conditions under which helplessness occurs in humans (Abramson et al., 1978; Abramson, Garber, & Seligman, 1980). Essentially, the reformulated theory still emphasizes that the expectation of noncontingency is the crucial determinant of symptoms of learned helplessness. It is meant only to clarify "under what conditions the *perception* that events are noncontingent in the past or present will be transformed into an *expectation* that events will be noncontingent in the future" (Abramson et al., 1980, p. 9). This is schematically presented in Figure 1.

The reformulated theory states that:

> the *attribution* individuals make for the noncontingency between their responses and outcomes in the here and now is an important determinant of their subsequent expectations for future noncontingency (Abramson et al., 1980, p. 9).

> *Objective* noncontingency → *Perception* of present and past noncontingency → *Attribution* for present or past noncontingency → *Expectation* of future noncontingency → *Symptoms* of helplessness.

Figure 1 Flow of events leading to symptoms of helplessness. *(From L. Y. Abramson, M. E. P. Seligman, & J. D. Teasdale (1978). p. 52. Copyright 1978 by the American Psychological Association. Reprinted by permission of the publisher and author.)*

These attributions can be categorized along dimensions of (a) internal-external, (b) stable-unstable, and (c) global-specific. The internal-external dimension defines the distinction between universal and personal helplessness. Universal helplessness occurs when outcomes are not contingent on one's own response or the responses of other people whereas personal helplessness occurs when there are responses that can produce the desired outcome in other people's repertoires but not in one's own. For example, universal helplessness is illustrated by the case of the parents of a child with a terminal illness. No one can save the child. Personal helplessness is illustrated by the case of the student who fails an exam despite spending a great deal of time studying and despite the fact that it is easily passed by other students in the class (Abramson et al., 1980). The stable-unstable dimension refers to factors which are perceived as long-lived and recurrent versus short-lived and intermittent. Finally, the global-specific attributional dimension refers to whether the factors occur in a wide variety of situations or only in specific situations.

What is important about the reformulated learned helplessness theory for the present purposes is its claims for applicability. The largest area of application has been that of depression (e.g., Huesmann, 1978; Garber & Seligman, 1980). Seligman (1975) initially argued that experience with uncontrollability produces the motivational, cognitive, and emotional components of depression. The attributional reformulation makes more specific predictions about the relationship between depression and learned helplessness and notes how each of the attributional dimensions can affect depression. There are four classes of deficit associated with depression: motivational, cognitive, affective, and self-esteem. According to Abramson et al. (1980), more global attributions lead to more general depressive deficits, more stable attributions will lead to more chronic deficits, and more internal attributions will lead to lower self-esteem. These attributions lead to depressive deficits only to the extent that they are able to generate global, stable, and internal expectations of future helplessness. In a further refinement of the theory, Peterson and Seligman (1984) argue that an explanatory style and its subsequent explanations determine the expectations of helplessness. The essential features of the theory remain unchanged, however.*

Like locus of control and self-efficacy theory, a central notion in learned helplessness theory is that the likelihood that one will engage and/or persist in a task will depend in large measure on one's expectations of control or judgments of success. Leaving aside the question of depression as a clinical construct per se, the core theoretical notion is avowedly asocial. In fact, its learning theory heritage virtually ensures it is so. But within the theory itself is embedded a social configuration no different from the homogenous backdrop to the locus of control construct. As McClure (1985) noted, learned helplessness theory assumes that contingencies are uncontrollable and inescapable. Therefore therapy consists of various philanthropic welfare arrangements (e.g., housing), relinquishing unattainable goals, and changing "unrealistic attributions" (Abramson et al., 1978). Note, however, that none of these proposals involves giving the depressed person more control over their contingencies. The question of the social origins of learned helplessness remains unaddressed as does the very constitution of the social world. Rather it is deemed both irrelevant and determined. It is the individual who must change and adapt in his/her isolation.

Self-efficacy Theory   The last theoretical statement concerned here with autonomy and control is Bandura's self-efficacy theory (Bandura, 1977a, 1977b, 1982). According to Bandura, any psychological procedure, such as psychotherapy, achieves its effect by altering the level and strength of self-efficacy. An expectation of personal efficacy consists of the conviction that one is able to execute successfully a required behavior. Along with outcome expectations, which are one's estimate that given behaviors will lead to certain outcomes, self-efficacy expectations are necessary cognitive factors that precede behavior change. Efficacy expectations determine both the initiation and the persistence of coping behavior. Bandura (1977a) states that:

> efficacy expectations determine how much effort people will expend and how long they will persist in the face of obstacles and aversive experiences. The stronger the perceived self-efficacy, the more active the efforts (p. 194).

---

*Other applications have also been proposed for the theory, largely in medically relevant areas of psychology (e.g., Taylor, 1979; Peterson, 1982). For example, Raps, Peterson, Jonas, and Seligman (1982) argue that long-term hospitalization may lead to learned helplessness, in part because hospitals require patients to forfeit control over most of the tasks they normally perform. The operative factor leading to learned helplessness, however, is the perception of noncontingency.

In a more sociological vein, Rabow, Berkman, and Kessler (1983) argued recently that learned helplessness was a good description of the "culture of poverty" found in the Southern Appalachians of the United States. By implication, the cure for extreme poverty is rooted in "changing negative expectations and interpretations into more hopeful ones so that the person will begin to believe that his or her responses will produce desirable outcomes" (p. 425). The authors have allowed the individualistic focus of learned helplessness theory to become central to their analysis of the culture of poverty.

Bandura then goes on to outline the dimensions of efficacy expectations, such as magnitude, generality, and strength, and their sources, namely performance accomplishments, vicarious experiences, verbal persuasions, and emotional arousal. Throughout however it is apparent that Bandura believes that in the presence of appropriate skills and adequate incentives, efficacy expectations are necessary for behavioral change.

In a more recent paper Bandura (1982) also argued that the self-efficacy mechanism has not only wide explanatory power but is central to human agency. However, as Kirsch (1985) has noted, for tests of ability self-efficacy has been operationalized in ways that are indistinguishable from Rotter's expectancy construct (Rotter, 1954). Both are assessed by having subjects predict the extent to which they feel they can be successful at a given task. Furthermore, there is considerable conceptual overlap between the two constructs (Kirsch, 1985). Much of self-efficacy theory may also be logically necessary rather than empirically testable. Smedslund (1978) has argued that the theory is derivable from

> the meaning of the terms involved, as defined by a dictionary and by the context in which they occur from other propositions already proved, or from propositions regarded as basic or self-evident (p. 3).

For example, the notion that self-efficacy expectations will affect whether people try to cope with given situations can be proven by three common sense theorems derived from this statement. Empirical tests of this notion would neither confirm nor disconfirm the theory but only indicate whether the conditions for its demonstration had been successfully established (Smedslund, 1978).

I briefly want to note two aspects of self-efficacy theory, specifically as they relate to control. First, the "onerous" side to personal control, according to Bandura (1982), is that the "self-development of efficaciousness requires mastery of knowledge and skills that can be attained only through long hours of arduous work" (p. 142). Furthermore, the

> exercise of personal control carries heavy responsibilities and risks . . . presidents of corporations are granted considerable controlling power, but they must bear personal responsibility for the negative consequences of their decisions and actions. . . . Attractive incentives, privileges, and heady social rewards are therefore needed to get people to seek control involving complicated skills, laborious responsibilities, and heavy risks" (p. 142).

In short, self-efficacy requires discipline.

The second aspect to note is Bandura's notion of collective efficacy. According to Bandura (1982), collective efficacy is rooted in self-efficacy. He states that "the strength of groups, organizations, and even nations lies partly in people's sense of collective efficacy that they can solve their problems and improve their lives through concerted effort" (p. 143). He goes on to argue that imbalances in social power may depend on the lack of influence exercised by people that is in fact theirs. People convinced of their inefficacy will not try to bring about social change even though these changes are attainable. "It is the internal barriers created by perceptions of collective efficacy that are especially pernicious because they are more demoralizing and behaviorally self-debilitating than are external impediments" (p. 144). This notion brings us full circle. The social and the psychological again mirror each other. In so doing they propose an artifactual social sphere that is ideologically grounded in individualistic and noncontextual theories.

Why are these constructs noncontextual and individualistic? Do they not accurately describe some aspects of advanced industrial civilization? What I wish to propose is that locus of control, learned helplessness and self-efficacy theory are only superficially social and can be viewed as theoretical productions that in fact limit social understandings through the interpretive practices of desocialization, deproblematization, deinstitutionalization, and dehistoricization (cf. Wexler, 1983). Interpretive practices constitute certain self-understandings that are made explicit when we view these works as texts equal to other texts that are products of culture. The appearance of accuracy is a function of their mesh with the dominant culture and their transposition of ordinary linguistic categories into a scientific discourse which maintains the embedded ideology found in those categories.

Textual Practices

Desocialization Desocialization "works by first abstracting the individual from her generative social context. Then the abstracted individual is recontextualized, but in a way which denies social constitution" (Wexler, 1983; p. 109). People interact but their interactions are only so many emanations from individuals who are wholly self-contained. Social interaction is a crude mechanical process.

How does this work with the problem of control? It works precisely because the conceptions of control discussed above appear to place the person within social interaction but, in reality, all interaction originates from the individual. Social relations are determined by individuals with expectancies and beliefs which, although socially acquired, are portrayed as natural human tendencies. The individual, filled with cognitive mechanisms, is repositioned in a social interaction and perceives him or herself to have or not to have control, freedom, agency, and so on. The relation between social structure and social interaction is missing. Lefcourt (1982) handily explains how the holocaust could have been prevented by recourse to a perception of personal causation.

Likewise, the application of learned helplessness to such socially constituted psychological events as depression creates the appearance of a socially based explanation while it, in fact, hinges on cognitive constructs. As the examples of the applications by the proponents of these theories make clear, each of their formulations individualizes social relations by translating a social process—control—into an individual perception.

Deproblematization   Deproblematization refers to the unproblematic way in which the structure of social relations enters theories of autonomy and control (Wexler, 1983). Each of the theories discussed translates their individual constructs to the social level. (In the case of Janowitz's notion of social control the societal is translated to the individual.) This deproblematization of social relations is a result of treating social structures, relations among contending groups, and concrete social processes as an entity, namely, society. Thus society "becomes the personified entity which acts with a single will, mirroring the rational, fair, self-seeking, isolated individual. . . . Social dynamic parallels individual dynamic" (Wexler, p. 110).

Janowitz's notion of social control requires the positing of a set of values so that social organizations may regulate themselves. Where do these values come from? For Janowitz the social scientist's role is simply clarification. Thus, the values are whatever is normative.* Aside from the minimization of coercion, social control "involves the capacity of constituent groups in a society to behave in accordance with their acknowledged moral and collective goals" (Janowitz, 1978, p. 29). The entire process occurs through the rational redefinition of societal goals. Society is a rational entity, devoid of internal contradiction.

In a similar manner, Bandura (1982, p. 145) has argued that:

> as a society we enjoy the benefits left by those before us, who collectively resisted inhumanities and worked for social reforms that permit a better life. Our own collective efficacy will shape, in turn, how future generations will live their lives.

Although both Janowitz and Bandura acknowledge the presence of numerous constituencies within society, neither acknowledges the problematic nature of social relations. In the case of self-efficacy theory, social interaction is reduced to a process whereby individuals, who have certain "cognitive structures," act in concert with others and thus constitute a rational society. On the other hand, Janowitz's notion of social control is the objectification of the personal. Social control is the social equivalent of a personal process. For each of the theories discussed above, social conflict is a state of diverging interests to be resolved

---

*By accepting societal "norms" and refusing to study them in their own right, an author can give a "democratic" rationale to his/her work and does not need to take responsibility for given standards. A contradiction exists here insofar as many control theorists acknowledge an interest in reforming society while they tacitly sanction its norms (cf., Mills, 1943).

rationally by interdependent opponents. They exclude domination conflicts which pit formal, socially recognized groups against oppressed but poorly identified or marginal groups (Apfelbaum & Lubek, 1976).

Deinstitutionalization Deinstitutionalization appears in control theories through the lack of interaction between the personal and the institutional. Nowhere is the interiorization of specific meanings attributed to the social order. Thus, the absence of social determination is accomplished through its externalization (Wexler, 1983). Society or state are theoretical entities, separate and distinct from individuals who are likewise self-constituted and self-regulating; masters of their own destinies. The environment is an external force that at no time impinges on development or is internalized (e.g., Mead, 1934; Sampson, 1983; Vygotsky, 1978). It is a monolith, defined as an agent that impinges on perceptions, expectancies, and so on, but is never part of the process of social interaction itself. Whereas deproblematization referred to the creation of a nonproblematic society, deinstitutionalization refers to the static interaction of this society with autonomous individuals. For example, learned helplessness theory begins from the assumption of an objectively noncontingent situation, but this is important only insofar as the situation creates the *perception* of noncontingency. Thus, if the perception of noncontingency occurs in the absence of such a situation, it is still possible to observe the cognitive, emotional, and motivational deficits associated with helplessness.

Bandura seems on the face of it, to have avoided this problem. A more careful analysis however reveals that he has merely given the *appearance* of dealing with it and in so doing has further confused the issue. For example, Bandura (1982) admits that society is not a monolith but rather is constituted of competing interest groups. Furthermore, human influence is never unidirectional but is instead reciprocal or, more specifically, subject to "reciprocal determinism" (Bandura, 1978). This means that "psychological functioning involves a continuous reciprocal interaction between behavioral, cognitive, and environmental influences" (p. 345). In Figure 2, Bandura differentiates reciprocal determinism from a unidirectional and partially bidirectional view of the relationship between behavior, persons, and the environment.

While clearly advocating the notion that rigid unidirectional rules of behavior are no longer tenable, Bandura has not provided any real alternative. First, the entire analysis is in danger of leading to an infinite regress (Phillips & Orton, 1983). Behavior influences cognitions which influence the environment which influences behavior. Does behavior therefore influence behavior? Although Bandura (1983) denies this charge he also does not adequately address the issue of what it means for things to be reciprocally determined and caused at the same time. At times he claims that B, P, and E are "interlocking determinants" (Bandura, 1978), whereas at other times he claims they involve "sequentiality of mutual influence" (Bandura, 1983). Second, while admitting to a

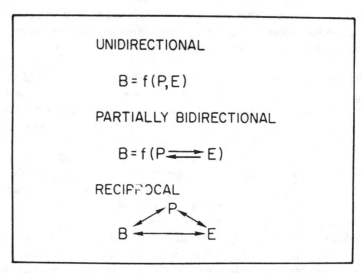

Figure 2 Schematic representation of three alternative conceptions of interaction. *B* signifies behavior, *P* the cognitive and other internal events that can affect perceptions and actions, and *E* the external environment. *(From Albert Bandura (1978). p. 345. Copyright 1978 by the American Psychological Association. Reprinted by permission of the publisher and author.)*

complex social world, Bandura's society is both deproblematized and deinstitutionalized by simply treating it as "environment." For example, in Figure 2, Bandura's P refers to internal personal factors such as conceptions, beliefs, and self-perceptions. Efficacy and outcome expectations can influence a person's behavior, which alters the environment, which in turn alters expectations.

> People activate different environmental reactions, apart from their behavior, by their physical characteristics (e.g., size, physiognomy, race, sex, attractiveness) and socially conferred attributes, roles, and status. The differential social treatment affects recipients' self-conceptions and actions in ways that either maintain or alter the environmental biases (Bandura, 1978, p. 346).

This position posits internal human processes that, despite their social origins, have the operative theoretical status of natural human tendencies—the problem of desocialization. Once this is accomplished, it is a small step to deinstitutionalization. Given that people have built-in cognitive structures, there is no necessity for originating those processes elsewhere. Therefore, while it appears that Bandura has included the social, he has in fact obscured it through the language of reciprocal determinism.

Dehistoricization In all control theories we can find the assumption of the necessity and naturalness for people to have control, or at least for people to perceive that they have control. Without it we are helpless, lack self-efficacy, fall prey to totalitarianism, and so on. In fact, some theorists have argued that the need for control is a basic human need state (e.g., Renshon, 1979) and that this is supported by "the culture-free results of relevant animal experiments"* (Perlmuter & Monty, 1979, p. 346). In other words, the need for control is dehistoricized, that is, removed from its sociohistorical context.

To counter this practice, it is necessary to understand the need for control as a prevailing cultural ideal rather than as a basic human need, and thus restore it to a historical construct. In it is embodied the Protestant ethic (Sampson, 1983). For example, as Bandura's vignette about the corporation president makes clear, it is important to be in control if one wishes to reap the rewards that come from positions of control. Thus, dehistoricization works in this case by applying an idealized social rule to the sphere of individual psychology. By doing so psychology is able to bypass questions about the nature of the sociohistorical constitution of this rule. Rather, it is legitimized as scientific fact and in this form can present social reality as the result of natural, individual motives (Wexler, 1982). The replacement of the historical with the natural however also precludes talk of social change. Natural categories do not reflect social conflict; historical categories do. Writing ordinary language constructs into scientific discourse removes them from the area of the social and the historical. By requiring control to serve as a basic human need state it is disguised as normative.

These four interpretive practices, I believe, are fundamental to the process of ideology production in the literature of psychological control. They silence some fundamental questions of control that are at the root of psychology's concern with autonomy, and instead, ensure that they are understood in a restricted, limiting context. It is not that psychology simply reflects or expresses ideology or cultural beliefs. Rather, it eclipses what is truly social and instead serves up a depoliticized, dehistoricized social sphere as the context of individual thought and behavior.

What are these fundamental questions of control that are at the root of psychology's concern with autonomy? They are questions that derive from the contradiction inherent in advanced industrial societies, namely, the press toward privatism in the form of overriding concerns with the family, personal career, and consumption while the state and socioeconomic forces increasingly intervene and dictate what was once deemed as personal and private (Marcuse,

---

*The argument that animal experiments are "culture-free" indicators of the need for control in human beings involves a host of untenable assumptions, namely, that it is in fact "control" that is being studied, that it is possible to generalize from animal models, etc. Needless to say, it also implies a wholesale acceptance of the tenets of logical positivism underlying experimental methodology.

1964; Habermas, 1975; Sampson, 1983). The ideology of individualism "fosters a belief in rational control and autonomy even as that control wanes and the key shaping forces operate behind the backs of those who should know but do not" (Sampson, 1983, p. 100). Illusory autonomy belongs to the self-directed and self-regulated individual who is in fact highly predictable and whose choices are governed by the forces of advanced industrial societies (Fromm, 1955; Sampson, 1983). It is the illusory autonomy of those who are essential to the process of reproducing culture (Sampson, 1983). Psychology's preoccupation with autonomy and control is consistent with this drive to privatism, or what Sampson (1983) has called self-contained individualism. As advanced industrial nations become more highly centralized and bureaucratized, there is an ever greater need for ideological interventions that emphasize individual freedom and responsibility. In psychology the healthy personality is construed within the framework of the self-contained individual. The underlying social contradictions are hidden from view however by the ideological productions of the psychological works themselves.

POWER AND IDENTITY

In the wake of this analysis what might a psychology of control look like if it also addressed problems of the social order, social inequality, and the possibilities of social change? What might a generative theory of control be, if by generative is meant theory to raise fundamental questions regarding contemporary social life (Gergen, 1982). What follows are several proposals that outline a different direction and perspective on the problem of control and self-control.

The first task is largely linguistic insofar as we abandon the notion of control and make explicit the problem of power contained in self-control theories. Lacey (1979) argues that a fundamental distinction is necessary between control over agendas and control over outcomes. Talk of agendas will at least recast the discussion of control into the language of power. When psychologists discuss control, it is usually along the lines of the control that can determine outcomes within specified situations, not situations themselves.* Perhaps labels such as "choice" are more appropriate to such discussions and we could then talk of control in the context of outcome agendas. The latter requires knowledge of the sociohistorical processes underlying existing domination in contemporary industrial societies (e.g., Akard, 1983; Marcuse, 1970).

Psychologists have on occasion pointed to the relationship between individualized constructs such as locus of control and power (e.g., Ng, 1980). This has never gone beyond an acknowledgement however and the implications of this

---

*Control theorists occasionally recognize this state of affairs but not its implications. For example, Langer (1975) noted that "when there are good reasons that it is either undesirable or impossible to remove restrictions on freedom, that is, when it is not possible to enable the exercise of real control, it may be advantageous to induce the illusion of control" (p. 326).

are not worked out; control theories themselves serve to contain and mask power relations of the dominant culture. The second task then is to examine the production of power relations. The production of power relations does not eclipse the issue of power but brings it to the fore. It denies the static and individualist frame of control theories. But two further questions are immediately raised; (a) what are power relations and (b) where is the juncture between power relations and psychology?

Before examining power relations, the very idea of power needs to be inspected. By power I do not mean what most psychologists have attributed to the term (Bennett, 1982; Henderson, 1981; Newbrough, 1980; Ng, 1980; Rappaport, 1981; Smith, 1981). These authors typically define power as sovereign or political power which as a commodity can be transferred or ceded through a contractual type of exchange. Marxist views of power are equally dependent on a contractual notion insofar as they rely on the concepts of class domination and the relations of production. According to Foucault (1980), the common point of these conceptions of power are their "economism" or their service of, and subordination to, the economy. That is, power is a *right* that is ceded to establish sovereignty or political power. The constitution of political power is modelled on a legal transaction that involves the contractual exchange of power, the limits of which demarcate oppression (Foucault, 1980). In short, power is a property which some have more of than others.

It is this view of power that is already implied in theories of control because the contractual nature of such power necessarily leads to questions of control, specifically, the control of those who have ceded their power to a sovereignty—even if this is a collective sovereignty that is democratized through the constitution of a public right. The concern of psychology with questions of mastery, autonomy, and control is in part a codification of this problem of the contractual nature of power. Thus if the psychology of control was rewritten and reconstituted using a conception power such as the one already implied in these theories, then we merely continue the obfuscation of the social. The conception of power that is used to recast the control problem must not reintroduce the problems of autonomy that are shed with the old theories. Hence the move from the construct of power-as-a-thing to power relations.

Giddens (1977) argues that power is held to be intrinsic to all interaction. For Giddens, power is present in human practice by its ability to transform nature and self. Power is a function of interaction and exists within the structure of social relations (Giddens, 1976, 1979). The transformative capacity of human action does not exist outside the interdependence of relations. Thus, argues Giddens, even those who are deemed relatively autonomous are dependent on the continuous production of resources by those who are subordinate. The resources produce and maintain the power relations.

Another relational conception of power is Foucault's (e.g., 1980) who likewise rejects the idea that power is possessed by some agents and not others but who, unlike Giddens, even eschews human subjectivity in his analysis. Within Foucault's problematic of "pouvoir-savoir" (power/knowledge)

> there are manifold relations of power which permeate, characterize and constitute the social body, and these relations of power cannot themselves be established, consolidated nor implemented without the production, accumulation, circulation and functioning of a discourse (1980, p. 93).

Power does not belong to some but acts as a "chain," or a "web" where the individual is always simultaneously undergoing and exercising power (see also Sheridan, 1980).

These reanalyses of the concept of power imply a fundamental reordering of our notions of control. Power exists not necessarily at the individual level but at subindividual and supraindividual levels simultaneously. To know domination is also to know the ways of domination inherent in the dominated. To be empowered requires simultaneous disempowering strategies; to act collectively requires the dismantling of the notion that power is not one individual's consolidated domination over others but something which individuals simultaneously undergo and exercise. As Foucault (1980) argues, "individuals are the vehicles of power, not its points of application" (p. 98). This is not to say that there are no structural forms of domination. There are slaves and slave-drivers. But to understand the functioning of power would be to analyse the historical condition of the slave and the slavedriver and follow this in a trajectory to forms of global domination.

We are now in a position to return to psychology via the concept of *identity*. By identity is meant the distinguishing characteristics that mark people as unique individuals and that are not attributable to normative characteristics of the self. According to Goffman (1961) for example, identity is always expressed, even in highly normative environments. And it is expressed as a distance from normative requirements which can either contravene norms or contribute to the smooth functioning of a social order. Although this definition does not speak to identity production it at least argues that identity is socially constructed. Wexler (this volume) has argued that identity is produced through an ordered social process of the commodification of "signs." In this symbolic economy of identity it is not discourse that creates identity but rather the structures of social interaction through which discourse functions. Apfelbaum and Lubek (1976) argue that identity evolves in the process of domination-recognition conflicts. The latter refer to conflicts between two fundamentally heterogenous opponents, "the inequality lying in the differential access to the decision-making covering values and rules that control our social future" (p. 83). They are "domination-recognition" conflicts because along with a struggle against domination is a struggle for the redefinition of a social identity. Refusing the identity imposed by domination leads an individual to produce an identity through the process of resistance.

Self-control strategies can now be recast as identity-securing strategies. They are attempts at domination/compliance; an individualistic use of symbolic resources to control/resist others. Control of self to dominate can be seen, for example, in Bandura's assessment of the disciplined executive. Control of self as compliance can be seen as an attempt to avoid identity-damaging disciplinary controls (Knights & Willmott, 1985). In either case, identity becomes the sphere in which power relations are played out. Strategies for self-control are themselves part of the symbolic economy of identity. Self-control as the domination of self fosters individualism and competition and retards social interdependence. Yet that very interdependence is necessary for identity production. Thus the discourse of self-control is eventually an identity-limiting discourse, encouraging the pursuit of individual self-interests and diminishing the productive power of collective interdependence (Knights & Willmott, 1985).

Notions of control, as exemplified by constructs such as locus of control, learned helplessness, and self-efficacy, are theoretical productions that simultaneously reproduce social conventions of individuality as well as define them. An analysis of the texts of these theories indicates their reliance on mechanical and cognitivist constructions of people and subjectivity. A rewriting of this literature would begin with an analysis of power relations and their interpenetration of human subjectivity. While space constraints make it impossible to produce a concrete case here, such work is already being done—albeit outside mainstream psychology (e.g., Janeway, 1980; Urwin, 1984). For example, Urwin (1984) presents an account of the development of language in infancy that relies on concepts developed from the work of Foucault and Lacan. In it she argues that the study of mother-child power relations in infancy belies the notion of unitary individuals and illuminates the processes that come to play in the production of human subjects.

The psychology of control is inextricably interwoven with psychology's conceptions of persons, behavior, and society. To question one is, ipso facto, to question the other. To rewrite the psychology of control is to begin rewriting psychology.

REFERENCES

Abramson, L. Y., Seligman, M. E. P., & Teasdale, J. (1978). Learned helplessness in humans: Critique and reformulation. *Journal of Abnormal Psychology, 87,* 49–74.

Abramson, L. Y., Garber, J., & Seligman, M. E. P. (1980). Learned helplessness in humans: An attributional analysis. In J. Garber & M. E. P. Seligman (Eds.), *Human helplessness: Theory and applications.* New York: Academic Press.

Akard, P. (1983). The "theory-praxis nexus" in Marcuse's critical theory. *Dialectical Anthropology, 8,* 207–215.

Apfelbaum, E., & Lubek, I. (1976). Resolution versus revolution? The theory of conflicts in question. In L. H. Strickland, F. E. Aboud & K. J. Gergen (Eds.), *Social Psychology in Transition*. New York: Plenum.

Arnkoff, D. B., & Mahoney, M. J. (1979). The role of perceived control in psychopathology. In L. C. Perlmuter & R. A. Monty (Eds.), *Choice and perceived control*. Hillsdale, NJ: Erlbaum.

Averill, J. R. (1973). Personal control over aversive stimuli and its relationship to stress. *Psychological Bulletin, 80,* 286–303.

Bandura, A. (1977a). Self-efficacy: Toward a unifying theory of behavioral change. *Psychological Review, 84,* 191–215.

Bandura, A. (1977b). *Social learning theory*. Englewood Cliffs, NJ: Prentice-Hall.

Bandura, A. (1978). The self system in reciprocal determinism. *American Psychologist, 33,* 344–358.

Bandura, A. (1982). Self-efficacy mechanism in human agency. *American Psychologist, 37,* 122–147.

Bandura, A. (1983). Temporal dynamics and decomposition of reciprocal determinism: A reply to Philips and Orton. *Psychological Review, 90,* 166–170.

Barthes, R. (1979). From work to text. In J. V. Harari (Ed.), *Textual strategies: Perspectives in post-structuralist criticism*. Ithaca, NY: Cornell.

Baxter, B. (1982). *Alienation and authenticity: Some consequences for organized work*. London: Tavistock.

Bennett, E. M. (1982). Native persons: An assessment of their relationships to the dominant culture and challenges for change. *Canadian Journal of Community Mental Health, 1,* 21–31.

Brewin, C. R., & Shapiro, D. A. (1984). Beyond locus of control: Attribution of responsibility for positive and negative outcomes. *British Journal of Psychology, 75,* 43–49.

Collins, B. E. (1974). Four components of the Rotter internal-external scale: Belief in a difficult world, a just world, a predictable world and a politically responsible world. *Journal of Personality and Social Psychology, 29,* 381–391.

Coward, R., & Ellis, J. (1977). *Language and materialism*. London: Routledge & Kegan Paul.

Culler, J. (1982). *On deconstruction: Theory and criticism after structuralism*. Ithaca, NY: Cornell.

de Charms, R. (1981). Personal causation and locus of control: Two different traditions and two uncorrelated measures. In H. M. Lefcourt (Ed.), *Research with the locus of control construct*. New York: Academic Press.

Dorfman, A., & Mattelart, A. (1975). *How to read Donald Duck: Imperialist ideology in the Disney comic*. New York: International General.

Eagleton, T. (1976). *Criticism and ideology: A study in Marxist literary theory*. London: New Left Books.

Fitzgerald, F. (1979). *America revised: History schoolbooks in the twentieth century*. Boston: Little & Brown.

Foucault, M. (1980). *Power/knowledge: Selected interviews and other writings*. (C. Gordon, Ed.). New York: Pantheon.

Fromm, E. (1955). *The sane society*. New York: Rinehart.

Furby, L. (1979). Individualistic bias in studies of locus of control. In A. R. Buss (Ed.), *Psychology in Social Context*. New York: Irvington.

Garber, J., & Seligman, M. E. P. (Eds.). (1980). *Human helplessness: Theory and applications.* New York: Academic Press.

Gergen, K. J. (1982). *Toward transformation in social knowledge.* New York: Springer-Verlag.

Gibbs, J. P. (Ed.). (1982). *Social control: Views from the social sciences.* Beverly Hills, CA: Sage.

Giddens, A. (1976). *New rules of sociological method.* London: Hutchinson.

Giddens, A. (1977). *Studies in social and political theory.* New York: Basic.

Giddens, A. (1979). *Central problems in social theory.* London: Macmillan.

Goffman, E. (1961). *Asylums.* Garden City, NY: Anchor.

Gregory, W. L. (1981). Expectancies for controlability, performance attributions, and behavior. In H. M. Lefcourt (Ed.). *Research with the locus of control construct.* New York: Academic Press.

Gurin, P., Gurin, G., & Morrison, B. M. (1978). Personal and ideological aspects of internal and external control. *Social Psychology, 41,* 275–296.

Habermas, J. (1975). *Legitimation crisis.* Boston: Beacon Press.

Henderson, A. H. (1981). *Social power: Social psychological models and theories.* New York: Praeger.

Huesmann, L. R. (1978). Special issue: Learned helplessness as a model of depression. *Journal of Abnormal Psychology, 87,* No. 1.

Jameson, F. (1981). *The political unconscious: Narrative as a socially symbolic act.* Ithaca, NY: Cornell.

Janeway, E. (1980). *Powers of the weak.* New York: Alfred A. Knopf.

Janowitz, M. (1978). *The last half-century: Societal change and politics in America.* Chicago: University of Chicago Press.

Kanungo, R. N. (1982). *Work alienation: An integrative approach.* New York: Praeger.

Kirsch, I. (1985). Self-efficacy and expectancy: Old wine with new labels. *Journal of Personality and Social Psychology, 49,* 824–830.

Knights, D., & Willmott, H. (1985). Power and identity in theory and practice. *Sociological Review, 17,* 22–46.

Kohn, M. L. (1976). Occupational structure and alienation. *American Journal of Sociology, 82,* 111–130.

Kohn, M. L., & Schooler, C. (1981). Job conditions and personality: A longitudinal assessment of their reciprocal effects. *American Journal of Sociology, 87,* 1257–1286.

Krause, N., & Stryker, S. (1984). Stress and well-being: The buffering role of locus of control beliefs. *Social Science and Medicine, 18,* 783–790.

Lacey, H. M. (1979). Control, perceived control, and the methodological role of cognitive constructs. In L. C. Perlmuter & R. A. Monty (Eds.), *Choice and perceived control.* Hillsdale, NJ: Erlbaum.

Langer, E. J. (1975). The illusion of control. *Journal of Personality and Social Psychology, 32,* 311–328.

Langer, E. J. (1983). *The psychology of control.* Beverly Hills, CA: Sage.

Lefcourt, H. M. (Ed.). (1981). *Research with the locus of control construct.* New York: Academic Press.

Lefcourt, H. M. (1982). *Locus of control: Current trends in theory and research.* Hillsdale, NJ: Erlbaum.

Mannheim, K. (1936). *Ideology and utopia: An introduction to the sociology of knowledge.* New York: Harcourt Brace Jovanovich.

Marcuse, H. (1964). *One-dimensional man.* Boston: Beacon Press.

Marcuse, H. (1970). *Five lectures: Psychoanalysis, politics, and utopia.* Boston: Beacon Press.

McClure, J. (1985). The social parameter of "learned" helplessness: Its recognition and implications. *Journal of Personality and Social Psychology, 48,* 1534–1539.

McKinney, J. P. (1981). The construct of engagement style: Theory and research. In H. M. Lefcourt (Ed.), *Research with the locus of control construct.* New York: Academic Press.

Mead, G. H. (1934). *The social psychology of George Herbert Mead.* (A. Strauss, Ed.). Chicago: University of Chicago Press.

Miller, S. M. (1979). Controlability and human stress: Method, evidence, and theory. *Behavior Research and Theory, 17,* 287–306.

Mills, C. W. (1943). The professional ideology of social pathologists. *American Journal of Sociology, 49,* 165–180.

Newbrough, J. R. (1980). Community psychology and the public interest. *American Journal of Community Psychology, 8,* 1–17.

Ng, S. H. (1980). *The social psychology of power.* London: Academic Press.

Palenzuela, D. L. (1984). Critical evaluation of locus of control: Towards a reconceptualization of the construct and its measurement. *Psychological Reports, 54,* 683–709.

Perlmuter, L. C., & Monty, R. A. (1979). Overview and appraisal. In L. C. Perlmuter & R. A. Monty (Eds.), *Choice and perceived control.* Hillsdale, NJ: Erlbaum.

Peterson, C. (1982). Learned helplessness and health psychology. *Health Psychology, 1,* 153–168.

Peterson, C., & Seligman, M. E. P. (1984). Causal explanations as a risk factor for depression: Theory and evidence. *Psychological Review, 91,* 347–374.

Pfohl, S. (1985). Toward a sociological deconstruction of social problems. *Social Problems, 32,* 228–232.

Phares, E. J. (1976). *Locus of control in personality.* Morristown, NJ: General Learning Press.

Phillips, D. C., & Orton, R. (1983). The new causal principle of cognitive learning theory: Perspectives on Bandura's "Reciprocal Determinism." *Psychological Review, 90,* 158–165.

Potter, J., Stringer, P., & Wetherell, M. (1984). *Social texts and context: Literature and social psychology.* London: Routledge & Kegan Paul.

Rabow, J., Berkman, S. L., & Kessler, R. (1983). The culture of poverty and learned helplessness: A social psychological perspective. *Sociological Inquiry, 53,* 419–434.

Rappaport, J. (1981). In praise of paradox: A social policy of empowerment over prevention. *American Journal of Community Psychology, 9,* 1–25.

Raps, C. S., Peterson, C., Jonas, M., & Seligman, M. E. P. (1982). Patient behavior in hospitals: Helplessness, reactance, or both? *Journal of Personality and Social Psychology, 42,* 1036–1041.

Renshon, S. A. (1979). The need for personal control in political life: Origins, dynamics, and implications. In L. C. Perlmuter & R. A. Monty (Eds.), *Choice and perceived control.* Hillsdale, NJ: Erlbaum.

Ricouer, P. (1971). The model of the text: Meaningful action considered as a text. *Social Research, 11,* 529–562.

Ross, E. A. (1901). *Social control.* New York: Macmillan.

Rotter, J. B. (1954). *Social learning and clinical psychology.* Englewood Cliffs, NJ: Prentice-Hall.

Rotter, J. B. (1966). Generalized expectancies for internal versus external control of reinforcement. *Psychological Monographs, 80,* (1, Whole No. 609).

Rotter, J. B. (1975). Some problems and misconceptions related to the construct of internal vs. external control of reinforcement. *Journal of Consulting and Clinical Psychology, 48,* 56–67.

Roucek, J. S. (Ed.) (1947). *Social control.* New York: Van Nostrand.

Sampson, E. E. (1977). Psychology and the American ideal. *Journal of Personality and Social Psychology, 35,* 767–782.

Sampson, E. E. (1981). Cognitive psychology as ideology. *American Psychologist, 36,* 730–743.

Sampson, E. E. (1983). *Justice and the critique of pure psychology.* New York: Plenum.

Schwendinger, H., & Schwendinger, J. R. (1974). *The sociologists of the chair.* New York: Basic Books.

Seeman, M. (1959). On the meaning of alienation. *American Sociological Review, 24,* 783–791.

Seeman, M., & Seeman, T. E. (1983). Health behavior and personal autonomy: A longitudinal study of the sense of control in illness. *Journal of Health and Social Behavior, 24,* 144–160.

Seligman, M. E. P. (1975). *Helplessness: On depression, development, and death.* San Francisco: Freeman.

Seligman, M. E. P., & Maier, S. F. (1967). Failure to escape traumatic shock. *Journal of Experimental Psychology, 74,* 1–9.

Seligman, M. E. P., & Miller, S. M. (1979). The psychology of power: Concluding comments. In L. C. Perlmuter & R. A. Monty (Eds.), *Choice and perceived control.* Hillsdale, NJ: Erlbaum.

Sheridan, A. (1980). *Michel Foucault: The will to truth.* London: Tavistock.

Singer, J. E. (1979). Diverse comments on diverse papers about choice and perceived control. In L. C. Perlmuter & R. A. Monty (Eds.), *Choice and perceived control.* Hillsdale, NJ: Erlbaum.

Smedslund, J. (1978). Bandura's theory of self-efficacy: A set of common sense theories. *Scandinavian Journal of Psychology, 19,* 1–14.

Smith, M. B. (1981). Themes and variations. In J. M. Joffe & G. W. Albee (Eds.), *Prevention through political action and social change.* Hanover, NH: University Press of New England.

Stam, H. J., & Spanos, N. P. (1982). The Asclepian dream healings and hypnosis: A critique. *International Journal of Clinical and Experimental Hypnosis, 30,* 9–22.

Strickland, B. R. (1977). Internal-external control of reinforcement. In T. Blass (Ed.), *Personality variables in social behavior.* Hillsdale, NJ: Erlbaum.

Strickland, B. R. (1982). Innovative assessment in locus of control. *Contemporary Psychology, 27,* 807–808.

Taylor, S. E. (1979). Hospital patient behavior: Reactance, helplessness, or control? *Journal of Social Issues, 35,* 156–184.

Taylor, S. E. (1983). Adjustment to threatening events: A theory of cognitive adaptation. *American Psychologist, 38,* 1161–1173.

Taylor, S. E., Lichtman, R. R., & Wood, J. V. (1984). Attributions, beliefs about control, and adjustment to breast cancer. *Journal of Personality and Social Psychology, 46,* 489–502.

Thompson, S. C. (1981). Will it hurt less if I can control it? A complex answer to a simple question. *Psychological Bulletin, 90,* 89–101.

Urwin, C. (1984). Power relations and the emergence of language. In J. Henriques et al., *Changing the subject.* London: Methuen.

Vygotsky, L. S. (1978). *Mind in society.* Cambridge, MA: Harvard University Press.

Wexler, P. (1982). Structure, text, and subject: A critical sociology of school knowledge. In M. Apple (Ed.), *Economic and cultural reproduction in education.* Boston: Routledge & Kegan Paul.

Wexler, P. (1983). *Critical social psychology.* Boston: Routledge & Kegan Paul.

Chapter 7

After Reflection: Psychologists' Uses of History

J. G. Morawski

INTRODUCTION

Clark Hull produced both theory and epistemology for psychology. Just as he diligently labored to translate the "older psychology into behaviorist terms," so he tried to transmute an older epistemology to correspond with behaviorism. His notebooks indicate that as early as 1925 he began sketching a behaviorist explanation of science and within four years he believed that the project was one of world-making.

> If a clear and convincing psychological basis could be worked out for such a theory of knowledge, it might have a far-reaching effect not only in the history of thought but on the course of civilization (Hull Papers, 1925).

In the end the neobehaviorist epistemology comprised just what is purportedly rejected in scientific thinking: a metaphysical thesis. These nonempirical foundations mean that it is impossible to empirically refute his system, but it

157

remains possible to reject it. Exploring Hull's behavioristic epistemology and theory with the tentacles of history dislodges the violations of logic, the loose play with language through subtle reliance on metaphor (Smith, in press), and the social devices ostensibly used to gain scientific precision but which actually yielded authority and defensiveness.

Historical studies unearth much more about the practice of science than these didactic anecdotes. The history of science illuminates the *reasons for* and *consequences of* enstating a particular model of reality. It can reveal how that model is found, constructed, retailed, violated, demolished. These were not always the interests of historians of science but over the last two decades they have become practically canonical. What remains largely unrecognized is that for psychology an historical attitude can do more. Given that psychology is the sole "science" whose subject matter, human actions and cognitions, is commensurate with the subject matter of history, then historiography may be relevant to our conceptual and methodological practices. An informed history of science, then, may yield more than sagacious retrospectives, more than caveats or moral lessons. Historical thinking conceivably may inform metatheory; it may even constitute a theory. History may form not only an "epistemological laboratory," to borrow a term an historian of science used some time ago (Dijksterhuis, 1959), but also a public domain for theory and practice.

That we, like Hull, seek consistency in our world making underscores my present objective: to consider the extent to which advanced historiography of psychology can guide the construction and evaluation of psychological theory. The procedure for this task involves, first, an account of why our science requires a substantially different historiography. From that point we can proceed to explore how that different historiography simultaneously enables a reformulation of our collective chronicle *and* affords transformation of our metatheory. Whereas this "new" metatheory shares much in common with other recent proposals for rethinking theory, the full implications of taking history seriously have yet to be laid out. The final step suggests the necessary moves toward a central tenet of the new metatheory, a transformation of our images of human nature.

AUDITS AND PURCHASES

Since 1929 thousands of psychologists have been weaned on E. G. Boring's (1950) *A History of Experimental Psychology.* The standards Boring set for the historiography of psychology were of presentism, inductivism, and internalism. He sold a Whiggishly presentist account of psychology's heritage that recorded those historical events bearing directly on contemporary research (presentism). Psychology was accorded a rational evolution (inductivism) whereby discoveries were duly collected and used as as bricks in an ascending scientific wall. Our past came to us purified for political, economic, and personal influences were not chronicled in Boring's history of psychology's internal events (Kelly, 1981; O'Donnell, 1979a). Psychology's maturation came to be depicted as an emergence from the murky depths of prenineteenth century speculative philosophy to an eventual fusion with experimental method. Moral ambitions and antiquated Baconian ideals of an immediately beneficial science were set aside for the priorities of disinterested and rigorous research. However influential his guidebook has been, Boring merely exemplifies a historiographical attitude that is still perpetuated in some contemporary histories (for criticisms see Danziger, 1979a; O'Donnell, 1979b; Samelson, 1974).

As for the philosophy of science, psychologists similarly shopped for readymade if not elegant formulas. Despite concerted early efforts to forge a self-identity independent of established philosophy, during the last fifty years psychologists have attempted a rapproachment of a rarified sort. With few exceptions, psychologists modeled their epistemology, not after physical science *per se,* but after the *philosophy* of physical science. Primed initially by nineteenth century materialism, positivism, and realism, psychologists eventually turned to the positivism of the Vienna Circle. Enraptured by their acquisition, psychologists were preeminent among intellectuals in their enduring commitment to a cult of empiricism. Here Hull can be summoned again, this time for his passionate devotion to the philosophy of science. In the last few decades the alliance has shifted to a much-popularized revision in the philosophy of science: Kuhn's thesis that scientists advance by embracing comprehensive pictures of the world, or paradigms. Kuhn's proposal liberated psychology from many problems encountered in logical empiricism and, hence, "Paradigm promotion became the new form of psychological commerce" (Koch, 1975, p. 480). Like its predecessors the paradigm theory, as loosely interpreted by psychologists, enabled the making of rational explanations for sometimes seemingly irrational research practices.

The formalist profile of psychology is being altered. The presumed rationality, logic, and intellectual purity of psychological practices are being challenged. Rational reconstructions are being replaced by dynamic historical accounts that resituate psychology within a social context of economics, politics, culture and personal relationships. The reconsidered history of intelligence tests, for instance, illustrates how politics, professional ambitions, and personal presuppositions were instrumental in research (Camfield, 1969; Samelson, 1975, 1979). Numerous instances where psychological theory encompassed politics, prophecy, or profit have been identified (i.e., Danziger, 1979b; Hale, 1980; Morawski, 1982a, Napoli, 1980; Sokal, 1984). Historical studies have shown that, once formulated, psychological theories have gained ascendency for a variety of reasons, and that empirical evidence was not always primary among those reasons (i.e., Apfelbaum & Lubek, 1976; Bleier, 1984; Furby, 1979, Harris, 1979; Israel, 1979; Morawski, 1985; O'Donnell, 1979a; Samelson, 1981).

While these reevaluations are in accordance with advances in the historiography of the natural sciences (e.g., Agassi, 1963; Teich & Young, 1973; Rosenberg, 1983), the revitalized historiography of psychology faces special problems as well as unique opportunities. This distinct status results from two conditions, the first of which is the *reactivity* and *reflexivity* contingent upon our being both the subject and observer of our research. The second condition pertains to the field's *peculiar institutional growth*. Unlike the natural sciences, psychology has staged a laborious, century-long struggle, not just for disciplinary independence but for self-identity and certainty. And in the enduring efforts, psychologists confronted research problems where their decisions about, say, what was the correct or most promising theory frequently carried implications for the discipline's very status as a science. That is, whereas in chemistry, the choice of a particular methodological approach would, at worst, lead to incorrect empirical conclusions, in psychology the choice of methodology had implications for whether or not the field was actually a science. These decision points encompass innumerable instances where psychologists' objectives were concealed, blurred, or represented in a somewhat duplicitous fashion. This is not to say that physical scientists' work or accounts of their work can be taken as direct and veridical (Gilbert & Mulkay, 1984; Shapin, 1984). Rather, abstruse accountings seem to be a much more distinctive feature of psychology's last century. Historical tasks thus require rigorous assessment of hidden motives and public persona. Studies of these features include analysis of the interpretations of Wundt's psychology (Blumenthal, 1976; Bringmann & Tweney, 1980; Danziger, 1979a), the moral intentions underlying scientific programs (Leary, 1979; Morawski, 1982a; Passmore, 1970), the plurality of interests in advancing psychology (White, 1980), and the political and professional dimensions of the success of behaviorism (Danziger, 1979b; O'Donnell, 1979b; Samelson, 1980).

These historical perspectives do not command a particular philosophy of science. Nevertheless, they tacitly eschew absolutist canons and realist figurations of epistemology. The recent historical work not only challenges formalist philosophies but also examines the functions served by the very espousal of such philosophies. For instance, psychologists' endorsement of a philosophical hierarch and unity of the sciences functioned to enhance psychology's prestige (Danziger, 1979b; Morawski, 1982a; 1983). Logical empiricism purportedly rescued the field from the perils of fragmented languages and observational bases as well as from normative theorizing (Sampson, 1978). These and other investigations suggest that what counts as rational and truthful, in this case a philosophy of science, changes over time and that at any particular juncture rationality attains meaningfulness only by virtue of its ulterior functions in that temporal context. As such, studies in the history of psychology can inform and perhaps form the study of epistemology.

THE HISTORICAL MODE OF (RE)READING

The reoriented historiography portrays a very different heritage of psychology and does so by using a different perspective on that past. The changes in what counts as evidence or as a coherent story amount to more than revisions in historical methodology. They constitute not merely a new purchase for looking at the past, but a different way of comprehending the world of social events, in this case the world of scientific work. In comparison, the two modes could be called the *rational reconstructivist* and the *historical* respectively. So far the discussion has shown how adopting one or the other mode of comprehension has implications for historical studies of psychology. The potential of using the historical mode in psychological theory itself is somewhat more complicated and requires acquaintance with the various dimensions of historical comprehension. The most fundamental features reside in what is taken to be an *explanation,* the *temporality* of events, and the *conceptual-methodological procedures* for devising that explanation.

Explanation

In the 1940s and 1950s conversations in the philosophy of history frequently entertained the possibility that historical explanations could or should be causal just as explanations in the natural sciences were held to be (law-like regularities and deductive methods). The idea was found problematic to say the least and the conversations shifted to considering what, if anything, was unique about historical understanding (Mink, 1965). Woven throughout these discourses are threads of a tolerant pluralism that recognized not only the need for modes of explanation compatible with practices indigenous to history but also the fact that there actually may be more than one mode of explanation. Aside from the limited positivist or "covering-law" explanations, historians formulate explanations where the connections between events (or intentions, utterances, or actions) require inferences other than those supposedly educed empirically, the empirical form being either inadequate or insufficient for the particular problem. Although generally termed "rational" explanations, this mode subsumes a number of distinct types, the most notable being the rational, contextual and narrative. The rational type posits that historical explanation requires knowledge not only of observable events but of the intentions and thoughts of the actor (Collingwood, 1946), or the reasonableness of the actor's doings (Dray, 1957). A type more contextualist in orientation holds that historical explanation is the representation of events through exposition of the full texture of the episode. Contextual explanations demand more than simply interrelating various threads of events; they require an unpacking of typical accounts such that:

> the distinction between cause and effect is itself a limited one, in the sense of being highly context-dependent. What is a cause in one context can be seen as itself a combination of cause and effect in another context (Scriven, 1966, p. 241).

Contextualism incorporates the situation of the historian:

> When we are looking for causes we are looking for explanations in terms of a few
> factors or a single factor; and what counts as an explanation is whatever fills the
> gap in the inquirer's or reader's understanding (Scriven, 1966, p. 256).

A third type of rational explanation, the narrative, need not exclude the other
two, but takes the very construction of a story as explanatory in itself. In its
most provocative form, this trope suggests that narrative, in accounting for real
events, actually demonstrates that:

> the reality of these events does not consist in the fact that they occurred but that,
> first of all, they were remembered, and second, that they are capable of finding a
> place in a chronologically ordered sequence (H. White, 1980, p. 23).

Both within and outside historiography have come attempts to identify and
classify what might be essentially different modes of explanation. The historiographical work on explanatory models, while inconclusive, does elucidate the
possible forms that the explanation of human events can take and some of the
assumptions about truthfulness that underlie these forms. It shows how mechanistic concepts of causality and explanation can be situated within a variegated
and complex mosaic of explanatory modes, and how adequacy, coherence, and
intelligibility of an explanation of human actions often requires more than the
hammering out of causal inferences (see Morawski, 1982b, 1984a). This view
shares much with that of pragmatism (Rorty, 1979, 1982) and perspectivism
(Lukes, 1982) in the philosophy of social action.

Temporality

A constitutive feature of all explanatory forms is temporality, the accounting for
change over time. Hence, models of change are typically though not overtly
stipulated in explanations. Those using a mechanistic-empirical framework
most often engage a highly compatible linear model of change, one that for
various historical reasons is often given a progressive or upward direction.
Historical work done within other explanatory frameworks utilizes a variety of
temporal models: homeostatic, evolutionary, revolutionary, cyclical, and degen-
erative, are among the most readily identifiable. The variety of possible temporal models obviously enriches possibilities for the development of theory and
the explanation of events (Morawski, 1984a).

Procedures and Practices

The assumed dichotomy of facts and values that has putatively excused psychologists from examining the limits of "objectivity" has not so mollified histo-

rians. The latters' skepticism toward positivism has prompted rigorous and continued reflection on values, human interests, and the subjectivity of intellectual practices. The benefit of inquiries on objectivity resides not in any conclusiveness of the arguments (to pretend any established consensus among historians on these issues would be erroneous), but in some very general provisions that have evolved. These provisions distinguish historiographical thinking on objectivity from its counterpart in psychology in several fundamental ways.

First, probably because historians usually are separated from their subject by time, and from any primary sense datum by two or more levels of evidence, many of them hold that the determination of empirical acts involves "constructing" by an active observer (the historian) and that this determination of facts must itself be viewed in dialectical and historical perspective. Consequently, these historians have avoided what William James called the "psychologist's fallacy"—the confusion of the observer's standpoint with that of her or his subject (James, 1890, p. 196). Historiographical analyses attend to the processes influencing the selection of materials: from decisions about what constitutes adequate data to the particular guiding interests and salient historical context of the historian. Even a moderate historian writing in the early 1960s could insist that

> the facts of history never come to us "pure," since they do not and cannot exist in a pure form: they are always refracted through the mind of the recorder. It follows that when we make up a work of a history, our first concern should be not with the facts which it contains but with the historian who wrote it (Carr, 1961, p. 22)

Many historians thus seriously examine their own historical situation, their modes of interpretation, or their imaginative understandings (i.e., Atkinson, 1978; Hexter, 1971; Humphreys, 1980). In psychological terminology, they practice reflexive thinking.

A related provision on objectivity and knowledge claims concerns pluralism and the adjudication of contending historical accounts. The incalculable number of perspectives from which an event can be observed and the potentially inexhaustible sources of evidence suggest that objectivity may require pluralism. Among the assorted historiographical positions there is general concurrence that pluralism is not "unnatural" and that questions of objectivity and competing interpretations are adjudicated through intellectual and professional rules of evidence, argument, and discourse.

The final provision is an ethical one based on the essential untenability of the positivist distinction made between research and the moral implications of that research. Rather, the historical models of subject and object relations just outlined stipulate assessment of the very relation of moral values to research (Hughes, 1964; Walsh, 1966). Again, this relation is viewed contextually and reflexively such that the historian's beliefs and standards of judgment are themselves part of history, and are as much subject to historical investigation as any other aspect of human behavior (Carr, 1961, p. 84). With a contextual conceptualization of values and moral responsibility, historians can eschew the positivist pretense of suspending moral entanglements by the conjectural separation of factual and evaluative enterprises.

BRINGING HISTORY TO THE PRESENT

There are at least two ways in which these general provisions of some contemporary historiography may be related to developing new theory in psychology. First, as the initial section of this paper indicates, using certain historical practices to excavate psychology's past compels us to reconsider our sometimes idealized models of scientific work and its underlying philosophical principles. Second, the historical practices delineated in this paper in many ways resemble the "new theory," or postempiricist models, currently being elucidated. These practices share much with critical theory, interpretive social science, ethogenics, dialectics, constructivism, contextualism and feminist analysis. Thus, historiography may guide psychological researchers who are attempting to develop, say, a contextualist understanding of labor negotiations, life-span narrative accounts of the concept of self, or social-ecological accounts of grieving. However lured by the challenge of developing different understandings, it remains that in most of the new theorizing we have yet to truly appreciate what theoretical (and epistemological) changes must be brought about, what habits must be broken and what new skills must be rehearsed. For these reasons, the history of psychology itself affords us an irreplaceable epistemological laboratory. In fact, that history is an imperative exercise in the development of theory.

Let us take three common concerns of postempiricist theorizing: *reflexivity, normative practices,* and the *context-dependence of meaning.* The terms may vary from work to work, but they represent broadly shared recommendations for transforming research. Reflexivity is the property of all human sciences whereby we are both the subjects who conduct inquiries and the objects of those inquiries. Regarding this property, the problems in the empiricist program have been either the abeyance of reflexivity or the inadvertent enactment of reflexive practices in research. Thus, Bertrand Russell could jest about how the infrahuman subjects of British researchers were found to exhibit stereotypically British behaviors while the animals in American research acted in a distinctly Yankee fashion (cited in Flanagan, 1981). Whether in critiques of conventional research or in proposals for new theory, the acknowledgement of reflexivity generally ends with just that, acknowledgement. Likewise there has been much excellent work on the normative dimensions of theory, and on the inevitability of this dimension, but few have gone further to correct, refine, or defend our normative practices. The same situation holds for the context-dependence of meaning, the claim that adequate interpretation of an event, utterance, or action requires understanding of the particular context in which it transpired. Admonishments and global proposals regarding these concerns are, of course, important. The reluctance to carry them into new undertakings suggests that we may not fully comprehend the phenomena, their powers, or their consequences. My proposals to return to history differs from others advocating historical psychology only in the sense that it considers the unfolding drama of the psychologists and not just the past actions of the ordinary social being who typically takes center stage in our research theatre. The examination of psychologist's past is both *part of* and *more than* historical psychology as it is usually construed. The kind of historical psychology advocated here sets aside the age-old search for scientific foundations and instead presents psychology, its subjects and its products, as a historical and interpretive enterprise.

MAKING SENSE OF MAKING PSYCHOLOGY

We tend to take experimental procedures and the scientific method for granted. With a clever eye we notice how it grew from psychologists' "physics' envy" or "method fetishism," from those early attempts to place psychology on the same pedestal that elevated the physical sciences. Of course our storytelling is more sophisticated, but in embracing this narrative we tend to forget that those earlier psychologists who inhabit the narrative, even with philosophy of science in hand or at least within reach, still had to manufacture concrete accounts of human behavior. We similarly tend to overlook the fact that our precursors had more than a professional interest in legitimating the science; in fact, legitimation was a means to accomplishing other interests. Consequently, it is not always recognized that we maintain some of those very interests, and that those interests include not just a desire to fully understand human actions but also aspirations to develop elegant and coherent theory and ultimately to convey acquired knowledge beyond the confines of the academic cabal. These interests and their heritage deserve attention as an essential component of psychological work. As trite as it may seem, where we are going depends to a great extent on where we came from and even more importantly, on where we *think* we came from.

Examination of these practices and interests is not unlike a stroll down a hall of mirrors. By looking back we seem common ambitions in the accomplishments of our predecessors, and in our predecessors' actions we see their confinement in the form of certain cultural constraints. If we wish to chance perpetual disorientation and look to yet another well-situated mirror across the hall, we can glance at the reflection of our historical gaze. The stroll certainly can be an exercise *reducto absurdum,* but it also can compel more self-conscious confrontation of our own interests and constraints. If used in this latter manner, the walk presents experiments in the fabrication of theory. It indicates just how psychology cannot be a positive science but a historical one.

The production of psychology during the interwar years (1919–1941) offers ample case studies. These years are germane to questions of theory and epistemology, for they mark the shift from loosely defined functionalism and pragmatism to more formalist theorizing, the final dissolution of introspectionism, the organization of psychologists' professional activities outside university departments, and the solidification of the commonly recognized methods of experimentation and quantitative analysis. Although hardly noticeable with our experimentally-oriented vision, these years were crucial ones for achieving consensus on what counts as an experimental event, and even less apparent to us, on what counts as the legitimate conduct and character of the subjects and observers of those experimental events.

It was during this period that scientific psychologists came to emphasize what was held to be the irrational core of human nature and accordingly, to argue for its pliability when exposed to the plethora of environmental pressures. Psychology would study this "other one" (Meyer, 1921) objectively, dispassionately, and with control. In fact, in one of the most popular textbooks, psychology was defined by the interest in control: "Ultimately it is a desire to get *control*" (Dashiell, 1928, p. 6). As Robert Woodworth (1929) described the state of the most promising theory, "Behaviorism handles the human subject without gloves, tears him apart with no compunction. Behaviorism prides itself in being 'hard boiled,' and as upsetting as possible" (p. 171). In keeping with larger social and intellectual trends, psychologists were changing the paradigm from a rational and morally autonomous human nature to one claiming that "reality constructs the person" (Buss, 1978; Flanagan, 1981). They were designing a particular discipline to ensure the "discipline" of others (Harris, 1984; Danziger, 1979b; Morawski, 1983, 1984b). But it is not generally realized that in unpacking and then reconstructing an image of human nature, psychologists were redefining themselves and their own authority accordingly.

The new image of the psychologists, defined in terms of a revised image of human nature, was grafted on to every stem of professional life, from the laboratory to the social arrangements among psychologists themselves. The underlying interests and the consequences of this image making can be elucidated through several examples. The first involves self-discipline. In making the transition to scientific research programs, psychologists were exceptionally preoccupied with control and order of themselves as well as of the "others." Immediately following World War I, they contemplated what social arrangements were appropriate for their own kind. Their planning for scientific work was frequently of corporate planning: researchers were executives serving the company. Edward Thorndike pronounced that:

> it seems fair to ask scientific men to work in the spirit of the business employee or contractor in certain cases, and to submit to certain irritations for the probable common good (Yerkes, 1921).

James Rowland Angell (1920) called for "a centralized device for planning," for "control," for a "democratic foundation" for research, and for replacement of individually-initiated research programs by "some definite purposeful cooperation." The writers of the classic schools and systems textbooks built their descriptions on a bedrock faith in an emerging, united psychology. One even spoke of psychology's progress in terms of the tactics and strategies of military science (Woodworth, 1929). Clark Hull made frequent notes about the research process as a gigantic machine, complete with well-fitted cogs (Hull Papers, Ideabooks, 1920–1940). However, and here is a clue to self-discipline, he also suggested that researchers like those he worked with at Yale needed a fuhrer to guide their activities (Hull, 1952). The self-discipline was a response to insecurities and to the fear that psychologists themselves were less than rational, were dangerously pliable. Thus the many controversies between psychological theories and schools were explained not in terms of the substantive problems inherent in devising a science of mental life but rather in terms of the human weaknesses—defensiveness, self-interest, emotionalism—of psychologists (e.g., Angell, 1919; Boring, 1929; Hull, 1935). As Raymond Dodge described the "perils" of experimental psychologists in 1926,

> he may get lost in the chaos of details and never emerge. I have known such lost souls. He may spend his time in fruitless quest, following trails that lead nowhere, at the peril of a wasted life. He is not altogether free from the peril of combat. He may find himself in conflict with his colleagues or with the native inhabitants of the dark continent of ignorance, who voluntarily choose darkness rather than light and prefer prejudice to information. Not all of them live in Tennessee (p. 129).

Dodge's text discloses the uncertainty of the alleged distinctions between the observer and the "other one," the subject: Trails or mazes? A wasted life or no reinforcement? Whose ignorance, prejudice, and darkness? John Dollard described the work of Yale psychologists of the 1930s in a similar tone:

> Life would be unbearable in a world where one was constantly having to choose. Uncertainty is exhausting and choice demands special psychological strengths and reserves. It is therefore a human necessity that the world be, to some extent, predictable. Behavior must flow along at least some of the time in golden quiet. Man needs orderly knowledge, scientific knowledge, a kind of knowledge which permits him to act most of the time without the excruciating necessity of choice. The block-busting scientific fact derives its power because it confirms or contradicts a theory or an expectation. Orderly knowledge is easier to teach and easier to learn because one item in theory suggests another. A correct theory simplifies human problems and makes individual choice easier (Dollard, 1964, p. 32).

The drives for cooperation, organized research, integration, and unified science undoubtedly served economic ends. But they were, above all, a rallying for consensus which would unit a fragmented discipline and ensure against irrationality and blind actions.

The second example is taken from the history of gender research (Morawski, 1985). For the first fifteen years of the century the study of gender differences had suffered from inconclusive findings (Rosenberg, 1982). That is, despite expectations to find gender differences through the new experimental studies of mental abilities, no such consistent pattern was unearthed. Some psychologists, those of the environmentalist position, expected these variable findings, but others less convinced of the influence of nurture continued to conjecture on the exact location of the real differences. The development of masculinity-femininity personality inventories, originally introduced by Lewis Terman and Catherine Cox Miles (1936) and followed by a considerable number of others, returned certitude to ascertaining the existence of gender differences. But to arrive at such conclusions the researchers first had to alter conceptions of the subject and the psychological entity. Femininity and masculinity were postulated as real entities, as natural concomitants of females and males, despite the fact that they were located beyond the corporeal and beyond the purview of the ordinary observer. The very elusiveness of the phenomena came to be taken as evidence of its primal force in everyday life (Lewin, 1984). Hence, it came to be held that the subject not only was unable to make correct self-observations but also was likely to mask his or her real inner mechanisms. Masculinity-femininity scales likewise came to be taken as revealing measures of mental adjustment. In short, to validate and preserve what was a cultural certainty, the uncontestable social fact that males and females were different, psychologists adopted an image of social beings as devious and self-denying and constructed an assessable psychological phenomena with the use of inferences and hypothetical reasoning. In doing so they both elevated their own cognitive powers and legitimated more or less novel methodological procedures (the most notable of these procedures being deception and projective techniques). As evidence of the enhanced acumen attained through their approach, Terman and Miles even demonstrated its superiority over the judgment of otherwise competent psychologists who failed to discern true masculinity and femininity as reliably as the tests did.

In both of these cases psychologists' tactics and solutions involved reflexive practices. While reflexivity takes a variety of forms, here it simply entailed reliance on common-sense conceptions of human nature. In the first instance those common-sense beliefs were initially self-imposed and then ostensibly eradicated, and in the other instance they constituted the grounds for denying the legitimacy of a host of observed actions, including the results of many experiments and the subject's knowledge of themselves. In these (though not in all) cases, the reflexive practices make certain normative interests transparent: interests of control, knowledge/power, and order. These cases exemplify how actions, whether of organizing groups or individual subjects, are intelligible only in context, and how these actions, stripped of context, may appear unproblematic. Psychologists' striving for professional order and cooperation is suspicious only in light of their ordinary conceptions of human nature and their own self-doubts. The continued search for underlying gender entities warrants interrogation only when related to concurrent decisions to proscribe subjective accounts, implement deceptive techniques, and practically disregard contrary evidence. Both cases illustrate a transformation of the image of human nature from the axiomatic premise that the person is the active producer of her or his perceptual world (person constructs reality) to one where the person is a passive receptor or simply reactor to the external world (reality constructs the person) (see Buss, 1978; Flanagan, 1981). The transformation required a yet unappreciated distinction between not just the technical expertise but the cognitive abilities of the observer and the observed.

CONCLUSIONS

The claims for the relevance of history—its lessons and potentially shared framework—has its sober side. One implication of my argument is that excursions into new theory are themselves firmly tied to our social traditions and professional practices. There are similar senses in which historical thinking itself is bound by conceptual habits. A belief in narrative explanations, the persuasiveness of rhetoric, and the moral authority ascribed to historical knowledge are inextricably part of what we do when we do history (i.e., Mink, 1978, Vann, 1976; White, 1980). There probably is no absolute exit. Such constitutive conditions or constraints require continual scrutiny, repeated unpacking and reinterpretation. Yet they do not mitigate our transformative or emancipatory projects. They actually compel us to routinely question our assumed grounding in "scientific method" and "rationality." Historical practices are necessary for gaining a coherent sense of our *attempts* to construct more adequate scientific understandings, and they are indispensible to the actual construction of those understandings.

REFERENCES

Agassi, J. (1963). Towards an historiography of science. *History and Theory,* Beiheft 2.

Angell, J. R. (1920). The organization of research. *Scientific Monthly, 11,* 25–42.

Apfelbaum, E., & Lubek, I. (1976). Resolution vs. revolution? The theory of conflict in question. In L. Strickland, F. Aboud and K. Gergen (Eds.), *Social Psychology in Transition.* New York: Plenum, 71–94.

Atkinson, R. F. (1978). *Knowledge and explanation in history: An introduction to philosophy of history.* Ithaca, NY: Cornell University Press.

Bleier, R. (1984). *Science and gender: A critique of biology and its theories on women.* New York: Pergamon.

Blumenthal, A. A. (1975). A reappraisal of Wilhelm Wundt. *American Psychologist, 30*, 1081–1088.

Boring, E. G. (1929). The psychology of controversy. *Psychological Review. 36*, 97–121.

Boring, E. G. (1950). *A history of experimental psychology* (2nd ed.). New York: Appleton-Century-Crofts.

Bringmann, W. G., & Tweney, R. D. (1980). *Wundt studies*. Toronto: Hogrefe.

Buss, A. R. (1978). The structure of psychological revolutions. *Journal of the History of the Behavioral Sciences, 14*, 57–64.

Buss, A. R. (Ed.). (1979). *Psychology in social context*. New York: Irvington.

Camfield, M. (1969). *Psychologists at war: A history of psychology and the first world war.* Unpublished Ph.D. dissertation, University of Texas at Austin.

Carr, E. H. (1961). *What is history?* New York: Macmillan.

Collingwood, R. G. (1946). *The idea of history.* Oxford: Claredon.

Danziger, K. (1979a). The positivist repudiation of Wundt. *Journal of the History of the Behavioral Sciences, 15*, 205–230.

Danziger, K. (1979b). The social origins of modern psychology. In A. R. Buss (Ed.), *Psychology in social context* pp. 27–46. New York: Irvington.

Dashiell, J. F. (1928). *Fundamentals of objective psychology.* Boston: Houghton Mifflin.

Dijksterhuis, E. J. (1959). The origins of classical mechanics from Aristotle to Newton. In M. Clagett (Ed.), *Critical problems in the history of science.* Madison: University of Wisconsin Press.

Dodge, R. (1926). Excursions in experimental psychology. *Scientific Monthly, 23*, 129–137.

Dollard, J. (1964). Yale's Institute of Human Relations: What was it? *Ventures Magazine of the Yale Graduate School, 3*, 32–40.

Dray, W. (1957). *Laws and explanation in history.* New York: Oxford University Press.

Flanagan, O. J., Jr. (1981). Psychology, progress, and the problem of reflexivity: A study in the epistemological foundations of psychology. *Journal of the History of the Behavioral Sciences, 17*, 375–386.

Furby, L., (1979). Individualistic bias in studies of yours of control. In A. R. Buss (Ed.), *Psychology in social context.* New York: Irvington, 169–190.

Gilbert, G. N., & Mulkay, M. (1984). Experiments are the key: Participants' histories and historians' histories of science. *Isis, 75*, 105–125.

Hale, M., Jr. (1980). *Human science and social order: Hugo Münsterberg and the origins of applied psychology.* Philadelphia: Temple University Press.

Harris, B. (1979). What ever happened to little Albert? *American Psychologist, 34*,

Harris, B. (1984). Give me a dozen healthy infants: John B. Watson's popular advice on childrearing, woman, and the family. In M. Lewin (Ed.), *In the shadow of the past: Psychology portrays the sexes.* New York: Columbia University Press, 126–154.

Hexter, J. (1971). *The history primer.* New York: Basic Books.

Hughes, H. S. (1964). *History as art and as science.* New York: Harper & Row.

Hull, C. L. (1925). Hull Papers. *Seminar Notes*. Sterling Library, Yale University, New Haven, CT.

Hull, C. L. (1935). The conflicting psychologies of learning: A way out. *The Psychological Review, 42*, 491–516.

Hull, C. L. (1952). Clark L. Hull. In E. G. Boring et al. (Eds.), *History of psychology in autobiography*, (Vol. 4, pp. 143–162.). Worcester: Clark University Press.

Humphreys, R. S. (1980). The historian, his documents, and the elementary modes of historical thought. *History and Theory, 19*, 1–20.

Israel, J. (1979). From level of aspiration to dissonance. In A. R. Buss (Ed.), *Psychology in Social Context*. New York: Irvington.

James, W. (1890). *The principles of psychology*. Boston: Henry Holt.

Kelly, B. N. (1981). Inventing psychology's past: E. G. Boring's historiography in relation to the psychology of his time. *The Journal of Mind and Behavior, 2*, 229–241B.

Koch, S. (1975). Language communities, search cells and the psychological studies. *Nebraska Symposium on Motivation, 23*, 477–560.

Leary, D. E. (1980). The intentions and heritage of Descartes and Locke: Toward a recognition of the moral basis of modern psychology. *Journal of General Psychology, 102*, 283–310.

Lewin, M. (1984a). Rather worse than folly? Psychology measures femininity and masculinity, I: From Terman and Miles to the Guilfords. In M. Lewin (Ed.), *In the shadow of the past: Psychology portrays the sexes*. New York: Columbia University Press, 155–174.

Lukes, S. (1982). Relativism in its place. In M. Hollis and S. Lukes (Eds.), *Rationality and relativism* Cambridge, MA: MIT Press, (pp. 261–305).

Meyer, M. (1921). *The psychology of the other-one*. Columbia, MO: Missouri Book.

Mink, L. O. (1965). The autonomy of historical understanding. *History and Theory, 5*, 24–47.

Mink, L. O. (1978). Narrative form as cognitive instrument. In R. H. Canary & H. Kozicki (Eds.), *The writing of history: Literary form and historical understanding*. Madison, WI: University of Wisconsin Press.

Morawski, J. G. (1982a). Assessing psychology's heritage through our neglected utopias. *American Psychologist, 37*, 1082–1095.

Morawski, J. G. (1982b). On thinking about history as social psychology. *Personality and Social Psychology Bulletin, 8*, 393–401.

Morawski, J. G. (1983). Psychology and the shaping of policy, *Berkshire Review, 18*, 92–107.

Morawski, J. G. (1984a). Historiography as methatheoretical text for social psychology. In K. J. Gergen and M. Gergen (Eds.), *Historical social psychology*. Hillsdale, NJ: Erlbaum, 37–60.

Morawski, J. G. (1984b). Not quite new worlds: Psychologists' conceptions of the ideal family in the twenties. In M. Lewin (Ed.), *In the shadow of the past: Psychology portrays the sexes*. New York: Columbia University Press, 97–125.

Morawski, J. G. (1985). The measurement of masculinity and femininity: Engendering categorical realities. *Journal of Personality, 53*, 196–223.

Napoli, D. S. (1980). *The architects of adjustment: The history of the psychological profession in the United States.* Port Washington, NY: National University Publications.

O'Donnell, J. M. (1979a). The "Crisis of Experimentalism" in the twenties: E. G. Boring and his uses of historiography. *American Psychologist, 34,* 289–295.

O'Donnell, J. M. (1979b). *The origins of behaviorism: American psychology 1870–1920.* Unpublished dissertation, University of Pennsylvania.

Passmore, J. (1970). *The perfectibility of man.* London: Duckworth.

Rorty, R. (1979). *Philosophy and the mirror of nature.* Princeton: Princeton University Press.

Rorty, R. (1982). *Consequences of pragmatism.* Minneapolis: University of Minnesota.

Rosenberg, R. L. (1982). *Beyond separate spheres: Intellectual origins of modern feminism.* New Haven: Yale University Press.

Rosenberg, C. E. (1983). American Science: A generation of historical debate. *Isis, 74,* 356–367.

Samelson, F. (1974). History, origin, myth, and ideology: Comte's discovery of social psychology. *Journal for the Theory of Social Behavior, 4,* 217–231.

Samelson, F. (1975). On the science and politics of the IQ. *Social Research, 42,* 467–488.

Samelson, F. (1979). Putting psychology on the map: Ideology and intelligence testing. In A. R. Buss (Ed.), *Psychology in social context.* New York: Irvington.

Samelson, F. (1980). J. B. Watson's little Albert, Cyril Burt's twins, and the need for a critical science. *American Psychologist, 35,* 619–625.

Sampson, E. E. (1981). Cognitive psychology as ideology. *American Psychologist, 35,* 730–743.

Sampson, E. E. (1978). Scientific paradigms and social values: Wanted—a scientific revolution. *Journal of Personality and Social Psychology, 36,* 1332–1343.

Scriven, M. (1966). Causes, connections and conditions in history. In W. H. Dray (Ed.), *Philosophical analysis of history.* New York: Harper & Row, 283–264.

Shapin, S. (1984). Talking history: Reflections on discourse analysis. *Isis, 75,* 125–130.

Smith, L. D. (In press). Metaphor of cognition and behavior in the history of psychology. In D. E. Leary (Ed.), *Metaphors in the History of Psychology.*

Sokal, M. M. (1984). James McKeen Cattell and American psychology in the 1920s. In J. Brozek (Ed.), *Explorations in the history of American psychology.* Lewisburg, PA: Bucknell University Press, 273–326.

Teich, M., & Young, E. M. (Eds.). (1976). *Changing perspectives in the history of science.* London: Heinemann.

Terman, L. M., & Miles, C. C. (1936). *Sex and personality.* New York: McGraw-Hill.

Vann, R. (1976). The rhetoric of social history. *Journal of Social History, 10,* 221–236.

Walsh, W. H. (1966). The limits of scientific history. In W. H. Dray (Ed.), *Philosophical Analysis of History.* New York: Harper & Row, 54–74.

White, H. (1980). The value of narrativity in the representation of reality. *Critical Inquiry, 7,* 5–27.

White, S. H. (1980). Psychology in all sorts of places. In R. A. Kasschau and F. S. Kessell (Eds.), *Psychology and society: In search of symbiosis.* New York: Holt, Rinehart and Winston.

Woodworth, R. S. (1929). Psychology. In W. Gee (Ed.), *Research methods in the social sciences.* New York: Macmillan.

Yerkes, R. (1921). *Human behavior: A plan for aiding the study of the human individual after infancy, to the end of discovering fundamental fact and laws of human nature and behavior.* Paper submitted to Carnegie Committee, p. 7. Sterling Library, Yale University. New Haven, CT.

Chapter 8

Transition, Revolution, and Metapsychology: A Theoretic Proposal for the Developments of Criticism in Social Psychology

Robert A. Boudreau

METAPSYCHOLOGY AND THE STUDY OF CRITICISM: A CONTEXTUAL ACCOUNT

Alongside traditional developments in psychology the faint traces of an emerging concern for what influences psychologists' activities have been appearing for the good part of two decades. Although this remains a turbid development for most of the discipline's constituency, early, singular contributions are starting to draw a larger audience as they multiply and combine to form a more formidable collective. Examples which comprise this growing, critical conscience of the discipline or metapsychology, include the historical (e.g., Baumgardner, 1976; Gergen & Gergen, 1984), philosophical (e.g., Mitroff, 1974; Rychlak, 1981), psychological (e.g., Coan, 1973; 1979; Grover, 1981), and sociological (Buss, 1975; Lindsey, 1978) elements which influence and contribute to psychology's knowledge base. Unfortunately, or fortunately, depending on the conservatism of one's point of view, metapsychology as a distinct field of inquiry presently lacks the poise necessary to make a difference within psychology. In the year of space shuttle launchings and viewings of

Halley's comet, the life form known as metapsychology is still not very well articulated or understood (cf. Brandt, 1982; Giorgi, 1970, 1981; McGuire, 1967; Smith, 1973, 1976).

One field where these developments are particularly transparent is social psychology. This subfield of psychology has been generally defined in North America as the science dealing with human interaction whose goal is the establishment of general laws through systematic observation. The formal beginnings of contemporary social psychology on this continent are usually associated with Triplett's (1898, cf., Haines & Vaughan, 1979) study on the effects of social facilitation and the seminal works of Ross (1908) and McDougall (1908). The core of social psychology, which is still predominantly grounded in the experimental laboratory science approach, consists of a great many research areas or content domains such as interpersonal relations, leadership, conformity, social influence, attitudes, social problems, humor, person perception, and aggression to name but a few (Fisch & Daniel, 1982; Riecken, 1960; Smoke, 1935). Over the last 80 years or so, there has been a vast proliferation of research output and publication based on these traditional themes of study.

Along with this research productivity on core topics has come a recent self-critical appraisal about what social psychologists actually do. The rubric term "crisis state" in social psychology has been used to describe a rather heterogenous collection of explicit critiques which have been levelled at the social psychological research enterprise. Such a notion of experiencing a state of crisis was borrowed from Thomas Kuhn's (1970) description of the structure of shifts or scientific revolutions in existing paradigms (see Berkowitz, cited in Smith, 1972). According to Kuhn, a crisis state is that period which usually precedes a scientific revolution and represents "the common awareness that something has gone wrong [and which supplies] a self-correcting mechanism which ensures that the rigidity of normal science will not forever go unchallenged" (p. 181).

Along with the many, specific labels for this critical approach in social psychology (e.g., the "general malaise," the "crisis of confidence," the "period of anguish," the "crisis of intellectual isolation," "the crisis of spirit," the "identity crisis," the "paradigmatic crisis," and the "discipline in transition"), there also have been many reasons and solutions offered to overcome the difficulties identified. Some of the reasons underlying the criticisms include: (a) the problematic use of the experiment as a means to study human functioning: (b) that theories do not explain enough and are not addressing real-world issues; (c) that our results are not generalizable because of subject and experimenter biases; (d) the concern for ethics or lack thereof in doing human research; (e) the absence of identified laws of human interaction; (f) the external pressures exerted on the researchers; and (g) the fallacious attempts to explain the dynamic functioning of human beings using only static models and techniques. Solutions to the seemingly endless array of problems are also plentiful and range from suggestions to hone the existing tools, through to a radical reorientation of how to approach the study of social interaction. Still others have phrased the question "So what?" and have either argued no crisis exists or if it does, the best way to overcome it is to continue business as usual because ours is just a young science suffering growing pains (see the early, significant efforts by Elms, 1975; Gergen, 1973; Katz, 1967; McGuire, 1973; Silverman, 1977; Triandis, 1975).

Beyond these individualized critiques, the concerns for crisis have been felt in the subdiscipline and in psychology overall. Support for this statement derives from the general commentaries on the critical literature in social psychology (e.g., Gergen, 1982; Hendrick, 1977), isolated outcries in other branches within psychology (e.g., Cronbach, 1975; Cummings, 1981; Kahneman,1968; Neisser, 1976; Payne, 1982), and selected interdisciplinary descriptions and comparisons of shared problematic issues (e.g., Boutilier, Roed, & Svendsen, 1980; House, 1977; Kuhn, 1970). To obtain a fuller appreciation of the varied forms of critical appraisal possible, however, one needs to sidestep the specific maladies or critical exemplars from the various disciplines and focus on the explicit treatment of the concept or process of criticism itself.

Psychology and the Critical Process

Since its inception, the discipline of psychology has continued to broaden its boundaries of concern as is evidenced by the plethora of subdisciplines. Moreover, central to this growth of psychological knowledge, there has been unappreciated development in the awareness and sophistication of the critical process for those involved in the discipline. For purposes of the present discussion, criticism is generally defined as the process by which individuals or groups analyze and evaluate phenomena with knowledge and propriety to better understand and/or effect change (Merriam-Webster, 1975). Such a definition for the psychological domain necessarily includes both the German meaning "to discern" and the English intention "to find fault with" (see Brandt, 1982). It is analogous with what Karl Popper (1963) describes as the "critical attitude"— "the readiness to change [laws and schemata]; to test them; to refute them; to falsify them, if possible" (p. 50).

> Criticism of our conjectures [our anticipations, guesses, or tentative solutions to our problems] is of decisive importance; by bringing out our mistakes it makes us understand the difficulties of the problem which we are trying to solve (p. vii).

According to Magee (1975), who has written a biography of Popper:

> he [Popper] . . . believes that only through criticism can knowledge advance. This leads him to put forward most of his important ideas in the course of criticizing other peoples: For instance most of his arguments in *The open society and its enemies* are advanced in criticism of Plato and Marx (p. 14).

The significance of critique as the fundamental concept for the advancement of knowledge is further underscored in the debate contrasting the views of Popper (1963) and Kuhn (1970) on the role of criticism in its revolutionary growth (see Lakatos & Musgrave, 1974, for a complete treatment of their differences). Briefly, for Popper (1963) criticism forms the heart of the scientific enterprise and is a necessary, ongoing process whereas Kuhn (1974) states that it is "the abandonment of critical discourse that marks the transition to a science" (p. 6); criticism will reoccur only at moments of subsequent "crises." Notwithstanding the import ascribed the critical process by these and other philosophers and historians of science as well as it representing the very cornerstone for what we choose to do and profess to know in science and psychology, there have been a dearth of attempts to examine the role of criticism in psychology.

The examples of critique which appear in the crisis literatures of psychology highlighted earlier, have tended not to deal with the construct of criticism explicitly. That is to say, the majority of social psychologists and psychologists in other fields offer their critiques and solutions without any attempt to reflect on the critical process they themselves are involved in. The few papers that do refer to criticism in psychology all seem overly circumscribed in either intent or perspective.

For one, Tedeschi, Gaes, Riordan, and Quigley-Fernandez (1981) assessed the character of research papers published in different social psychology journals. They reported that only 3.6% or 15 of all the papers reviewed for the years 1976 and 1977 in the *Journal of Personality and Social Psychology (JPSP)* and the *Journal of Experimental Social Psychology* fit the category of criticism, defined as the "examination of the methods or conclusions of prior studies or . . . a reply to such an examination" (p. 163). This finding was compared with the articles published in *JPSP* in 1967 where no "criticism" articles were found. The authors concluded such a change:

> indicates an increased concern about methodological and statistical problems associated with laboratory research. Of course, changes in editors over the comparison years may also be a relevant factor (Tedeschi et al., 1981, p. 170).

A second example of this explicit analysis of criticism in psychology involves a series of efforts which taken collectively, offer a taxonomy for the types of criticism found in the crisis literature of social psychology. Specifically, Duck (1980) distinguishes between attacks on method and the crises of theory, utility, intellectual isolation, practice, and identity. Minton (1984), Pepitone (1976) and Rosnow (1981) all refer to methodological, ethical, and metatheoretical categories of criticism, while Parker (1979) in his doctoral dissertation identifies critics of the empiricist and critical positivist persuasions. According to this last author, "neopositivism" as the presently dominant tradition of science encompassing most of psychology, defines the boundary limits of current criticisms. In order for this crisis to be resolved, though, the critical analysis must reach to the level of fundamental neopositivist assumptions. Philip Wexler (1983) in a recent effort distinguishes between a critique of knowledge and the internal critique of social psychology. For him the former refers to a "basic kind of remembering, a reminder that theories are socially, historically, and humanly constructed" while the latter refers to actually two sub-forms of groups of criticisms: Conventional critique which has arisen from the center of social psychology and received the most attention. It "is mounted by prestigious researchers in social psychology and limits itself to methodological and conceptual repair" (p. 13); and a dissenting critique which developed on the periphery of the subdiscipline and "displays a commitment to a radical alternative in social psychology, but lacks the theoretical base which could produce such an alternative" (p. 3).

Finally, a third set of exemplars characteristic of this increased awareness in the use of criticism involves the contributions by Manicas and Secord (1983) and Buss (1978, 1979b). In two related papers, Buss (1978) initially offers a "conceptual" critique of the cause-reason distinction used by attribution theorists which he follows up with a discussion of forms of "metascience" critique (i.e., empiricism, hermeneutics, and hermeneutic-dialectic) and how these may also apply to the problems of attribution theory. Manicas and Secord (1983) extend this discussion of the types of criticism with their offer for a new philosophy of science for psychology. They highlight the "Kuhnian or paradigmatic" and the "realist" critiques as alternatives to the "standard view" of science.

So far the chapter has featured selected discussions of metapsychology, the crisis literature of social psychology, and explicit treatments of criticism in the discipline. The next section of the paper represents a working synthesis of all these literatures insofar as they contribute to the proposed formulation of a theory of critical development for the subdiscipline of social psychology. Unlike any of the contributions previously reviewed, the remainder of this work offers a stylized and systematic analysis of the forms and development of critical attitudes derived mostly from the social psychology literature. Now we can turn to the details of this theoretical proposition.

TOWARDS A THEORY OF CRITICISM FOR SOCIAL PSYCHOLOGY

Structure Considerations

Basically, all of the critical efforts referred to above can be grouped into one of the three possible forms: material, method, or meta. This tripartite classification is offered as a simplified introduction to the eight forms of criticism which will be discussed shortly. The actual terms used to designate these three forms of criticisms were derived from those already available in the published literature (i.e., Duck, 1980; Kuhn, 1977; Pepitone, 1976).

Material criticism refers to a view dedicated solely to the advancement of content domains and the existing knowledge base of the subdiscipline. In the case of social psychology, material forms of criticism involve the study of representative topics like attitudes, emotion, intraversion-extraversion, leadership, marriage, and prejudice (Smoke, 1935). *Methodological criticism* reflects a great many of the explicit concerns that have been levelled at the hypothetico-deductive laboratory venue—the sine qua non of experimental social psychology. Under this rubric of methodological criticism, one might include the critical commentaries on artifacts, the "applied" alternative, and ethics of research (e.g., Adair, 1973; Kelman, 1967; Ring, 1967). *Metatheory/metamethod (Meta) criticism* generally involves examinations of the process of discovering social psychological knowledge. This form of criticism narrowly refers to the explicit discussions of the driving force behind the choice of philosophies and methodologies by members in the subdiscipline. It includes both calls for support as well as abandonment of the status quo (e.g., Buss, 1975; Harré & Secord, 1972; Schlenker, 1974).

For purposes of the present approach, the three types of material, method, and meta criticism have been further translated into eight distinct forms:

- material—variable/theory and empirical/conceptual;
- method—method/artifact, ethical, and paradigmatic;
- metatheory/metamethod (I, II, & III)—positivist-empiricist, hermeneutic-ethogenic-historical-interdependence, and critical-dialectical.

A brief description of each of these explicit forms of criticism with exemplars will be given, beginning with the two forms of material critique.

Variable/Theory.   This first type of criticism represents discussion of the appropriate choice of variables and/or theoretical explanations of interest. Variable/theory criticism typically assumes the form of a standard experimental social psychology study whereby certain constructs, variables, or theoretical positions are examined using information from a sample of respondents. Beginning with Triplett's (1898, cited in Hendrick, 1977) study of the effects of social facilitation there have been vast numbers of variables and theories examined and proposed in social psychology. Two of the more recent, traditional themes of study within the subdiscipline include the work in leadership effectiveness and training (e.g., Fiedler, 1967, 1978) as well as stress and burnout (e.g., Cooper & Payne, 1978, 1980; Lazarus & Folkman, 1984; Paine, 1982).

Empirical/Conceptual.   In contrast to variable/theory, the second form of material criticism, empirical/conceptual, refers to more detailed discussions or updates as to whether research is following the appropriate empirical and/or conceptual routes given existing notions and available data; such attempts may also offer alternatives to the existing research trends. These critical reviews can be for specific, popular concepts or theories in social psychology, or they can involve a form of overview of research/publication trends in the entire discipline for a certain period of time. Exemplars for this form of criticism include published reviews of specific content domains such as cognitive dissonance (Chapanis & Chapanis, 1964), and the survey by Fisch and Daniel (1982) of research and publication trends in experimental social psychology for the period 1971-1980. As well, *meta-analysis* reports for cumulating research findings across studies devoted to a particular content topic (see Hunter, Schmidt, & Jackson, 1982) as well as many of the narrative reviews contained in social psychology serials (e.g., *Annual Review of Psychology, The Handbook of Social Psychology, Advances in Experimental Social Psychology,* and *Review of Personality and Social Psychology*) reflect the empirical/conceptual form of criticism.

Method/Artifact. The first of three forms of methodological criticism in this approach is designated method/artifact. It is characteristic of those treatments aimed at identifying subject and experimenter artifacts which may affect the methods used and data collected in social psychological experiments. Examples of some of the artifactual issues identified in the literature include evaluation apprehension (Rosenberg, 1965), the deutero-problem (Riecken, 1962), demand characteristics (Orne, 1962), and experimenter expectancy (Rosenthal, 1963; see also Rosenzweig, 1933 for an earlier discussion of some of these problems).

Ethical. This next form of criticism is concerned with the effects such factors as deception, threat in the experimental setting, and the degree of confidentiality of responding have on measured outcomes. The rights of subjects are often juxtaposed with the potential scientific gains of research. Probably the most well-known instance of this form of criticism is the Baumrind-Milgram (1964) exchange on the behavioral studies of obedience.

Paradigmatic. The third type of methodological criticism is framed around the struggle for relevancy of social psychological research as it applies to the human condition. Specific arguments center on the decision between alternatives such as an applied or theoretical social psychology, a field versus lab approach, correlational as opposed to manipulational research, or a pure versus applied science orientation. Explicit critiques of this form involve not only a choice of research methods and/or locales, but also include the issues of usefulness, external and ecological validity, and generalizability of the research findings. Kenneth Ring's (1967) discussion of fulfilling the Lewinian vision for social psychology is the prototype for paradigmatic critique.

The final three forms of criticism to be detailed fall under the general heading of epistemological or metatheory/metamethod. Presently, there still exists a good deal of debate concerning the number of distinct forms available or even possible (i.e., 2 to 5). As has been documented elsewhere however (Boudreau, 1985), this distillation to three forms of meta critique seems to represent a fair reading and synthesis of overlapping epistemic themes which have recently appeared in the crisis writings of social psychology.

Metatheory/Metamethod (Meta) I. To begin, criticism of the metatheory/metamethod I or dominant variety usually takes the form of positivist/empiricist, abstract, and valueless approach to social psychological knowledge. A characteristic feature of this type of criticism is that some underlying assumption(s) of the positivist/empiricist philosophy of science and/or the hypothetico-deductive model are made explicit and defended. Arguments in support of metatheory/metamethod I criticism include psychology is a science along with pleas to strive for greater methodological and theoretical pluralism. McGuire (1973) and Schlenker's (1974) published contributions are two examples of Meta I criticism.

Metatheory/Metamethod (Meta) II. The second form of epistemological criticism represents a hybrid of the hermeneutic tradition (e.g., Buss, 1979b; Hendrick, 1977), the study of ethogenics (Harré & Secord, 1972), the historical thesis posited by Gergen (1973), and the interdependence position adopted by Pepitone (1976, 1981). Here the emphasis is on understanding, reason, and interpretation in order to achieve valid intersubjective meaning. All the examples for a Meta II alternative (e.g., Cronbach, 1975; Thorngate, 1975) share a common call for the study of the subdiscipline of social psychology to become more contextual, ideographic, and social in their rejection (weak or strong) of positivist-empiricist ideals and traditional methodology.

Metatheory/Metamethod (Meta) III. The eighth and final form of Meta criticism is referred to as the critical-dialectical form (for a more complete review see Buss, 1979a, 1979b, Georgoudi, 1983, & Gergen, 1982). The emphasis of Meta III critiques is on the concrete, value-laden basis of knowledge. Guiding assumptions of the positivist-empiricist approach are rejected while the study of actions, change, conflict, and contradiction replace the focus on equilibrium and stability. Relevant exemplars for critical-dialectical metatheory/metamethod include: calls for a psychology and sociology of psychological knowledge (e.g., Buss, 1975; Coan, 1973); critical discussions on the history and future of the subdiscipline itself (e.g., Baumgardner, 1976; Sampson, 1977, 1978), as well as social psychological analysis of power and aggression in social psychology (Lubek, 1976, 1979) and the philosophy of science (Mitroff, 1979).

This concludes the treatment of *structure* considerations and the eight forms of criticism identified for this approach. The purpose up to this point in the discussion has been to provide the reader with a substantive appreciation of the background literature leading up to this focus on criticism. But the presentation of the actual, theoretic proposal for critical use remains half-done. To complete the account we ask the reader to consider the *process* of critical use; more specifically, this includes the two most salient and distinguishable properties for the proposed theory of critical use in social psychology—development and spirality.

The Process of Development

Based primarily on the aforementioned review, a diagrammatic representation for a proposed *spiral* theory of criticism development is given in Figure 1. The eight types of criticism are ordered in the sequence of material, method, and then meta forms. The shaded diagonal signifies the hypothesized course of "normal" development found in social psychology while the empty cells above or below the diagonal reflect possible positions ahead or lagging behind normal development, respectively (derived in part from Buss, 1979b, chap. 5).

It should be emphasized that the theoretical description detailed here, is more than just a classificatory scheme inasmuch as it reflects real, natural

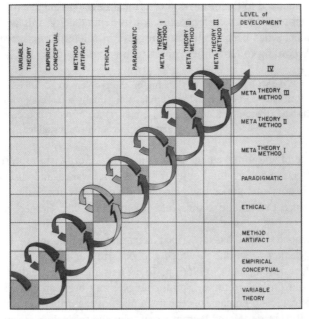

FIGURE 1.   Spiral theory of critical development in social psychology. Ordinate: levels of development; abscissa: hypothesized temporal sequence; entries: stages of critique; shaded diagonal; hypothesized course of normal development.

changes, a kind of evolution in the critical thinking process within the subdiscipline of social psychology. The forms and order of criticism reflect actual historical change and focus in the writing, thinking, and acceptance of ideas by social psychologists since they began the business of studying human social interaction (see Rosnow, 1981 for a comparison).

The Process of Spirality

In addition to the process of development in critical use, a second process consideration for the proposed theory of critical use is the notion of spirality. With any structural account like this, the question of movement and how this occurs must also be addressed. Unlike many of the developmental-type theories available (e.g., Erikson, Greiner, Piaget), the present view favors the process heuristic of helical or spiral change versus a lineal or cyclical process for describing movement across the various forms of criticism. Such an emphasis seems most appropriate given the limitations with these latter types of processes. The focus on spiral change also fits most closely with the kinds of dynamic properties envisioned for critical development within the present account. Not very much has been written about the implications of these kinds of process differences. However, a few selected examples from the psychological literature have been identified by this author. Three of these which are relevant and can be extended to the discussion of critical development are offered here:

1. An emphasis on recurrence and not just spontaneity; this notion of recurrent tendency has been applied to progress in scientific and psychological research. According to Crutchfield and Krech (cited in Adair, 1973):

> we seem to detect a tendency for thinking on the problem to go full circle. But this usually turns out to be not really a circle, not simply a regression to an earlier stage. Instead, there is a kind of *spiral,* a recurrence of older conception but at a more advanced level of complexity and sophistication (italics added, p. 2).

Any type of spiral movement across the forms of criticism represents more than just a return to origin. For example, the relevance and discussions of topics like history and ethics have changed dramatically for many social psychologists since the middle sixties (cf., Baumrind 1985; Gergen & Gergen, 1984).

2. Raymond Cattel has described scientific research as an "*inductive-hypothetico-deductive* spiral, in which a good array of alternative hypotheses are in constant development" (1966, p. 18). The same can be said about developments in our critical attitudes. Spiral change either between or within any of the forms of criticism emphasizes the dynamism of the critical process.

3. Finally, there is Heinz Werner's *psychogenetic principle of spirality* as it applies to development at various levels of functioning. With the attainment of higher levels, lower levels are not lost; they are subordinated to more advanced

levels of functioning but may come to the fore under special circumstances (Werner, 1948; Werner & Kaplan, 1963). Similarly, it may be possible to function in a number of critical forms simultaneously. Individuals or disciplines could conceivably operate in one or more forms which still differ from the types of critique they employ in the majority of their published communications.

To summarize, in a "conservative" sense what you have before you is a means for viewing the types of criticism that have evolved in social psychology. In another more "radical" sense, (see Cummings, 1981, for a use of these terms) the approach may be seen as both an explanation and means for better understanding the emergence of metapsychological inquiry and the future development of psychology proper. No doubt the reader's preference of alternatives will depend in large part on the type of criticism (i.e., material, method, or meta) each one favors.

At this juncture a caution must be offered. Even though this proposed theory stands as an inaugural effort to better understand the critical process and how the subdiscipline progressed, it is far from being a completely adequate description. Indeed, many more questions than answers remain which cannot be addressed in the space of this paper. A sampler of these queries might include: Where do individual social psychologists or other scientists fit in terms of "normal" development and this theory? What are the alternative forms of criticism not described here? Are there any fixed entry points or directions of movement in critical development? How does time, ability, and editorial policy limit the use of the different types of critique identified? Can subdisciplines in psychology be distinguished in terms of levels of critique achieved, frequency of use, and differences between preferred and actual forms of criticism used? And in what ways can this theory of critical development be applied to other social and natural science disciplines?

Essentially, this theoretic approach offers a jumping-off point to gain further self- and disciplinary awareness into a process we all use often but seldom take the time to reflect on. In the same way that Mitroff and Mason (1983) describe the fundamental purpose of Carl Jung's typology, this spiral theory of critical development attempts:

> to give people a framework and a series of concepts, a vocabulary, for, first of all, recognizing their differences and, second, working through them . . . The [theory] is not meant to imply rigid classification or permanent fixity for all of one's life (Mitroff & Mason, 1983, p. 154).

Applications from This Study of Criticism

Notwithstanding the relative newness for the proposal of a spiral theory in critical development, a number of applications are suggested.

In an attempt to investigate further the individual-subdiscipline relationships, a biographical analysis of the use(s) of criticism appears warranted. It would be very informative to establish how individual use of criticism (e.g., Buss, Gergen, & McGuire are three potential candidates for study) corresponds and differs from the disciplinary developments traced in the present study. Such an idiographic focus would also allow for greater insight into the actual *process* of critical use.

Description of the various forms of criticism could also be employed as a heuristic device to educate as well as examine those directly involved with the publication process in social psychology. Establishing whether there is a publication imbalance in the material, method, and meta forms of criticism, may be just the kind of information necessary for initiating any editorial changes and the acceptance criteria for publication in social psychology journals.

A third application from this present work might involve a sociometric study of critical use along the lines of the psychosocial which have recently appeared in the literature (e.g., Kimble, 1984; Krasner & Houts, 1984; Nederof & Zwier, 1983). In the first instance this would involve just social psychologists, but it could be easily extended to other subdisciplines and even include a cross section of psychologists from the entire discipline.

In an attempt to further examine the developmental nature of critical use, other established fields within psychology (e.g., I/O or comparative psychology) also need to be closely studied. For example, in research just completed, the present author (Boudreau, 1985) used the theory to examine critical development in a selected occupational stress and burnout literature. The most significant finding was the overwhelming use of material and variable/theory forms of criticism for this relatively new and evolving field of study.

Only when information from all these forms is obtained will the real benefits be felt (e.g., increased awareness and maybe even an acceleration in the developmental process of critical use) and the value—the generative capacity (Gergen, 1978) of the study of criticism for metapsychological inquiry and the general discipline—be fully realized. As Goldstein (1980) has noted:

> the more sensitive we are to what we, as social psychologists, do and why we do it, the more likely it is that we will make contributions to both the knowledge of social behavior and the solutions to social problems" (p. 35).

CONCLUSIONS

This chapter represents a proposal for a spiral theory of criticism in social psychology. While such an effort is necessary and timely vis-á-vis its attempt to consolidate the many divergent opinions and literatures, it is still overly restrictive and untested. The theory is best viewed as a benchmark from which social psychologists can take reference. Moreover, this focus on improving self- and disciplinary-awareness through the description of critical use in social psychology is contained within a larger proposition—the development and acceptance of the new discipline of metapsychology (cf., Gergen, 1985; Rappoport, 1984).

REFERENCES

Adair, J. G. (1973). *The human subject: The social psychology of the psychological experiment.* Boston: Little, Brown.

Baumgardner, S. R., (1976). Critical history and social psychology's "crisis." *Personality and Social Psychology Bulletin, 2*(4), 460–465.

Baumrind, D. (1964). Some thoughts on ethics of research: After reading Milgram's "Behavioral study of obedience." *American Psychologist, 19,* 421–423.

Baumrind, D. (1985). Research using intentional deception: Ethical issues revisited. *American Psychologist, 40*(2), 165–174.

Boudreau, R. A. (1985). *Transition, revolution, and metapsychology: A theoretical proposal for the developments of criticism in social psychology with an application to a selected occupational stress and burnout literature.* Unpublished doctoral dissertation, The University of Calgary, Alberta.

Boutilier, R. G., Roed, J. C., & Svendsen, A. C. (1980). Crises in the two social psychologies: A critical comparison. *Social Psychology Quarterly, 43*(1), 5–17.

Brandt, L. W. (1982). *Psychologists caught: A psycho-logic of psychology.* Toronto: University of Toronto Press.

Buss, A. R. (1975). The emerging field of the sociology of psychological knowledge. *American Psychologist, 30*(10), 988–1002.

Buss, A. R. (1978). Causes and reasons in attribution theory: A conceptual critique. *Journal of Personality and Social Psychology, 36*(11), 1311–1321.

Buss, A. R. (Ed.). (1979a). *Psychology in social context.* New York: Irvington.

Buss. A. R. (1979b). *A dialectical psychology.* New York: Irvington.

Cattell, R. B. (1966). Psychological theory and scientific method. In R. B. Cattell (Ed.), *Handbook of multivariate experimental psychology* (pp. 1-18). Chicago: Rand McNally.

Chapanis, N. P., & Chapanis, A. (1964). Cognitive dissonance: Five years later. *Psychological Bulletin, 61*(1), 1–21.

Coan, R. W. (1973). Toward a psychological interpretation of psychology. *Journal of the History of the Behavioral Sciences, 9*(4), 313–327.

Coan, R. W. (1979). *Psychologists: Personal and theoretical pathways.* New York: Irvington.

Cooper, C. L., & Payne, R. (Eds.). (1978). *Stress at work.* Chichester: John Wiley & Sons.

Cooper, C. L., & Payne, R. (Eds.). (1980). *Current concerns in occupational stress.* Chichester: John Wiley & Sons.

Cronbach, L. J. (1975). Beyond the two disciplines of scientific psychology. *American Psychologist, 30*(2), 116–127.

Cummings, L. L. (1981). Organizational behavior in the 1980s. *Decision Sciences, 12,* 365–377.

Duck, S. (1980). Taking the past to heart: One of the futures of social psychology? In R. Gilmour & S. Duck (Eds.), *The development of social psychology* (pp. 211–237). London: Academic Press.

Elms, A. C. (1975). The crisis of confidence in social psychology. *American Psychologist, 30*(10), 967-976.

Fiedler, F. E. (1967). *A theory of leadership effectiveness.* New York: McGraw-Hill.

Fiedler, F. E. (1978). The contingency model and the dynamics of the leadership process. In L. Berkowitz (Ed.), *Advances in Experimental Social Psychology* (Vol. 11, pp. 59-112). New York: Academic Press.

Fisch, R., & Daniel, H. D.(1982). Research and publication trends in experimental social psychology: 1971-1980—a thematic analysis of *The Journal of Experimental Social Psychology,* the *European Journal of Social Psychology* and *The Zeitschrift Fur Social Psychologie. European Journal of Social Psychology, 12*(4), 395-412.

Georgoudi, M. (1983). Modern dialectics in social psychology: A reappraisal. *European Journal of Social Psychology, 13,* 77-93.

Gergen, K. J. (1973). Social psychology as history. *Journal of Personality and Social Psychology, 26*(2), 309-320.

Gergen, K. J. (1978). Toward generative theory. *Journal of Personality and Social Psychology, 36*(11), 1344-1360.

Gergen, K. J. (1982). *Toward transformation in social knowledge.* New York: Springer-Verlag.

Gergen, K. J. (1984). An introduction to historical social psychology. In K. J. Gergen, & M. M. Gergen (Eds.), *Historical social psychology* (pp. 3-36). Hillsdale, NJ: Erlbaum.

Gergen, K. J. (1985). The social constructionist movement in modern psychology. *American Psychologist, 40*(3), 266-275.

Gergen, K. J., & Gergen, M. M. (Eds.). (1984). *Historical social psychology.* Hillsdale, NJ: Erlbaum.

Giorgi, A. P. (1970). *Psychology as a human science: A phenomenologically based approach.* New York: Harper & Row.

Giorgi, A. P. (1981). Humanistic psychology and metapsychology. In J. R. Royce & L. P. Mos (Eds.), *Humanistic psychology: Concepts and criticisms* (pp. 19-47). New York: Plenum.

Goldstein, J. H. (1980). *Social psychology.* New York: Academic Press.

Grover, S. C. (1981). *Toward a psychology of the scientist: Implications of psychological research for contemporary philosophy of science.* Washington: University Press of America.

Haines, H. & Vaughan, G. M. (1979). Was 1898 a "great date" in the history of experimental social psychology? *Journal of the History of the Behavioral Sciences, 15,* 323-332.

Harré, R., & Secord, P. (1972). *The explanation of social behavior.* Blackwell: Oxford.

Hendrick, C. (1977). Social psychology as an experimental science. In C. Hendrick (Ed.), *Perspectives on social psychology* (pp. 1-74). Hillsdale, NJ: Erlbaum.

House, J. S. (1977). The three faces of social psychology. *Sociometry, 40*(2), 161-177.

Hunter, J. E., Schmidt, F. L., & Jackson, G. B. (1982). *Meta-analysis: Cumulating research findings across studies.* Beverly Hills, CA: Sage.

Kahneman, D. (1968). Method, findings, and theory in studies of visual masking. *Psychological Bulletin, 70,* 404-425.

Katz, D. (1967). Editorial. *Journal of Personality and Social Psychology, 7*(4), 341–344.

Kelman, H. C. (1967). Human use of human subjects: The problem of deception in social psychological experiments. *Psychological Bulletin, 67*(1), 1–11.

Kimble, G. A. (1984). Psychology's two cultures. *American Psychologist, 39*(8), 833–839.

Krasner, L., & Houts, A. C. (1984). A study of the "value" systems of behavioral scientists. *American Psychologists, 39*(8), 840–850.

Kuhn, T. S. (1970). *The structure of scientific revolutions* (2nd ed. enlarged). Chicago: The University of Chicago Press.

Kuhn, T. S. (1974). Logic of discovery or psychology of research? In I. Lakatos & A. Musgrave (Eds.), *Criticism and the growth of knowledge* (corrected edition) (pp. 1–23). London: Cambridge University Press.

Kuhn, T. S. (1977). *The essential tension: Selected studies in scientific tradition and change.* Chicago: The University of Chicago Press.

Lakatos, I., & Musgrave, A. (Eds.). (1974). *Criticism and the growth of knowledge* (corrected edition). London: Cambridge University Press.

Lazarus, R. S., & Folkman, S. (1984). *Stress, appraisal, and coping.* New York: Springer.

Lindsey, D. (1978). *The scientific publication system in social science.* San Francisco: Jossey-Bass.

Lubek, I. (1976). Some tentative suggestions for analyzing and neutralizing power structure in social psychology. In L. H. Strickland, F. E. Aboud, & K. J. Gergen (Eds.), *Social psychology in transition* (pp. 317–333). New York: Plenum.

Lubek, I. (1979). A brief social psychological analysis of research on aggression in social psychology. In A. R. Buss (Ed.), *Psychology in social context,* (pp. 259–306). New York: Irvington.

Magee, B. (1975). *Popper* (4th impression with corrections). Great Britain: William Collins Sons.

Manicas, P. T., & Secord, P. F. (1983). Implications for psychology of the new philosophy of science. *American Psychologist, 38*(4), 399–413.

McDougall, W. (1908). *An introduction to social psychology.* London: Methuen.

McGuire, W. J. (1967). Some impending reorientations in social psychology: Some thoughts provoked by Kenneth Ring. *Journal of Experimental Social Psychology, 3,* 124–139.

McGuire, W. J. (1973). The yin and yang of progress in social psychology: Seven koan. *Journal of Personality and Social Psychology 26*(3), 446–456.

Merriam-Webster. (1975). *Webster's new collegiate dictionary.* Toronto: Thomas Allen & Son.

Milgram, S. (1964). Issues in the study of obedience. *American Psychologist, 19,* 848–852.

Minton, H. L. (1984). J. F. Brown's social psychology of the 1930s: A historical antecedent to the contemporary crisis in social psychology. *Personality and Social Psychology Bulletin, 10*(1), 31–42.

Mitroff, I. I. (1974). *The subjective side of science: A philosophical inquiry into the psychology of the Apollo moon scientists.* New York: Elsevier.

Mitroff, I. I. (1979). Eminent psychologists and selenologists: A comparative study of their images of science. In A. R. Buss (Ed.), *Psychology in social context* (pp. 307–328). New York: Irvington.

Mitroff, I. I., & Mason, R. O. (1983). Stakeholders of executive decision making. In S. Srivastva (Ed.), *The executive mind* (pp. 144–168). San Francisco: Josey-Bass.

Nederof, A. J., & Zwier, A. G. (1983). The "crisis" in social psychology, an empirical approach. *European Journal of Social Psychology, 13,* 255–280.

Neisser, U. (1976). *Cognition and reality: Principles and implications of cognitive psychology.* San Francisco: W. H. Freeman.

Orne, M. T. (1962). On the social psychology of the psychological experiment: With particular reference to demand characteristics and their implications. *American Psychologist, 17,* 776–783.

Parker, L. (1979). *Existentialism, neopositivism, and the crisis in social psychology.* Unpublished doctoral dissertation, Cornell University.

Paine, W. S. (Ed.). (1982) *Job stress and burnout: Research, theory, and intervention perspectives.* Beverly Hills, CA: Sage.

Payne, R. (1982). The nature of knowledge and organizational psychology. In N. Nicholson & T. D. Wall (Eds.), *The theory and practice of organizational psychology* (pp. 37–67). London: Academic Press.

Pepitone, A. (1976). Toward a normative and comparative biocultural social psychology. *Journal of Personality and Social Psychology, 34*(4), 641–653.

Pepitone, A. (1981). Lessons from the history of social psychology. *American Psychologist, 36*(9), 972–985.

Popper, K. R. (1963). *Conjectures and refutations: The growth of scientific knowledge.* New York: Harper & Row.

Rappoport, L. (1984). Dialectical analysis and psychosocial epistemology. In K. J. Gergen & M. M. Gergen (Eds.), *Historical social psychology,* (pp. 103–124). Hillsdale, NJ: Erlbaum.

Riecken, H. W. (1960). Social psychology. *Annual Review of Psychology, 11,* 479–510.

Riecken, H. W. (1962). A program for research on experiments in social psychology. In N. F. Washburne (Ed.), *Decisions, Values and Groups* (pp. 25–41). New York: Pergamon.

Ring, K. (1967). Experimental social psychology: Some sober questions about some frivolous values. *Journal of Experimental Social Psychology, 3,* 113–123.

Rosenberg, M. J. (1965). When dissonance fails: On eliminating evaluation apprehension from attitude measurement. *Journal of Personality and Social Psychology, 1*(1), 28–42.

Rosenthal, R. (1963). On the social psychology of the psychological experiment: The experimenter's hypothesis as unintended determinant of experimental results. *American Scientist, 51,* 268–283.

Rosenzweig, S. (1933). The experimental situation as a psychological problem. *Psychological Review, 40,* 337–354.

Rosnow, R. L. (1978). The prophetic vision of Giambattista Vico: Implications for the state of social psychological theory. *Journal of Personality and Social Psychology, 36*(11), 1322–1331.

Rosnow, R. L. (1981). *Paradigms in transition: The methodology of social inquiry.* New York: Oxford University Press.

Ross, E. A. (1908). *Social psychology.* New York: Macmillan.

Rychlak, J. F. (1981). *A philosophy of science for personality theory* (2nd ed). Malabar, FL: Krieger.

Sampson, E. E. (1977). Psychology and the American ideal. *Journal of Personality and Social Psychology, 35*(11), 767–782.

Sampson, E. E. (1978). Scientific paradigms and social values: Wanted. . . . a scientific revolution. *Journal of Personality and Social Psychology, 36*(11), 1332–1343.

Schlenker, B. R. (1974). Social psychology and science. *Journal of Personality and Social Psychology, 29,* 1–15.

Silverman, I. (1977). Why social psychology fails. *Canadian Psychological Review, 18*(4), 353–358.

Smith, M. B. (1972). Is experimental social psychology advancing? (L. Berkowitz, personal communication to Smith, September 14, 1970). *Journal of Experimental Social Psychology, 8,* 86–96.

Smith, M. B. (1973). Is psychology relevant to new priorities? *American Psychologist, 28*(6), 463–471.

Smith, M. B. (1976). Some perspectives on ethical/political issues in social science research. *Personality and Social Psychology Bulletin, 2*(4), 445–453.

Smoke, K. L. (1935). The present status of social psychology in America. *Psychological Review, 42,* 537–543.

Tedeschi, J. T., Gaes, G. G., Riordan, C. & Quigley-Fernandez, B. (1981). Social psychology and cumulative knowledge. *Personality and Social Psychology Bulletin, 7*(1), 161–1782.

Thorngate, W. (1975). Process invariance: Another red herring. *Personality and Social Psychology Bulletin, 1*(3), 485–488.

Triandis, H. C. (1975). Social psychology and cultural analysis. *Journal for the Theory of Social Behavior, 5*(1), 81–106.

Werner, H. (1948). *Comparative psychology of mental development.* New York: Science Editions.

Werner, H. & Kaplan, B. (1963). *Symbol formation: An organismic-developmental approach to language and the expression of thought.* New York: John Wiley & Sons.

Wexler, P. (1983). *Critical social psychology.* Boston: Routledge & Kegan Paul.

Chapter 9

Hearing the "Un-Saids:" An Essay on the Role of Folkloristics in Metapsychology

T. B. Rogers

INTRODUCTION

One of the central theses that is woven throughout this volume is that certain unstated assumptions have pervasive effects on how we approach the discipline of psychology. Whether thought of as ideology or world view, it seems clear that there are a number of "un-saids" that shape the way in which analyses, values and methodologies are embraced within psychology. The goal of this essay is to introduce a methodology that will help render visible these typically invisible value statements. By so doing, it will be possible to identify certain weaknesses within contemporary psychology, and perhaps, with some luck, suggest alternatives to prevailing approaches to the discipline.

In order to document "un-said" assumptions it is necessary to find a situation in which their effect is accentuated. Such a situation exists in what some might view a rather unexpected place. Basically, the informal interchanges between psychologists, as reflected in the stories, personal narratives and the jokes they tell each other are pregnant with statements of the value system that underlies their activity in the lab. So too do the rules of conduct of psychologists in certain institutional settings (e.g., the colloquium) contain indicators of the underlying value structure. Perhaps an examination of some of these casual, informal aspects of the discipline will provide a useful means for coming face to face with the "hiddens" of scientific psychology.

The fundamental thesis of this essay is that an informal, shared belief system is a significant part of how scientists (in particular, scientific psychologists) do their work. This system pervades the day to day interactions and cognitions of scientists and directs their behavior in what are sometimes very subtle ways. These beliefs are not written down anywhere; rather they are passed on orally within the group. They are learned by novitiates as they work their way through graduate school. They are reinforced at conventions and formal meetings and are the fabric of daily interactions between colleagues. These beliefs, often not consciously held, guide behavior through the unsettled waters of academia by offering a set of values that can be used to evaluate not only theoretical analysis, but also colleagues, students and a wide range of sensitive issues. These "un-saids" are not easy to demonstrate, or for that matter define, as they are relatively hidden and rarely discussed explicitly in the scientist group. They are a bit like a fog, easy to see from a distance, but very difficult to see when you are in the middle of it. But they are there, and they do exert a very significant influence on the way in which scientists value analyses within their discipline.

THE "UN-SAIDS" IN ACTION

It is appropriate at this point to ask whether the "un-saids" of psychology are worth investigating. If they cannot be shown to have an important effect on the final product of the discipline, then why bother trying to uncover them? Perhaps the most important place where they exert their effects is in the decision of whether to accept or reject a given theoretical proposition. Each psychologist is faced with this valuing decision every time an article is read, and the eventual outcome of the decision making process, considered collectively, shapes the progress of the discipline. The formal, written documentation of the discipline suggests that the acceptance of a theory (or, more properly, the failure to reject it) rests on the empirical evidence that is brought to bear. But there is more to it than that. Indeed, the "un-saids," which exist independently of the empirical data related to the theory, exert a very pervasive effect in this process.

This process of acceptance or rejection of a theoretical proposition based on extra-empirical factors can be seen in a number of settings. Several months ago I was asked to present a lecture on hemispheric lateralization of musical behaviors to a group of music students. I outlined the relevant research and gave a speculative explanation of the findings (Rogers, 1983b). I also concluded with significant caution regarding hemispheric lateralization accounts of behavior—offering a very strong (and to my mind devastating) critique of this position, particularly if held in the extreme. In fact, I spent at least 10 minutes of the 50 minute presentation debunking some of the current thinking in the field. But several days later I ran into some students who had attended the lecture. While most positive in their comments, it became very clear to me that these students had completely ignored the caveats I placed on the left-right analysis of musical behavior. They were citing my lecture as gospel regarding the validity of a lateralization account. I was not only angered by this, but a bit frightened as it became clear that no amount of rational discussion (e.g., "but don't you remember that I said most of these ideas are fiction. . . ." etc.) would dissuade them that I had not made a strong pro-lateralization presentation. Some aspect of the music student's value system had prompted them to ignore the caveat I had placed on the lateralization data. My guess is that they found the idea of the emotional and rational aspects of music being in different parts of the brain (and thereby independent) very appealing. The appeal, for these students, rests with the observation that most being performers, were having trouble rationalizing the teaching and requisite logical analysis of the subject with the affective and artistic dimensions of actually playing. In other words, the personal need to explain the independence of the rational and emotional aspects of music outweighed the empirical data (and attending reservations about lateralization), to the point that they over-interpreted the empirical evidence and dismissed the caveats as irrelevant.

The music students are not scientists, and it may be possible to argue that trained scientists are not prone to making this kind of "selective interpretation." However, I will argue that exactly the same kind of problem does occur in psychology, and, I believe, in social science generally. It emerges in a much more subtle way than the music student example, but it is there, and the same kinds of effects are evident.

In the late '60s I was involved in research in personality assessment. The focus of my work was the Minnesota Multiphasic Personality Inventory (MMPI). Our research group was exploring the reasons why people respond in specific ways to inventories such as this (see Jackson and Messick, 1962; Rogers, 1971). By the early 1970s several things were most clear: (1) the MMPI was not particularly well-designed and validated; (2) there were several much better tests available on the market—no matter what criterion you used to define "better"; and (3) there were more effective ways than the MMPI of making the kinds of statements one can make from the test. As I moved out of this area I thought the MMPI was history and the field had demonstrated some progress. Needless to say I was most surprised when I heard from a friend of mine that he had been forced to take the MMPI at a local in-patient unit—just several months ago! Upon asking, I found that this test is still viewed as "state of the art" by many clinicians, and the empirical case against the MMPI was, somehow, irrelevant.

As with the music students, clinicians are not typically active scientists, so perhaps a "kind" argument can be offered here too. Not trained in scientific evaluation, these clinicians cannot be expected to examine the nuance of empirical debate. But better tests are available. Do clinicians not have the responsibility to keep up-to-date with the technology of their field? To be sure, a radiologist who does not keep abreast of technology will soon find it hard to retain a job. So perhaps the "kind" argument is not totally justified. More important here though, is that the survival of the MMPI despite the awesome empirical case against it, reflects the activity of an informal, unwritten belief system among clinicians. While debatable, it seems likely that the core belief underlying this is the manner in which the MMPI reifies the "psychiatrist as master" ideology in mental health settings. The MMPI was developed to predict psychiatrist ratings of patients, and continued use of the test reinforces the supraordinate role of the MD. The test, then, offers the psychologist a way of showing the psychiatrist that the discipline "has something to say" at the same time not threatening the position of the medical practitioner. While other factors may also be operative (e.g., inertia, the general conservative ethic in mental health settings etc.), it seems clear that factors other than the data are involved in the survival of the MMPI in clinical settings. It is the equivalent of this belief system in scientists that we must understand if we wish to comprehend how nonempirical factors shape scientific evaluations.

A third example, and one which is particularly germane to the present paper, comes from my research into the "self" (see Rogers, 1981 for a review). I can recall the first major paper that I published in this area with great clarity (Rogers, Kuiper and Kirker, 1977). Without going into the details, this paper had a *major* flaw in it. The inferences I was drawing from my data were not defensible (see Bower and Gilligan, 1979; Keenan and Baillet, 1980; Kuiper and Rogers, 1979 for subsequent elaborations). I confess that the flaw had escaped my attention prior to submitting the article. When I heard from the journal, two reviewers waxed ecstatic, while the one who spotted the flaw was not quite as happy. Much to my surprise, the editor was willing to overlook the objections of this one reviewer and accepted the paper with minimal revisions. The extent of the flaw had not really dawned on me as I sent in the revised manuscript. Only later did I realize what had happened. The editor was so interested in the theoretical idea of the self that he was willing to ignore the flawed empirical case documented in the article. Something had led him to suspend the traditional rules of evidence in the interests of getting my analysis into the literature. More than the data were at issue here. On reflection, I believe that a number of factors contributed to this decision. Among these was that the paper involved the adaptation of a current "hot" construct in human experimental research to the self (Craik and Tulving's "depth of processing" model), and I believe the paper offered a degree of legitimization to self research. In addition, the journal was trying to upgrade its image as a theoretical leader (in contrast to an outlet for one-shot empirical papers). These factors (along with others, I am sure) interacted to produce a situation in which the flawed paper was allowed to enter the open literature.

I have not told this story to blame any specific individual or suggest that a particular area is prone to doing "bad" science. Rather my intent of presenting this story is to provide an example of how nonempirical beliefs are implicated in the scientific enterprise. Here we are not dealing with scientifically naive readers such as (some) music students, but we are dealing with respected, revered and accomplished scientists. But what happened is identical to the kinds of events associated with scientifically naive persons. I submit that this is not an isolated scenario. Rather, I believe that this kind of event is very frequent in virtually all areas of scientific activity.

These three examples (lateralization, the MMPI and the "self") serve to demonstrate the means in which hidden assumptions of "un-saids" can be seen to exert effects on the scientific valuing process. The fundamental problem with the foregoing analyses is that the content of the hidden beliefs are strictly conjectural at this point. My analyses of the beliefs underlying these case histories represent one reading of any number possible. An important question at this point, then, is whether there are ways that will allow us to converge on a more consensual definition of the content of the belief system as it applies to scientific psychologists.

SOME HELP FROM OUR SOCIAL SCIENTIFIC NEIGHBORS

The "un-saids" of scientific psychology can be thought of as components of the subculture shared by members of the group. To the extent that these are not part of the formal, written documentation of the discipline, they can be thought of as informal, unwritten components of this subculture. The discipline of folklore is concerned directly with the collection, categorization and interpretation of exactly these aspects of oral culture, and it is now to this field that we direct our attention in search of a means of uncovering the content of the "un-saids" of scientific psychology.

While most of us associate folklore with myths and old wives tales, contemporary approaches to this discipline are explicit in their concern with unwritten beliefs. For example, Brunvand (1968) suggests:

> Folklore comprises the unrecorded traditions of people; it includes both the form and content of these traditions and their style or technique of communication from person to person. The study of folklore (or "folkloristics") attempts to analyze these traditions (both content and process) so as to reveal the common life of the human mind apart from what is contained in the formal records of culture that compose the heritage of a people (p. 1).

Toelken (1979) considers the discipline as follows:

an informal system for learning the daily logic and world view of the people around us. What we learn is more in the way of style and performance than specific content. We may say that folklore itself is characterized by (1) certain cultural rules that determine strongly what gets articulated and how and when, and (2) by a looseness, and informality, an inclination toward rephrasing and change, that will eventually result in an individuation on the surface of all articulations (p. 27).

Both of these definitions impart a concern with the nonformal aspects of the interchanges of a group. My thesis is that we can learn a significant amount about how we do our science by examining the folklore of the group of people we call "scientific psychologists." By analyzing their folklore and rules of conduct we will begin to gain an understanding of the kinds of factors that shape the eventual acceptance or rejection of a particular scientific analysis.

Folklorists tend to break down the area into various genres or forms of expression (see Dorson, 1972 for an illustration). The underlying ethos (or "un-saids") of the group are present in these genres in varying degrees. So too are various genres more appropriate to certain groups (e.g., there is not a large corpus of "scientific psychologist" folk songs . . .). For our purposes, stories in circulation among the group are particularly relevant. These can vary from a specific joke through to institutional lore that is being passed on from member to member of the group in various informal communication contexts. A particularly relevant local example relates to our Religious Studies programme. This group submitted an application to the powers that be (no pun intended) to develop a graduate program. Their proposal was—without doubt—the best proposal from among many, including several sciences. Accordingly it was assigned a high priority in the queue of proposals awaiting governmental funding. I was consulting with the Faculty of Science shortly thereafter on another matter and the following story was told just before the agenda of the meeting was initiated:

> You know there was a real funny thing that the Religious Studies crowd pulled in their proposal to Grad Faculty? They had all of this stuff about the importance of Religious Studies and a list of names of Faculty they would hire. One of the names was "S. Beagle." Can you imagine, a Dr. S. Beagle, being part of that group? The "S," of course, was for "Snoopy." They sure pulled a fast one!

This story brings the inevitable conflict between religious and scientific approaches into very sharp focus. Particularly when viewed in a context of competition for limited fiscal resources, this story has a very real bite to it in its efforts to debunk the Religious Studies proposal to a science audience. Whether or not the story is true is irrelevant—the key point is that this particular story of many other possible was the one selected for telling in this group of scientists. The nods and sardonic chuckles that emanated from the telling of this story indicated that it was in wide circulation in the group. By reinforcing the territoriality of the scientific group, in the mocking of the Religious Studies proposal, this story serves as an insightful indicator of some of the group values. It is this kind of story—casual, informal and oral—that begins to give us purchase on the underlying beliefs of a group.

This kind of story or folklore is typically performed in a specific context. For the scientific group, the time for performance of these kinds of stories and lore is "in the cracks" between various formal proceedings. Be it in the warming up period before a meeting, in the Faculty Club after a guest lecture or in off-campus social gatherings, it is the time when the formal guarding of the values is dropped, and the "un-saids" become very knowable.

These stories and lore are not part of the official, written documentation of the group. Rather, they exist in oral circulation among members. They are appended, as it were, to the formal aspects of the group, serving to reinforce, support and verify the important group maintenance values that they so aptly reflect.

THE COLLOQUIUM: AN EXAMPLE

Another place that folklore oftimes reveals itself is in the kinds of rituals and customs that are adopted by a given group. In classic folklore studies these behaviors and rituals are easily seen and their meaning readily extrapolated (e.g., the "end of year" festivities celebrating the birth of a new cycle can be seen as functional and important rituals for an agricultural culture). In the scientific group these rituals are, perhaps, not as easily seen (particularly as we are a part of the group), but there are some very interesting ideas that follow from the observation of casual behavior in various activities of the group.

A particularly relevant example is the psychology colloquium. Here a speaker presents an analysis (typically involving data) to a group of colleagues and students with an eye to sharing current work and ideas in a specific field. There are definite unwritten, orally transmitted rules that govern conduct in these meetings. Should a speaker violate these rules, the probability of gaining a positive response from the audience is greatly diminished. In our department, the acceptance of a colloquium seems to vary directly with the number of slides presented. But within this, it is important that the performance should have some rough edges—too slick a presentation raises some questions about the speaker. This is reflected in a number of formulaic behaviors and expressions that are a part of the colloquium. For instance, the audio visual equipment must *not* work properly, and the presenter should somehow fumble with the slide projector. So too is the expression "I've just collected these data, but haven't had a change to analyse them yet" an expected part of the colloquium. In addition to these formulaic behaviors, there is also an expected dress code or uniform—tweedy for men, tailored for women, which contrasts with downtown "slick" (read $400 suit) dress codes for the business world.

All of these aspects of the colloquium indicate that unpolished performance is tolerated. It is interesting to ask why this should be so. After all, virtually all of us spend hours a week in front of students making very similar types of presentations in our classes. In fact, one behavior that is almost universally well rehearsed in the academic scientist group is the oral presentation of data and theory. Why then does the group tolerate unpolished performance? A provocative answer to this question is that the communication systems adopted by the group have evolved to make access to the fundamental ideas more difficult—thereby making it harder for members of the out-group (or those thinking of joining it) to acquire the knowledge. An obfuscated communication system serves to protect the group from intrusion by outsiders thereby strengthening it.

INFORMAL ATTITUDES TOWARD TEACHING EVALUATION: MORE LORE

Interpreting the informal aspects of the colloquium as reflecting an intentionally obfuscated communication system is indeterminant as there are a number of other readings possible (e.g., scientists have been selected for their scientific aptitude, not their communication skills etc.). It would seem appropriate, then, to examine other aspects of the lore of the scientist group to determine if the suggested reading has validity.

Very few topics generate more heated conversations among scientists than teaching evaluation. At Calgary we have a relatively well-developed system of collecting students' opinions about their teachers. Department Heads sometimes use these ratings to evaluate faculty, and a number of firmly-held beliefs have evolved in this context. Perhaps the most pervasive one is that a faculty member who gets "rave" reviews from students is clearly suspect. Some of the comments I have heard are: "Must be telling lots of jokes" . . . . "Anybody can get good ratings if they have the juicy courses" . . . . "Can't be teaching very well if the students like him that much!" . . . . "No pain, no gain!" A social science department head confided that all good teaching evaluations mean is that the person has the "gift of the gab," thereby relegating the utility of good communication skills to the coffee room and faculty club. These comments clearly reflect the same concern for polished presentation of material that was seen in the discussion of the colloquium. In fact, when asked whether he thought the teaching evaluation program was useful, one Head of a science department replied: "My better teachers all get lower ratings, so the survey must be screwed up." Again, the truth-value of these beliefs is not important— what really matters is that these beliefs are the ones held by the group, reflected in their continued oral circulation among members.

The fundamental point of this discussion of colloquia and teaching evaluation is to demonstrate that there are hidden, unwritten rules that have pervasive effects on how a group of scientists accepts or rejects a specific presentation and presenter. These rules focus on the style of presentation, and both tolerate unpolished performance and induce skepticism if they are too "slick." This is not to suggest that the content of the presentation at a colloquium is irrelevant, rather the point is that the style in which a presentation is given is an important determiner of peer evaluation—and that this style is dictated by informal, un-written rules. In the academic scientist group being too flashy, too slick, too good, a speaker is likely to cause concern and negative evaluation. Scientists' tendency to heavily criticize colleagues who work closely with the media (e.g., David Suzuki in Canada) is another indicator of this evaluative system.

The unwritten rules regarding communication mentioned above are a part of the folklore of the scientific psychologist group. They have been shaped by generations of peer evaluation and are taught to "new boys" by example and via certain rites of passage (e.g., PhD oral examinations). Violations of these rules result in severe reprimands from the group elders. Yet these rules are not written down anywhere. Their reality exists in oral transmission within the scientific community and only through careful observation of the effects of these rules can their presence be established and their content discerned.

The central thesis of my argument is that these unwritten rules reflect underlying value systems within the group. The rules regarding communication style articulated above appear to reflect a concern for the maintenance of the ownership of the ideas and content of the discipline. After all, if the ideas are rendered in a completely understandable form, would it not be possible for *anyone* to acquire them and thereby threaten the group? The devaluing of pol-ished presentation appears to suggest a basic territoriality within the discipline, wherein ideas are thought to be possessions (material things that are owned) and communication systems have evolved to protect these precious entities. That ideas are usually associated with persons in the field (e.g., Hull's theory of learning, Festinger's cognitive dissonance, Skinner's operant conditioning, etc.) reinforces the interpretation that ideas are seen as things to be owned and protected. It should be noted that this idea of the ownership and protection of ideas runs counter to the formally-stated policies of the institutions supporting the research from which the ideas came. Specifically, most of the work has been done in universities, whose explicit goal is the dissemination and sharing of these ideas—not their protection by obfuscation and unpolished presentation. There is a hint, then, that the folklore and the formally-stated policies of the universities are somehow at odds with each other.

JOKES IN ACADEME: A FURTHER INDICATOR
OF PREVAILING FOLKLORE

Another genre of folklore that is rife with information about the group value system is the jokes that are in circulation. We all hear a fair number of jokes in our daily interactions with colleagues, and only certain ones are "good" enough to be told and retold throughout a given group. A joke that does survive does so because it touches some common core of meaning within the group, and it is in this that an examination of jokes can serve as an especially potent compliment to the folkloristic observations tendered in the earlier part of this essay.

Dundes (1980) has published a number of jokes from academe that were in circulation at the time. Several examples are:

> A chemist, a physicist, and an economist are marooned on a desert island without food. Suddenly a cache of canned goods is discovered, but there is no opener. The chemist begins looking about for chemicals in their natural state so he can make a solution that will dissolve the tops of the cans. The physicist picks up a rock and begins calculating what angle, what force, what velocity he will need to strike the can with in order to force it open. The economist merely picks up the can and says, "Let's assume we have a can opener" (p. 13).

> A physicist, a statistician, and a mathematician were in an airplane flying over Montana. They looked out and saw below a herd of sheep all of which were white, except one which was black. The physicist began calculating the number of black sheep in the universe, based on the sample. The statistician began calculating the probability of a black sheep occurring in any given herd. The mathematician, on the other hand, knew that there exists at least one sheep that is black, *on top!* (p. 13)

The unifying thread of these jokes is "poking fun" at the other disciplines. This is congruent with the supposition that one of the prevailing attitudes of the scientist group is a territorial concern, where boundaries between disciplines are very tightly drawn so as to mark out one's turf. Clearly, this is similar to the materialization of ideas that was suggested as the value underlying the communication style within the scientist group. In both cases, the concern is with ownership of certain aspects of the academic world (ideas or disciplines). It is interesting to note that these jokes converge with the Religious Studies story about Snoopy presented earlier in this chapter.

WHAT PROFS SAY ABOUT STUDENTS: MORE EVIDENCE
OF TERRITORIALITY

Another source of information that helps to elucidate the underlying values of the scientific psychologist group is the stories in circulation among professors about students. Teaching is a significant aspect of the academic's life, and there are a large number of stories that are told about students, particularly with respect to attempts to gain a higher grade. I am sure most will recognize the following motifs:

—the voluptuous (handsome) female (male) student who will do "just anything" to improve her (his) grade. (I heard a local variant recently. This narrative was told by a professor about his advisor in a casual, social situation. A physiological psychology professor was visited by a female student who announced that she would do anything to get a higher grade. "Anything?" he asks. "Yes" she replies, "I must get into med school." "Anything?" he asks again softly, closing the door. "Yes" she replies, eyes downcast. The professor then whispers softly into her ear, "Why don't you try studying"!)

—the poor, confused student who asks Dr. Jones where he can find Dr. Jones because he missed the one class when the midterm was given.

—the older student whose family obligations resulted in a lower grade, which should be raised.

—the tearful female undergraduate who promises to do better on the next exam if only you would raise her midterm.

—the (aggressive) male student who insists that he should be graded on what he meant on the exam, not what he actually wrote.

—the varsity athlete whose dedication and sacrifice for the university should be rewarded with higher grade than earned.

Each of these story motifs reflects the power relationship between student and professor, and suggests (unsuccessful) methods used to try and breach it. As with the jokes, there is territoriality implied in these stories. The professor has (owns) something (presumably knowledge and standards) and these are his to protect and dole out when earned. Students who try to gain this precious possession by devious pursuits are celebrated in the stories which professors tell each other in various informal contexts.

WHAT STUDENTS SAY ABOUT THEIR PROFESSORS: SOME CONVERGENT EVIDENCE

Perhaps more than any other group, students are the brunt of the communication style that is so much a part of the scientific psychologist's world. Day after day the undergraduate has to sit through lectures that are presented with varying degrees of concern for communication skills. Of course, students have their own folklore and it is instructive to examine this to determine if there is evidence for the territoriality noted in the previous sections. Most of the narratives in circulation among the student group focus on successful attempts to "out fox" the professors. One local story that spread like wild-fire at the University of Calgary was about the would-be exam-pilfering student who tried to gain access to a professor's office by crawling above a partition through the suspended ceiling. He fell during this perilous journey and broke both of his wrists. The victim in this tale was soon accorded the status of folk hero in the local student folkways. The popularity of this story in the student group indicates a shared perception of the importance of the things which professors own, and focus on attempts to gain these. As above, this lore converges on the "materialization" and territorialization of ideas within the academic community.

There are a series of stories related to professors' use of blackboards that have particular relevance here. Toelken (1968) reports two stories in circulation in the US.

> . . . there is another professor who writes on the board with his right hand and erases as he goes with his left; anyone who cannot take immediate notes is lost. But since the professor has given the same final examination for twenty-three years, everyone always gets an A (p. 378).

> . . . one hears tell of a professor who writes equations so rapidly on the board that a graduate student assistant must follow and erase the board behind him. Since the student erases faster than anyone can take notes, most of the material is irretrievably lost (p. 378).

These two stories are compatible with the interpretation that communication styles have developed within academe that serve to obscure the content being communicated. This general type of story has received some particularly interesting updating recently at the University of Calgary. Two such narratives emerged this term. One relates to a professor who has his lecture notes painstakingly handwritten on the continuous rolls of an overhead projector. Apparently the professor comes in and installs these rolls (aptly dubbed "the great scrolls" by the students) and winds through them as he lectures. Of course he winds much too fast for the students to take notes. The second variant relates to a female professor who uses the scrolls but with a different twist (so to speak). Described as "winding the overhead like it was a music box" this professor rolls through the required material while at the same time *talking about something entirely different!* This style of presentation appears to overtax the information processing capacities of the students and is the subject of quite a bit of conversation. As above, these stories affirm the thesis that communication styles within the academic community have the implication of obscuring the material that is being communicated. In the eyes of their students, it seems the profs go to extremes to make their precious possession (knowledge) very difficult to acquire.

There is also evidence of the lay community having noted the tendency of academics to be obscure (and protective) in their communications. A case can be made for the "absent minded professor" stereotype deriving from this. A recent New Yorker cartoon nicely reflected this in showing a very tweedy, middle aged gent approaching a New York policeman and saying, "Pardon me sir, I'm an academic. Where am I?" Several student stories show this as well.

One relates to a professor who concluded a mid-campus conversation with a student by asking, "Which way was I going when we stopped?" and on being told answered, "Oh, then I *have* eaten lunch" (Toelken, 1968, p. 375). The apparent bumbling behavior of professors in the classroom is revealed in this story:

> One professor lectures only to the best looking girl in the class, looks only at her, and checks her face after every attempt at humour and on making every point (of course she nods constantly throughout all lectures, to show that she understands everything he is saying). One day, late in the quarter, however, she is absent. The professor enters, opens his book, put on his glasses, and looks out over the class to her empty seat; after a puzzled moment he asks, "Where is everybody today?" (Toelken, 1968; p. 378).

These stories reflect the perception of the professor as blunderer—inept in the ways of effective communication, and acting as though ideas are best shrouded in a blanket of obfuscation. While the "absent minded professor" narratives poke fun at these communications behaviors, they have a real edge to them in their focus upon the essential territoriality implied in trying to make content and substance difficult for the learner to attain. The stories appear to reflect a kind of intellectual fence building that serves to delineate (and protect) the region of the professor.

Combining the "absent minded professor" stories with the narratives that professors tell about students and vice versa, as well as the comments of performance style in colloquia, begins to uncover a basic profile of the underlying value structure, or the "un-saids," of the scientific group. There is a fundamental materialism that suggests that knowledge and ideas are something that is owned by the scientist. When jokes are told, they are structured about this ownership. When professors talk about students they focus upon efforts to steal this precious possession. When presenting ideas to colleagues in a colloquium a communication style oriented toward protecting the knowledge by obfuscation is adopted. Not unlike our phylogenetically less advanced neighbors in the animal kingdom, the scientist has adopted a series of behaviors that are oriented toward protecting this territory. These behaviors, of course, are less overtly aggressive than those found in the animal kingdom, being reflected in more academic aspects of communication, but they serve exactly the same functions; namely, the protection of precious territory. (Librarians are, no doubt, pleased that this group has chosen to mark its territory in intellectual ways, rather than adopting the practices of some of our more canine cousins—although some cynics have suggested that such marking is appropriate to the substance of most of the holdings). Examination of the casual aspects of communication styles within the group (e.g., stories, jokes, lecturing styles etc.) reveals substantial evidence to verify this aspect of the "un-saids" of the scientist group.

It is important to realize that there is a conflict between the "un-saids" articulated in this essay and the written or formal documentation that is part of the group. To be sure, virtually every scientist ascribes to the code of clear and concise communication of the results of their research in the interests of scientific progress. One cannot deny the countless hours spent by editors trying to make articles more understandable to their readership. All of these aspects of the group appear to be at odds with the territoriality suggested from examination of the folklore of the academic group. But such a conflict between the formal and informal in a cultural group is not at all uncommon. There are the continual formal proceedings of a group that are overlaid on the day-to-day informal business of virtually every group. The fundamental thesis of this chapter is that the informal aspects of the group are preeminent if we chose to try and articulate the hidden or "un-said" assumptions that guide the behavior of the scientist.

SOME CONCLUSIONS

This essay began by suggesting that "more than the data" were involved in psychologists' decisions about acceptance or rejection of theoretical propositions. It was suggested that various "un-saids" were important, and that examining the content and style of informal communications within the group could provide some useful insight into these hidden values. The present examination of the folklore of academe has pinpointed a basic materialization or territorialization of ideas in the discipline which can be seen to underlie significant proportions of the day-to-day activities of scientific psychologists.

It would seem that this "un-said" will exert itself in a number of different ways in terms of the acceptance or rejection of theoretical propositions. For example, rather than being a simple "data based" decision about the utility of a theory, acceptance can be seen as "territorial negotiation." Under the influence of this "un-said," the acceptance of a new idea is tantamount to relinquishing a piece of territory. This boils down, then, to a fundamental decision about what the individual scientist has to give up in order to embrace a new idea. In other words, decisions of worth about theoretical propositions are more cost-benefit analyses at the individual level than they are "data driven," rational decisions. The "cost" of relinquishing a cherished piece of territory can be significant, particularly when important values are integral to the perceived loss in giving up an old idea in favor of a newer one. Hence, the more central an old idea is to the value structure of the scientist, the less likely are the chances that it will be replaced by a newer idea—regardless of the empirical case presented. In a field like psychology, which deals with phenomena so firmly embedded in the cultural context, the probability of observing increased costs of relinquishing old ideas is greatly enhanced, suggesting significant difficulties for the discipline if this aspect of its activity is not acknowledged.

The three illustrations of ignoring empirical data described at the start of this essay (music students' embracing hemispheric lateralization, clinicians' views of the MMPI and the publication of a flawed empirical case for a theory of the self) are examples of this territorial negotiation in action. In each of these cases the value systems of the evaluators were stronger than the empirical case presented thereby leading to the acceptance of a proposition for nonempirical reasons. While not as crucial with the music student example, it is clear that the impact of the value system as illustrated with the MMPI and self examples has important implications for the discipline of psychology. Without explicit knowledge of the values held by the evaluator, the acceptance or rejection of a specific theoretical proposition will be a fundamentally indeterminant act. Whether masked in elegant empirical evidence or not, the decision to embrace a specific theoretical analysis can just as readily be attributed to a value statement as to anything else. This is certainly a sobering thought to a radical positivist who firmly believes that the data serve as the final arbiter of "truth."

The territoriality outlined above is one aspect of an "un-said" value system shared by most members of the scientist group. It seems likely that a detailed analysis of the folklore of the group will reveal a number of other values that are part of a constellation of "un-saids" that direct scientists' behavior. In fact, a number of the chapters in this volume suggest other possible candidates (e.g., power, political ideology). It is beyond the scope of this chapter to attempt a full discussion of the entire set of "un-saids." Rather, the fundamental goal has been to demonstrate how an examination of the folklore of the group can provide a useful lever to begin investigation of these hidden assumptions that are such an important (and oftimes denied) part of how work proceeds in the discipline. Much more work is needed to fully elucidate this position.

A detailed analysis of the hidden value systems employed by psychologists would, no doubt, prove useful in the identification of various areas of the discipline where one is apt to find problems. For example, I believe aspects of the value system have had a significant impact on psychology's failure to make what most would view as meaningful progress in the study of emotion. A number of researchers have noted our poor record in dealing with this topic (e.g., see Rogers, 1983a for a review), pointing out the failure to obtain the kind of cumulative gain expected from proper application of scientific methodology. A fair number of researchers do some preliminary work in the field, and then retreat to "easier" domains of study. Perhaps the need to treat ideas as "material" or "territory" forces a kind of logical system on the study of emotion that is not appropriate to the topic. I believe that the current constellation of "un-saids" within the discipline literally force us to ask the wrong kinds of questions about emotion. In true Procrustean fashion, we try to force the topic into the prevailing metatheory, and the failure to realize benefits from this exercise is due, in part, to the "un-saids" and their impact on how we do our science. It will be necessary to do much more work to explicate the content of the value system and note its impact on the study of emotion, before this possibility can be fully elucidated. For now, the point in mentioning it is to suggest that a detailed analysis of the "un-saids," uncovered with the help of systematic investigation of the casual communication styles and folklore of the discipline, has the potential of making a significant contribution to the understanding and improvement of the discipline.

It should be stressed that this essay is not (necessarily) a condemnation of the value system that is presently directing the discipline. There can be little doubt that the materialization and territorialization of ideas is very functional—particularly within our current cultural context. Indeed, in the physical sciences, there is no doubt that the value system has generated some exceptionally significant ideas and concepts. So too, has the borrowing of the physical scientists' tool box by psychologists resulted in some meaningful analyses of humanity. The fundamental point is that we could be doing a lot better than we are, and that one way of improving would be to come to grips, in an explicit manner, with the "un-saids" that have such an effect on how we do our work. Not only would this cleanse the discipline of a number of significant misconceptions that it has about itself, but it would also suggest ways in which we might be able to carve out a new meta-theory that is of especial relevance to the problems with which psychology deals. By clearly stating and understanding the "un-saids" (rendering them "said"), we will be in a much stronger position in our quest for the solution to problems of the human condition. Failure to clarify the hiddens of our discipline will, in the long run, weaken the potential of the discipline of psychology, and its potential for making a meaningful contribution to humanity.

However, while not condemning the value system, per se, it should be made clear that proceeding without explicit knowledge of the value positions is highly undesirable. Business as usual is not an adequate solution to the improvement of our science. Radical positivism is seductive in its apparent objectivity and valueless stance. The foregoing, and indeed most of the chapters in this book, make it clear that the formal doctrine of objectivity is at odds with what actually happens in our labs. The acceptance of theoretical propositions, and other evaluative transactions in our labs, are firmly embedded in the current social context, and we must be aware of how this is affecting our work. Only by facing up to these realities of doing science can we hope to see psychology develop a sound future. On the basis of the analysis presented here, I hope it seems evident that an important next step in the evolution of our discipline will be explicit value clarification.

It is instructive to ask what effects the clarification and explication of the values underlying the enterprise of scientific psychology will have. At the simplest level, it will allow for a better understanding of the underpinnings of the discipline, and perhaps (as was suggested with emotion) indicate some of the areas that the value system appears to be interfering. Considered more broadly though, the value clarification exercise carries the potential of inducing significant change to the very fabric of the discipline. To the extent that the choice to adopt a particular approach to psychology is embedded in an implicit value system, the explication of the values may have the effect of forcing changes in the system itself. To be sure, every time we use a psychological test, or construct an operational definition or defer to empirical validation, we are making a series of assumptions about the very nature of our subject matter. The question is whether explication of these assumptions and values would cause us to realize that the assumptions we are making are not appropriate, forcing, as it were, a set of unsuitable constraints on how we might better understand humanity.

At a very fundamental level, it may well be that the scientism which is so much a part of today's psychology is itself the folklore of the 1980's. While couched in twentieth century language and conceptual framework, it is conceivable that the guiding assumptions of the discipline are just as much folklore as the proverbs, personal narratives and legends that were passed on to us by our forefathers of earlier centuries. The underpinnings of psychology can be considered folklore to the extent that they represent a communal, shared value system that pervades the membership of the group calling itself "scientific psychologists" and direct (in subtle and unknowing ways) the behavior of group members. The data and arguments presented here suggest that this may indeed be the case. The present paper can be seen as a first step in developing the thesis that the fundamental tenets of scientism in psychology are today's folklore.

The basic point of this paper has been to suggest that an examination of the folklore of the discipline is a useful lever in explicating the "un-saids" of the group called "scientific psychologists." It is in casual conversation that these hidden values are most likely to be knowable. It is as though the institutional guard has been dropped during casual communication and the vulnerable jaw of hidden assumptions exposed. Examination of communication styles provides an alternate approach which, by virtue of its independence from the actual formal documentation of the discipline, provides a kind of methodological independence that allows us to know the "un-saids" from outside. I submit that this approach has a very rich potential for helping us clarify the very core of the prevailing values of the discipline of psychology. Careful attention to our institutional or disciplinary folklore holds the key to a powerful understanding of the discipline and holds the promise of helping direct future developments that are based on an explicit understanding of the presently "un-said" aspects of our discipline.

REFERENCES

Bower, G. H. and Gilligan, S. G. (1979). Remembering information relating to one's self. *Journal of Research in Personality, 13,* 420–432.

Brunvand, J. B. (1968). *The study of American folklore*. New York: Norton.

Dorson, R. M. (1972). *Folklore and Folklife*. Chicago: University of Chicago Press.

Dundes, A. (1980). *Interpreting folklore*. Bloomington: Indiana University Press.

Jackson, D. J. and Messick, S. (1962). Response styles on the MMPI: Comparison of clinical and normal samples. *Journal of Abnormal and Social Psychology, 65,* 285–299.

Keenan, J. M. and Baillet, S. D. (1980). Memory for personality and socially significant events. In R. S. Nickerson (Ed.), *Attention and performance VIII*, Hillsdale, NJ: Erlbaum.

Kuiper, N. A. and Rogers, T. B. (1979). The encoding of personal information: Self-other differences. *Journal of Personality and Social Psychology, 37,* 499–514.

Rogers. T. B. (1971). The process of responding to personality items: Some issues, a theory and some research. *Multivariate Behavioral Research Monographs, 6*(2).

Rogers, T. B. (1983a). Emotion, imagery and verbal codes: A closer look at an increasingly complex interaction. In J. C. Yuille (Ed.), *Imagery, memory and cognition*, Hillsdale, NJ: Erlbaum.

Rogers, T. B. (1983b). Music and neuropsychology. *Notes, 8,* 9–17.

Rogers, T. B., Kuiper, N. A. and Kirker, W. S. (1979). Self-reference and the encoding of personal information. *Journal of Personality and Social Psychology, 35,* 677–688.

Toelken, B. (1968). The folklore of academe. In J. H. Brunvand, (Ed.) The study of American folklore. New York: Norton.

Toelken, B. (1979). *The dynamics of folklore*. Boston: Houghton Mifflin.

Chapter 10

Dialectical Materialism as Psychological Metatheory

Charles Tolman

INTRODUCTION

The practice of any science necessarily rests upon some kind of understanding of that with which the practice is conducted. Historically, this understanding has not always been explicit, but clearly it promises to be more effective if it is, since it thus becomes accessible to rational evaluation.

The current discussions in psychology around metatheory, simply another word for the understanding presupposed by our scientific practice, are therefore to be welcomed. The self-examination which these discussions imply was long neglected under the positivist hegemony which relegated many important metatheoretical questions prematurely to the scrapheap of "metaphysics." It is now becoming clear to an increasing number of psychologists, as well as philosophers, that not all metatheoretical concerns can be reduced to questions of logic, that questions of ontology and epistemology, even of ethics, are essential concerns of scientific practice that do not disappear when ignored.

My purpose here is to advocate dialectical materialism as an appropriate set of understandings upon which psychological scientific practice can be based. Indeed, I will maintain that dialectical materialism is the *only* metatheory appropriate to any truly scientific practice. Having said that, it will be necessary to persuade the reader that such a strong claim is not based on sheer arrogance, but upon fully rational considerations.

Current concerns about metatheory have their origins in the late 1950s and 1960s. During that period we experienced what many observers referred to as the "demise" of positivist hegemony, not only in psychology but in other sciences as well—indeed the "demise" came later in psychology, on average, than in philosophy and the much idolized physical sciences. Owing to the fact that current discussions can justifiably be characterized as "post-positivist," it will be useful to begin my explication of dialectical materialism with an examination of positivism and its presumed demise.

THE DEMISE OF POSITIVISM?

I have ended the heading with a question mark for reasons which, I hope, will become clear presently.

From its beginnings in the early 19th century, positivism represented an attempt to make philosophy useful to science. What was clearly not useful, and which ran entirely against the grain of scientific self-consciousness, was armchair speculation. It was wholly wrong-headed to imagine that a person given the right sort of premises arrived at through speculation could, by purely rational procedure, arrive at a concrete knowledge of the world. The world was simply not to be conjured up out of pure reason. Rather it was given in our perception of it—in our sense-data. From the start, positivism was an outgrowth, a further scientific development, of empiricism, most particularly the empiricism of Hume. Positivists, both old and new, generally accepted Humean views on causality, induction, and the priority of sense experience. The various factions of positivism quibbled over problems of meaning and verification, of language and logic, but remained true to their fundamental Humean scientism.

Earlier critiques of neopositivism (i.e., the forms of positivism that have been influential in the 20th century) often focussed mainly on ethical implications (e.g., Joad, 1950) but these had little impact on the scientific community. At the heart of later critiques which we now associate with the period of demise (e.g., Bridgman, 1959; Carnap, 1956; Polanyi, 1959) were concerns that positivists had sought their goal of objectivity at the utterly destructive expense of subjectivity, and of social knowledge at the costs of the individual and the personal. The developing antipositivist reaction therefore set out to redress these wrongs by taking up the cause of the individual subject.

In the resulting renewal of interest in philosophy, psychologists turned for support to two distinct philosophical movements. The first was the existential-phenomenological, about which no more will be said here because the resultant so-called "third force" never captured more than a dissident fringe of practicing psychological researchers owning to its overtly antiscientific character. The second and more important grouping to which psychologists turned were certain philosophers of science such as Polanyi (1959), Kuhn (1962), Hanson, (1958), and to some extent Feyerabend (1962). It is this "line" which appears to dominate discussions of psychological metatheory today.

There are two important observations to be made about this background to present discussions. First is that, as Wertheimer (1972) has cogently demonstrated, positivism, particularly in its psychological "operationist" form, although overtly and totally preoccupied with objectivity and the social character of knowledge was all along covertly individualist and subjectivist in the worst way. Wertheimer's argument runs roughly as follows: X is objectively true if and only if it is agreed upon by experts; but who is to certify the objectivity of the agreement itself? Obviously this cannot be done except through an infinite regress of agreements, none of which can transcend the individual's willingness to grant that such agreement exists. The positivist's position is, in short, fundamentally solipsist, that is, individualist and subjectivist. This, of course, comes as no real surprise considering the Humean origins of modern neopositivism.

The second observation to be made is that much of the antipositivist reaction, both in philosophy and psychology, appears to have committed the reciprocal of the error ascribed to neopositivism. That is, the individual and subjective have been emphasized at the expense of the social and objective. This is nowhere clearer than in Wertheimer's own conclusion from the argument mentioned above. This was that the positivists were wrong to believe that solipsism could be overcome by special procedures and that philosophers and scientists should simply resign themselves to their solipsistic condition.

Now if Wertheimer is at all representative of the post-positivist New Psychologists, and I am sure that such a case can be made, then what they have done in fact is not reject positivism; they have preserved in a newly emphasized form its scientifically most objectionable characteristics, the Humean metaphysical assumptions which form the root of all its problems. Obviously a more "radical" solution is needed.

MATERIALISM IS NOT POSITIVISM!

I will indicate that I believe dialectical materialism is the more radical solution that we need. It will therefore be useful, indeed even necessary, to affirm here as clearly as possible that materialism is not positivism.

It is true that there are significant historical links between the two positions, and they share many important attitudes and beliefs. Most philosopher-scientists from Francis Bacon onward were materialists. Even the idealist Kant acknowledged with his thing-in-itself the unavoidability of some degree of onto-logical materialism and the great scientists of the 19th century such as Helmholtz showed strong evidence of materialism in their thinking despite the rising tide of positivism. Both materialism and positivism were scientifically motivated philosophies. This is clearly reflected on their common emphasis on objectivity, methodology, and scientific theory building.

But more fundamentally there are opposing philosophies. The materialist ontology opposes the essentially antiontological position of the positivists and it requires as a result a quite distinct epistemology. These differences will hope-fully become clear in the following sections of this chapter.

That specifically *dialectical* materialism and positivism (in whichever form) are distinct and fundamentally opposed is evidenced by the fact that positivism was consistently and vigorously opposed in some of the most impor-tant polemical works of Marx, Engels, and Lenin. Of these, Lenin's *Material-ism and Empirio-Criticism* (1972) remains one of the most biting critiques of positivist thought in the entire philosophical literature. The more recent *In Defense of Philosophy* (1950) by the British Marxist, Maurice Cornforth, is one more of a great number of examples that can be cited.

THE MATERIALIST WORLDVIEW

What, then, is materialism? The essence of this position is expressed in the following three fundamental theses (based on Cornforth, 1975, p. 25):

1   The world is by its very nature material. Everything which exists comes into being on the basis of material causes, arises and develops in accord-ance with the laws of motion of matter.

2   Matter is objective reality existing outside and independent of the mind; and far from the mental existing in separation from the material, every-thing mental or spiritual is a product of material processes.

3   The world and its laws are knowable, and while much in the material world may not be known there is no unknowable sphere of reality which lies outside the material world.

The first is the ontological thesis that matter is what is, and what is is matter. It is important to note that this thesis, in contradistinction to the more ancient metaphysical materialisms, does not specify the physical nature of mat-ter. It does not require that it be made of irreducible Democritean atoms or take any other presupposed form. The physical characteristics of matter are for science to discover. Thus the modern view of matter as energy or motion is not a contradiction of materialism, at least in its modern or dialectical form.

The second thesis specifies the relationship of mind and matter. It asserts, first, the important epistemological principle of mind independence of matter, and therefore of the material object of knowledge. This object of knowledge is not the creation of the knowing process but is discovered as thing-in-itself. This is not to say that the knowing process cannot distort the object nor does it imply that the object is given absolutely at any point in the process. False knowledge is possible and partial knowledge is almost inevitable. Historically, the implication is that we, collectively, are getting to know the world as object better and better. This is achieved through practice in the world, and feeds back to make that practice more and more effective, that is, effective in bringing about changes in the world in accordance with our conscious aims and desires.

The second thesis has a second part asserting a psychophysical monism. Minds are certainly separate from their objects, but they do not constitute a separate order of existence: they are of the same "stuff." As long as matter was thought of as something hard and static the temptation of dualism was irresistible, but the modern conceptions of matter as process are entirely supportive of a materialistic monism.

The second part of this thesis also specifies an evolutionary view of mind. Mind is a process or function of highly organized matter that has got that way by an orderly process of development. This is true whether we are concerned with phylogeny or ontogeny. Both the human species and the human individual *were* before they *knew* they were. This idea is also occasionally expressed as the "priority" of matter over mind.

The third thesis asserts the principle of knowability of the material world. There is indeed much that we do not know and at this point in historical time that we cannot know, but there is no limit to knowledge *in principle*. The history of human thought is replete with examples of those who prematurely proclaimed limits to knowing. They or their followers, however, have repeatedly suffered the embarrassment of seeing those limits dissolve in the advance of real knowledge. In terms of strategy alone it is foolish to declare such limits. But it is no mere strategic consideration that leads materialists to adopt this thesis. It follows rationally both from the first two theses and from our experience of collective human history. Over and again the latter has demonstrated that only ignorance stands between the knower and the thing-in-itself.

Modern materialism originates in and retains a close association with the practice of science. As such it is entirely consistent with and supportive of what Scheffler (1976) has called the "standard view" of scientific practice:

> . . . this view affirms the objectivity of science; more specifically, it understands science to be a systematic public enterprise, controlled by logic and empirical fact, whose purpose it is to formulate the truth about the natural world. . . . Any two theories of the same domain of phenomena may be compared to see if either is superior in accounting for the relevant empirical facts. . . . When one hypothesis is superceded by another, the genuine facts it had purported to account for are not inevitably lost, they are typically passed on to its successor, which conserves them as it reaches out to embrace additional facts. Thus it is that science can be cumula-

tive at the observational or experimental level, despite its lack of cumulativeness at the theoretical level. . . . (Scheffler, 1976, pp. 8–9).

The last point in the excerpt from Scheffler is worth special notice. The materialist asserts a gradual historical increase in real knowledge. But this requires from time to time a radical alteration in how we codify that knowledge. According to this view, then, the Newtonian and Einsteinian "revolutions" were not revolutions in knowledge, but only in theory—which by no means minimizes the enormous significance of those events. The materialist view of the history of science is, however, clearly at variance with the idealist views of Thomas Kuhn (1962).

Some Negative Arguments

Supporting arguments from materialism are both negative and positive. The negative arguments are directed at opposing views and positive arguments offer direct support for the advocated view. We shall first examine some representatives of the former.

Materialism opposes idealism. It is maintained that there can be no other philosophical worldviews: the opposition is exclusive and exhaustive. The reason for this is that in contemplating anything, we are necessarily confronted with two things, the object contemplated and the idea of the object. The fundamental question is: Which is prior? Or, which determines the other? Wherein lies the essence? The question has been put in many ways. The case of invention offers a homely example of the issue. Did a steam engine exist before Mr. Watt had the idea of one? Obviously not. The idealist might take this as a *prima facie* case in his or her favor: the idea clearly existed first and then determined the characteristics of its object, much as the whole material world existed first as idea in the mind of God. More secular versions of this world view are found in the philosophies of Plato, Aristotle, Descartes, Leibniz, Kant, Hegel, Kuhn, and hundreds of others.

The materialist, however, will point to the fact that Mr. Watt did not live in a social and historical vacuum and that the idea of a steam engine was not new with him, and that it was itself the result of (determined by) a long history of material practice with machines, heat, etc. Furthermore, this is no "chicken and the egg" problem. The objects of practice are ultimately prior to practice, and practice itself is prior to consciousness of practice. There clearly were things and organisms, and action of the latter upon the former, long before ideas (mind) emerged to guide practice as Mr. Watt's idea guided his.

But still, someone might ask, what is *wrong* with idealism? In order to facilitate answering this question it will be useful to make a distinction between two historical forms of idealism. These can be labeled "objective" and "subjective." The objective form shares much in common with materialism. For instance, it maintains that the objective world exists and that it is knowable.

Christian theology and Platonism are classic examples. The former gives ontological priority to divine idea, the latter to universal ideas of which the things of
this world are imperfect copies.

The implication of objective idealism that most distinguishes it from materialism is methodological. In order to know things, we are advised to discover
and study the ideas which determine them, i.e., universals or divine will. The
principal argument against this view is also methodological. It points to the
ultimate dogmatism upon which any knowledge-conclusions must be based. In
theology this dogmatism may be cloaked somewhat by appeal to some nonle-
gitimate epistemological principle such as revelation or faith. But in any case,
how are we to resolve the differences if I discover universals that are different
from Plato's, or divine principles different from the Christian's? There is no
appeal except to dogmatism. Now, Christians long ago recognized this fact and
resigned themselves to it, and therefore do not take this as an argument against
their position. Scientists, by contrast, have recognized the need to remain
within normal epistemological limits, and from their point of view, therefore,
this kind of idealism would be regarded as bad science, and to point to its
dogmatism would constitute a legitimate negative argument. Objective idealism
is rejected on precisely the same grounds that lead us to abjure the "naming
fallacy." The invention of a Good or universal idea no more explains things
than does naming them.

The subjective form of idealism is more complex, but generally refers all
knowledge back to individual—as opposed to universal—ideas. This ordinarily
does not entail a denial of an external objective world: that would be blatant
solipsism. Rather it tends to be expressed as an insurmountable dependence of
knowledge on some, usually distorting, individual, subjective contribution to
the knowing process. Protagoras claimed, for example, that "man is the measure of all things," meaning roughly that reality is whatever we make it out to
be. More modern forms of subjective idealism follow the Humean skeptical
model or the Kantian constructivist model. In either case the external world is
not denied, but our knowledge of it is hopelessly entangled in the knowing
process itself. The individual can know only his or her own sense perceptions,
or else the world can be known but only as constructed or construed by the
innate categories of the mind.

The materialist must grant a degree of truth to subjective idealist claims
that knowledge is often distorted by bias, prejudice, or other limitations. The
materialist must also grant that knowledge is often hopelessly far from
absolute. The materialist objects, however, to the claim that knowledge is necessarily, insurmountably, and for all times limited or distorted by such factors.
The materialist agrees with the subjective idealist that truth is relative, but
would not agree that it is relative only to some set of arbitrary personal (or even
social) frameworks. Knowledge, for the materialist, is relative only to
ignorance, that is, in the sense that knowledge is at any point in history only

partial. We may never know the whole truth, but we are learning more and more of it.

The arguments against subjective idealism are of two sorts. On the one hand we can point to a kind of dogmatism such as we find in objective idealism. A restriction is here being placed on the knowing process that is unwarranted and arbitrary. As mentioned earlier there is too much historical evidence opposed to subjective idealist claims about such limits to give them any real credence.

The second main line of argument is either a *reductio ad absurdum* or, what amounts to the same thing, a demonstration of an underlying solipsism. Owing to the limitations on the knowing process mentioned above, subjective idealists usually claim that theories are ultimately untestable. But this itself is a theory. How can such a claim be made, as if it were true, when it is itself untestable. The theory itself does not compel anyone to believe it. Subjective idealism inevitably undermines itself in this and other similar ways. We have already alluded to the solipsistic nature of logical positivism. Such is to be discovered in all subjective idealist positions because the self (individual consciousness or perception) is the only acknowledged final reference for the certainty or truth of all claims.

Some Positive Arguments

A favorite argument of the idealists, particularly the subjectivist variety, runs somewhat as follows: "If you materialists are so certain that real objects exist independent of your consciousness or perception of them, then prove it." Any materialist who now accepts this challenge at face value, as every good idealist well knows, will fail in the attempt at proof, thus confirming the idealist in the certainty of his or her beliefs (as dogmatic or absurd as they may ultimately be).

Now there is much that can be said here about the nature of argument, proof, and belief, but I shall restrict myself simply to an outline of what I believe to be the correct response to the idealist's challenge. This is that anyone, idealist or materialist, who takes the questions of mind-independence to be a matter for proof is quite mistaken, and anyone who makes this mistake is philosophically lost. What the idealist is demanding is an argument, with as yet unspecified premises, the conclusion of which is the mind-independent existence of objects. But what could such premises be? At most they would themselves be idealist (e.g., "God created objects"), and again the materialist loses. What must be seen is that there is no more fundamental premise than the mind-independent existence of objects. Mind-independence *is* the most fundamental premise, the one from which ultimately all other proofs proceed. Reasonable people can debate the existence of God; they can debate individual interpretations of the world; but they cannot debate the existence of the pen in my hand. I prove its existence by showing it. Its existence is its own proof and anyone who persists in denying its existence after having been shown it would be deemed unreasonable.

At this point the idealist may take a different tack. He or she may say that mind-independent existence of objects never was the *main* item of contention. It might be granted that there is such existence, but it would be asserted that we cannot know these objects as they are in themselves. Now this line of idealist argument is also based upon a mistake which, when revealed, can be turned into an argument in support of materialism. A little probing reveals that this idealist argument rests upon a representationist theory of perception which is almost always taken simply for granted and therefore hardly ever acknowledged, let alone examined.

The representationist theory of perception, also known as the "Lockean" theory, assumes three distinct levels or moments in the perceptual process: object, sensation, idea. Ideas are always of sensations, never of objects directly. This being the case we cannot be sure how well the sensation represents the object since we have no access to the object except through sensation. It is entirely likely—indeed experience seems insistent upon it—that sensations are in fact largely determined by ideas. Thus there is no way of sorting out the influence of object and idea: the object-in-itself is hopelessly out of reach.

But the representationist theory of perception is, on the surface at any rate, no more justified than the alternative theory of "direct" perception. According to this theory what we perceive are not sensations or other representations of objects, but objects themselves. When I look at the pen in my hand, I see the pen. The introspective evidence is decidedly in favor of direct perception. I believe the theory is favored by all other evidence, and reason as well, but to make the case would take us well beyond the scope of the present chapter. It will be sufficient here if the reader sees how different the philosophical issues appear if a convincing case were to be made for direct perception. If we perceive objects, then we *can,* in principle, sort out the competing influences of object and idea, we can learn about objects-in-themselves, and we can assert their existence as the ultimate premise of our arguments. Materialism flows naturally and necessarily from the theory of direct perception, and arguments and evidence supporting such a theory are, *ipso facto,* arguments and evidence for materialism.

DIALECTICS: MAKING MATERIALISM WORK

Certainly, materialism is, and has been since the time of the presocratic scientist-philosophers, the preferred philosophy of science. This is because it supports the possibility of discovery of objective qualities, and of genuinely objective knowledge. It permits the formulation of unequivocally testable theories, and supports an historical view of cumulative knowledge. Clearly its alternatives, including positivism, are irredeemably plagued with either dogmatism or absurdity, or both.

But materialism, in its classical form, from Thales to Moleschott, had its characteristic difficulties. In the modern (from Bacon on) mechanist form these difficulties were most acute and apparent. Most of all, materialism had problems with motion and mind, both of obvious importance to psychology. These problems can be illustrated by the philosophy of Thomas Hobbes (to which the materialist psychologies of Jacques Loeb and John B. Watson bear a strong resemblance). For Hobbes the mind was reduced to the workings of a clock-like body. For all practical purposes mind was epiphenomenal. Such a treatment is entirely unsatisfactory for those of us whose introspections confirm the very unmachine-like manner in which we think, plan, and make decisions, not to mention the obvious reality of our own consciousness. It is not surprising that the dualist understandings of mind, like that of Descartes, had greater popular acceptance.

Also for Hobbes, the movements of the bodily machine to which mind was reduced could not be any more spontaneous in the human body than in an egg-beater. All motion was thus conceived to originate in external stimulation. The motion of our bodies was nothing more than the motion passed on to them by other moving things.

Now this all appears quite tidy until one asks how it happens that those other things are moving. The problem of infinite regress becomes immediately obvious. The materialist seemed to have two choices: either give in to idealism and admit God (or some other abstraction) as the prime mover, or retreat into some kind of obstinate (dogmatic) refusal to deal with the problem. Again, no surprise that idealism was preferred for popular consumption.

Clearly, if we can find reasonable solutions to the problems of motion and mind within the constraints of the materialist worldview, as I believe we have for the problem of perception, then we will have not only a scientifically preferred philosophy, but a genuinely workable one as well.

Dialectics is what makes materialism work, by providing solutions to problems like those of motion and mind. How does it do this? In order to answer this question, even in outline, we shall have first to understand something of what Hegel, the discoverer of the modern dialectic, was up to.

Hegel was concerned that there was such a poor correspondence between the world, as people were coming better to know it in the early nineteenth century, and the philosophy that purported to account for it. In particular, the world was experienced as an organic unity while the categories of philosophy resembled more a rag-bag assortment of arbitrarily selected qualities. There had to be a way in which categories could be generated which reflected the true unity and internal relatedness of the world. Surely, he reasoned, the world had to start in some simple condition and evolve into the complex form we know (Kant had already advanced an evolutionary cosmology). But the starting point was crucial in that all subsequent complexity must be deducible from it. It could not therefore be arbitrary.

On carefully reasoned grounds, Hegel selected Being as his initial category. He then discovered that absolute undifferentiated Being was identical to its opposite, Nothing. In fact as one thought of the first category, one found oneself inevitably slipping into the second. Neither Being or Nothing were really static; they were inherently in motion. And it was this inherent motion in Being and Nothing that generated a third category, Becoming. From there, Hegel found, a category system embracing the whole of human experience could be generated. The end product was, like the world, a diversity, but one that, also like the world, formed an organic unity, what he called a "self-determining monism." The unity was guaranteed by the fact that each category was *genetically* (and therefore necessarily) related to all other categories. This genetic relationship, in turn, came about owing to the fact and specific nature of the internal motion of the categories. Logic could no longer be regarded simply as the rules by which categories are combined, but was rather the laws governing the self-generation of categories.

We may justifiably raise our eyebrows at the substance of Hegel's system, but we should not be thereby distracted from the really significant insights that it contains. These are basically the ideas of universal inherent motion and universal genetic interrelation. It is worth mentioning here that these insights are essentially the same as are found in Darwin's theory of evolution. If we substitute species for categories the resemblance is striking.

Now with respect to motion, dialectics is effectively a theory of inherent motion. We need not go into the details of this theory; it is sufficient to see that if motion is conceived (correctly, I believe) as inherent to matter, then there need be no appeal to prime movers. A principled solution to every problem of motion (mechanical, process, transformation, transmutation) becomes possible.

The problem of mind also finds a solution in the dialectical view of motion and genetic relationship. If mind, or consciousness, is seen as a property of highly evolved matter, then we have a basis for asserting that mind is indeed distinct from the body (which all organisms possess), as the dualists held, but at the same time the two form a unity since mind has evolved from other bodily functions. Psychology thus necessarily becomes an evolutionary science charged with, among other things, discovering the process by which mind has developed phylogenetically. The old dualisms and monisms are now seen to have been based on a static logic, and thereby to have abstracted either side of a dialectical opposition from its actual concrete unity.

DIALECTICS, REDUCTIONISM, OBJECTIVISM, AND INDIVIDUALISM

In Hegel's system the reality of Being could only be discovered in its internal relation to Nothing. Being and Nothing are distinct but also identical. Being, taken as distinct only, out of relation to Nothing, is abstract. To be understood concretely Being must be seen in its opposition to Nothing—in its identity with Nothing. For dialectics, the truth is always concrete, that is, "in relation," never abstract.

The reductionism of Hobbes (and Loeb and Watson, and many other psychological theorists) is untrue because it is abstract. Surely the mind can be reduced to bodily function, but that does not mean that it is merely bodily function. Descartes' view of mind was equally abstract because it asserted only its distinction from bodily function and overlooked its identity. Mind, concretely and therefore truly understood, must be seen in its distinctness from, as well as its identity with, bodily function. And the key to the relationship between these opposites is a developmental one. A dialectical view, therefore, is neither dualist nor reductionist; it is one of process. This applies not only to the mind-body relationship, but to all complex phenomena which earlier materialists sought to understand by reduction to simpler or apparently more basic ones.

It will be recalled that positivism was rejected because of its one-sided emphasis on objectivity and social knowledge. From a dialectical point of view this was an abstract and untrue philosophy. Concretely understood, objectivity is achieved only in the preservation and correct appreciation of the subjective (and vice versa). Both must be explained: neither can be explained away. But this is not done by merging the two sides into an abstract identity. Reciprocal errors do not correct one another. The subject exists only in relation to an object. We are never merely conscious, only conscious-of. . . . And objects, as we become conscious of them, become objects-for-us. That is the nature, the essence, of science, of getting-to-know.

Likewise knowledge is social. Our whole existence is social. But knowledge and existence are also individual. One cannot stand (concretely) without the other. To understand one requires appreciation of the other. To reduce knowledge or existence to one or the other would be to abstract it into unreality. Everything I know or do is part of a social history, touched in endless ways by an infinite number of others. Yet that social history consists of the actions of others who are individuals. Can one exist without the other? Of course not.

What I am saying here is, I hope, patently obvious, hardly worth the effort of saying—except that so much of our philosophy and psychology appears to overlook it. Dialectics helps us to retain the concrete two-sidedness of things and thereby also to produce better theories of real events and processes.

SOME IMPLICATIONS FOR PSYCHOLOGY

Implications of dialectical materialism will to some extent be apparent from what has already been said. My purpose here will be to draw out a few more in somewhat greater detail. These will concern psychology as a science, the subject matter of psychology, and mental development.

Psychology as a Science

Scientific practice, as Francis Bacon recognized with his concepts of *experimenta fructifera* and *experimenta lucifera,* is simply an extension of ordinary human practice in which work is done upon an object in order to alter it in some predetermined way. Scientific practice has the additional goal of gaining systematic knowledge of the object. By seeking to alter the object according to historically determined principles of scientific method, the object reveals to us its properties. Our knowledge of these properties is then codified into theories which then guide further ordinary or scientific practice. Clearly if all this is to be the case, then the object must have independent existence and must be accessible to our knowing. This is what dialectical materialism asserts.

The theory, being a codification of properties of the object learned about through practice, is a conscious or cognitive reflection of the reality of the object. This does not mean, however, that the theory cannot be wrong, biased, or incomplete. It will almost certainly be incomplete since we have good reason to believe that the properties of objects are infinite. But incompleteness does not render the theory nonobjective—as long as what it represents reflects the object correctly, that is, objectively. The theory may be biased or wrong for any number of reasons, and to the extent that it is, it is also nonobjective. But because the object is the final arbiter in theoretical questions and disputes, further practice with the object can, in principle, reveal and finally correct the bias. Only the mind independence and accessibility of the object make this correction possible. Indeed these conditions are the *sine qua non* of resolving theoretical differences and testing theories. Science, in any meaningful sense of the word, would be impossible if we were to make concessions on these two vital conditions. There is no such things as a science worthy of the name whose theories are, by self-proclamation, untestable.

With respect to these broad scientific requirements, psychology is no different from any other science. If we are interested in the process of language acquisition by children, are we not to direct our attention to that process itself, to study it in order to discover *its* properties? What would be the point of going through these motions if we cannot, in principle, gain an objective account of the process. If all we can get is some arbitrary construction or interpretation, would we not be better off calling it "poetry" from the start? Why all the pretense of science? But science is not a pretense. We know from much historical experience that real knowledge can be had from objective investigation of processes, whether psychological or physical.

The Subject Matter of Psychology

The basic requirements of a scientific psychology may be identical to those of physics, but that does not rule out significant differences stemming from subject matter. The anti-reductionism of dialectical materialism asserts from the beginning that the subject matter of psychology, although developmentally related to and therefore ultimately forming a unity with that of physics and biology, is qualitatively distinct and therefore requires its own peculiar methods and theories. Psychology, from this point of view, is a distinctly human science. Something has evolved in human functioning that is evolutionarily new and marks human beings as qualitatively different from all other living creatures.

The surface features of this difference are obvious to all who care to look. We have culture, history, complex divisions of labor, language, etc. No ape, however clever it might otherwise be, has ever written an essay aimed at persuading other apes that a particular worldview was necessary in support of their scientific activities. The differences are obvious, but specifying what it is that lies at the core of all this, and that should form the subject matter of psychology is more difficult. (By "subject matter" I mean that in terms of which psychology is defined, i.e., "psychology is the science of. . . .")

It is easier to decide what it is not. For example, it is not behavior. And there are all sorts of good reasons why. Behavior flagrantly ignores precisely what we are trying to grasp—that which has evolved such as to drastically mark off human existence as unique. After all, paramecia, mussels, and rats behave. And if it turns out they do so according to the laws of conditioning, then we should be inclined to think that these laws belong to biology and not uniquely to psychology.

But there is another reason, based on dialectical considerations, for rejecting behavior. It is too abstract. The fact that all organisms behave already suggests abstractness, but this is all the more apparent when we consider that even organs and cells behave. Physical particles behave. Stock markets behave. And so on. Even if we tried restricting the meaning to "what whole human organisms do," we have not solved the problem. Consider how the behavior conception has historically been expressed in terms of responses that can be attached to or detached from stimuli. The response here is conceived as essentially out of relation: it is abstract. Suppose we restrict the meaning further to S–R relationships (of whole human organisms). It is still abstract insofar as it implies (as indeed it has in most behaviorist psychology) a one-way street, a reaction of the organism to external stimulation. What we know of actual concrete human action is that it most often flows from us and is more often guided by stimuli than instigated by them. (It should be recognized that Skinner's concept of the "operant" goes a long way toward meeting these objections, but from a dialectical materialist point of view not nearly far enough.)

Psychology's subject matter also cannot be consciousness. It is many ways more satisfactory than behavior, but it, too, suffers from abstractness. This is nowhere more clearly seen than in the early experimental psychologies of Wundt, but particularly of Titchener, whose psychology was the epitome of arid and largely useless abstraction. The "act" psychologists and early functionalists came closer to what we are seeking. "Act" and "mental life" were concepts aimed at making consciousness more concrete, putting it back into relation.

Certainly it is this kind of consciousness for which psychology must account. We have already pointed out that psychology, from a dialectical materialist point of view, is an evolutionary science. To give an account of consciousness, therefore, is to discover the context in which consciousness has evolved (or, ontogenetically developed). This context is what Leontyev (1981) and others have called "activity." This differs from behavior in that it is a unit that encompasses both subject and object (similar to Dewey's 1896 concept of "coordination"). Motives, goals, means, etc. are not "added" to activity but are intrinsic to it. In the course of evolution, activity becomes conscious. Labor is the prototypical conscious activity, particularly as exemplified in the manufacture of tools. In order to make a stone tool, the primitive human had to have "in mind" the use to which it would be put. This consciousness of purpose then guided the tool making activity. This, in turn, became the basis of the social division of labor in which planned, coordinated activities of different individuals are guided by the shared consciousness of a common goal. The importance of language, meaning and its communication, in this development is obvious.

We could go on to elaborate the details of this view, but hopefully sufficient has been said to indicate the need for a concrete conception of our subject matter, however it may be labeled.

Mental Development

It should be clear by now that development forms a major preoccupation for *dialectical* materialists. To understand virtually anything is to understand it in its development. The developmental process, therefore, becomes a focus of theoretical concern.

What has prevailed until recently in our psychology might be called an "accretion" theory of development. This entails a view of the process in which nothing new emerges. It is understood entirely as quantitative increments of something already present, with some occasional rearranging of elements. In this view, the concept of stages is to be avoided altogether or used simply as a linguistic convenience. The adult is viewed as simply a bigger and more complex or more differentiated child. Usually the principles of learning, readily reducible to a mechanical stimulus and response substitution model, are taken as providing all the explanation that is needed.

At this point it should not be necessary to say that dialectical materialists abhor such a view as a travesty, an unworthy distortion of the rich and complex reality of the developmental process, one that will never lead us to an understanding adequate to that reality. Recalling Hegel, we need a theory that better matches what is actually going on. As many psychologists have recently begun to recognize, dialectics is what we need to move us in that direction.

The adult human is qualitatively different from the human infant child. The use of language is different, cognitive processes are different, the use of plans and conscious guidance of action are different, etc. To get from child to adult we need a logic of transformation, of the production of new qualities, a logic that allows us to affirm that children and adults are both the same and different, that facilitates our grasping the real process by which the child becomes the adult. What's more, we need a logic that is not merely of our invention, but one that is discoverable in the developmental process itself, one that can be codified in theory and tested against the reality of actual children becoming actual adults. Dialectical materialism provides the philosophical, metatheoretical support for such a project. I am not aware of any other philosophy that does this (least of all positivism in any of its forms). This is why I stated so confidently at the beginning that dialectical materialism is the only metatheory appropriate to any truly scientific psychological practice.

CONCLUDING REMARK

Since at least the time of Democritus, scientific thinkers have gravitated to materialist philosophy. The reasons are plan to see. It is the only philosophy that unequivocally affirms both the real existence and genuine knowability of the objects that excite scientific curiosity. Anything short of this undermines the very possibility of scientific understanding.

But modern materialism is not the materialism of Democritus. The position has grown since then, and dialectical materialism is the latest stage in that growth. In modern times we have moved from a mechanical materialism, such as that espoused by Newton and Hobbes, that was unable adequately to grasp development and was even forced to deny subjectivity, to dialectical materialism which retains all the scientific advantages of the older position and, as well, embraces development and subjectivity as essential categories. Such a claim by itself should warrant more serious attention than has ordinarily been paid this philosophy in Western countries. Perhaps it is time to put ideology aside—for psychology's sake.

BIOGRAPHICAL NOTES

I have avoided numerous references in the text. Therefore I propose here to inform the reader where he or she might go to get more complete information on the topics discussed. What follows is by no means exhaustive, but is intended only as a starter for readers who wish to pursue further the matters dealt with in this chapter.

Somewhat elementary discussions of dialectical materialist philosophy are to be found in Cornforth (1973, 1975), Politzer (1976), and Sommerville (1983). Selsam and Martel (1963) provide a good selection from the "classics" with clear introductory comments on various topics. More advanced discussions are found in Kharin (1981), Konstantinov (1974), which is a very comprehensive work, and Ruben (1979). Goldstick (1980) gives an excellent exposition of the problem of perception.

Nonmarxist materialists should also be consulted. Good examples are found in Bhaskar (1978, 1979) and Bunge (1973). A comprehensive treatment of perception is provided by Armstrong (1971).

Regarding dialectics in particular, the best introduction to Hegelian dialectics, in my view, is found in Stace (1955). After such an introduction, Hegel (1975) is actually quite readable. Two of my own papers may help to tie all this into psychology (Tolman, 1983a, 1983b).

Good summaries of arguments around the problem of objectivity are found in Cunningham (1973), Cunningham and Goldstick (1979), and Scheffler (1967). A superb collection of essays dealing with both sides of the issue can be found in Hollis and Lukes (1982). Some examples of dialectical materialist psychology are found in Lawler (1978), Leontyev (1981), Levitin (1983), Strickland (1984), Talysina (1981), Vygotsky (1981),and Wertsch (1981). A highly accessible treatment of the evolutionary conception of human nature can be found in Woolfson (1982).

The best known "refutation" of dialectical materialism is that of Popper (1961, 1962, 1963), now a "classic" of its genre. This "refutation," like most others, proves to have been founded upon distortions, often grotesque, of its target, as was brilliantly demonstrated in a rejoinder by Cornforth (1968). The difficulty was anticipated by Hegel already in 1830: "No great expenditure of wit is needed to make fun of the maxim that Being and Nothing are the same, or rather to adduce absurdities which, it is erroneously asserted, are the consequences and illustrations of that maxim" (Hegel, 1975, p. 129).

REFERENCES

Armstrong, D. M. (1961). *Perception and the physical world.* London: Routledge & Kegan Paul.

Bhaskar, R. (1978). *A realist theory of science.* Sussex: The Harvester Press.

Bhaskar, R. (1979). *The possibility of naturalism.* Sussex: The Harvester Press.

Bunge, M. (1973). *Method, model and matter.* Dordrecht: D. Reidel.

Carnap, R. (1956). The methodological character of theoretical concepts. In H. Feigl & M. Scriven (Eds.), *Minnesota studies in the philosophy of science, I* (pp. 38–76). Minneapolis: University of Minnesota Press.

Cornforth, M. (1950). *In defence of philosophy: Against positivism and pragmatism.* London: Lawrence and Wishart.

Cornforth, M. (1968). *The open philosophy and the open society: A reply to Dr. Karl Popper's Refutations of Marxism.* New York: International Publishers.

Cornforth, M. (1973). *The theory of knowledge.* New York: International Publishers. (Original work published in 1955).

Cornforth, M. (1975). *Materialism and the dialectical method.* New York: International Publishers. (Original work published in 1953).

Cunningham, F. (1973). *Objectivity in social science.* Toronto: University of Toronto Press.

Cunningham, F. (1973). *Objectivity in social science.* Toronto: University of Toronto Press.

Cunningham, F., & Goldstick, D. (1979). Marxism and epistemological relativism. *Social Praxis, 6,* 237–253.

Dewey, J. (1896). The reflex arc concept in psychology. *Psychological Review, 3,* 357–370.

Feyerabend, P. L. (1962). Explanation, reduction, and empiricism. In H. Feigl & G. Maxwell (Eds.), *Minnesota studies in the philosophy of science, III.* Minneapolis: University of Minnesota Press (pp. 28–97).

Goldstick, D. (1980). The Leninist theory of perception. *Dialogue (Canadian Philosophical Review), 19,* 1–19.

Hanson, N. R. (1958). *Patterns of discovery.* Cambridge: Cambridge University Press.

Hegel, G. W. F. (1975). *Hegel's logic.* London: Oxford University Press. (Original work published in 1830).

Hollis, M., & Lukes, S. (Eds.). (1982). *Rationality and relativism.* Oxford: Basic Blackwell.

Joad, C. E. M. (1950). *A critique of logical positivism.* London: Victor Gollancz.

Kharin, Y. A. (1981). *Fundamentals of dialectics.* Moscow: Progress Publishers.

Konstantinov, F. V., et al. (1974). *The fundamentals of Marxist-Leninist philosophy.* Moscow: Progress Publishers.

Kuhn, T. S. (1962). *The structure of scientific revolutions.* Chicago: University of Chicago Press. (Enlarged edition published 1970).

Lawler, J. M. (1978). *IQ, heritability and racism.* New York: International Publishers.

Lenin, V. I. (1972). Materialism and empirio-criticism: Critical comments on a reactionary philosophy. *Collected Works, vol. 14.* Moscow: Progress Publishers. (Original work published in 1980).

Leontyev, A. N. (1981). *Problems of the development of the mind.* Moscow: Progress Publishers.

Levitin, K. (1983). *One is not born a personality.* Moscow: Progress Publishers.

Polanyi, M. (1958). *Personal knowledge.* Chicago: University of Chicago Press.

Politzer, G. (1976). *Elementary principles of philosophy.* New York: International Publishers.

Popper, K. R. (1961). *The poverty of historicism.* New York: Harper & Row.

Popper, K. R. (1962). *The open society and its enemies.* (4th ed.). London: Routledge & Kegan Paul.

Popper, K. R. (1963). *Conjectures and refutations.* London: Routledge & Kegan Paul.

Ruben, D. H. (1979). *Marxism and materialism.* (2nd ed.). Sussex: Harvester Press.

Scheffler, I. (1967). *Science and subjectivity.* Indianapolis: Bobbs-Merrill.

Selsam, H., & Martel, H. (1963). *Reader in Marxist philosophy.* New York: International Publishers.

Sommerville, J. (1983). *The philosophy of Marxism: An exposition.* Minneapolis: Marxist Educational Press. (Original work published in 1967).

Stace, W. T. (1955). *The philosophy of Hegel.* New York: Dover Publications. (Original work published in 1924).

Strickland, L. H. (Ed.). (1984). *Directions in soviet social psychology.* New York: Springer-Verlag.

Talysina, N. (1981). *The psychology of learning.* Moscow: Progress Publishers.

Tolman, C. (1983a). Categories, logic, and the problem of necessity in theories of mental development. *Studia Psychologica, 25,* 179–190.

Tolman, C. (1983b). Further comments on the meaning of "dialectic." *Human Development, 26,* 320–324.

Vygotsky, L. S. (1981). *Mind in society.* (M. Cole, V. John-Steiner, S. Scribner, & E. Souberman, Trans., Eds.). Cambridge: Harvard University Press.

Wertsch, J. V. (Ed.). (1981). *The concept of activity in soviet psychology.* Armonk: M. E. Sharpe.

Woolfson, C. (1982). *The labour theory of culture.* London: Routledge & Kegan Paul.

Part Three

Metatheoretical Applications

Chapter 11

After Social Psychology

Philip Wexler

INTRODUCTION

I see social psychology, like any other academic or mass discourse, as an aspect of historically changing forms of social organization and collective social practices. What I think is happening now is that not only social psychology, but also the critical theory that has been its loyal opposition, are both being replaced by historically newer discourses. Social theory is giving way to literary theory. First, I want to describe that discursive shift.

The importance and effectiveness of literary theory is not, I think, due to its intellectual superiority to the earlier kinds of social theories, but to its historical appropriateness to broad new forms of sociocultural organization and possibilities. Second, I want to indicate what I think are some of these social and cultural changes.

Social change does not, I think, occur by one social form or type simply

The thesis of this paper was presented at the American Psychological Association 1984 meetings in Toronto.

advancing to take the place of another. Rather, new forms of social life result from the dynamic tensions and oppositions of the present. I try to locate changes in discourse and society especially within one such dynamic tension. Third, I describe this dynamic tension as one of commodification and dereification: a process in which social relations become like commodities and obscure the human social work through which they are made; but are also subject to decomposing "dereification," a display of the processes of making, of composition and production. I try to show specifically what this dialectic means for current forms of social speech and social practice.

Last, as I look toward the future I want to identify historically vibrant social practices, and the conditions which either enhance or inhibit their development. The theoretical debates are ultimately about which of these social practices are going to prevail.

THESIS

American social psychology is an historical discourse. The object that it helped construct and operate was the ideological apparatus of corporate liberal capitalism—the more institutionally organized, expert-driven historical successor to free-market, so-called "laissez-faire" capitalism. Corporate liberalism has "managed" the conflict of classes by the incorporation, accommodation and partnerships of labor and capital. As a later transnational corporate capitalism, and a newly restored set of private market arrangements and language have began to supplant the corporate liberal phase of capitalism, social psychology's discursive social value has begun to diminish. It is not, I think, the force of the critiques against it, but these specific changes in the social formation which are rendering social psychology less interesting. Indeed, it now appears that the critiques too—with all the vituperative spite and hatred by which they aimed to flee from social psychology's ideologically mediating meliorism—belonged to the same passing social epoch.

Critical theory was liberalism's bonded negation. Along with the liberal social psychology that it opposes, "radical" critical social theory is also losing its power to persuade. Both liberalism and its cultural radical negation—even in the limited expression of social psychology and critique—are retiring to the work of revision and ordinary paradigmatic routinization.

It is literary theory that now supplants not merely critical theory, but also social theory. The language and rhetoric of academic ideological labor is changing. The terms "society" and "individual" that social psychology and its critics enunciated and argued about are disappearing. This does not mean to say that some new literary discourse will not also play an ideologically active role that parallels the historic social function of social psychology. It already plays that role: to contain and block societal movements toward socialization.

But the ideological process of containing contradictions and blocking change is different. It is less mediated by the cultural liberalism, and the familiar academic terms of social psychology. Instead, new areas of social life are denaturalized and demystified for social use as commodities. When social practices and beliefs are denaturalized, they are open-to-question and lose the status of "taken-for-granted." In the process of naturalization, the natural world becomes a more transparent social world, but also a world more manipulable as an object of commodification.

Nothing less than the twin pillars of bourgeois ideology are now denaturalized and readied for commodity-use. They are the ideological elements culture-as-nature and individualism. Within this space, this gap where ideology is at first denaturalized only to then become a commodity, new social practices and discourses are created that have the power to illuminate and revision the social order—and also to confirm it by blocking the imagination of change.

The most evident new discourse created in this gap is, I think, "literary theory," and more narrowly, textualism. Here, it is the category "culture" and its constituent processes that are denaturalized or dereified. The activity of symbolic labor or signification, that composes or makes "culture" is more transparent. The discourse of dereified culture, in literary theory and textualism generally, and in poststructuralism particularly, can however, be made opaque, become commodified and so be reintegrated into a semiotic class society, (Baudrillard, 1981). New forms which the denaturalization of individualism takes are in less familiar terms of a symbolic economy of identity. An economy of identity, in which interactional resources are constantly mobilized to create loci of value, as individual identity, can be centralized, rationalized, and then appropriated, leaving only defensive, "minimal selves" (Lasch, 1984).

The outcome of this dynamic, this opening and closing of social possibility, depends on collective action. For it is not simply that the discourses of literary theory and economy of identity necessarily historically supplant social psychology and its critics. Rather, the articulation of the newer discourses enables different historically specific collective practices. In the present historical situation, I suggest that the displacement of social psychology and critical theory by literary theory and textualism enables a better understanding of such practices as collective criticism and collective cultural creation. Similarly, an economy of identity makes collective production and private appropriation of symbolic identity value transparent, and leads toward questions of the ownership of socially produced identity values. In sum, we face as a practical social dynamic an expansion of commodification that includes even pillars of the ideological apparatus—naturalized culture and individualized identity—on one side, and on the other, a possibility of the collectivization or the socialization of value—in the media of meaning and identity. This is a new version of the old dynamic of social production and individual appropriation in which social psychology originated, and played its role against earlier collectivizing or socializing tendencies in American history (Wexler, 1983). In the new context, the conflict over social labor—now in cultural and psychological media—and the private ownership of these media as commodities, becomes simultaneously deeper and more evident.

DISCURSIVE SHIFT: LITERARY THEORY AND TEXTUALISM

The historic disintegration of corporate liberalism carries away with it ideologically mediating academic languages, like social psychology. Among the newer forms of academic speech (excepting the language of information machines), none is now more pervasive than literary language. Not merely social psychology and its critics, but social theory generally is being recast and replaced by literary theory. Rorty, for example, asserts that the influence of literary theory extends beyond social theory (1982, p. 155), to: ". . . the plausible claim that literature has now displaced religion, science, and philosophy as the presiding discipline of our culture . . ." He uses the term "textualism" to refer to the intellectual movement of historians, social scientists, and philosophers, as well as literary theorists, who (Rorty, 1982, p. 137) ". . . write as if there were nothing but texts." Textualism is a cultural form, which though it inherits idealism's distrust of science and Romanticism's literariness, is itself a "postphilosophical form." It takes final shape passing through Pragmatism, which does not claim to represent the discovered truth of reality, but only a more useful way of talking. Textualism, as the historical effect of Idealism, Romanticism and Pragmatism, has its counterpart in literary modernism, (1982, p. 153) ". . . which prides itself on its autonomy and novelty rather than truthfulness to experience or its discovery of preexisting significance."

In quite a different vocabulary, Geertz also asserts a replacement of traditional social theory by literary theory. His way of saying it is that there is (1980, p. 168) a "revised style of discourse in social studies." The revision is that the analogies which are the bases of understanding ". . . are coming more and more from the contrivances of cultural performance than from those of physical manipulation. The imagery of the humanities now supplants physical and mechanical metaphors as the mode of understanding in the social sciences. These images of cultural performance are those of games, dramas, and (1980, p. 175): "the text analogy . . . in some ways, the broadest of the recent configurations of social theory, the most venturesome, and the least well-developed."

The view of social life as a text, underlines the so-called "interpretive turn" (Rabinow and Sullivan, 1979) in modern social science, and a contextualist approach to symbolic action. It takes Geertz close also to Rorty's antifoundationalism, and Pragmatism's noncorrespondence approach to "reality." Unlike Rorty, Geertz doesn't want to abandon the "mirror of nature." But he does, however, want to understand social life differently; not as an object to be reduced by imposing physical metaphors, but as symbolic action to be interpreted by reading.

The interpretive turn carries analogies of the humanities, particularly literature, to the heart of social science understanding. The reasons for this change are unclear. In Geertz's terms, the change is a "genre mixing," a "cultural shift" that represents a new interpretive convention, part of a "democratic temper" and an accommodation to a (1980, p. 166): ". . . situation at once fluid, plural, uncentered, and ineradicably untidy."

Marxism would read the rise of textualism and the discursive shift from social to literary theory not merely as that of a new "interpretive convention," but as part of social history. In an attempt to grasp this change, Marxism could offer an explanation alternative to those of intellectual history or cultural shifts. While he is not writing about modern literary theory, Perry Anderson's (1976) view of the history of "Western Marxism" can be extended to explain the displacement of social theory by textualism.

In Anderson's view, since the political defeats of the post First World War period, Western Marxism has been characterized by a (1976, p. 29): ". . . structural divorce of this Marxism from political practice." What Anderson calls Marxism's "unending detour" away from the masses and from political practice was the result of a series of political defeats that have so deeply affected the Marxist tradition that it is possible to say, as Anderson does, that (1976, p. 42): "The hidden hallmark of Western Marxism as a whole is thus that it is a product of defeat." The "formation in defeat" has meant a neglect of concrete materialist analyses of strategies of class struggle and studies of modes of production and "political machinery." Instead, Marxism became a theory of academic philosophers, who brought it into the ambit of (1976, p. 55) "contemporary bourgeois culture." The theoretical representation of this cultural embourgeoisement was that the central topic of study in Western Marxism became "superstructures." "Theoreticism"—the separation of theory from practice—that has characterized this Marxism, is ahistorical, except that it follows the historical path of bourgeois academic culture. "The most striking single trait of Western Marxism as a common tradition," writes Anderson (1976, p. 56), "is thus perhaps the constant presence and influence on it of successive types of European idealism."

Extending Anderson's argument, textualism, as the successor to idealist and romantic philosophy, is simply the most recent instance of Western Marxism's (and social theory's) detour into bourgeois culture and the study of superstructures. Continuing to underline the defeat of revolutionary practice, this latest idealism does not simply concentrate on superstructure. It declares that the theory of superstructure is all that there is to social theory. To say, with poststructuralist philosopher Derrida that there "is nothing outside of the text," seems to eliminate not only political practice, but also social history. Textualism can then be understood as a fitting culmination to Western Marxism's (and social theory's) historic pattern of denying political practice.

This move toward theories of superstructure, first in philosophy and now in literary theory, may re-present historic forms of social life and practice as socially-abstracted academic theories. But, is not part of the work of "theory-for-practice" to socially replace such discursive displacements and to recover the possibilities of political practice which they deny?

SOCIOCULTURAL CHANGE: SEMIOTIC SOCIETY

The new social formation from which textualism speaks, is necessarily different from the corporate liberal industrialism that social psychology served. The change occurs at a number of levels: a significant move away from the general cultural climate of liberalism; important changes in the organization of social institutions; alterations in the basic productive forces of society, in the forms of cultural representation and communication, and in the organization of personal life. Taken together, these changes present the outlines of a new type of society.

The most evident sociocultural change of the past decade is the partially successful effort of a variety of social movements to effect a restoration of historically earlier cultural commitments. The cultural restoration has its forerunners. Marx commented on the restoration of Louis Bonaparte (1959, pp. 323–329):

> Society now seems to have fallen back behind its point of departure . . . They had given out the watchwords of the old society, "property, family, religion, order" . . . Every demand of . . . the most ordinary liberalism, of the most formal republicanism, of the most shallow democracy is simultaneously castigated as an "attempt on society" and stigmatized as "socialism."

Although the current "restoration" may express similar cultural content, it is the result of a peculiarly contradictory twentieth century dynamic. On the one side, the language and premodern social practices of local attachments and integration to family, religion and nation become highly valued. At the same time, there is an intensified social rationalization, instrumental and technical regulation of everyday social life, and marketization and privatization of social domains like schooling which had formerly belonged to the sphere of public institutions. What appears on the surface as a cultural restoration turns out to be part of a much more profound reorganization of social life; a reorganization toward a form of society that its critics call "corporatist."

Corporatism is increasingly the most general new institutional form that is emerging in response to capitalist crises. Corporatism surpasses the internal contradiction of groups of market-commodity actors. It wipes the slate clean of pre-capitalist feudal forms by realizing their integrative possibilities within the logic of commodity production. Panitch (1977, p. 66) defined the corporatist model as:

". . . a political structure within advanced capitalism which integrates organized socioeconomic producer groups through a system of representation and cooperative mutual interaction at the leadership level and of mobilization and social control at the mass level . . ."

Among corporatism's distinguishing features, (Panitch, citing Bowen, 1977, p. 62) are that it operates through ". . . collective agreements concluded among solidly organized 'communities of interest,' " and that it is (1977, p. 63) centered on the integration of central trade union and business organizations in national economic planning and incomes policy programmes and bodies." The important thing about corporatism is that it appears not to be state imposed, but only state coordinated. The cooperation of corporate capitalist and corporate labor bodies' representatives appears to be equal. But corporatism does not mean the end of class society. On the contrary, (quoting Jones, a British industrialist and corporatist theorist of the fifties), Panitch (1977, p. 71) emphasizes the fallacious pretense of egalitarianism in the corporate organization of society:

> Authority remains with the employer, it is he who still controls. But those who are controlled are taken into his confidence; their views are solicited; and so the control, by becoming less of an imposition, is made to operate more effectively.

Corporatism is hailed as the solution to the current crisis by business-intellectuals, on Wall Street, and in the academies and think-tanks. Rohatyn (1981, p. 16), for example wants not only a "reindustrialization," a "second Industrial Revolution," but also a social "restructuring." This would begin with a more planned investment policy, and the regulation of capital through a Reconstruction Finance Corporation. In its control of the flow of capital, this corporation would be "publicly accountable but [is] run outside of politics." According to Rohatyn, capital and wages require new organizational forms of regulation because (1980, p. 24): "The body politic is so splintered and balkanized that the impotence of the political establishment is a perfectly valid reflection of the negativism and lack of interest of the electorate." The answer (1981, p. 20): "a new pattern of cooperation."

> If the country soon wakes up, it will not do so by way of laissez-faire; nor will it do so by way of the old liberalism which has proven itself incapable of coping with our present problems, it will do so only by building a mixed economy, geared mostly to business enterprise, in which an active partnership between business, labor, and government strikes the kind of bargains—whether on an energy policy, regional policy, or industrial policy—that an advanced Western democracy requires to function . . .

Traditional conservatives, like Kevin Phillips, also see a corporatist possibility—though less sanguinely than the fiscal reconstructors and industrial evolutionists (1982, p. 27):

> . . . the new government-business partnership will probably be more corporatist than liberal, and will put high emphasis on economic growth. Accordingly, the terms "liberal" and "conservative" will tend to become irrelevant.

Corporatism poses at least a serious possibility at the form of social reorganization that will solve the capital and labor problems of the current crisis; and also resolve the antinomy between the marketizing, atomistic tendency of commodity exchange and the organicist solidarity patterns of premarket antirationalist forms of social integration. Corporatism provides for social integration according to functional relation to the commodity. The conflicting demands of exchange and integration, of calculation and loyalty, of distantiation and communicative connection, now come to the fore as the underlying contradiction beneath a historical transient corporate liberalism. The importance of the new corporatism as a social form is that it surpasses or supercedes the contradiction with a "higher" and less democratic form of capitalism. Corporate liberal capitalism is replaced by corporatism.

The corporatist reorganization serves not only the ideology of restoration, but ultimately a market, commodity society that shapes the form of all social relations. One example of this change is in education. Educational change, as part of a larger historical movement, begins to transform education into a commodity. This change requires the establishment of market practices internal to the operation of schools and then, externally, the establishment of educational markets. The final stage in educational corporatism is fiscal; private financing and ownership of what was formerly the public common school. There is evidence for the occurrence of each of these processes in this fundamental sequence of institutional change (Wexler and Grabiner, 1985).

Beneath the cultural restoration, and even more basic than the emergent tendency to organize social life along corporatist lines, there are other deep and large-scale social changes on the horizon. Fundamental changes are taking place in social production, in the culture of consumption, and in the structure of persons which, I believe, are part of a broad social transformation. Whether seen through the Marxist language of a "revolution in the forces of production," or the postindustrial language of changes in "transforming resources" (Bell, 1979) a historic change is occurring in the productive basis of society. A major change in social life is that signification has itself become a force of production to unprecedented degree. The basic productive energy or force of production is becoming information. Information is becoming central in production, distribution, communication and services. Luke summarizes the economic reorganization of "informationalism" (1983, pp. 61–64):

American producers increasingly are engaged either directly in the production of information or indirectly in the informationalization of goods-production and services provision . . . industrial capitalism has been greatly augmented if not nearly displaced by American informational capitalism . . . informational capital has not eliminated industrial or agricultural capital. Rather, it has begun to informationalize industrial production . . . just as industrial capital industrialized agriculture."

The new informationalism is organized by transnational corporations to resolve the economic crisis which corporate liberalism could no longer contain (Schiller,1984). There is a less evident, but no less important, change in the cultural organization of consumption. It is no longer a question simply of whether advertising is important; it has already been recognized as a preeminent cultural form within the "sales effort" of a consumer culture (Ewen and Ewen, 1982). The issue is that the cultural form of advertising is itself changing. The "sign," which acts as an associatively effective signal, replaces more traditionally coherent narrative and relational symbols as the cultural means of engagement in consumption (Baudrillard, 1981). This is a shift in cultural genres, from realist narrative representation to a dispersed, modernist, and nonrepresentational use of cultural resources. Realism versus modernism is not simply a dispute among the literati; it is a historical conflict within the sales culture of an emergent new society, and a change in a mass cultural forms.

Change in the structure of persons, or in the language of poststructuralism (Young, 1981), "subjects," occurs along with changes in production and consumption. The diffusion or so-called "de-centering" of traditional narrative culture, corresponds to a historically different sort of subjectivity. The structure of a new type of personal functioning is better characterized by polymorphous fluidity rather than moral integration. There is already extensive debate about the existence and value of this historically "new self" (Wexler, 1983, pp. 117-140; Lasch, 1984).

Taken together as the outline of a new society, these changes open the way toward alternative possibilities of social organization. For example, in production, informationalism makes possible a greater degree of Taylorization—a fragmentation and degradation and deskilling in the labor process. In consumption, signalling that replaces symbolic representation as the cultural sales medium, facilitates a new type of symbolic incapacitation. For the power of ambiguous understanding and the mutuality of human social relations, the symbolic and narrative realism that liberal culture possessed, even in commercial sales culture, are now endangered by uni-directional cultural conditioning. According to Baudrillard (1981), we are already living in a de-narrativized "political economy of the sign." In person structure, fluidity and decenteredness are potential ego weaknesses that make new selves susceptible to the mass appeals of authoritarian unifiers. In sum, degradation, meaninglessness, and authoritarianism represent one configuration of resolutions to emergent social changes.

On the other hand, informationalism promises release from surplus labor and an electronic community that will redefine and revive democratic society. The diffusion of cultural narratives can unchain the means of signification from their emplacements in traditional cultural commitments. The attack on coherent representational realism frees signs for less burdensome use in continuously negotiated rather than fixed meanings. Similarly, the decentered subject is liberated from the weight of selfness. The desire of energy of such a "new self" is no longer an individualized replay of a coercively integrated collective past that is recast as "morality."

Textualism is part of this qualitatively new, complex social formation. It is a rationalized, reflexive, and academically specialized aspect of the culture of this new social formation: the semiotic society.

DYNAMIC TENSION: DE-REIFICATION AND COMMODIFICATION

Where discourse has become, as Finlay-Pelinski (1982) argues, a dominant condition of production, where signification is a central means of informational production and coordination, literary theory and textualism are historically appropriate forms of social speech.

There is a contradiction in the relation of the language of textualism to its social formation. On the one side, what the academic discourse of literary theory does is to take naturalized "culture" and decompose and dereify it, displaying an apparently unitary entity of culture as the product of processes of symbolic activity. On the other side, the elevated importance of symbols in the emergent semiotic society is that they do the work of commodities, and even serve as a catalyst for further commodification of social life.

Naturalized culture, which is a central pillar of bourgeois ideology ("the natural," the "taken-for-granted") moves between this dynamic: de-reification of culture into processes of signification, and commodification of signs and symbols as boosters for the general logic of commodity life. Literary theory is about processes of signification. It aims to show how the operation of relations among signs produces the effect of meaning. Its intent is to take apart those thing-like cultural essences that stand over and block the transparent fluidity of processes of symbolic movement. Structuralist and poststructuralist analyses of texts, by drawing analytic attention to the signifying practices and symbolic codes of language, literature, cinema and television, effect a continuous de-naturalizing of culture and ideology.

The practical, political, historical importance of textualism then is that it offers a de-reification of the sign and of those concepts of culture and meaning which block and deny significatory activity. Textualism plays a role like critical social theory's analysis of commodity fetishism. It disperses the essential "thing," and reveals its constituent activities. Foucault writes (1972, p. 47): "What, in short, we wish to do is to dispense with 'things' . . . To substitute

for the enigmatic treasure of 'things' anterior to discourse, the regular formation of objects only in discourse." The relation of the work of poststructuralist
analysts like Foucault and Derrida, or of modern literary and film theorists to
the social formation is neither direct nor uniform. But, as I have argued (Wexler, 1987), their attack on the discourses of "humanism" is a critique of the
historic cultural bases of liberalism. Even more, it is a critique of the commodification of language and culture. The importance, (often unwittingly) of the
textualist critique is that it anticipates the struggle over the means of discursive
production in an informational, semiotic society.

The dialectic of dereification and commodification is that the sign which
literary theory de-naturalizes is soon reclaimed by the logic of commodity production. The same nonreferential, bottomless chessboard of poststructural theory that de-reifies the sign, also operates as a new logic of commodity consumption. Baudrillard writes of the "object" of consumption that (1981, pp.
65, 67):

". . . it finds meaning with other objects, in difference, according to a hierarchical
code of significations . . . The definition of an object of consumption is entirely
independent of objects themselves and exclusively a function of the logic of significations."

A society of the political economy of the sign is one in which the sign plays the
same role that the commodity once did in industrial society. It is the abstract,
reductive generalization of the "labor of signification." Like the commodity in
the labor process, the sign is a reification of the symbolic process. The other
side of cultural de-naturalization is that the environment becomes "semanti-
cized," and even more extensive cultural resources can be used in the interac-
tionally destructive and exploitative production of commodities.

This process—in which cultural elements are first crystallized and articulated as oppositional and transformative cultural statements, and then absorbed
into the cultural commodity apparatus—is exemplified in the absorption of subcultures into mass produced fashion advertising (Hebdige, 1979; Ewen and
Ewen, 1982). What I am talking about, however, is the dereification and commodification of symbolic processes in society generally. What is at stake is the
form, ownership and use of meaning.

The same dialectic that operates in the medium of meaning, works also
through identity. Textualism's insistent assertion that "discourse forms the subject" overlooks the structure of social interaction through which discourse operates in society. In our current research (Wexler et al., forthcoming), we show
how signs are used in an ordered social process in which individual identity is
produced. I call this a "symbolic economy of identity" because while the medium of relation is symbolic (with a heavily coded use of subcultural and mass
cultural signs), the process of relation among the signs is mediated through

interactions that follow the form of capital-logic, particularly of exploitation and commodification. Identity, like "things" and apparently natural "culture," is a reification of a symbolic economy. This economy combines labor and sign, as interactional resources like trust and status are produced and distributed symbolically.

Identity, however, is not ordinarily being de-reified in academic discourse. Rather, any historic unfreezing of selfhood that reached popular awareness during the cultural revolution of the sixties, has been re-placed into direct process of self-commodification (Wexler, 1983, pp. 120–126) and naturalizing individualist ideologies of survivalism (Lasch, 1984). The working-up of identity-elements for entry into a symbolic economy of identity remains a generally opaque process, and the rules of that economy are still ignored in favor of the iconized identity commodity of the individual self.

How identity and meaning both operate within a dynamic of de-reification and commodification circumscribed by the value logic of capital may become evident only with the realization of those practices which breach that logic: practices of socialization.

PRACTICE: SOCIALIZING MEANING AND IDENTITY

Textualism, and symbolic economy are forms of social speech appropriate to a society where discourse is a central means of social production and where the mobilization of collective energies is mediated through individual identity. These symbolic practices potentially offer a display of the processes which constitute their apparently stable and integral products: cultural meaning and personal identity. The contradiction of these practices is that while they can denaturalize social life by decomposing it, that same decomposition lends itself to an easier incorporation of transparent cultural and personal elements into structured processes of capital. The cultural restoration, the institutional reorganization toward corporatist forms, and the shifts in production, culture and person that, together, outline what I have called the semiotic society, have not dislodged the commodification and exploitation of value that defines capitalism as a social system.

What has changed is that pillars of the ideological apparatus, natural culture and personal identity, have been drawn out of hiding into the operation of the social relations of capital. What has also changed is that symbolic practices, like textualism, that increasingly supplant the academic ideologies of social theory generally, and social psychology in particular, do not work ideologically by simply containing social contradictions, as social psychology once did. Instead, they work through oscillation, from the illuminating and critical moment of denaturalization, to the inclusion of newly transparent cultural and social dynamic elements into the cycle of exploitative commodity production. It is this re-commodification that leads Baudrillard to call, not for the further denaturalization or de-reification of culture, but for the destruction of the sign (1981: 162): "Only total revolution, theoretical and practical, can restore the symbolic in the demise of the sign and of value. Even signs must burn." The "symbolic" that he wishes to restore is the "reciprocity of speech" that has been abrogated by the transformation of socially mutual symbolic relations into the monological mass media commodity of the sign. For him, the transgressive discourse of the streets, grafitti, overcomes the commodification of signs.

An alternative is to block the reintegrative commodity phase by an intervening appropriation of dereified cultural and personal "things." Such an appropriation would engage the display of the constituent processes of culture and identity in its own process of formation. Unlike social psychology, which was an ensemble of symbolic practices for containing socializing movements, the intervention that I am talking about would use the transparent moment of the dereification/commodification dynamic for its own formative empowerment. Concretely, that means the collective production of meaning and identity.

Collective production ruptures the natural-seeming private ownership of the value of significatory and identity labor. It is too early in the analysis of our own research, as it may also be in social history, to know what the practices are which transform a private symbolic economy of identity into a social one. But we know that they are practices which persuade the participants in the economy that the identity value of others is being produced at their expense, and that identity is a social value rather than a private "thing" or attribute. Under conditions of such awareness and a balanced mixture of identity-commitments and deprivations, the symbolic apparatus can be willfully altered. Collective action, in a social system that mobilizes energies through the privatization of the economy of identity, must include the socialization of identity value.

The discourse of textualism is now a more familiar discursive movement than that of identity economics. If textualism is now the academic discourse of the semiotic society, criticism is its potentially transformative intervention. If literary theory is the socially sublimated theory of a semiotic society, its conventional practice, literary criticism, is the starting point for a counter-practice. Criticism does not mean either individualist impressionism or scientistic formalism. Criticism reads through the text, using its transparency for the process of social/self formation. Criticism means socially transformative reading, and cultural literacy as the conscious cultural reconstitution that blocks re-commodification.

I am talking about a practice of an expanded meaning of literacy and criticism. In the semiotized, signified society, self-formation means the ability to write-over, to express the process of group formation, in which criticism is the interpretive moment. This points toward a new literacy and a new meaning of reading and writing, of which an extreme example are the subway grafitti "writing gangs" engaged in the collective production of group identity by collective "writing over." In the semiotic society, *criticism means discursive reap-*

propriation through socially formative action. The reciprocal symbol defeats the unilateral sign when writing restores social relations.

The historicity of social psychology should become increasingly apparent, as we exit corporate liberal industrial capitalism. The newer discourses, textualism and the as-yet underdeveloped symbolic economy of identity, are also, like social psychology once was, midpoints between privatization and socialization—in the media of culture and identity. The difference is that these discourses open, if only for a moment, an understanding of the historical means of the production of culture and person. Whether or not we shall choose that moment to realize a socialization of meaning and identity which that understanding enables, is difficult to say. Perhaps we can gauge the likelihood of that socialization by observing the ease with which we can distance ourselves from the historic ideology of social psychology.

REFERENCES

Anderson, P. (1976). *Considerations on Western Marxism*, London, NLB.

Baudrillard, J. (1981). *For a critique of the political economy of the sign*. St. Louis: Telos Press.

Bell, D. (1979). Communications technology: for better or for worse, *Harvard Business Review*, May-June, pp. 20–42.

Ewen, S. and Ewen, E. (1982). *Channels of desire*, New York: McGraw-Hill.

Feuer, L. S. (Ed.). (1959). *Basic writings on politics and philosophy: Karl Marx and Friedrich Engels*, Garden City, NY: Anchor Books.

Finlay-Pelinski, Marike. (1982). Semiotics of history: From content analysis to contextualized discursive praxis. *Semiotica, 40*(3, 4), pp. 229–266.

Foucault, M. (1972). *The archaeology of knowledge*. New York: Harper Torchbooks.

Geertz, C. (1980). Blurred Genres: the Refiguration of Social Thought, *The American Scholar, 29*(2), Spring.

Hebdige, D. (1979). *Subcultures: The meaning of style*, London: Methuen.

Lasch, C. (1984). *The minimal self: Psychic survival in troubled times*. New York: Norton.

Luke, T. (1983). Informationalism and ecology, *Telos, 54*, Summer, pp. 59–73.

Panitch, L. (1977). The development of corporatism in liberal democracies, *Comparative Political Studies, 10*(1), pp. 61–90.

Rabinow, P. and Sullivan, W. M. (Eds.). (1970). *Interpretive social science*, Berkeley, CA: University of California Press.

Rohatyn, F. (1981). Reconstructing America, *The N.Y. Review*, February 5, pp. 16–20.

Rorty, R. (1982). *Consequences of Pragmatism*. Sussex, England: Harvester Press.

Schiller, H. I. (1984). *Information and the crisis economy.* Norwood, New Jersey: Ablex.

Wexler, P. (1983). *Critical social psychology.* Boston: Routledge and Kegan Paul.

Wexler, P. (1987). *Social analysis of education: After the new sociology.* Boston: Routledge and Kegan Paul.

Wexler, P., et al. (Forthcoming). *Becoming somebody: Studies in high schools.*

Wexler, P. and G. Grabiner. (1985). The education question: America during the crisis. In R. Sharp (Ed.), *Capitalist crisis, education and the state: A comparative politics of education.* Melbourne: MacMillan.

Young, R. (1981). *Untying the text: A poststructuralist reader.* Boston: Routledge and Kegan Paul.

Chapter 12

Social Psychology in the Soviet Union

Lloyd H. Strickland

INTRODUCTION

One of the concomitants of social psychology's passage through its paradigmatic "crisis" has been an increasing awareness of alternative models of the field's methodology and subject matter. Over the last two decades, the attention of North American psychologists has been drawn to developments in Western Europe and the UK, probably given their most important exposition by Israel and Tajfel (1972) and by Harré and Secord (1972), respectively. Within North America, some attention has been drawn to the development of a Canadian social psychology that seems to embody components of both the West European emphasis on intergroup relations and the cultural context (Gardner and Kalin, 1981) and the more experimental/individualistic features of U.S. social psychology (Rule and Wells, 1981). Here and there have appeared outlines of social psychologies in Eastern Europe and the USSR (Derlega, 1978; Krauss, 1976; Strickland, 1979; 1984).

The possible functions of these alternative social psychologies are several for a North American or "mainstream" audience. They may serve as ground for the structural figure of our own efforts to develop a social psychology that makes the most sense in our own society. As well, they may serve as positive or negative anchors, against which we can evaluate the quality of our own efforts. They may of course serve as sources of useful ideas we may otherwise have overlooked. They may be highly interesting in their own right, as developing templates through which to view the important states or problem areas of a society's social relations. Finally, they may provide the instances which serve as evidence for or against claims about the interrelationship of political ideology and social psychological research.

With respect to Soviet social psychology, as the author has been concerned with it over the past half-decade (Strickland, 1979, 1980, 1981, 1984; Petrovskii, 1983a, b), it would appear that all of these functions have been performed. As will be seen in the following pages, Soviet social psychology certainly contrasts starkly with the version of the field with which most Westerners are familiar; it may be particularly interesting to note that theirs has boasted for some time of many of the features that we have more lately begun to address: for example, our recently increased concern with application (compare Elms, 1975 and Fisher, 1977 with comments by Soviet psychologists in Strickland, 1980, 1981), our current preoccupation with issues of theory and metatheory (compare Gergen, 1978, 1982 with Petrovskii, 1971), an explicit linkage of psychological theory with the social context (compare Tajfel, 1972, with Andreeva, 1984), and so on. Secondly, as examples of useful ideas, the important Soviet concept of *activity*, to be discussed below, is beginning to receive attention in the West (Wertsch, 1981), and, of course, Vygotskii's emphasis on the importance of the developmental approach (Cole, John-Steiner, Scribner, and Souberman, 1978) as the basic method of a psychological science has found a progressively widening audience here. Third, the social psychology of the USSR is certainly interesting in its own right, and its design and focus of course tells us much about Soviet society, its priorities, and problems.

IDEOLOGY AND CONTENT OF SOCIAL PSYCHOLOGY

The discrepancies between Soviet and US social psychology of course have a multiplicity of historical antecedents. Those most relevant for the theme of the present conference involve the degree to which a political ideology has explicitly or implicitly set certain limits on the development of the field's metatheoretical parameters, which, in their turn, have stipulated the sort of social psychological research that is "correct" or, at least, appropriate. An ideological analysis of US social psychology which stimulated useful debate was given careful articulation by Sampson (1977, 1978, 1981). Also, a provocative and searching examination of the role of ideology within Soviet social psychology has been provided by Billig (1981, 1982) in an analysis and critique of the initial attempt to bring Soviet and Western social psychologists into confrontation (Strickland, 1979). Billig has discussed the degree to which the Soviets' adoption of Marxist/Leninist starting points for the progression towards specified societal goals has defined both the mold of Soviet society and the metatheoretical dimensions and limits of a social psychology designed to further that society's aims. He further contrasts the explicit acknowledgement of these dependencies by the Soviets with the apparent ignorance of them by the North Americans who participated in the exchange.

Both this first book (Strickland, 1979) and Billig's (1981) analysis were published at a time when little was known in the West about the *products* of modern Soviet social psychological research. In effect, because so few Westerners read Russian, the Soviets' rules were to be learned before their "game" could be watched. Subsequent publications (Petrovskii, 1983a, b; 1984; Strickland, 1984) now make possible an examination of some of the Soviet field's content, and it is to this that the following chapter is devoted. It may be clear by its final paragraphs that the path from ideology to the design of a research instrument or laboratory experiment may under some circumstances be easily drawn.

METATHEORETICAL CONSIDERATIONS: METHODOLOGICAL AND ANALYTIC PRINCIPLES IN SOVIET SOCIAL PSYCHOLOGY

Our own social psychology texts are normally initiated with a chapter on research methodology in social psychology, so before examining what the Soviets study we shall examine the framework of how, in general, they study it.

Levels of "Methodology" in Soviet Social Psychology

III General Methodology—e.g., Marxist dialectics
II Special Methodology—e.g., of social psychology *vs.* sociology
I Methodics—e.g., data collection techniques

Our books tend to employ the word "methodology" in a way that merges all three of the levels identified in the outline above. In contrast, the Soviets are usually quite clear about the level on which they are operating; indeed, they are often constrained to be explicit about what ideological/philosophical assumptions, from Level III, are involved in the assignment of a problem (say, leadership in collectives) to attack by social psychologists as opposed to sociologists, at Level II, or the use of specific data-collection strategies, in Level I.

In addition to the requirement for clarification of levels of methodology, is the Soviets use of certain *principles of analysis,* construable here as salient metatheoretical dimensions, which give both orientation to their research efforts and meaning to their data. Primary among them is the *Principle of Activity (deiatel'nost')* (Leont'ev, 1975). When they examine, for example, cognitive events of interest, it is usually acknowledged that they have been generated, either directly or *via* mediation by language, through the person's goal-directed *activity*, and they are interpreted in that light. This has a number of consequences, not all of which can be considered here, but the notion of "getting inside via the outside" and of relating the two aspects in terms of this keystone psychological concept is a starting point of any, including social, psychological analysis.

A second dimension involves the notion of *Principle of Development*. The behaviors to be considered are examined over the course of time, instead of as responses emitted in a usually brief interval, such as the hour of a social psychology experiment, or the millisecond of a grimace or a change in voice pitch. This so-called "developmental approach" does not necessarily refer to studies with children, although its mentor, Vygotskii, has certainly had some important observations about child development. Rather, as Blonskii has been quoted: "Behaviour can be understood only as the history of behaviour" (1921). Phenomena are examined genetically, sometimes through the use of approximating strategies such as cross-cultural techniques.*

A third methodological principal is the *Principle of Obshchenie*. This last word is normally translated as "communication," although a more faithful translation would be "interaction." This principle demands that meaningful social activity be looked at in terms of its continuing development through communication with others.. The use of these principles may be clearly illustrated through examination of the subject matter of Soviet social psychology.

Activity

As suggested above, the most important notion in Soviet psychology is that elaborated by Leont'ev (1975), i.e., activity (*deiatel'nost'*). The reader now may discover that "activity" serves both as an organizing principle and as a primary, broad dependent measure category. To help conceptualize it in the second way, as a focus of study, one may for a moment first consider what North Americans say they study. Almost all our introductory social psychology texts state or imply that we are primarily concerned with the scientific study of social behavior, or of behavior in response to socially significant stimuli, etc. To be sure, some definitions of our field also make reference to cognitive processes—attributions, opinions, attitudes, etc.—but we traditionally try to link "behavior" to the less public states of our social psychological subject. Into the hopper of "social behavior" we tend to dump everything from the flicker of an eyelid or other nonverbal cue, through elaborate role-plays, to the

---

*This cross-cultural strategy, as a kind of first-order comparative folk psychology, was not begun by the Soviets despite its usual identification with Luria; rather, under the auspices of the Russian Geographical Society, it seems even to have predated Wundt by a half century (Budilova, 1984).

deliberate casting of a vote for a political candidate. Again, the Soviets are careful to distinguish among such different events.

The category *deiatel'nost'* has three levels, labelled *activity, action,* and *operation.* According to a recent analysis by Wertsch (1981)

Levels of Activity (deiatel'nost') in Soviet Social Psychology
(after Wertsch, 1979, p. 18)

III Activity—distinguished on basis of socially learned motive and object toward which they are motivated

II Action—distinguished on basis of goals

I Operation—distinguished on basis of conditions under which they are performed

". . . *activities* are distinguished on the basis of their motives, and the object toward which they are oriented; *actions,* on the basis of their goals; and *operations* on the basis of the conditions under which they are carried out" (p. 18). To paraphrase Andreeva (1979, p. 117), in performing an operation a speaker may remove his or her glasses and blink; one might not have a special goal for this, it may be a conditioned response to an audience situation, but it could very well have social psychological significance. At a higher level, one could perform a social action—stop speaking and head for the washroom; this would have clear goal direction, and it would have social significance, but it would not be social *activity.* What one would interpret as social activity is the fact that the speaker is among friends and colleagues, discussing issues of metatheory and social psychology; this would be influenced not by immediate goals, but by higher level motives, that might include one's perception of the importance of social psychology, about the general value of exchange among scientific colleagues, etc.

However, it is also clear that a single, simple social "event" could be analyzed at any of these levels—an eyeblink could be an operation, an automatic response to social stress; it could be an action, a goal-directed indication of assurance to a session chairman nervous about time; or it could be activity, the signal for the start of an assault on the podium by certain members of the audience.

It is useful to apply the other principles of analysis mentioned to the concept, activity. According to Wertsch's analysis, activity has the following defining features. First, it may be analyzed at different levels (as we have seen). Second (also mentioned) it involves notions of goal and goal-directedness, ideas that have received little attention in the West for decades. Third, activity is *mediated* through the use of both tools and sign systems, but especially through speech. It is not the case:

that sign systems simply mediate some activity that would exist without them—that is, they are not viewed as being handy tools for making an existing activity easier.

Rather, as in the case with all forms of mediation, they allow, and even lead to, the creation of types of activities that would not otherwise exist (Wertsch, 1981, p. 26).

The fourth feature of the theory of activity is its emphasis on the *genetic* or developmental explanation, discussed above as a principle of analysis. The fifth characteristic of activity is that it, and the way it is mediated, has been acquired during the course of *social interaction (obshchenie)*, usually between the child and an adult, then between children, and so on; a lecturer's eyeblink would not signal the start of the audience rebellion unless there has been some preceding discussion. This ties in with a sixth characteristic, *internalization:* "activity" can refer to complex mental events as well as observable physical events.

The foregoing paragraphs only identify the main features of the most important concept in Soviet psychology, *deiatel'nost';* the reader may be able at least to sense the tremendous amount of thought that has gone into this concept, making it both a unit of observation and a principle of analysis, much as "reinforcement" has been for us. However, the lines between activity theory and Marxist theory have been drawn and debated from the start, while the relationship between reinforcement and capitalist assumptions have been drawn lately and tentatively.

Social Perception

As with activity, one of the principles of analysis that distinguish Soviet social perception research (they more usually have spoken of "social cognition") from our own version is the preoccupation with change over time of the social processes within which they are concerned. A second is that Soviet social perception research is almost never conducted outside the context of *communication* between the subject and object of perception, or, in our own familiar terms, between perceiver and perceived.

It is useful to note the wide range of problems that Soviet person-perception researchers have addressed. According to recent reviews by the putative founder and senior representative (Bodalev, 1979, 1984) of this area, they include the following:

1 The formation of the definition of a social situation that results from the verbal contacts which participants have to establish with each other.
2 The development of understanding of personality characteristics related to bodily characteristics during the communication process.
3 The effect of psychological characteristics (e.g., memory) and "personality" characteristics of interactors on their cognition of one another, and on the communication itself.
4 The dependence of social cognition processes on the emotional states of participants in the interaction.
5 The effect of *salient* person attributes on the interaction process and

consequent changes in social cognition (here we refer to things like age, sex, profession—variables we more frequently treat as role components).

6 What a person's reference group might think of him, his place in the collective, the emotional climate of the collective, etc.

Bodalev also cites studies on spatio-temporal characteristics of communication settings and their role in the development of the formation of "knowledge" about others. Finally, in what may have anticipated our own recent concern with "self-fulfilling prophecies" (Darley and Fazio, 1980; Fiske and Taylor, 1984), and consistent with their philosophical concern for the relation between theory and practice, there appear to be recent studies of how "concrete-imaginal" and verbal-conceptual knowledge possessed by man about other people mediate various individual acts, both in the communication area and beyond it; how this knowledge interacts with knowledge by the individual about the other aspects of reality, and how they may jointly control his behavior in the most important situations that he faces in his life (Bodalev, 1979, p. 146).

As a concrete example it is useful to quote Bodalev on a prototypical study paradigm:

> It is interesting to study the cognition of one person by another, but it is more important to discover the *significance* of the way people imagine other people to be. What are the consequences of the impressions that we gain from other people for the regulation of our behavior towards that person? What we are studying is, essentially, the interdependence of our reflection of other people, our emotional response to them, and the type of behavior we choose on that basis. Accordingly, a number of works have been carried out in our country, where the people to be studied are physicians and patients, or teachers and schoolchildren, manager and subordinate personnel, sport trainers and athletes, and many other groups which represent the same relationship of manager and worker, or actors and spectators. The object of the study is to comprehend the interdependence of the reflective, emotional and behavioral components of the communication process. As an example, we could consider a teacher and a student. An observer will study over a long period of time what method the teacher employs—both his behavior and his attitude toward the student. What qualities he attributes to his students are recorded with questionnaires and scales. And even using this extremely simple method, we can find profound differences between master teachers and novice teachers.
>
> From memory, I will describe a recently completed work on wrestlers who had not met each other previously in a wrestling bout. First one determines the way they picture their opponent and how they assess their own potential. After that they start the wrestling bout, and following the actual fight they are again questioned, and we determine how their opinion of themselves and of their opponent has changed. The important thing is the wrestler's initial self-concept and his evaluation of his opponent; we ask him what strategy he is going to employ in this wrestling bout based on his self-concept and his evaluation of the opponent. We find that there is a most striking difference in the accuracy of evaluation of the opponent

between a beginning wrestler and an experienced one, each one meeting a new opponent that he has not wrestled with before.

We also carry out this type of study with personnel managers, and we compare the evaluation of a job applicant and inexperienced personnel managers. (Bodalev, 1979, 147).*

Descriptions by this investigator of other experiments can be found in English (e.g., Bodalev, 1970, 1971, 1972, 1984; Bodalev et al., 1970).

Such efforts seem to North Americans to have an "old fashioned" ring, to be ridden with design, measurement, and other methodological traps, and, finally, to be largely descriptive instead of theory—or even mini-theory—oriented. But in terms of method, they are concerned with real people and not laboratory subjects, with changes over the course of interaction instead of with a brief interval of time, and, in general, with the activity-related consequences of the processes of "cognizing" others. Most importantly for the focus of this conference, the society which forms the context of these theories is itself defined and explained in terms of their major socio-psychological theory, Marxism, so such developmental and interactional research *cannot* really be atheoretical.

Attitude

The concept *attitude* shares a hierarchicalism with other core social psychological notions. It has been closely linked historically with the concept of "set" (*ustanovka*), an important concept in the development of Russian general psychology. The Institute of Psychology at the Academy of Science of the Georgian SSR, Tbilisi, was the source of "The Psychology of Set" (Uznadze, 1966); the Tbilisi Institute has remained the base of most of the prominent conceptual and, to a lesser degree, empirical work with "attitudes."

Attitudes belong to the class of *fixated sets,* along with other familiar concepts (e.g., *einstellung*), which Uzandze distinguished from *primary sets* (see Figure 1). While primary sets are newly developed each time new goal-directed behavior is appropriate, attitudes and other fixated sets are schemes based on prior experience; their function is to ensure the purposefulness of behavior. Attitudes are a prominent part of the Soviet conception of personality, and much of the educational process is seen as a process of developing desirable social psychological attitudes. The primary context for empirical attitude research has been industrial social psychology (see Kus'min and Trusov, 1984; Magun, 1985; Strickland, 1980, 1981).

Another theorist who has addressed himself specifically to socially-related "attitudes" is V. A. Iadov, of Leningrad State University. Iadov (1975) focuses

*Reprinted with permission from Strickland, L. H., *Soviet and Western Perspectives in Social Psychology,* Copyright 1979, Pergamon Press.

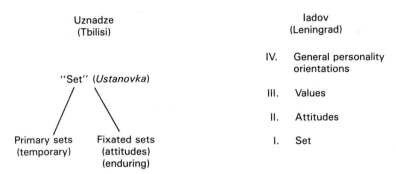

FIGURE 1. Conceptions of "attitude" in Soviet social psychology.

on the dispositional aspect of concepts in his hierarchy (see Figure 1): at the lowest level he places *set* in the sense that it is used by Uznadze, a disposition that helps man meet his simplest needs, or act in simple situations. *Attitudes* are, for Iadov, higher level dispositions, serving higher level (social) needs and relevant for more complex situations. Level three involves *values* and finally, at the level of highest social needs and the most complex social situations in which the person acts, we discover what Iadov has posited as *general orientation of personality*. Such hierarchicalism in Soviet social psychology should by now be familiar; it will be discovered again in the final content area examined here.

Groups

Group psychology is divided along the lines in Figure 2, this scheme taken from a recent Russian social psychology text (Andreeva, 1980, p. 194). One should give special attention to the efforts at developing research and theory concern-

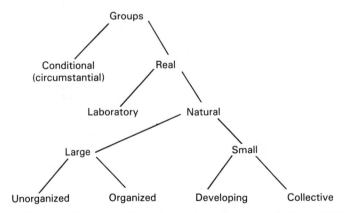

FIGURE 2. Groups in Soviet social psychology (after Andreeva, 1980, p. 194).

ing the *collective*, because in addition to the fact that it is interesting in its own right (and something North Americans study infrequently), the theory illustrates an attempt to relate other key notions we have discussed separately, such as attitude or activity, to a concept of central societal, ideological, and hence, social psychological concern.

The name most often associated with the concept of the collective is that of Artur V. Petrovskii, of the Moscow Pedagogical Institute. Petrovskii's name is most prominently linked with the development of yet another hierarchical social psychological concept, the *stratometric conception of group structure and activity*.

The notion of *kollectiv* is not an invention of recent ideologues. McLeish (1975) has asserted that the idea itself is as old as anything recorded in Russian history:

> Russian thought is steeped in the notion of a physical unity generated by communal life—in the *mir* (village community), the family, State and Church. This feeling for *kollectiv*—any group endowed with a common purpose, mutual trust, and empathetic unity—explains the outrage expressed by Russian thinkers of all persuasions (Khomyakov, Hertzen, etc.) when brought face-to-face with Western individualism (p. 263).

The first use of "collective" as a social psychological term has been ascribed by Budilova (1984) to the Russian journalist Iadrintsev, who wrote about the needs for activity and communication among prisoners in the Archangel region, where he was himself in exile.

During the 1960's a modern social psychology of the collective was needed; much effort at production had been, often forcefully, "collectivized," ranging from that of groups of laborers to that of scientists in research institutes, yet little formal theory relevant for specific settings existed beyond the fascinating accounts of Makarenko's efforts with post-civil war collectives of orphans (1951).* Makarenko was himself no friend of academic psychology, and his seminal insights and great successes with his collective-based rehabilita-

---

*The problem which Makarenko faced was the regeneration of a group of young criminals—thieves, murderers, and bandits—rendered homeless and initiated into a life of crime by the First World War, the Russian Revolution and the succeeding Civil War. In 1920 he was entrusted with the task of organizing a colony for homeless children, later named the Maxim Gorki Labor Colony, near Poltava. There he spent eight years, working out his distinctive methods and rehabilitating hundreds of children brutalized by the conditions of war, famine and revolution. In 1928 he took over a similar colony, the Dzerzhinsky Labor Commune, on the outskirts of Kharkov. In these two situations Makarenko worked out the implications of Marx's expressed ideas on education—three ideas in particular: combining productive labor with book-learning, the principle of the union of mental training, physical, and aesthetic instruction, and the idea of polytechnical instruction, that is, a general education in science centered on learning the basic principles of *all* the sciences and technology. McLeish (1975, p. 153).

tion attempts were not of the level of analysis most useful for development of social psychology theory.

Petrovskii (1983a, b) writes of how the Soviet psychologists read and tried to apply to groups what they knew from Western social psychology, especially that of the early Cartwright-Zander-Bales group dynamics school, and how it did not "fit." The reasons why Western group psychology did not work for the Soviet collective became the bases of much subsequent criticism of Western social psychology. It is interesting to relate these "errors" to notions in our own self-criticism of the past twenty years. Among them were: (a) a "tendency to regard a small group as a sum of interactional and communicative acts" (p. 6); (b) to define the small group in terms of qualities which were too psychological, that is, taken out of a broader social context and reduced to surface connections and, primarily, emotional relationships involving limiting reliance on a single methodological tool, sociometry; (c) to ignore long-term aims and tasks of a group in favor of short-term goals, often those newly established in the hour of a social psychological experiment; (d) to be locked into one paradigm: "In the end, a social psychological study turned out to be based on the sacred stimulus-response principle, encasing the researchers within a circle of already known behaviourist schemes and constructions" (Petrovskii, 1983a, p. 8). Petrovskii and his colleagues have labored mightily to develop a Soviet alternative theory, called the *stratometric theory of group development;* the collective is seen to be at the highest of several levels of that development (Petrovskii, 1983b).

Identification of a group as a true collective depends on several of the principles discussed earlier. A collective is a group in which interpersonal attitudes or *relations (otnoshenia),* have been *developed* and *mediated,* over *time* through the group's *activity,* said activity being in harmony with the *goals* of the society. This is illustrated in Figure 3.

Group I represents a genuine collective, one in which group members are

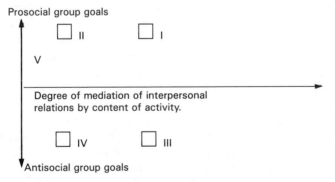

FIGURE 3. Activity mediation of interpersonal relations, social goals, and level of development in five different types of groups. (After Petrovskii, 1983).

united through adherence to a goal approved of by society, and in which the interpersonal relations between people are mediated through the performance of their shared activity.

Group II has some things in common with Group I, but the interpersonal relationships have not been mediated by participation the group's activity. Rather, they may be based on such things as interpersonal liking, or first impressions, as in a newly formed group, one assembling to achieve some positive goal.

Group III shares certain features with Group I, the joint activity and the resulting mediation of interpersonal relationships, but lacks social approval for its goal—as, say, within an effective criminal group. Group IV would simply be best represented by a group of new acquaintances sharing only antisocial motives. It is of more than incidental interest to note that Group V, which the Soviets would term a "diffuse group," is what they feel that Western social psychologists have studied the most—groups with no particular pro- or antisocial goal and no shared activity to define the relationships between members. Ongoing research in Petrovskii's laboratories has been directed at refining this theoretical conception (Petrovskii, 1984, 1985). Outside the laboratory, of course, collectives are studied constantly (for recent reviews see Chernyshev, 1984; Zhuravlev and Shorokhova, 1984).

Effects of Interpersonal Communication (Obshchenie)

With respect to all of these content areas previously considered, great emphasis is placed on one process, communication, also discussed above as a principle of analysis. The name most closely linked at present with *obshchenie* is that of Boris Lomov, Director of the Institute of Psychology of the Academy of Science of the USSR in Moscow. Lomov is a rare combination—by training and reputation a top rank ergonomist, a specialist in visual processes, but who is committed to demonstration of the importance of social communication in determining and modifying what we would normally think of as individual psychological events (see discussions of his views in Lomov, 1978, 1979a, b, 1982, 1984). As indicated already, just as attitude is more than set, and collective is more than group, *obshchenie* is more than communication—and in its way as difficult for English speakers to understand. *Obshchenie* has been called as "communication in the broad sense" (Andreeva, 1979, 62–63). If one thinks of *obshchenie* as meaning "interpersonal contact," or perhaps "interpersonal commerce" one can see how textbook headings like person perception, or interpersonal attitudes, or interaction could be subsumed under such a rubric.

Lomov effectively defined the importance of communication over a decade ago after the 24th Communist Party Congress, when he reflected for psychology the important role it would play "to further develop our own uniquely socialist ways of fusing science with production" (Lomov, 1972, p. 329).

At that time he said:

Most concrete investigations examine primarily objective, practical activity, and in some specialized areas, intellectual activity.

But man's actual way of life, which determines his mental makeup, is not exhausted by practical, objective activity. This activity constitutes only one aspect of man's way of life, of his behavior in the broad sense. The other aspect is communication as the specific form of a person's relations with other people. It is precisely in the process of communication that, above all, the exchange of ideas and interests and the "transmission" of character traits takes place; it is here that a person's attitudes and viewpoints are formed. In the process of communication (whether it is direct or mediated through the communications systems developed in modern society), the concrete individual assimilates the experience accumulated by mankind as a whole.

Unfortunately, the problem of communication has yet to acquire the status in psychology that it deserves. Almost no research is being done on this problem. For a long time, the problem of communication was at best considered only in connection with the communicative functions of speech. The future prospects for a general theory of psychology urgently demand elaboration of this fundamental problem, the study of dynamics, mechanisms, and means of communication, their development in human ontogeny, and their interrelations between activity, communication, and knowledge. Many areas and specialized branches of psychology have been involved in working out this problem. It can rightfully be counted as one of psychology's pivotal problems, one of the problems that embraces certain aspects of the aggregate set of problems faces by general psychology: from mental processes to personality. There are grounds (including experimental grounds) for assuming that the conditions of communication exert a considerable influence on the dynamics of perception, thought, and memory. This applies also to mental states, and in even greater measure to collective human activity, since communication is, so to speak, the internal mechanism of the life of a collectively (or social group) (p. 356)

If one reads Lomov's work, either that mentioned briefly (Lomov, 1982) or described in detail (Lomov, 1979a, 1984), one may discern the provocative possibilities offered by research on social psychophysics (joint scaling under conditions of communication) or social memory and recall (the memory of interacting, as opposed to individual, learners), etc.

SUMMARY AND COMMENT

First, the field of Soviet social psychology tends to be organized around important principles of analysis that are congenial with Marxist theory; cross-cutting these principles are the subject matter areas which would sound like the sections of our own textbooks. Each major subject matter area tends to be identified with one, possibly two, research institutes, either in a university department or a branch of the Academy of Sciences. Further, these subject matters and institutes tend to be primarily associated with one project at one research collective and one senior investigator's name. All of this speaks to the close relationship among ideology, general theory, special theory, research practice and application.

Regarding research practice, one may observe that what North Americans would consider a series of well-controlled and precisely executed laboratory experiments is comparatively rare in the USSR; applied observational, questionnaire and interview studies are much more common. Also, in experiments that *are* done, concerned with such matters as from effective leadership in collectives to interpersonal cognition in teachers and pupils, one seldom sees a preoccupation with mapping and testing group differences which are distributed around some overall average; rather, comparisons are made with respect to some high standard, one that reflects the goals or values of the society. In experimental analysis of leadership in the collective, for instance, it is the performance of good leaders and collectives that is studied first; then performance of inexperienced leaders or groups is compared with them, and then changes over time in these initially inexperienced units are examined, and so on. With respect to interpersonal cognition, similar comparisons of experienced and inexperienced teachers, experienced and inexperienced policemen, and so on, provide the starting points of research efforts. This has obvious consequences for the course of collection, analysis and interpretation of data which will not be pursued here. Suffice to say that we shall not find anything like our own exhausting pursuit of the determinants of the erstwhile "risky shift," or behavior in nonzero sum games, in Soviet social psychology.

What we may learn from examining the development of Soviet social psychology? There are a number of profitable approaches and answers to this question, and we turn first to Graham's (1980) discussion of why one should study Soviet science at all.

If one selects the first of the three proposed motives for such study, and hence tries to learn something about the Soviet Union, one may examine foci of Soviet social psychology; from identification of high-profile research areas, one may make some reasonable inferences about their derivation from problems acutely important for the society as a whole. In a way, there is really no other sensible inference to be drawn from the activities of mission-oriented social psychologists in such a goal-dominated social system.

If one elects to learn something about science in general, one may review, with respect to social psychology, those reasons outlined by Gustafson (1980) to answer his own question, "Why doesn't Soviet science do better than it does?" One may discern the degree to which social psychology seems to have (or have not) followed the same developmental paths as other sciences, and note and anticipate corresponding strengths and weaknesses. Perhaps more focally for present purposes, we have an object lesson concerning the way in which an ideology, which determines what sorts of theory will be acceptable or not, ultimately shapes the research questions that will be asked and, to the degree one might expect, the answers that will be found.*

For our own closing conjecture, we are inclined to pick the most modest of Grahams's (1980) three goals, that is, to gain a better understanding of specific scientific problems common to East and West. It may be enlightening here to view the Soviet and North American social psychologies in their alternating figure/ground relationship, mentioned at the beginning of this paper. Doing so, one notes that North Americans and the Soviets have started from opposite poles, and seem to be moving toward, possibly past, one another. We have often begun a research project with a set of naive observations, we try to say what sort of hypothesis would make sense of them, and we move on to search for confirmation of our hunches. They start with an official ideology and sociopsychological theory, which make the most sense of their society and its short- and long-term goals, and which stipulate what sets of observations would fit with the theory most meaningfully. We write books, and meet at conferences, in which we are trying to figure out where we have come from and what we are doing (e.g., predicting the world or changing it) and, if we answer these questions, how we are best advised to go about our task (e.g., via historical research or more familiar data collection and number-crunching techniques). We have too many and too heterogeneous "mini theories" to make our undergraduate textbooks coherent, and we (and our students) occasionally long for a broad paradigm, however incomplete, which we may help flesh out. The Soviets, on the other hand, do not need general theory, but rather may yearn for what we seem to have too much of. Their overall theory, heavily historical, is one in which goals are regularly examined and articulated, that says what social events should be as well as what they have been. Yet Marxist metatheory is not easily translated into such situation-constrained mini-theoretical statements as we may quickly generate over the course of a weekend conference (witness the decade of development and verification of Petrovskii's strato-metric theory); without sensitive and straightforward hypothesis systems, it is difficult for them to devise methods of data collection and analyses of much delicacy.

Social psychologists of both East and West may with profit remind themselves of Thorngate's (1976) discussion of the futility of trying to develop theories that are simultaneously general, simple, and accurate. We and the Soviets will spend our time better in exchanging general or limited theories and observations than in mutual disparagement. The disparity between societies and

---

*It is ironic to note Billig's (1981) observation that: "There is a confusion between the different senses of the concept of ideology, for, whatever else they may be, the Soviet social psychologists are not ideological analysts of their own ideology. Acceptance of the official ideology is the precondition of their discipline and will continue to be so as long as Soviet social psychologists assume that the 'goals of psychology' can be identified with the 'principles that guided the great October Socialist Revolution and that have become a living reality in the development of socialist society constructed by the Soviet people under the leadership of the Communist Party' (Lomov, 1979, p. 60.)"

ideologies is sufficiently wide that neither "side" need fear easy seduction, but there may be some enriching experiences from a period of flirtation. To echo the conclusions of Campbell and Wertsch (1980), it is time to start a dialogue, at least.

REFERENCES

Andreeva, G. M. The development of social psychology in the USSR. In Strickland, L. H. (Ed.), *Soviet and Western perspectives in social psychology.* Oxford: Pergamon, 1979.

Andreeva, G. M. Social psychology *(Sotsialnaia psikhologii)* Moscow: University of Moscow Publishing House, 1981.

Andreeva, G. M. Cognitive processes in developing groups. In L. H. Strickland (Ed.), *Directions in Soviet social psychology.* New York: Springer-Verlag, 1984.

Billig, M. Ideology within Soviet and Western social psychology. *Current Pscyhological Reviews,* 1981, *1,* 193–204.

Billig, M. *Ideology and Social Psychology.* New York: St. Martins, 1982.

Blonskii, P. P. *Essays in scientific psychology.* Moscow: State Publishing House, 1921.

Bodalev, A. F. Individual and developmental differences in interpersonal understanding. *Soviet Psychology,* 1970–71, IX, 2, 157–169. (*Problemy obshchenie sotsial'noi i inzhenernoi psikhologii*) 1968, 2, 127–136.

Bodalev, A. A., Kynitsyna, V. N., Maksimova, R. G., Panferov, V. N., Pikel'nikova, M. P., Stekkin, Yu, P., and Fedotova, N. F. New data on the problem of social perception: A person's perception and conception of another person. *Soviet Psychology,* 1972, *XI, 1,* 85–99, (*Voprosy psikhologii,* 1970, *3,* 126–131).

Bodalev, A. A. On the study of some cognitive processes in Soviet social psychology. In L. H. Strickland (Ed.), *Soviet and Western perspectives in social psychology.* Oxford: Pergamon,1979.

Bodalev, A. A. Psychology of interpersonal cognition in the Soviet Union during the past twenty years. In Strickland, L. H. (Ed.), *Directions in Soviet social psychology.* New York: Springer-Verlag, 1984.

Budilova, E. A. On the history of social psychology in Russia. In L. H. Strickland (Ed.), *Directions in Soviet social psychology.* New York: Springer-Verlag, 1984.

Campbell, D. C., and Wertsch, J. S. (Eds.), Soviet perspectives on American social psychology. *Soviet Psychology,* 1980, *XIX,* 1 (whole special issue).

Chernyshev, A. S. Experimental research on self-discipline of collectives of pupils and students. In L. H. Strickland (Ed.), *Directions in Soviet social psychology.* New York: Springer-Verlag, 1984.

Cole, M., John-Steiner, V., Scribner, S., and Souberman, E. (Eds.), *L. S. Vygotskii: Mind in society.* Cambridge, MA: Harvard University Press, 1978.

Darley, J., and Fazio, R. Expectancy confirmation processes arising in the social action sequence. *American Psychologist,* 1980, *35,* 867–881.

Derlega, V. J. Social psychology in Poland. *Personality and Social Psychology Bulletin,* 1978, *4,* 613–637.

Elms, A. C. The crisis of confidence in social psychology. *American Psychologist,* 1975, *30,* 967–976.

Fisher, R. J. Applied social psychology: A partial response to Sarason's suggested divorce. *Canadian Psychological Review,* 1977, *18,* 346–352.

Fiske, S., and Taylor, S. *Social cognition.* Reading, MA: Addison-Wesley, 1984.

Gardner, R. C., and Kalin, R. *A Canadian social psychology of ethnic relations.* Toronto: Methuen, 1981.

Gergen, K. J. Toward generative theory. *Journal of Personality and Social Psychology,* 1978, *36,* 1344–1360.

Gergen, K. J. *Toward transformation of social knowledge.* New York: Springer-Verlag, 1982.

Graham, L. Reasons for studying Soviet science. In L. L. Lubrano and S. G.Solomon (Eds.), *The social context of Soviet science.* Boulder, CO: Westview, 1980.

Gustafson, T. Why doesn't Soviet science do better than it does? In L. L. Lubrano and S. G. Solomon (Eds.), *The social context of Soviet science.* Boulder, CO: Westview, 1980.

Harré, R., and Secord, P. E. *The explanations of social behavior.* Oxford, Blackwell, 1972.

Iadov, B. A. *Concerning the dispositional regulation of persons' social behaviour (O dispozitsionnoi reguliatsii sotsial'nogo povedeniia psikhologii).* Moscow, 1975.

Israel, J., and Tajfel, H. (Eds.), *The context of social psychology: A critical assessment.* New York: Academic Press, 1972.

Krauss, R. Social psychology in the Soviet Union: Some comments. In S. A. Corson and E. O. Corson (Eds.), *Psychology and psychiatry in the USSR.* New York: Plenum, 1976.

Kuz'min, E. S., and Trusov, V. P. Industrial social psychology. In L. H. Strickland (Ed.), *Directions in Soviet social psychology.* New York: Springer-Verlag, 1984.

Leont'ev, A. N. *Deiatel'nost', soznanie, lichnost' (Activity, consciousness, personality).* Leningrad: Izadatel'stvo politicheskoi literaturi, 1975.

Lomov, B. F. Present status and future development of psychology in the USSR in the light of decisions of the 24th Congress of the Communist Party of the Soviet Union. *Soviet Psychology,* 1972, *XI,* 329–358 *(Voprosy psikhologii,* 1971, *5,* 3–19).

Lomov, B. F. Psychological processes and communication. *Soviet Psychology,* 1978, *XVII,* 1, 3–22. (From E. V. Shorokhova (Ed.). *Methodulogiia i metody sutsialnoi psikhologii,* 151–164).

Lomov, B. F. Mental processes and communication. In L. H. Strickland (Ed.), *Soviet and Western perspectives in social psychology.* Oxford: Pergamon, 1979. (a)

Lomov, B. F. Sixty years of Soviet psychology. *Soviet Review,* 1979, *20,* 46–60. (b)

Lomov, B. F. Soviet psychology: Its historical origins and contemporary status. *American Psychologist,* 1982, *37,* 580–586.

Lomov, B. F. Mental processes and communication. In L. H. Strickland (Ed.), *Directions in Soviet social psychology.* New York: Springer-Verlag, 1984.

Magun, V. S. Work performance and job satisfaction: A coexistance of positive and negative correlations. In Strickland, L. H., Trusov, V. P., and Lockwood, E. (Eds.), *Applied social psychology in the USSR.* (under review).

Makarenko, A. S. *The road to life* (2nd ed.). Moscow: Foreign Languages Publishing House, 1951.

McLeish, J. *Soviet psychology: History, theory, content.* London: Methuen, 1975.

Petrovskii, A. V. Some problems of research in social psychology. *Soviet Psychology,* 1971, *IX,* 4, 382–398.

Petrovskii, A. V. Toward the construction of a social psychological theory of the collective. *Soviet Psychology,* 1983, *XXI,* 2, 3–21 (*Voprosy filosofii,* 1973, 12, 71–81).

Petrovskii, A. V. The new status of psychological theory concerning groups and collectives. *Soviet Psychology,* 1983, *XXI,* 4, 57–78 (Voprosy filosofii, 1977, 5, 48–60).

Petrovskii, A. V. The theory of activity mediation in interpersonal relations. In L. H. Strickland (Ed.), *Directions in Soviet social psychology.* New York: Springer-Verlag, 1984.

Petrovskii, A. V. Some new aspects of the stratometric conception of groups and collectives. *Soviet Psychology,* 1985 (in press). (*Voprosy psikhologii,* 1976, 6, 33–44.

Rule, B. G., and Wells, G. L. Experimental social psychology in Canada: A look at the seventies. *Canadian Psychology,* 1981, *31,* 459–466.

Sampson, E. G. Psychology and the American ideal. *Journal of Personality and Social Psychology,* 1977, *35,* 767–782.

Sampson, E. G. Scientific paradigms and social values: Wanted—a scientific revolution. *Journal of Personality and Social Psychology,* 1978, *36,* 1332–1343.

Sampson, E. G. Cognitive psychology as ideology. *American Psychologist,* 1981, *36,* 730–743.

Strickland, L. H., Aboud, F. E., and Gergen, K. G. *Social psychology in transition.* New York: Plenum, 1976.

Strickland, L. H. (Ed.), *Soviet and Western perspectives in social psychology.* Oxford: Pergamon, 1979.

Strickland, L. H. (Ed.), Social psychology in the Soviet Union. *Personality and Social Psychology Bulletin,* 1980, *6,* 363–360.

Strickland, L. H. (Ed.), Applied social psychology in the USSR. *Soviet Psychology,* 1981, *XX,* 1, 81–89.

Strickland, L. H. *Directions in Soviet social psychology.* New York: Springer-Verlag, 1984.

Tajfel, H. Experiments in a vacuum. In H. Tajfel and J. Israel, (Eds.), *The context of social psychology: A critical assessment.* London: Academic Press, 1972.

Thorngate, W. Possible limits on a science of social behaviour. In L. H. Strickland, F. E. Aboud, and K. J. Gergen (Eds.), *Social psychology in transition.* New York: Plenum, 1976.

Uznadze, D. *The psychology of set.* New York: Consultants Bureau, 1966.

Wertsch, J. V. *The concept of activity in Soviet psychology.* Armonk, NY: M. E. Sharpe, 1981.

Zhuravlev, A. L., and Shorokhova, E. V. Social psychology problems of managing the collective. In L. H. Strickland (Ed.), *Directions in Soviet social psychology.* New York: Springer-Verlag, 1984.

Chapter 13

Toward a Diachronic Social Psychology: Pointing with More than One Finger

Mary M. Gergen

INTRODUCTION

Most social psychologists trained in the profession within the last thirty years have been indoctrinated into a synchronic, or cross-sectional, social psychology. It is a psychology primarily focused on the relationship between two or more events (often construed as independent and dependent variables) occurring in close temporal proximity and isolated from the range of events either preceding or following this focal relationship. The extensive role that this social psychology-of-the-moment has played in the creation of the modern paradigm cannot be overestimated. Yet the social psychology that depends on the findings obtained in a single investigation, or series of single investigations within a brief time span, is severely limited by these very temporal constraints. Within this chapter the synchronic approach to the study of social phenomena will be contrasted with the diachronic, or cross-time, form. First several assumptions inherent in the synchronic approach and the problems raised by them will be considered. Then the advantages of the diachronic approach to these problems will be addressed.

SYNCHRONIC SOCIAL PSYCHOLOGY: THE LIMITS OF A CROSS-SECTIONAL SCIENCE

In general, paradigmatic social psychologists have built the science on the assumptions that relationships under study are stable, events are isolated, and the ideal methodology is experimental. These characteristics of synchronic social psychology will be explored below. For the most part, those who chose to isolate psychological phenomena and test the immediate effects of given conditions on these phenomena assume that the relationships under study are *constant* unless disturbed by outside forces. This constancy is typically produced by psychological constructs, including structures, mechanisms, dispositions or traits. Such constructs are stable, it is proposed, either because they are built into the physical system (such as processes or perception, memory or motivation) or have been structured by long-term learning experiences (as is said to be the case with schemata, traits, cognitive heuristics and personality styles). Within the synchronic literature, the human is, metaphorically, a machine, with the stability of such an object (Overton & Reese, 1972). Congenial to this view is the assumption that reactions of the organism to given stimulus conditions will also be stable, and thus predictable. If responses were random, chaotic or unreliable, it would be impossible to generate general laws having predictive value. In effect, from the synchronic perspective we must assume that the relationships under study perdure, thus enabling any investigator at any time to scrutinize the same phenomenon.

The second characteristic of the synchronic program is its assumption that an isolated phenomenon may be understood in and of itself. Each pattern or relationship (typically between a stimulus and response unit) is treated as a decontextualized whole. As it is assumed, the scientist may thus understand the relationship between conditions of helplessness and depression, between communicator variables and attitude change, and between environmental annoyances and aggression, for example, independent of each other and independent of the historical context more generally. Each S–O–R linkage has an integrity apart from any other segment of reality. Scientific understanding does not require an S–O–R unit to have a past, a future or a link to other concurrent events. Analytic bits of a predetermined size become the starting points for understanding.

The third essential of the synchronic approach is methodological. Synchronic theory favors research techniques in which action is suspended in time; a cut is then made through the fiber of social life baring one unit for intense scrutiny. Social psychology, long enamoured of the controlled laboratory experiment, is circumscribed by this form of endeavor. The controlled experiment, either in the laboratory or in the field, is a conscientious attempt to disrupt the fiber of on-going social life. The ideal of the controlled experiment is to trace the effects of selected "independent" variables on one or more designated dependent variables. It is considered a threat to the validity of the experiment if too much time elapses between the presentation of the stimulus and the measurement of the response. Unplanned events in a lapse of uncontrolled time lend themselves to contamination by uncontrolled variables. Standards of rigorous experimentation thus require that research be truncated in terms of time.

Each of these interdependent assumptions can be sustained so long as one remains committed to a synchronic perspective. However, if one adopts a temporally sensitive or diachronic view of how to conduct social psychology, each of these assumptions is rendered problematic. First, serious questions are raised over the stability of phenomena across time. As Kenneth Gergen has emphasized (1973, 1982) social phenomena are lodged within specific socio-historical conditions. To assume that contemporary patterns are replicable across history is perilous, if not foolish. Further, if one takes a diachronic perspective, the assumption of the human being as a stable pawn unless moved by stimulus events is thrown into jeopardy. When people are observed across extended periods of time, it is less compelling to view them as mere products of their environments. Rather, their actions are more likely to appear internally motivated. People seem to be seekers of situations enabling them to express potentials rather than products of situations in which they happen to find themselves.

We further find that a diachronic perspective is required if one is to make sense of human action. That is, one cannot comprehend the actions of persons in a temporally disembedded way. A nod, a smile, or a decontextualized phrase is virtually uninformative. It is when we know the history of the person or relationship of which these actions are a part that we begin to comprehend their meaning. The controlled experiment as the major vehicle for warranting theory thus becomes suspect as well. To the extent that the experiment narrows the temporal period of concern, it obscures the processes in which the phenomenon may be embedded and indeed, which give it meaning. The experimental method in itself creates the individual as automaton and ultimately fails to render action comprehensible.

CONTRASTING PERSPECTIVES WITHIN A DIACHRONIC SOCIAL PSYCHOLOGY

It is against this backdrop that a number of social psychologists have begun to explore the potential of a diachronic social psychology, one that would escape these various perils insofar as possible and open new vistas for inquiry. A diachronic social psychology would be especially concerned with social phenomena over time, where time may be considered in units ranging from minutes to millenia, depending on the problem at hand. Such a psychology would be particularly sensitive to the ways social patterns are embedded within particular historical conditions. Relationships among events as they unfold over time would also be of focal concern, as would the cross-time interaction between science and society. A diachronic social psychology would also serve a critical, reflexive function in social life. As Kenneth Gergen (1979) has defined it, the function of the science would be generative, that is questioning traditional assumptions of reality and preparing the way for alternative and potentially more fulfilling constructions.

Important examples of the diachronic orientation have been collected together in a recently published volume, *Historical Social Psychology* (Gergen & Gergen, 1984). Within this volume three major perspectives on an historical social psychology are outlined. The differences among these perspectives relate to their orientation to change and to how change over time is to be analyzed. These orientations to change can be classified as one of the following: Temporal stability; ordered change; and, disordered change. It is useful to consider each in more detail.

Certain investigators agree with the traditional attempt of synchronically oriented psychologists to posit universal patterns of relationships among variables. However, they differ from the traditionalists in their concern with historical conditions as realizations of specific variables (or values along a continuum). From this perspective, whether or not a given social pattern is manifested depends on systematic aspects of the historical condition. In effect, history furnishes a set of natural experiments. The work of Marcia Guttentag and Paul Secord (1983) on gender-ratio effects is exemplary of this approach. These authors have looked at the ways in which the ratio of men to women in a culture affects various cultural patterns. As they attempt to demonstrate, an oversupply of women in proportion to men leads to such diverse effects as promiscuity, a predominance of girl babies and women's liberation movements. During historical periods in which there is a scarcity of women, one finds monogamy, traditional female roles, and early marriage. The general mechanisms underlying these effects are traced to basic principles of exchange theory, along with male dominance. Research by Dean Simonton (1984) on the historical conditions fostering scientific innovation, creativity and originality also employs a basic stability model, as does McClelland's (1961) classic work on achievement level as it relates to economic development.

A second group of historical social psychologists follow an ordered change orientation. The concern of this group is with the orderly progression that occurs in social phenomenon over time, whether based on innate, evolutionary, cyclical, dialectic or other processes. This perspective opposes a situationist viewpoint and draws attention to the orderly aspects of what otherwise might appear to be random or chaotic alterations in activity. James Davies (1962) and Faye Crosby (1976) have developed theories of revolution that are exemplary of this approach. Such theories attempt to trace the orderly patterns of revolutionary developments and isolate the conditions favoring such developments. Colin Martindale's work (1981, 1984) on historical changes in aesthetic tastes also follows this form. Martindale adopts a variation on Freudian theory in arguing that in order to capture popular interest artists in any domain must continue to increase the expression of primary processes within their work. The history of rock music, British poetry, and Renaissance art all follow the same patterns, according to Martindale's research. The music becomes louder and more aggressive, poetry more emotionally and sexually expressive, and art more sensual and vibrant over years of development within the same form.

The third, and most radical variant within diachronic social psychology is the disordered or aleatoric orientation. From this view, social patterns across time are not held to be prefixed or necessarily reiterative. Rather it is assumed that social phenomena may vary across history without orderly pattern. Many life-span developmentalists have begun to favor such a view. For example, research on cohort analysis showing broad, historically contingent variations in life-span trajectories is consistent with the aleatory perspective (cf. P. Baltes, Reese & Nesselroade, 1977; M. Baltes & P. Baltes, 1986). For some, the aleatoric perspective is consistent with the view that social patterns can be altered by virtue of self-reflexive scrutiny. That is, as people come to understand the patterns of action in which they are engaged, they may initiate change. Alice Eagly's (1978) review of persuasibility and gender differences over time is an exemplar of a reflexive science at work. By taking account of the way women have become less persuasible over the decades, people may begin to cast off past images of women; social psychologists may consider how this analysis affects their evaluations of contemporary theories of persuasion. Investigators in the aleatory mode often take as their model of the person a voluntary agent. As such, individuals are free to remake their images and create new relationships and ways of being without constraint. The remainder of this chapter will describe this work and its relationship to the diachronic perspective more generally.

THE NARRATIVE APPROACH TO LIFE-SPAN ANALYSIS

As Thomas Blank (1982) has described it, social psychological accounts of human behavior are much like a scrapbook of snapshots. Here we have people reacting to reinforcement, there we have people stereotyping, and on other pages they are reducing dissonance, reacting to noise, or following decision rules. Nothing sticks together. Yet, in looking at a scrapbook, we may have an advantage over the reader of a social psychology journal. We may be accompanied by a storyteller who sits by our side as we thumb through the album. The storyteller fills us in on the relationships among pictures. Understanding of daily lives indeed seems to require that we tie together events over time. This "tying together" seems best accomplished with the stories that we tell ourselves and others. As Bettleheim (1976) has proposed, such creations of narrative order may be essential in giving life a sense of meaning and direction. Without the strands of narrative that connect one thing to another, events, even substantial ones, may be lost forever. Novelist Milan Kundera in the *Book of Laughter and Forgetting* describes Tamina, a young widow, who has fled Prague for the West. Her memory of her husband is fading, and she is desperate to retain the fleeting remembrances of their married life together.

> There she sits on a raft, looking back, looking only back. The sum total of her being is no more than what she sees in the distance behind her. And as her past begins to shrink, disappear, fall apart, Tamina begins shrinking and blurring. She longs to see her notebooks so she can fill in the fragile framework of events in the new notebook, give it walls, make it a house she can live in. Because if the shaky structure of her memories collapses like a badly pitched tent, all Tamina will have left is the present, that invisible point, that nothing moving slowly toward death (p. 86).

For Kundera, the narrative of the past is essential to give meaning to the present.

The Study of Narrative Forms

Elucidating the process of narrative formulation raises many interesting questions. How are we to understand the organization of narrative forms? How do such narratives function in the life of the individual and in the society more generally? How do narrative constructions relate to real life events? And how do such constructions change over time? The present chapter is not the appropriate context for a full review of this work. However, it is possible to touch on several illustrative aspects, which themselves tell a story. This study of narrative began with a search for a method of characterizing narratives and differentiating among narrative forms. It seemed that most well-formed narratives in Western culture are characterized by two features. First, narratives seem to furnish a *directionality* to events across time. One is not provided simply with a sequence of events, but a sequence that seems to be going in some direction. Second, narratives provide a sense of *coherence* or connectedness to elements of the story. Further the sense of direction in narrative relies on the establishment of an endpoint or goal around which the events may be organized. To achieve coherence, events are then entered into the story in ways that indicate whether the goal is or is not being reached. Extraneous events are usually weeded out, put in a parenthesis, or accompanied by an apology. For example, to tell the story of a love affair typically requires the glorification of the loving relationship itself, thus establishing a goal state. The story is then composed of elements that bring the lovers closer to their goal or that frustrate or destroy them. Other events, such as what one ate for dinner, the exchange rate for the pound, or Aunt Martha's gout are excluded because of their irrelevance to the goal. A good story-teller will adhere to these prescriptions, while the poor story-teller may be described as disorganized or boring.

In a simple narrative, three prototypical forms can be identified. These forms are illustrated in Figure 1. First, the *stability narrative may be envisioned, in which all events lead in one direction with equally favorable or unfavorable outcomes. In this story line the protagonist remains unchanged. Someone who tells a life story that is always happy or always miserable would have a stability narrative. A second rudimentary form is the progressive narrative,* in which the story line becomes more positive as it unfolds. The third form, its complement, is the *regressive narrative.* Here the story line becomes more negative as it unfurls. The dramatic forms we use in our culture reflect the combination of these forms; tragedy, for example, would commence with a high stable plateau, and then develop into a rapidly regressing narrative. Comedy, in most instances, ends with a progressive narrative, with the happily-ever-after denouement. A melodrama combines the progressive and regressive narratives in a roller-coaster format that contains many reversals, but after much struggle usually ends happily. It would appear that the cultural preferences for a particular narrative form, its shape and style, the angle of the slopes, and the number of reversals that the plot is allowed to contain may constrain the way in which dramas are allowed to be played, lived, or described.

Do people actually account for their lives according to these forms? Consider a study carried out with a group of undergraduates at Swarthmore College who were asked to account for their personal histories by drawing a continuous line depicting their feelings of generalized well-being from their childhood to the present. From these various depictions we were able to develop an average

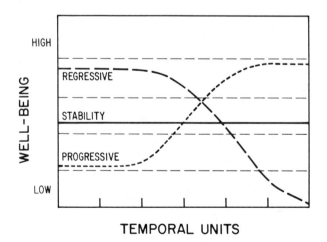

FIGURE 1. Three types of narratives.

"life line" that was descriptive of the sample. As revealed in Figure 2, among these students, the typical life pattern revealed a "comic" form of narrative. The story seemed to go as follows: Basically, I had a happy childhood, with few ups and downs. Around adolescence something went wrong, (e.g., we moved, parents got divorced, I lost my friendship group) and then slowly I came out of it, and now I am increasingly happy again. Recent high points included falling in love, overcoming adversity, and having intense sensual or aesthetic experiences. To determine whether the students possessed differing narrative forms for different aspects of their lives—as opposed to using only one general form— they were also asked to chart the history of their relationships with each parent and their academic careers. In general, each of these narrative lines followed a somewhat different course. With parents, progressive narratives were the rule, with students becoming more pleased with these relationships over time. The slope for the academic achievement narrative was regressive, however, and seemed to indicate that this area of life did not fit the slope described by their general feelings of well-being. College represented a time of crisis in the intellectual history of the students, with past glories crumbling in the face of keener competition from peers.

It seemed plausible, from these examples and from general conclusions about narratives, to conclude that people can create a multiplicity of narratives about various areas of life. In addition, even those events that seem to support one type of narrative might be reworked at another time to support a contrary one. A failing grade on a midterm might be viewed as evidence that a previous belief that one is a genius is false; all previously garnered A's might be reinterpreted as the result of favoritism, guile, luck, cheating, poor testing, or insuffi-

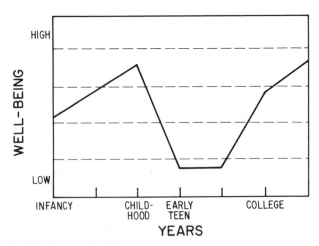

FIGURE 2. Students' narrative line.

cient challenge. It is crucial to appreciate that narratives like other social psychological phenomena are subject to the aleatoric confluence of events. We will explore this further.

The Social Dependency of Personal Narrative: History in Motion

Much current research on narratives has asked respondents to construct life accounts. From such accounts an attempt is made to extract dominant forms of narrative. Yet, such research is also misleading in one major respect: It suggests that narratives themselves are frozen in time and thus militates against the same diachronic orientation that it otherwise attempts to champion. This misleading indication must now be redressed. Specifically, it is important to emphasize the continuously unfolding character of narrative constructions. The shifting of narrative constructions over time is chiefly dependent on their basis in social interdependency.

While it is possible for an individual to tell a multiplicity of stories about oneself, in order to be sustained the self-narrative must meet a standard of shared meaning within the community. If one's self-narrative is too far from the norms of the social group, it is vulnerable to being rejected, along with the story-teller. Occasionally people try to validate story lines that are unsubstantiated by others. For example, an elderly woman recently died still proclaiming that she was Anastasia, the surviving daughter of the Russian Czar's family, the members of which were all supposedly killed by the Bolsheviks during the Russian Revolution. Her claims were not generally accepted, and she could not actually sustain the life she felt was her due. Her narrative was not validated within society.

Clear cases of the social interdependence of narrative construction occur when people describe a shared experience. One member of a group may describe how wonderful the group's vacation had been, and how the weather, by and large, had been fine. Another might remind the rest that it had rained the first few days, but that the weekend festivities had made it all worthwhile. A third vacationer might mention that the place was a veritable paradise, with exquisite vegetation and lush surroundings. A fourth might comment on the prompt service and friendly and helpful staff. Together they might knit a story that allows them all to share a common history, that of the wonderful vacation. Comments about rain, overpriced rooms, bugs, and bad wine would all be suppressed, or cast into footnote status in the tale. In the end, this product, the history of the vacation, is a communal or joint product. Not so much a reflection of reality as a communal artifact. As Jorge Luis Borges has framed it, "Reality may be too complex for oral transmission; legend recreates it in a manner which is only accidentally false and which allows it to go about the world, from mouth to mouth" (p. 122).

The Interdependency of Narratives: The Plot Thickens

As is exemplified in the vacation story, narratives typically require a supporting cast. That is, other persons' actions are typically insinuated into one's own narrative. To include others in this way requires that they are indeed willing to play the assigned roles. To portray oneself as generous and loving rather than selfish and obnoxious requires supporting characters who are willing to support this self-characterization. If supporting characters wish to reinterpret the relationship to give themselves a better part, the previously balanced interplay of characters in one's narrative may be jeopardized. This interdependence and reliance of one actor upon another seems fundamental to social life. In Wilhelm Schapp's terms (1976) each of us is knitted into others' historical constructions as they are into ours.

This delicate interdependence of constructed narrative suggests that a fundamental aspect of social life is an ongoing reciprocity in the negotiation of meaning. Because one's narrative construction can be maintained only so long as others play their proper supporting roles, and in turn because one is required by others to play supporting roles in their constructions, the moment any participant chooses to renege, he or she threatens the array of interdependent constructions. An adolescent may explain to his mother that she is a bad mother who does not understand him. The mother may, in turn, declare that the child has taken all of the bad traits of his father's family, and she does not consider him truly her child. Each is then left bereft of their normal interdependent construction of themselves as a mother-child combination. The intolerability of this situation might lead to one or the other casting about to find means to reknit the torn narrative fiber between them.

In order to maintain the precious reciprocity in narrative construction various strategies may be deployed. For example, one strategy is to engage in the objectification of the relationship itself. That is, the relationship between parties is given its own narrative identity to which one's personal narrative is attached. For example, the *Marriage,* the *Friendship,* the *Affair* or the *Feud* become entities that have their own narrative. To the extent that the participants can agree on the narrative of the relationship, they may rest more secure in the stability of their related narratives of self. Other strategies of maintaining reciprocity may include the use of guilt, deception in the management of one's public identity, and reward, when the other supports your story.

Science and the Shaping of Narratives: The Case of Aging

Although the present analysis has emphasized the interdependence of narratives at the dyadic level, the range of influences over one's narrative accounts may be far greater. One critical concern in this regard is the potential influence of the social sciences on narrative construction within the culture. The sciences furnish ample portrayal of what is the natural and normal course of development. Within the classroom, the media, and the popular book accounts, scientific authorities deliver messages on what constitutes "normal" youth, adulthood, and old age. These depictions furnish scientifically accredited models for people's life formulations. To construct a narrative at extreme variance with the scientifically established models might incur public derision for the individual.

The crucial importance of these social science models is particularly evident in the case of aging. While scientific literature has generally painted childhood and adolescence as a period of rapid acceleration in skills, knowledge, and overall physical development, and adulthood as a plateau, old age has been portrayed as a period of decline. This inverted U or rainbow form of narrative, constructs the elderly as "over the hill." Yet as emphasized earlier, narratives are essentially literary constructions. Whether one is declining or advancing largely depends on what goals one establishes, and the events one selects as relevant to these goals. In this sense, the sciences may render an unwitting injustice to the elderly—essentially informing them that they are undergoing a period of decline.

Do these scientifically substantiated narratives have such an impact? This is difficult to ascertain. Relevant to this question is an in-depth interview study with a group of elderly people (M. Gergen, 1980). These individuals, ranging in age from 63 to 93, each lived in their own dwellings, independently. Each was asked to recount various aspects of their lives, with probes made as to how their current life activities and interests compared with their activities of the previous five years. They were also asked to talk about when in their lives they had been happiest, and what time life was the best. In effect, they were asked to furnish an interpretation of their general well-being as it had waxed and waned over the years.

As these interviews revealed, most of these elderly people saw their well-being in terms of the rainbow narrative suggested by the scientific literature. That is, they saw the early years as being one of challenge and development as they climbed to the zenith of life, while middle-age furnished a happy, high level plateau. Old age, in contrast, seemed to be largely a regressive phase, down hill after the middle years. While it is difficult to ascertain the extent to which social science models are implicated in these views, at a minimum this literature has served as a sustained accompaniment to broadly held cultural beliefs. To the extent that social science models do influence the larger public consciousness, those who work in the field of life-span development might become aware of this relationship. With more creative conceptualizations of life-span narratives, the social sciences could play a more beneficial role in the way people talk about, and live, their lives. While social scientists cannot single-handedly create the perennial sought fountain of youth, they can retouch the rainbow and bring rejuvenating hope to a vast audience of adults.

CONCLUSION

As described, the concern with cross-time change in social patterns invites inquiry into a variety of topics, along with the development of new theoretical and methodological tools. In the present case we have focused on how people account for cross-time processes, particularly in their own lives. As it was proposed, the major device for making such accounts, the narrative, could take a variety of different forms. These forms were viewed as social constructions, subject to wide-ranging alteration as the social context changed and supporting characters affirmed or withdrew from their assigned places in one's narrative. At least one sample of young persons was found to account for the history of their general well being with comic narrative forms. In this sense, their preferred narrative approximated the same form most frequently used in television dramas and situation comedies. In contrast, a sample of elderly persons accounted for their lives with a rainbow-like narrative, in which the early years seemed to be ones of growth and development, and the latter years of decline. This narrative form is similar to the stereotype of the aging process characterized in much behavioral science literature. In the future as more attention is paid to diachronic forms of social inquiry, new possibilities for life narratives will be generated.

REFERENCES

Baltes, M. & Baltes, P. B. (Eds.). (1986). *Aging and control.* Hillsdale, NJ: Erlbaum.
Baltes, P. B., Reese, H. W., & Nesselroade, J. R. (1977). *Life-span developmental psychology: Introduction to research methods.* Monterey, CA: Brooks/Cole.
Bettleheim, B. (1976). *The uses of enchantment.* New York: Knopf.
Blank, T. (1982). *A social psychology of developing adults.* New York: Wiley.
Borges, J. L. (1967). *A personal anthology.* New York: Grove Press.
Crosby, F. (1976). A model of egotistical relative deprivation. *Psychological Review, 83,* 85–113.
Davies, J. C. (1962). Toward a theory of revolution. *American Sociological Review, 27,* 5–19.
Eagly, A. H. (1978). Sex differences in influenceability. *Psychological Bulletin, 85,* 86–116.
Gergen, K. J. (1973). Social psychology as history. *Journal of Personality and Social Psychology, 1,* 309–320.
Gergen, K. J. (1978). Toward generative theory. *Journal of Personality and Social Psychology, 36,* 1344–1360.
Gergen, K. J. (1982). *Toward transformation in social knowledge.* New York: Springer-Verlag.
Gergen, K. J. & Gergen, M. M. (1982). Form and function in the explanation of human conduct. In P. Secord (Ed.), *Explaining social behavior: Consciousness, human action and social structure.* Beverly Hills, CA: Sage.
Gergen, K. J. & Gergen, M. M. (1983). Narratives of the self. In K. Scheibe & T. Sarbin (Eds.), *Studies in social identity,* New York: Praeger.

Gergen, K. J. & Gergen, M. M. (Eds.). (1984). *Historical social psychology,* Hillsdale, NJ: Erlbaum.

Gergen, M. (1980). *Antecedents and consequences of self-attributional preferences in later life.* Doctoral Dissertation, Temple University.

Guttentag, M. & Secord, P. (1983). *Too many women? The sex ratio question.* Beverly Hills, CA: Sage.

Kundera, M. (1981). *The book of laughter and forgetting.* (Trans. Michael Henry Heim), Harmondsworth, England: Penguin Books.

Martindale, C. (1981). *Cognition and consciousness.* Homewood, IL: Dorsey.

Martindale, C. (1984). The evolution of aesthetic taste. In K. Gergen & M. Gergen (Eds.), *Historical social psychology.* Hillsdale, NJ: Erlbaum.

McClelland, D. (1961). *The achieving society,* New York: Van Nostrand.

Overton, W. R. & Reese, H. W. (1973). Models of development: Methodological implications. In J. R. Nesselroade & H. W. Reese (Eds.), *Life-span developmental psychology: Methodological issues.* New York: Academic Press.

Schapp, W. (1976). *In Geschichten Verstrickt zum Sein von Mensch and Ding.* Weisbaden: B. Heymann.

Simonton, D. K. (1984). Generational time-series analysis: A paradigm for studying sociocultural influences. In K. Gergen & M. Gergen (Eds.), *Historical social psychology.* Hillsdale, NJ: Erlbaum.

Chapter 14

Artificial Intelligence: What, if Anything, Can Machines Teach Us about Human Psychology?

Robert G. Weyant

It is the case that, in certain areas of psychological theory, concepts have a kind of self-referential quality. An obvious example involves the attempt to understand the process of "understanding." Here, theory attempts to define a concept and apply to that concept the appropriate psychological process represented by that concept. In scientific theory generally, early attempts at understanding make explicit use of metaphors, models, and reasoning by analogy as the theorists attempt to place the unfamiliar (i.e., not understood) concepts and phenomena within a framework of familiar (i.e., understood) concepts and phenomena, in an effort to understand them. Since we understand relatively little about "understanding," much of our language in discussing the phenomenon, such as my previous sentence, is overtly metaphorical. Where the use of metaphors, models, and reasoning by analogy is explicit enough to be obvious, some attention to the process may help us understand how we attempt to understand. Thus the importance of occasional discussion about the theoretical background of a discipline's research assumptions. Such a case is presented by current work in artificial intelligence (AI) that attempts to apply the (largely understood) functioning of machines to the (largely not understood) functioning of human beings.

To begin with the question that forms the title of this paper, "What, if anything, can machines teach us about human psychology?" the answer is almost surely "nothing" if we are referring simply to the machines themselves, the computer hardware. It is the software, the programs, from which we might conceivably learn something abut human psychology. But even with this caveat the question, for many individuals, is stillborn. The proper study of mankind, as Pope observed, is man, not machines or programs. What, then, are we to make of the study of artificial intelligence in relation to the problems of human psychology?

The very term "artificial intelligence" is itself misleading since it is often used to refer to at least two quite distinct activities. The first is the mimicking or reproducing of human behavior as an end in itself. The second is the development and testing of theories of human psychology. John Searle has, among other things, attempted to deal with this distinction in asking whether there is any psychological and philosophical significance in recent efforts at computer simulation of human cognitive processes (Searle, 1981). Searle makes a distinction between what he refers to as "weak" AI and "strong" AI. Weak AI, according to Searle, claims only that the computer is a very powerful tool in the study of the human mind. It is a tool that allows for more exact formulation and testing of psychological hypotheses. Strong AI, Searle argues, goes further in claiming that, over and above the computer's use as a tool, an appropriately programmed computer literally has cognitive states such as "understanding."

Most of Searle's attention is directed at what he characterizes as the claims of strong AI, although it is not entirely clear whose claims he is refuting (but see the comments of Douglas Hofstadter and Daniel Dennett, 1981), so we are not provided with examples of the use of the computer as a tool in weak AI. That is, we are never specifically told how a computer might be used for the more rigorous and precise formulation and testing of hypotheses or even what "rigorous" and "precise" might mean in relation to computer formulation and testing of hypotheses. Whether, for example, the reference here is to more quantitative hypotheses or hypotheses that refer to finer detail in human behavior is not discussed. Nor is it clear what would constitute a "test" using the computer as a tool. Searle does go on to say of strong AI that, because the claim is made that the programmed computer actually has cognitive states, then the programs are not simply tools, but, rather, they are explanations of the psychological processes. Presumably, for this claim to be substantiated the cognitive states of computers would have to be assumed to be identical with the cognitive states of humans (a stronger claim that Searle indicates) and the term "explanation" would be taken to mean something like "can produce identical cognitive states."

There is no question that some extreme claims have been made for artificial intelligence. Some twenty years ago James Culbertson claimed to be able to create artificial states of consciousness in robots (Culbertson, 1963, preface). These extreme claims are much less common, although not nonexistent, among more recent researchers in the field. If extreme claims are being made, they might be expected to be found within the context of work in which human higher mental processes are being mimicked. Such work is reported, for example, by Frank H. George, writing in 1970 on models of thinking, who recognizes that what he is using are formal models to "simulate" human systems (George, 1970, p. 15). Roger Schank, writing in 1982 on dynamic memory, pointed out that it is important for a program to be "extensible" in the natural world if it is to have any value as a psychological theory (Schank, 1982, p. 11). Michael G. Dyer, in a 1983 volume on in-depth understanding, argued that people are the only in-depth understanders that we have and that what he was proposing in his book was simply a model of "those knowledge constructs, inference strategies, and memory search processes which are prerequisite for in-depth understanding" (Dyer, 1983, p. xiii).

What the claims that have been made in these more recent discussions have in common is not that human cognitive processes are being duplicated, but that the programs are incomplete representations of human psychological processes. There is an emphasis on the modelling nature of the researchers' activities rather than the identity of human and machine processes.

It is an obvious point that the language we use in describing phenomena causes us to think about those phenomena in particular ways. Hidden assumptions are frequently smuggled on board an argument in crates labeled "purely descriptive language." The language used by workers in artificial intelligence has clearly been a problem. It is a descriptive language that employs cognitive terms. It is commonplace to speak of computers as "remembering," "learning," "knowing," "understanding," and so on. Indeed, "understanding," has probably received more attention from researchers in cognitive science over the past twenty years than it had received from psychologists over the previous two centuries.

When we examine our students for the purpose of assessing their comprehension of course materials, we may simply test for retention of information, of facts, or we may attempt to test for "understanding." Essentially, we do that by asking questions of the students that require them to use the information they have acquired in new and novel ways rather than simply repeating it verbatim. We test to see if they can perceive relationships, significance, implications, etc. If they are able to answer such questions to our satisfaction then we feel comfortable with saying that they "understand" the material, at least to the degree tested. It would seem particularly perverse to argue that this behavior did not really indicate understanding because the students had to be provided with the necessary information in some form before they could understand it or that they had to be taught such skills as integration, extrapolation, and reasoning. On the other hand, if a computer could produce answers indistinguishable from those produced by our students, many individuals would be reluctant to conclude that the computer had an understanding of the material. The argument would typically be made that humans had to "feed" the computer the information and program it to respond correctly. What grounds do we have for applying one set of criteria to identifying a phenomenon in humans, but believing it to be inappropriate to apply that same set of criteria to identifying the phenomenon in machines?

One of the traditional criticisms of work in artificial intelligence, referred to by Alan Turing in 1950 as "Lady Lovelace's objection," is that computers can do only what we program them to do, that we must supply them with the information as well as the processes by which the information is manipulated (Turing, 1950). This criticism is usually countered in one of two ways. The first countering argument takes the point of the criticism to be that the responses of a computer are always predictable while the responses of human beings are not, and argues that computer programmers often write programs that are very complicated or that contain branching choice points such that neither the programmer nor anyone else can, in fact, predict the outcome. The second countering argument questions whether the situation is any different for human beings who are, it is argued, "programmed" by a combination of heredity and experience to behave in ways that would be predictable if we had sufficient information. The point of both arguments is to question whether there really is, in principle, a fundamental difference of any importance between machines and humans in relation to the information and processes needed to produce their respective behavior.

If there are not crucial, relevant differences then we may be justified in using a word such as "understand" to indicate that the computer is responding in ways that, if the behavior was produced by human beings, we would call "understanding." At present, however, the language is metaphorical. It is not assumed that computer "understanding" and human "understanding" are identical processes, although they may be. This is a crucial point that seems to be forgotten in discussions of the relationship between artificial intelligence and human psychology. What advantage is there to using such cognitive descriptive terms metaphorically when we know that there is the potential disadvantage of the terms being taken literally and misunderstood? The situation has been described, in part, by Margaret Boden who argues that the use of such terms encourages potentially fruitful theoretical insights into the analogous processes. That the use of psychological terms in relation to computer processes is an analogous use, Boden claims, is argued on two counts. First, existing programs are puny in their abilities when compared to the human mind. Second, and philosophically more controversial, human cognitive processes, but not computer processes, involve "intentional" interests that are essential to the literal application of cognitive terms.

So in the relationship between human and computer psychological processes we are faced with a descriptive language that is metaphoric. Does this set this area of research apart from all other scientific research? The answer to this question is, of course, controversial, but W. H. Leatherdale has recorded an extensive history of the use of analogies, models, and metaphors in science (Leatherdale, 1974) and Roger Jones, among others, has gone so far as to liken the scientist to the poet in *creating* meaning in a search for understanding and has argued that all physical science is a metaphor (Jones, 1982, p. ix).

To return to the specific case of the use of the word "understanding" in relation to computers, there is a further criterion that must be met and that Boden alludes to when she refers to using cognitive terms while making explicit "the precise functional details of the program concerned" (Boden, 1981, p. 34). The response cannot be a "canned" response. That is, it cannot be a response that the computer has been programmed to produce whenever a particular cue appears. In the eighteenth century the brothers Maillardet constructed a mechanical magician. You could present the magician with one of a very limited number of prescribed questions about your future and the magician would go through much of the external behavior associated with thinking—it would nod, incline its head, rest its chin in its hand and so forth. Then it would produce a canned answer that was always the same no matter who asked the question. There is no record of anyone believing that the magician really understood the questions that it answered. Joseph Weizenbaum's program known as *Eliza* had a canned response, ("tell me more about your family") to the first mention of a family member (mother, father, sister, etc.), that had the appearance of intelligent intentionality about it (Weizenbaum, 1976, p. 4). Modern computer programs have been written, such as the story telling programs of Roger Schank and his associates, that appear to provide for the appropriate extrapolation of background information to new situations. That is, they exhibit what in human beings we might call "understanding" behavior. The points to be determined in each are (1) whether these are simply cleverly concealed canned responses and (2) how they differ from human responses in similar situations.

When our students demonstrate understanding on an examination they may do so in a number of different ways at a number of different levels. Correctly filling in their name, student number and so on demonstrates an understanding of instructions but it is not behavior that we find very impressive, rare though it may be. Some limited ability to extrapolate and discuss the more obvious implications and relations may indicate an understanding, but a rather shallow understanding, of the material. Recognizing less obvious extrapolations may indicate a deeper understanding. The problem of determining whether a particular student understands a particular point is superficially similar to testing a computer program but, it is likely to be argued, the crucial difference is that we *know* that the human student is capable of the process of understanding, whether or not any understanding of the particular point is demonstrated, and we know no such thing about the computer. This is, of course, a philosophically debatable assumption.

Margaret Boden has argued that machine understanding is the ability to carry out the appropriate processes when the machine has been given the appropriate instructions. This is basically an automatic or "blind" process built into the machine's hardware (Boden, 1977, p. 8). But if there is something odd about refusing to accept as a criterion for machine "understanding" something that one is quite willing to accept for human "understanding," there also seems to be something odd about saying that a machine which simply carries out its programmed instructions "understands" unless, of course, we recognize that the word is being used metaphorically. Given this definition, we should have to accept the Maillardet magician as an understanding machine. Boden goes on to point out that machines can also "understand" higher level symbols and that a machine, like a human being, would have to "think rather harder" if asked to find the second noun phrase in the sentence "The cat sat on the mat" than it (or the human) would if asked simply to find the words "the mat." This is surely moving us closer to what we usually mean by "understanding," but it still is not clear why we should find this example any more congenial than the simple carrying out of instructions.

We might look to John Searle as providing a reasonably typical discussion of the problems relating to understanding. After having made the distinction between weak AI and strong AI, Searle turns to a *gedankenexperiment.* Suppose:

1 Searle is locked in a room with a large batch of Chinese script;
2 Searle knows no written or spoken Chinese;
3 Searle is then given a second batch of Chinese script together with a set of rules for correlating the second batch with the first batch (note that Searle says here that the rules are presented in English and that he "understands" these rules as competently as any native speaker of English);
4 Searle is then given a third batch of Chinese script together with instructions in English that enable him to correlate elements of the third batch with the first two batches;
5 Searle is also given instructions in English on how he is to give back certain Chinese symbols with certain sorts of shapes in response of certain sorts of shapes given to him in the third batch.

Now, Searle says, unknown to him the people who are giving him all of these symbols call the first batch "a script," they call the second batch "a story," they call the third batch "questions" and they call the symbols he gives back to them in response to the third batch "answers to questions," while the set of rules they gave him in English they call "the program." Suppose further, that the people giving him all these Chinese scripts do the same thing with English writing. From their point of view, Searle argues, the same thing is happening in the case of the Chinese scripts as with the English writing. That is, he is answering questions in both cases. But, Searle argues, from his point of view two different things are happening. In the case of the Chinese script he is producing answers by manipulating uninterpreted formal symbols according to a set of rules, that is, he is acting like a computer. But the English language case he argues, is very different.

Searle contends that "understanding" implies "both the possession of mental (intentional) states and the truth (validity, success) of these states" (Searle, 1981, p. 287) but that he is concerned only with the former. Thus, it would seem that intentionality is the crucial difference between his processing of the Chinese script and his answering of the English language questions. The concept of intentionality in psychology has a long history going back to Aristotle and, more recently, to Franz Brentano. Included in the concept are such psychological phenomena as "desires," "hopes," "wishes," "expectations," "beliefs," and "assumptions." The objects of these activities need not, in reality, exist so their objects are taken to be mental representations, not physical things. Thus, I can believe that you will take me for a ride in your new Mercedes even if such a ride is never forthcoming. Indeed, I may hope for such a ride even if you do not, in fact, own a new Mercedes. It is, then, these intentional states that are lacking in computer processes for Searle and for many other critics of AI. And these intentional processes, they argue, are crucial for true psychological functioning. What computers engage in, according to Searle, is manipulation of formal symbols, not intentional processes.

The point of this elaborate *gedankenexperiment* is to repute the claims of strong AI within the context of a situation similar to that used by Roger Schank and his associates with computer programs. As an interesting aside, Searle acknowledges in a footnote that Schank has not made strong AI claims for his work, so it is not clear whose claims Searle is demolishing. Nevertheless, there is some face validity to the proposition that the psychological processes involved in answering the English language questions are not the same psychological processes as those involved in processing the Chinese script. But how much more than this can we say? It is not, for example, clear in what specific ways the two processes differ. The processing of the Chinese script is not without some element of understanding since, as Searle points out, he would have to understand the English language instructions and, as he does not point out, that recognizing differences in shapes itself involves some element of understanding. Are we to take Searle's admission that he would have to understand the instructions as support for Boden's view that what constitutes machine understanding is the ability to carry out appropriate processes when given appropriate instructions? It is unlikely that Searle meant to be providing such support. Moreover, Hofstadter and Dennett (1981, pp. 373 ff.) have seriously questioned the possibility of a person being able to behave at all in the way that Searle has indicated.

Searle's arguments deserve far more consideration than we can provide here (for further discussions see the comments that appeared with the original article, Flanagan, 1984, chap. 6, Hofstadter and Dennett, 1981, chap. 22 and Cummins, 1983, chap. 3). Searle is *not* arguing that machines cannot think because he believes that we *are* machines. Nor is he arguing that man-made machines, even digital computers, cannot think. What he does claim to be arguing against is the thesis that something could think or understand *solely* because it is a computer with the correct program (Searle, 1981, p. 300). His argument is that such a computer would be nothing more than a formal symbol manipulator without intentionality. What might provide such a computer with intentionality? Searle does not give us any clear answer to that question, but he does say that it would require the same causal powers as brains and he relates this to specific biochemical processes (Searle, 1981, p. 305).

This is neither an unreasonable nor an uninteresting position and if computer designers make effective use of biochips, Searle may be moved to modify his thesis. Even if Searle's points on intentionality are granted and it is agreed that computer processes and human processes are not identical, we are still left with the question, "What, if anything, can the incomplete psychological processes of computers teach us about human psychological processes?"

To provide one example of the type of research that might prove useful, take the concept of "intuition." Some years ago Malcolm Westcott reported a number of studies of what he termed intuition in which he presented human subjects with various sorts of numerical and verbal problems to be solved on the basis of increasing amounts of information. He found that a significant number of correct solutions could be produced on the basis of logically "incomplete" information (Westcott, 1968, chap. 5). There would seem to be some relationship between this kind of ability and the abilities demonstrated by computers using Roger Schank's storytelling programs. One would want to look in great detail at any program that claimed to allow the computer to go beyond the evidence provided, just as one would like to know more about the processes at work in Westcott's subjects. But certain kinds of questions are clearly suggested. Could such studies be duplicated with computers and what kind of information and programs would enable the machine to demonstrate "intuition?" How far would the analogy hold if the computers could produce the required behavior and what clues might that analogy provide us that would be of use in further studies with human subjects? What conceptual errors are we likely to commit if we begin to refer to properly programmed computers as being "intuitive?"

Research psychologists most commonly use a simple "predictive" model of science. That is, beginning with either a full-blown theory, a formal hypothesis or a relatively informal guess (which they subsequently tend to write about as if it had been a formal hypothesis), they conduct an empirical test of the theory/hypothesis/guess and, if their prediction is more-or-less in conformity with the outcome of the empirical test, they consider the theory/hypothesis/ guess to have increased to some degree in the probability of its being correct. If the prediction is not in conformity with the outcome of the empirical test, any one of a number of responses may ensue ranging from rejection of the theory/ hypothesis/guess through its modification, to a decision that the empirical research was not, after all, an adequate test of the prediction. This, the niceties of discussions among philosophers of science notwithstanding, seems to be the model of science most psychologists have in mind when they are actually performing research.

Some discussions of research on artificial intelligence have suggested that this research may be thought of in a slightly different way. Aaron Sloman, for example, has argued that science may be viewed as having four aims, the discovery, description, explanation, and limits of possibilities. He is particularly interested in the process of testing the limits of what may be possible in nature since he sees this as being how laws of nature are determined (Sloman, 1978, Chap. 2). Margaret Boden has made some similar points within the context of a discussion of the computational metaphor and analogical reasoning in psychology (Boden, 1981, p. 35).

Referring specifically to the artificial intelligence—human psychology relationship, much of the work of developing intelligent software to model human behavior seems to involve asking questions such as "can we get the machine to produce this particular type of behavior?" and "if so, what kinds of operations and information are required?" We have already seen that research in artificial intelligence involves use of a metaphoric language, we now turn to models and analogies.

Argument by analogy is a recognized form of argument in logic. Its basic form is:

Objects of type A have properties X, Y and Z.
Objects of type B have properties X, Y and Z.
Objects of type A also have property P.
Therefore, objects of type B have property P.

Clearly, as with all inductive reasoning, one is not compelled to accept the conclusion, but analogical reasoning has proven to be useful in many areas including science and law. Perhaps one of the best known arguments by analogy in science was Galileo's argument that because Jupiter and its moons had certain observable properties in common with Earth and its moon, and since Jupiter and its moons were clearly moving through space, then it was possible that Earth and its moon were also moving through space.

It has been asked whether argument by analogy and description by metaphor is unavoidable in scientific theory. A few arguments might be given in the affirmative. First, if the language of scientific description (or the language of psychological description) is a social artifact, then all theory may be seen as being a metaphor relating the description of the observations to the social context. (See Kenneth Gergen's paper in this volume.) One might press the matter further and say that since no two natural objects are, so far as we can tell, absolutely identical then all empirical argument in science is, in that sense, analogical. When we extrapolate from one falling body to another, from one human being to another, or from the averaged behavior of a thousand persons to any one person, we are using analogical arguments. We normally think of analogical argument as a sub-set of inductive argument but, of course, what we are doing when we extrapolate from the behavior of a hundred first-year university students to the behavior of all human beings is to assume implicitly (and often incorrectly) that the analogy holds because there are no *relevant* differences. Arguments by analogy do not depend on a one-to-one identity of the properties of objects. Parts of analogous psychological processes and behavior may very well be missing and this may or may not be crucial to the analogy. The question to be asked is whether it matters for our purpose once we realize that our purpose is not to recreate human mental life and behavior in its entirety. For example, feeling pleasure is a part of human mental life. It has been recognized by philosophers such as Aristotle and Locke that one function of feeling pleasure is to cause us to repeat certain behaviors. But if we are only concerned, for our purposes, in the effects of repetitive behavior (as, for example, in learning) and if repetition can be programmed in other ways, then it may not matter for this particular purpose that a computer cannot feel pleasure. It may still be able to learn from repetition and we may still be able to learn something from how it learns.

The crucial point, therefore, is the determination of the properties that are shared by the objects or classes of objects being compared, *where these properties are relevant to the analogy being drawn.* If, for example, we are interested in making analogical arguments between human beings and some other species in relation to the phenomena of learning, we would probably consider the shared property that both humans and chickens have two legs to be irrelevant to the learning process analogical argument. On the other hand, although humans and dolphins do not share the property of having two legs, they do share other properties such as the size and complexity of the brain that might make an analogical argument in relation to learning stronger and of more interest to us. A major problem, of course, involves how we determine that the number of legs is not a relevant property but the size and complexity of the brain are relevant properties, where the process of learning is concerned. The determination of the relevance of a given property or properties to a particular analogical argument involves testing the limits of the analogous relationship. That is, setting a range of analogical arguments that are strengthened by the similar, shared properties.

Thus, part of the activity of scientists is directed towards determining to what extent any analogical argument is valid, which properties are relevant and/

or crucial for the analogy to be valid, and which valid analogical arguments are interesting. If our primary focus is on human beings, we are not likely to spend much time testing the limits of analogical arguments that relate humans to inanimate objects such as stones (unless we happen to be interested in behavior when pushed off a high ledge). Some psychologists seem to have found it interesting to study the limits of analogical arguments that relate humans to plants by attempting to determine if it helps to say "good morning" to your boston fern. Even more psychologists have been interested in testing the limits of analogical arguments that relate humans to rats, pigeons, dolphins and chimpanzees. Of greater interest have been the limits of analogical arguments relating humans to other humans.

One could construct a continuum of psychologists' interest in analogical arguments with humans at one end of the continuum and stones at the other end. In general, animate objects such as higher primates, rats, and pigeons would be separated from inanimate objects such as stones by a wide gap of interest. The one exception to the animate-inanimate dichotomy would be computers and computer programs. This is of some interest for a number of reasons. First, it may illustrate, as some writers have claimed, that the advent of microchip technology has changed our conception of "machines" in a very fundamental way. Margaret Boden, for example, has observed:

> The new concept of "machine" provided by artificial intelligence is so much more powerful than familiar concepts of mechanism that the old metaphysical puzzle of how mind and body can possibly be related is largely resolved. (Boden, 1977, p. 4)

Second, a particularly important shared property in strengthening such analogical arguments involving the psychology of humans and other species has always been thought to be similarity in the structure and functioning of the central nervous system, including the sensory organs. Computers, of course, do not have central nervous systems. They do, however, have a functioning circuitry that is, in some ways, similar to a central nervous system while in other ways there are great differences. Physically, there is little in common between the system of carbon based neurons on the one hand, and the system of metallic wires and silicon based crystals on the other. Functionally, the binary action of computers in transmitting impulses bears some resemblance, but only some, to the combination of binary functioning, graded functioning and chemical exchange of ions that takes place in the human central nervous system.

The crucial similarity between humans and computers on which, at their foundation, all of the arguments by analogy between human and computer functioning seem to rest is that both humans and computers process information. If this is, in fact, taken to be *the* major crucial and relevant similarity then the strength of all of the analogical arguments rests largely on this shared property. The differences in human and computer hardware or the way that hardware functions are, it might be argued, details not relevant to the analogical argument so long as what the hardware does is process information.

Hubert Dreyfus has specifically questioned the assumption that, since humans process information, at least in some general sense of the phrase "process information," there must be an information processing level of activity, including a program, in the human mind. He refers to this as the "psychological assumption." Dreyfus argues that "information processing" is an ambiguous phrase. Dreyfus's point is worth raising, for what he is saying is that if the arguments by analogy that relate human to computer functioning are grounded on the similarity that both classes of objects are information processors, then we should carefully test the limits of that analogy. It is an empirical question whether or not the brain functions at some basic level as a digital computer, to be answered, in time, through research. He quite correctly points out that just because the biochemical processes that take place in human "information processing" can in principle be calculated directly, this does not mean that any discrete processes are actually occurring (Dreyfus, 1979, p. 168).

However, we still need to ask whether this possible difference between humans and computers is crucial for any of the arguments by analogy we may wish to draw. Dreyfus argues that:

> For psychological *explanation,* a *representation,* somehow stronger than a mere *simulation,* is required. . . . That is, equivalence in the psychological respect demands machine process, *of the psychological type.* (Dreyfus, 1979, p. 168).

Note that Dreyfus seems to have moved, without noticing it, from "representation" to "equivalence," which is part of the basis for much of the confusion in AI-human psychology discussions. He indicates that he is referring to psychological processes such as searching, sorting, and storing rather than physiochemical processes, but it is not entirely clear what kind of searching, sorting, and storing behavior in a computer would count, for Dreyfus, as being processes of the psychological type.

The crucial point here is that Dreyfus, and others, have assumed that work in AI must involve the production of equivalent systems. This is incorrect if, in fact, one is dealing with analogies, with representations. Representations, by their very nature, are not equivalencies and are not intended to be equivalencies. They "represent," they do not "duplicate." At its base, this is part of the familiar argument about whether the function of scientific theory is to represent reality or to duplicate reality.

John Searle has also questioned th "information processing" analogy between the human brain and the comr .er, but from the other direction. He has argued that the computer does not engage in information processing but, rather, in the manipulation of formal symbols. The crucial point for him is whether the concept of information processing implies intentionality as a part of the process.

The appeal to intentionality, as has already been pointed out, is an appeal to what is at least a debatable philosophical point and can hardly be taken as settling the question (see Dennett, 1981).

Our exploration of the AI-human psychology relationship has raised a number of very fundamental issues. They include our view of the nature of machines, our view of the nature of human beings, our view of what constitute adequate descriptions of psychological phenomena and the use of analogies, metaphors and models in science. A combination of positions on these issues will, to a large degree, define an individual's position on the issue of the relevance of AI research to psychology. Having asked a number of questions, the adequate answers to which require a good deal more consideration than we can give them here, what can we say about our original question? If we hold the classic mechanistic view of machines and also hold the classic view that human beings possess some totally unique property that is crucial to true psychological functioning and which must be included in all adequate descriptions of psychological phenomena, then we shall probably conclude that, no matter what the role of analogies, metaphors and models in science, little or nothing can be learned about human psychological processes from research on machine intelligence. That may be an unfortunate conclusion both because it rules out what might conceivably be a fruitful source of analogical insights into human psychology and also because it may be based more on cultural prejudices than on methodological considerations or empirical evidence. (For further references to these and related issues see Anderson, 1984 and Dennett, 1982 and 1984).

Indeed, it is clear that we have already learned from AI research. Recently, M. Mitchell Waldrop has discussed the possibility that one important insight which AI research has given us is that reasoning ability plays a less important role in intelligence than we believed and "having lots of highly specified knowledge about lots of things" plays a more important role than we had previously suspected. Waldrop sees this realization as having led to a concentration of effort in AI research since the mid-1970s, on three issues. First, the representation of knowledge (equivalent to human memory). Second, the control and use of knowledge (equivalent to human problem solving and planning). Third, the acquisition of knowledge (equivalent to human learning) (Waldrop, 1984, p. 1280).

Research on specific aspects of machine intelligence from storytelling to translating has been centering on the background information necessary to allow a machine to form a world view within the context of which something analogous to human understanding can occur. It is not at all obvious that this research will be useless in providing us with insights into the acquisition and development of human contexts of understanding.

It is tempting to engage in some speculation about the effects of future efforts in the development of computer hardware and software on the computer/human relationship. Anyone with any knowledge at all of the chaotic past development of the computer industry and the inaccuracy of predictions made by those who should know, will realize the folly of such speculation. Even experts in AI will argue that the advent of truly "intelligent" computers is anywhere from five to fifty years in the future. All that a sane individual can safely say here is that, as the range of abilities of computers becomes greater, the limits we wish to place on our arguments by analogy will stretch accordingly. When the external behavior of the machines matches that of humans, then we may be provided with further motivation to look again at the historical concept of "intentionality." For the time being, computers may be our servants, they may be our friends, but they are not our equivalents. That does not, however, appear to keep them from providing us with insights by analogy.

One last set of comments on the social psychology of views on the artificial intelligence-human psychology relationship relates to an attitude expressed with admirable bluntness and clarity by Charles Spezzano, a psychotherapist, in a popular magazine article. Spezzano noted:

> A machine's blasphemous attempt to mimic us deserves to be labeled artificial. . . .
> No matter what the animal psychologists or sociobiologists try to tell us, deep in our hearts we cling to the belief that no other creature on earth really deserves to be called intelligent. . . . We not only find that heretical, it's repulsive. We're not sure we want it even if it was possible. (Spezzano, 1983, p. 60)

Notice the language, "blasphemous," "we cling to the belief," "heretical," "repulsive." Spezzano has accurately caught the tone of many discussions of artificial intelligence. It is difficult not to wonder why some writers on the AI-human psychology relationship have taken such time and gone to such lengths to attempt to refute arguments for strong AI that are rarely made and, having dismissed strong AI for whatever reasons, also dismiss the usefulness of weak AI. Part of their motivation may involve vaguely conceived ideas about the human-computer analogy that can be explicated within the context of the logical form of the argument by analogy. They are that the human properties include one ("mind," "rational soul," "intentionality," or whatever) that is both pertinent and crucial to any analogy about psychological functioning (this part of the argument is so common that it has been given a name, the "hollow-shell strategy," by John Haugeland). The argument then continues that since machines cannot engage in true psychological functioning, we are unlikely to be able to learn anything about human psychology from them. The gaps in this argument should now be clear. First, it assumes something about the invalidity of the arguments by analogy that should really be approached by testing the limits of the analogies, that is, by empirical tests. Second, it confuses identity of properties with modeling and, since it is assumed that the first cannot occur, the second is dismissed.

James S. Albus has commented:

Such is the stuff of lively conversation and philosophical disputation. All such arguments are speculation and reasoning by analogy. The answer to the question of whether machines ever will, or even can, possess a general level of intelligence comparable to humans' is unknown and may be unknowable. (Albus, 1981, p. 229)

Certainly, if we are ever going to know we must continue, like John Locke, to remove the rubbish that lies in the way to knowledge by giving some thought to the logic of the questions we ask and perhaps even our motivation for asking them.

REFERENCES

Albus, J. S. (1981). *Brains, Behavior, and Robotics*. Peterborough, NH: Byte (McGraw-Hill).

Anderson, J. R. (1984). Cognitive Psychology. *Artificial Intelligence, 23,* 1–11.

Boden, M. A. (1977). *Artificial intelligence and natural man*. New York: Basic Books.

Boden, M. A. (1981). *Minds and mechanisms: Philosophical psychology and computational models*. Ithaca, NY: Cornell University.

Culbertson, J. T. (1963). *The minds of robots*. Urbana, IL: University of Illinois.

Cummins, R. (1983). *The nature of psychological explanation*. Cambridge, MA: MIT.

Dennett, D. (1981). Intentional systems. In John Haugeland (Ed.), *Mind design,* Cambridge, MA: MIT.

Dennett, D. C. (1982). Recent work in philosophy of interest to AI. *Artificial Intelligence, 19,* 3–5.

Dennett, D. C. (1984). Recent Work in Philosophy II. *Artificial Intelligence, 22,* 231–233.

Descartes, R. (1662). *Treatise of man*. (Trans. By Thomas Steele Hall) Cambridge, MA: Harvard University, 1972.

Dreyfus, H. (1979). *What computers can't do: The limits of artificial intelligence* (Rev. ed.). New York: Harper & Row.

Dyer, M. G. (1983). *In-depth understanding: A computer model of integrated processing for narrative comprehension*. Cambridge, MA: MIT.

Flanagan, Jr., O. J., (1984). *The science of the mind*. Cambridge, MA: MIT.

George, F. H. (1970). *Models of thinking*. London: Allen and Unwin.

Hofstadter, D. R., & Dennett, D. (1981). *The mind's I*. New York: Basic Books.

Jones, R. S. (1982). *Physics as metaphor*. Minneapolis: University of Minnesota.

Leatherdale, W. H. (1974). *The role of analogy, model and metaphor in science*. Amsterdam: North Holland.

Locke, J. (1690). *An essay concerning human understanding. (Annotated by Alexander Campbell Fraser)* New York: Dover, 1959.

Schank, R. C. (1982). *Dynamic memory: A theory of reminding and learning in computers and people*. Cambridge: Cambridge University.

Searle, J. R. (1981). Minds, brains and programs. In John Haugeland (Ed.), *Mind design*. Cambridge, MA: MIT. (This paper, with extensive comments, originally appeared in *The behavioral and brain sciences,* 1980, vol. 3 and has also been reprinted in Hofstadter and Dennett, 1981.)

Sloman, A. (1978). *The computer revolution in philosophy: Philosophy, science, and models of mind.* Sussex: Harvester.

Spezzano, C. (1983). The Human Factor. *Micro Discovery,* October.

Turing, A. M. (1950). Computing machinery and intelligence. *Mind, LIX* (236).

Waldrop, M. M. (1984). The necessity of knowledge. *Science,* 23 March, Vol. 223.

Weizenbaum, J. (1976). *Computer power and human reasoning.* San Francisco: W. H. Freeman.

Westcott, M. R. (1968). *Toward a contemporary psychology of intuition.* New York: Holt, Rinehart and Winston.

Chapter 15

Establishing Applied Social Psychology: An Exercise in Pragmatic Transcendence

Ronald J. Fisher

INTRODUCTION

The theme of this volume and indeed the central thrust of Metapsychology communicates a sense of standing back, of analyzing where we are in the discipline of psychology, and of thinking about where we are going. In doing so, we must also ask what are the alternatives in looking toward the future and which way do we turn? These questions of course involve the assumptions that there are realistic choices to make and that making no changes is in fact a choice. Therefore, in articulating a purpose for this chapter, I see the need to challenge the field of social psychology to seek alternative directions that are different from the existing state of affairs.

In short, we need to ask the question "Whither social psychology?" as part of the broader enterprise of psychology. Previously I have indicated there are three potential directions in which our field might go in the foreseeable future (Fisher, 1982a). In the first place, from my perspective, it can indeed go no-where! In other words, social psychology can continue with a "business-as-usual approach" in the aftermath of the identity crisis of the late 60's and early 70's. That is, mainstream social psychology can remain an insulated interplay of theory and research concentrating on social cognition that largely ignores social problems and thereby some degree of social reality. This orientation of theoretical-experimental social psychology appears to me to be part of the problem rather than part of the solution.

In the second place, we could take what might be seen as a radical left turn toward "Marxist social psychology" following the lead of some number of our contemporaries in sociology. This orientation emphasizes the centrality of class conflict in understanding social behavior and ultimately seeks to use social psychology as part of the revolution. While this perspective provides some useful analyses of contemporary Western society, it appears to me to be generally unrealistic, overly cynical, and much too narrow in focus. For these reasons, I do not see it as the wave of the future in social psychology.

In the third instance, I have prescribed what I consider to be a "middle-of-the-road" orientation which would involve the rejuvenation and full development of applied social psychology within the discipline. This perspective would place social psychology in the service of human welfare and constructive social change. Because of a greater connection to social reality, largely through a focus on social problems, the theories and methods of the discipline itself would be revitalized. This middle of the road orientation is really a moderate left turn toward a humanistic value base and away from a conservative, status quo position. I therefore see it as a positive approach which is cognizant of the often quoted Chinese proverb: "It is easier to curse the darkness, than to light a candle." Let us see if indeed we can light a candle for social psychology.

Following from these considerations, and the theme of metapsychology to get above and beyond what is, it makes sense that the thrust of this chapter requires an element of transcendence. By *transcendence* in this context, I mean the quality of exceeding the usual limits imposed by our definition of social psychology and our socialization experiences within it. This entails going beyond the limits of our current norms and knowledge to see if we can envisage new identities and priorities for ourselves from a fresh and radical perspective. However, at the same time this transcendence must be realistic and useful, with definite implications for action. In other words, it must be *pragmatic* in the sense of being practical and workable in the current interface of social psychology and society. We need an analysis whose implications can in fact be implemented within the broad challenge of redefining and reorientating our field. I do not use pragmatic to the exclusion of intellectual or idealistic, but call for complementary fusion of all three of these qualities in a constructive representation of social psychology. These lines of reasoning lead me to consider this chapter as an initial exercise in *pragmatic transcendence.*

In order to meet the purpose of the chapter, I will first present a brief critique of mainstream social psychology so that we can see what needs to be transcended. In order to gain a fuller understanding of the potential processes of pragmatic transcendence, I will then look at current expressions of applied social psychology, the implications of pragmatic transcendence for social psychology, and the benefits of such change for society.

CRITIQUE OF MAINSTREAM SOCIAL PSYCHOLOGY

In answer to the question "What would I like to change by lighting a candle," let me provide you with what I label as my snide definition of mainstream social psychology. This flows out of my frustration with what I perceive as the moribund nature of the current expression of my discipline. I define mainstream social psychology as the *experimental philosophy of contemporary social cognition*. Let me comment briefly on each of the major terms in this definition.

I specifically say *experimental* as opposed to empirical in order to highlight the almost total reliance in the discipline on simplistic and artificial laboratory experimentation for gathering data on social behavior. The limitations of this myopia should be so apparent by now that further comment is not required.

To refer to mainstream social psychology as a *philosophy* is not intended to slight true philosophers whether they be within psychology, philosophy, or elsewhere. It refers, however, to a superficial, pseudo-scientific approach to understanding social behavior in which the search for truth takes place primarily through logical reasoning rather than complex, factual observation. The problem with theoretical-experimental social psychology is that most laboratory experimentation is so contrived, so artificial and so trivial that one can only assume that logical reasoning must be the primary vehicle to carry the work forward! At the same time, there is such a detachment from the social reality in which most behavior occurs that one can only assume that the reality of the work itself is being constructed primarily in the minds of the experimenters.

It is in these ways that this endeavour is a "philosophy" as opposed to a science based in a combination of empirical observation and social reality. Even as strong an experimentalist as McGuire (1973) has indicated that experiments are primarily conducted to confirm hypotheses which the researchers have every reason to believe will in fact be confirmed. In order to have this chain of events occur, simplistic theories are put to trivial tests thus yielding results which are open to numerous criticisms.

The use of the term *contemporary* is an acknowledgement of the work of Gergen (1973) and others which sees social psychology as primarily a descriptive endeavor producing an account of contemporary North American history. It is essential that we come to recognize the time-limited and culture-bound nature of our activities and seek to broaden our enterprise on these dimensions whenever possible.

Finally, it should come as no surprise that the focus of mainstream social psychology is seen as the study of *social cognition,* that is, of intrapsychic cognitive processes that may relate only minimally or at best partially to the existing social world. This is not to deny the power nor the uniqueness of the basic phenomenological approach of social psychology. However, when the study of social cognition is focused almost solely at the individual level of analysis to the detriment of understanding complex social reality through a multilevel approach, then the field must be seen as fundamentally limited and deficient.

The definition and functioning of contemporary social psychology give rise to a series of interrelated issues which I have described in more detail elsewhere (Fisher, 1982a). Due partly to the artificial and contrived nature of the research endeavor, the field generally lacks relevance to complex human social behavior and to pressing social problems. Too many of the measures and procedures which are used lack validity, depth and meaning. There continues to be an air of triviality within the discipline which is at times expressed through a fun-and-games approach, but is also evident in the observation that research fads around particular topics appear to be more important than substance. This is not to deny the basic importance of social scientists having the freedom and the flexibility to study topics of choice, but it is to stress that lines of investigation often seem determined by expediency and conformity rather than other priorities. Partly as a result of these characteristics, the discipline lacks utility as measured by jobs for its graduates and benefits for society at large. It is therefore not surprising that research dollars are shifting in a more applied direction. Another issue, which should hardly be surprising to social psychologists, is that the field tends to mirror the norms and priorities of contemporary North American society. The danger here is that social psychology automatically takes a status quo orientation and ignores what *should* be in terms of an identified and articulated value base. Finally, social psychology is rife with socio-political biases of both an individual and a social nature. One good example of this type of bias is shown in the person-blame-attribution bias of much social-psychological research, even that which is supposedly problem directed (Caplan & Nelson, 1973).

PRAGMATIC TRANSCENDENCE

If definition and issues relating to contemporary social psychology represent the darkness, the question follows: "How do we attempt to light a candle?" What I would propose as an alternative is a social psychology that is a socially concerned field that works to understand human behavior as a complex, multidetermined process, and that seeks to ameliorate social problems through the application of theories, research methods, and practice skills (Fisher, 1982a, 1982b). In this direction, I have offered a definition of applied social psychology as social-psychological research and practice in real world settings directed toward the understanding of human social behavior and the amelioration of social problems.

In conjunction with this definition, I have offered seven "touchstones" which may serve as guides along the way (Fisher, 1980). Touchstones were used in times gone by to test the purity of precious metals—particularly gold and silver. A sample was rubbed across the face of the black touchstone and the resulting streak was judged for its purity. I suggest we need some touchstones to assess the genuineness of our aspirations and activities in applied social psychology. I would like to follow these touchstones in order to illustrate in a more detailed fashion the ways in which pragmatic transcendence might be accomplished.

A Central Focus on Fundamental Social Problems at All Levels of Analysis

It is essential that social psychology begin to transcend the array of trivial topics that have permeated the field for some time, and begin to transcend the individual level of analysis. With regard to trivial topics, I am convinced that dozens if not hundreds of productive lives can be spent documenting and elaborating the almost infinite nuances of human social behavior, without much impact on the improvement of human welfare or our basic understanding of society. Following the hundreds of dissonance studies, we now have hundreds of attribution studies, each one taking away from the significance of the seminal work in an expedient flood of diminishing returns. What is required is a reorientation that takes social problems as the starting point of inquiry, as has happened at some points in our history (for example, a concern with racial, religious, and ethnic prejudice underlying the work on attitudes). I suggest that our attention be directed to a wide range of social problems from the apparently mundane (e.g., poor interpersonal communication, ineffective organizational functioning) to the overtly dramatic (e.g., racism, violent crime, environmental degradation). In this way, our theorizing will be challenged to comprehend and explain complex social reality, and our research and practice activities will have greater potential for contributing to the quality of life.

In order to further transcend the limited focus of the experimental philosophy of contemporary social cognition, it is also essential to adopt a multiple levels of analysis approach. Thus, we should initially investigate a phenomenon at the appropriate level of analysis and blend in concepts from other levels as appropriate. The levels of analysis included here range from the individual through the interpersonal, the group, the intergroup, the organizational, the community, the societal, to the international or global (Fisher, 1977). In doing so it is essential to maintain the phenomenological approach which is part of the basic social-psychological perspective. Thus, variables at the individual level of analysis, including those associated with perception, cognition and communication, would be emphasized, but would be blended in with variables from other levels of analysis to more fully understand the topic at hand. A laudable example of this is found in a true social psychology of organizational behavior as developed by Katz and Kahn (1966, 1978). A more recent example of this useful approach is to be found in the conceptualization of cognitive community psychology (O'Neill, 1981) and in the related approach of community consultation (O'Neill & Trickett, 1982). Finally, the potential of social psychology to contribute to understanding and improving international relations in this manner has been with us for some time (Fisher, 1982a, Chapter 12; Kelman, 1965).

The Continuous Integration of Theory, Research, and Practice

It is essential to transcend the current insulated separation of theory and research from practice, that is, application to real world settings and problems. In particular, we should find ways of sharing and testing our knowledge through the dissemination of theories and research results and through the use of theory in the formation of social programs and public policy. In this way we would come to potentiate our social knowledge through theoretical application and social practice (Gergen & Basseches, 1980). Further interplay among theory, research and practice will be described in one of the current expressions of applied social psychology presented below.

The Development of Middle Range Theories Stressing
the Reciprocal Interaction of the Person and the Environment

Following this touchstone would allow us to transcend the study of simplistic, linear notions of intrapsychic processes by appreciating the significance of the social environment in shaping behavior and in turn being shaped by that behavior. Theoretical-experimental social psychology has shown a predisposition to concentrate much activity on minitheories of individual functioning such as cognitive dissonance or casual attribution with a consequent neglect of middle range theories such as group development or organizational motivation which link two or more levels of analysis. Transcending this state of affairs would also be partly accomplished by developing generative theory along the lines proposed by Gergen (1978)—theory which could challenge what exists and offer alternatives for social life. In managing this transcendence it would be very important to take account of Thorngate's impostulate regarding theory in social psychology: "It is impossible for an explanation of social behavior to be simultaneously general, simple and accurate" (1976, p. 126). In other words, general and accurate theories of social behavior must necessarily be complex, and a multilevel, interactive approach is necessary to capture the fullness of social reality.

The Application of a Variety of Complementary Research Methods

There is no doubt that the laboratory experiment provides precision and control, but its overuse in mainstream social psychology has led to constriction and sterility. The emphasis in research should be to transcend this heavy reliance on laboratory experimentation and 2 × 2 designs which investigate simplistic, linear relationships between a limited number of variables. We require multivariate, longitudinal, and historically sensitive field research to adequately capture social reality. To maintain precision and control in our methodological repertoire we should make greater use of complex laboratory simulations which balance internal and external validity and allow us to study a collection of multilevel variables interacting naturally over time. In line with these initiatives, I am proposing that we maintain our empirical and positivistic base as a pragmatic necessity for dealing with social phenomena that can be described and logically related to one other. Such an approach yields a wide range of time-proven research methods for describing and analyzing social behavior (see, for example, Fisher, 1982a, Chapter 3). This expanded positivist-empiricist view sees social reality as an ongoing, multiply determined process in which cause and effect, that is, influence, is to be found within mutual, reciprocal relationships.

The Expansion of Practice Expertise Partly Through Interdisciplinary Collaboration

Social psychologists must transcend their disdain of social practice and in doing so their disciplinary ethnocentrism which separates them from professions such as social work and public administration. We should move out of the universities and the research institutes and apply social-psychological concepts to illuminate issues and processes in society at large. We should not be hesitant to move (with adequate preparation) into the field of practice, that is, into purposeful, systematic, and skilled involvement as technical and social consultants at a number of levels of functioning. Practice roles include those of applied researcher, research consultant, social technologist, human relations trainer, program development consultant, group and organizational consultant, and social advocate (Fisher, 1982a). Each of these roles requires a conceptual base that is shared historically with other disciplines and that requires addressing issues in identity, training and certification (Fisher, 1982b). A shift toward practice activities is required for a sizable (but not complete) portion of social psychologists if we are to develop a truly applied focus for our field.

The Adherence to a Clearly Articulated Humanistic Value Base and a Professional Code of Ethics

If we are to overcome irrelevance and futility, we need to transcend our alleged objectivity and neutrality which is too often an implicit cover for supporting the status quo. The humanistic value base demands that we facilitate the democratization of social systems and that we place our science in the service of improving human welfare. By implementing our applied efforts on the basis of humanistic and scientific ideals we can contribute to the mutual respect, dignity, and growth of individuals and societies. This idealistic bent is essential so that our efforts at being pragmatic do not place us in the service of the highest bidder or the most powerful decision maker. Adherence to a humanistic value base and a related code of ethics will work to proscribe manipulative and exploitative applications of social technology or other practice roles. We therefore need to transcend through expansion our currently limited conception of ethics which is primarily concerned with protecting the welfare of the individual in the face of experimental deception and manipulation. We need to develop and apply comprehensive ethical codes of research and practice for professional social psychologists (Fisher, 1982b).

A Commitment to Continuous Professional Development and Role Versatility

In order to bring about the revitalization and continued development of our field we must transcend our tendency to be over-socialized during our graduate studies and to become fossilized thereafter. A broader commitment to graduate training along the lines of the touchstones would place us in a much better position to continue our professional development following the awarding of the doctoral degree. We need to develop and maintain a general competence as scholar/practitioners in which each individual social psychologist will acquire his or her unique mix of theory, research, and practice in relation to a manageable number of specialities. One way to foster life-long learning toward these goals is to complement academic training with professional practitioner training such as that provided by the NTL Institute for Applied Behavioral Science (NTL Institute, 1985).

The process of pragmatic transcendence captured by the implications of the touchstones is already underway. It is demonstrated primarily by a shift toward an applied emphasis within social psychology. The current extent, the details, and the ultimate outcomes of this shift are difficult to discern—one can only gain broad impressions to be further documented as data become available. Nonetheless, it is clear that the face of social psychology is changing.

CURRENT EXPRESSIONS OF APPLIED SOCIAL PSYCHOLOGY

The shift toward applied social psychology has been evident for some years now, but has not been a uniform process. There are at least three discernible directions in which the shift is occurring (Fisher, 1982b), and each of these expresses pragmatic transcendence to varying degrees.

Applying Social Psychology

A good deal of contemporary activity in social psychology involves the application of mainstream theories to social, that is often, personal, issues. A good example is provided by Frieze, Bar-Tal, & Carroll (1979) which in part applies contemporary theories of social cognition, particularly attribution theory, to problems such as alcoholism, loneliness, and depression. It is interesting to note that theories about intrapersonal processes appear primarily to have clinical as opposed to social applications. The major difficulty with applying social psychology is that it attempts to explain real world behavior by using theories developed mainly from laboratory research (Fisher, 1982a, Chapter 1). Methodologically, the concern here is with external validity in that theories and results from limited and contrived manipulations fail to capture and explain behavior in complex, interactive social systems. Morally and ethically, it can be argued that much laboratory experimentation mirrors the ways that people typically behave toward each other rather than offering new, and more humanistic, forms of social behaviors (Argyris, 1969, 1975). It is therefore not surprising that several existing minitheories (e.g., dissonance theory, reactance theory) can be used to influence people without their knowledge and not necessarily in their best interests. Social technology as developed and advocated by Varela (1971, 1977) is one of the clearest (and most effective) examples of this form of social engineering. It is disturbing that several commentators have praised Varela's work as an example of applying social psychology while overlooking the serious ethical concerns that it raises.

Applying social psychology is also demonstrated by laboratory experiments on topics of social concern and by field replications of laboratory findings. The first response to the call for relevance has been documented by analyses such as those provided by Helmreich (1975) and McClure et al. (1980) which demonstrate that many apparently applied studies in mainstream journals *(Journal of Personality and Social Psychology, Journal of Applied Social Psychology)* follow the traditional mold of laboratory experiments using college students as subjects. Furthermore, these studies typically use the individual level of analysis for conceptualizing the problem. The second response envisages applied work primarily as an opportunity to validate minitheories developed in laboratory settings. There was a definite growth in this type of activity in the 1970s in areas such as helping behavior and social influence, but the yield in terms of developing a more applied social psychology is actually quite limited. Primarily, the focus is on field validations of restricted minitheories, rather than seeing real world settings as a legitimate and perhaps superior arena in which to develop and test middle range theories that have greater utility in understanding social problems.

The Research Emphasis

One of the strongest developments in recent years has been to adapt the research design and analysis skills of social psychologists to social experimentation and program evaluation (Bickman, 1980; Campbell, 1973; Saxe & Fine,
1980). This is perhaps due to the powerful combination of a wide range of
research skills with the phenomenological, interactive perspective of social psychology in understanding the behavior of individuals in the context of social
systems. The conducting and evaluating of large scale social experiments in
which different policy or program alternatives are compared is one way that
social science can contribute to ameliorating social problems. Hopefully, this
will also involve the development and/or testing of differing theoretical propositions which underlie the alternate policies. In a related manner, program evaluation has come to occupy a central role in the activities of applied social
psychologists. In this area, we need to move beyond the application of research
expertise to the application and creation of social-psychological theories that
improve program development and functioning. Here lies a golden opportunity
for social psychologists to operationalize the scholarly side of their identity in
ways that have payoffs for program managers and clients as well as social
theoreticians. The research emphasis is also demonstrated by the interplay of
laboratory and field research within a mutually reinforcing cycle (Cialdini,
1980). This linkage goes beyond the simple validation of laboratory findings in
field settings to encompass a reciprocal interaction in which natural observation
of social phenomena lends direction to experimentation the results of which are
then verified through further natural observation. The yield should be more
valid and useful theories of human social behavior.

The Integration of Theory, Research, and Practice

My own prescription for applied social psychology is a rejuvenation of the
Lewinian vision in which theory, research, and practice form an integrated and
mutually reinforcing cycle (see Figure 1). Theory guides both research and
practice and is reciprocally informed by them. Research evaluates and redirects
both theory and practice. Practice provides essential contact with social reality
and clearly connects the discipline to the improvement of human welfare. The
major forms of practice are seen as program and policy development (based on
social-psychological theories) and social intervention (training, consultation,
advocacy), each complemented respectively by evaluation research and action
research. Theory development continues to be informed by the interplay of field
and laboratory research. This conceptualization results in a picture of social
psychology that is radically different from that presented in most textbooks and
journal articles which usually focus on individual-level theory and results in
mainstream areas such as attitudes, attribution, aggression, altruism, and attraction (the so called five A's). The alternate picture stresses person-setting interaction at multiple levels of analysis and elevates practice to a priority similar to

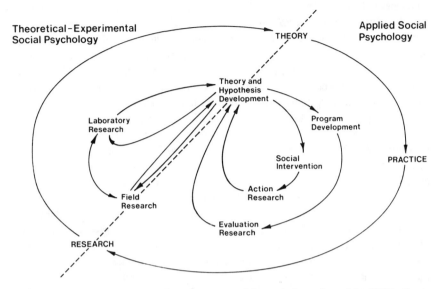

FIGURE 1. Theory, research and practice in social psychology. Copyright 1981, Canadian Psychological Association. Reprinted by permission.

that of theory and research (Fisher, 1982a). Whether such a picture comes to be a stronger reality in the field depends on the degree of success in pragmatic transcendence.

IMPLICATIONS OF PRAGMATIC TRANSCENDENCE FOR SOCIAL PSYCHOLOGY

Regardless of the expression of applied social psychology which is adopted, there are definite implications for the discipline. The theory-research-practice expression carries the most radical implications. The general implications fall primarily into two admonitions. The first states that we should train social psychologists differently, and the second prescribes that we should conduct our research, theory, and practice activities differently. In short, we should train social psychologists to be scholar/practitioners who are able to integrate theory, research, and practice around specific, manageable and yet socially significant topics. Let me briefly describe two examples of pragmatic transcendence: one in training and one in research.

Training Social Psychologists

Some would see the new directions for training which flow from the touchstones as being restricted to the applied area. However, it is becoming increasingly apparent that these prescriptions lead to a new view of training for generic social psychologists who can function in either a basic or an applied fashion.

Elsewhere (Fisher, 1981, 1982b), I have commented on the training of applied social psychologists in terms of the rationale, the essential elements, and the issues which must be addressed for continued advancement. The basic thrust is that we must look for new combinations of experiences in the training of social psychologists in order to move the discipline forward both theoretically as well as professionally. The essential elements of such training are an adequate coverage of scientific and professional competencies, an integration of theory, research and practice, continuous real world involvement of students in interdisciplinary field settings, and a combination of apprenticeship training with the traditional demands for independent, scholarly work. There now exist a number of training programs which implement these essential elements in ways that are appropriate given their faculty resources and community settings.

Our experience at the University of Saskatchewan began with the initiation of a two year masters program to train applied social researchers (primarily program evaluators) and research consultants who are able to work in a variety of organizational and community settings. In addition to a combination of basic and applied course work, the program involves an ongoing practicum, a full-time, four month internship, and a master's thesis. Recently, our offerings have been extended to the doctoral level with the objective of training scholar/ practitioners who can function effectively in either academic or applied settings. Course work stresses advanced social research (particularly the dissemination and utilization of results in policy formation) and consultation (primarily program development, group, and organizational consultation). The practicum and internship sequence is supplemented if students choose by completion of the NTL Institute's Graduate Student Professional Development Program.

Although a number of difficult issues confront training in social psychology (Fisher, 1982b; Fisher, Grant & Callahan, 1984), our experience to date demonstrates that pragmatic transcendence in training is a viable possibility. One major problem in applied training is to create a viable role for theory development and testing in areas such as program development and policy formulation. Too often, applied work is atheoretical relying mainly on expertise in research methodology with the necessary complementary social skills, and therefore does not heed Lewin's truism that there is nothing so practical as a good theory. In theoretical-experimental or academic training, the role of practice is neglected or regarded as something that should just come "naturally" in areas like field research or program evaluation. The discipline as a whole must come to grips with ways of respecting the need for both strong theoretical work and good practice.

The Study and Resolution of Intergroup Conflict

A great deal of past and current endeavour in social psychology can be seen as initially stemming from a interest in intergroup conflict. Much of the study of attitudes and behavior, prejudice and discrimination, cognitive consistency, and attribution theory has been concerned with the issue of how groups in conflict see each other and behave toward each other. Unfortunately, within all of this activity, the core process of intergroup conflict, particularly in terms of variables at the group and intergroup levels of analyses, has become almost completely lost. A recently formed research and practice team at the University of Saskatchewan provides a potential example for conducting activities that are in line with pragmatic transcendence. This team is composed of two faculty and several graduate students who share an interest in the study and resolution of intergroup conflict. The team has been functioning for three years, and has a longterm research agenda. Hence, this description will be comprised more of a statement of objectives than of products. Nonetheless, these objectives illustrate one way of integrating theory, research and practice within the process of pragmatic transcendence.

The first objective of the research team is to develop an eclectic, social-psychological theory of intergroup conflict. This theoretical development would be based in realistic group conflict theory as proposed by Campbell (1965). At the same time, an attempt will be made to blend in the predominant social-psychological perspective as exemplified by such contributors as Deutsch (1973) and Tajfel and Turner (1979). An initial attempt toward developing an eclectic theory demonstrates the complexity that needs to be incorporated (Fisher, 1985).

In the research domain, the second objective of the team is to develop a realistic simulation of intergroup conflict in order to systematically study processes and outcomes as well as the effects of ameliorative interventions. At present, the team has developed and piloted an adequately complex laboratory simulation including the phases of ingroup development, intergroup conflict, and conflict resolution (Hall, 1985). This approach follows the general paradigm pioneered by Sherif and his colleagues in a field setting (Sherif, Harvey, White, Hood, & Sherif, 1961), but allows for much greater precision and control of variables thus yielding an optimum balance of internal and external validity. In the longterm, this work, if successful, will help re-introduce and extend the longitudinal, multilevel, multivariable study of intergroup conflict in social psychology. This simulation will be used to study theoretical relationships over time among a variety of variables at the individual, group, and intergroup levels. Within this paradigm, it will also be possible to relate both processes and outcomes to conflict resolution interventions such as third party consultation (Fisher, 1972, 1983).

The third objective relates to practice, that is: to develop an intergroup conflict training laboratory and to undertake ongoing applications of ameliorative interventions to real world conflicts. Such practice would be based on the theory and research findings and would take its lead from pioneering work such as that of Blake and Mouton (Blake & Mouton, 1961; Blake, Shepard, & Mouton, 1964) for training conflict resolution skills and for managing intergroup conflict in organizational settings. The training laboratory would be designed to illuminate for participants the processes of intergroup conflict and to provide alternative behaviors that would lead to collaborative resolutions. The ongoing applications would attempt to move groups toward the constructive resolution of their differences through third party consultation and related problem-solving strategies (e.g., Kelman & Cohen, 1976). If the conflict research and practice team is successful in meetings its objectives, it will provide an illustration of a radically different way of doing social psychology than is represented by the majority of mainstream endeavors.

BENEFITS FOR SOCIETY

To the extent that a rejuvenated social psychology is able to attain pragmatic transcendence, a number of beneficial ongoing outcomes for society will be realized. The first of these will be the documentation through research and the amelioration through practice of social problems. In this way, social psychology can make a contribution to constructive planned change (Bennis, Benne, & Chin, 1985). Related benefits will accrue through the development and evaluation of effective social programs and policies. There is much unrealized potential for the appropriate use of theories of human social behavior in the development of effective programs and policies directed towards improving human welfare. It is readily apparent to most social scientists involved in the real world that a large proportion of program planning and policy development is carried on with only a hint of systematic and comprehensive conceptual understanding of the underlying dynamics of human social behavior. At the same time, the application of our considerable expertise in research methodology is very useful for evaluating the processes and effects of programs and policies implemented in a world of complexity and confusion.

Finally, in line with the humanistic value base, social psychologists with generic professional training can, in concert with other trained professionals, serve as models of ethical and humanistic behavior. It is not uncommon in the fields of program management and policy implementation to come across decision makers whose training has not equipped them with the necessary ethical sensitivity to the welfare of individuals or the needs of society. Thus, in many ways social psychologists can make a meaningful contribution to a more humane and equitable world. This will only occur, however, to the degree that we are able to overcome our existing limitations and fully engage ourselves in the process of pragmatic transcendence.

REFERENCES

Argyris, C.(1969). The incompleteness of social-psychological theory: Examples from small group, cognitive consistency, and attribution research. *American Psychologist, 24,* 893–908.

Argyris, C. (1975). Dangers in applying results from experimental social psychology. *American Psychologist, 30,* 469–485.

Bennis, W. G., Benne, K. D., & Chin, R. (Eds.). (1985). *The planning of change* (Fourth ed.). New York: CBS College Publishing.

Bickman, L. Introduction. In L. Bickman (Ed.). (1980). *Applied social psychology annual* (Volume 1). Beverly Hills, California: Sage.

Blake, R. R., & Mouton, J. S. (1961). *Group dynamics: Key to decision making.* Houston, TX: Gulf.

Blake, R. R., Shepard, H. A., & Mouton, J. S. (1964). *Managing intergroup conflict in industry.* Houston, TX: Gulf.

Campbell, D. T. (1965). Ethnocentric and other altruistic motives. In D. Levine (Ed.), *Nebraska symposium on motivation* (Volume 13). Lincoln, NE: University of Nebraska Press.

Campbell, D. T. (1973). The social scientist as methodological servant of the experimenting society. *Policy Studies Journal, 2,* 72–75.

Caplan, N., & Nelson, S. D. (1973). On being useful: The nature and consequences of psychological research on social problems. *American Psychologist, 28,* 199–212.

Cialdini, R. B. (1980). Full-cycle social psychology. In L. Bickman (Ed.), *Applied social psychology annual* (Volume 1). Beverly Hills, CA: Sage.

Deutsch, M. (1973). *The resolution of conflict: Constructive and destructive processes.* New Haven, CT: Yale University Press.

Fisher, R. J. (1972). Third party consultation: A method for the study and resolution of conflict. *Journal of Conflict Resolution, 16,* 67–94.

Fisher, R. J. (1977). Applied social psychology: A partial response to Sarason's suggested divorce. *Canadian Psychological Review, 18,* 346–352.

Fisher, R. J. (1980). Touchstones for applied social psychology. In R. F. Kidd, & M. J. Saks (Eds.), *Advances in applied social psychology* (Volume 1). Hillsdale, NJ: Erlbaum.

Fisher, R. J. (1981). Training in applied social psychology: Rationale and core experiences. *Canadian Psychology, 22,* 250–259.

Fisher, R. J. (1982a). *Social psychology: An applied approach.* New York: St. Martin's Press.

Fisher, R. J. (1982b). The professional practice of applied social psychology: Identity, training, and certification. In L. Bickman (Ed.), *Applied social psychology annual* (Volume 3). Beverly Hills, CA: Sage.

Fisher, R. J. (1983). Third party consultation as a method of intergroup conflict resolution: A review of studies. *Journal of Conflict Resolution, 27,* 301–334.

Fisher, R. J. (1985). *The social psychology of intergroup conflict: Toward eclectic theory and effective practice.* Paper presented at the Annual Meeting of the Canadian Psychological Association, Halifax, June.

Fisher, R. J., Grant, P. R., & Callahan, M. J. (1984). *The potential role of theory in the training of applied social psychologists.* Paper presented at the Annual Meeting of the Canadian Psychological Association, Ottawa, June.

Frieze, I. H., Bar-Tal, D., & Carroll, J. S. (Eds.). (1979). *New approaches to social problems.* San Francisco: Jossey-Bass.

Gergen, K. (1973). Social psychology as history. *Journal of Personality and Social Psychology, 26,* 309–320.

Gergen, K. J. (1978). Toward generative theory. *Journal of Personality and Social Psychology, 36,* 1344–1360.

Gergen, K. J., & Basseches, M. (1980). The potentiation of social knowledge. In R. F. Kidd & M. J. Saks (Eds.), *Advances in applied social psychology* (Volume 1). Hillsdale, NJ: Erlbaum.

Hall, D. G. (1985). *The design of a laboratory simulation to study the development and resolution of intergroup conflict.* Paper presented at the Annual Meeting of the Canadian Psychological Association, Halifax, June.

Helmreich, R. (1975). Applied social psychology: The unfulfilled promise. *Personality & Social Psychology Bulletin, 1,* 548–560.

Katz, D., & Kahn, R. L. (1966). *The social psychology of organizations.* New York: Wiley.

Katz, D., & Kahn, R. L. (1978). *The social psychology of organizations* (2nd ed.). New York: Wiley.

Kelman, H. C. (Ed.). (1965). *International behavior: A social psychological analysis.* New York: Holt, Rinehart, & Winston.

Kelman, H. C. & Cohen, S. P. (1976). The problem-solving workshop: A social-psychological contribution to the resolution of international conflicts. *Journal of Peace Research, 13,* 79–90.

McClure, L. et al. (1980). Community psychology concepts and research base: Promise and product. *American Psychologist, 35,* 1000–1011.

McGuire, W. J. (1973). The Yin and Yang of progress in social psychology. Seven Koan. *Journal of Personality and Social Psychology, 26,* 446–456.

NTL Institute. (1985). *1985 Programs.* Arlington, VA: NTL Institute for Applied Behavioral Science.

O'Neill, P. (1981). Cognitive community psychology. *American Psychologist, 36,* 457–469.

O'Neill, P., & Trickett, E. J. (1982). *Community consultation.* San Francisco: Jossey-Bass.

Saxe, L. & Fine, M. (1980). Reorienting social psychology toward application: A methodological analysis. In L. Bickman (Ed.), *Applied social psychology annual* (Volume 1). Beverly Hills, CA: Sage.

Sherif, M., Harvey, O. J., White, B. J., Hood, W. R., & Sherif, C. W. (1961). *Intergroup conflict and cooperation: The Robbers Cave experiment.* Norman: University of Oklahoma Book Exchange.

Tajfel, H., & Turner, J. (1979). An integrative theory of intergroup conflict. In W. G. Austin, & S. Worchel (Eds.), *The social psychology of intergroup relations.* Monterey, CA: Brooks/Cole.

Thorngate, W. (1976). Possible limits on a science of social behavior. In L. H. Strickland, F. E. Aboud, & K. J. Gergen (Eds.), *Social psychology in transition.* New York: Plenum.

Varela, J. A. (1971). *Psychological solutions to social problems: An introduction to social technology.* New York: Academic Press.

Varela, J. A. (1977). Social technology, *American Psychologist, 32,* 914–923.

Index